# FINAL FANTASY

## LOST STRANGER

STORY: **Hazuki Minase**

VOLUME **7**

Translation: Melody Pan    Lettering: Bianca Pistillo

FINAL FANTASY LOST STRANGER Volume 7 ©2021 Hazuki Minase, Itsuki Kameya/SQUARE ENIX CO., LTD. ©2021 SQUARE ENIX CO., LTD. All Rights Reserved. First published in Japan in 2021 by SQUARE ENIX CO., LTD. English translation rights arranged with SQUARE ENIX CO., LTD. and Yen Press, LLC through Tuttle-Mori Agency, Inc., Tokyo.

English translation © 2022 by SQUARE ENIX CO., LTD.

Yen Press
150 West 30th Street, 19th Floor
New York, NY 10001

Visit us at yenpress.com
facebook.com/yenpress
twitter.com/yenpress
yenpress.tumblr.com
instagram.com/yenpress

First Yen Press Edition: May 2022
The chapters in this volume were originally published as ebooks by Yen Press.

Yen Press is an imprint of Yen Press, LLC.
The Yen Press name and logo are trademarks of Yen Press, LLC.

Library of Congress Control Number: 2018948073

ISBNs: 978-1-9753-4481-8 (paperback)
978-1-9753-4482-5 (ebook)

10 9 8 7 6 5 4 3 2 1

WOR

Printed in the United States of America

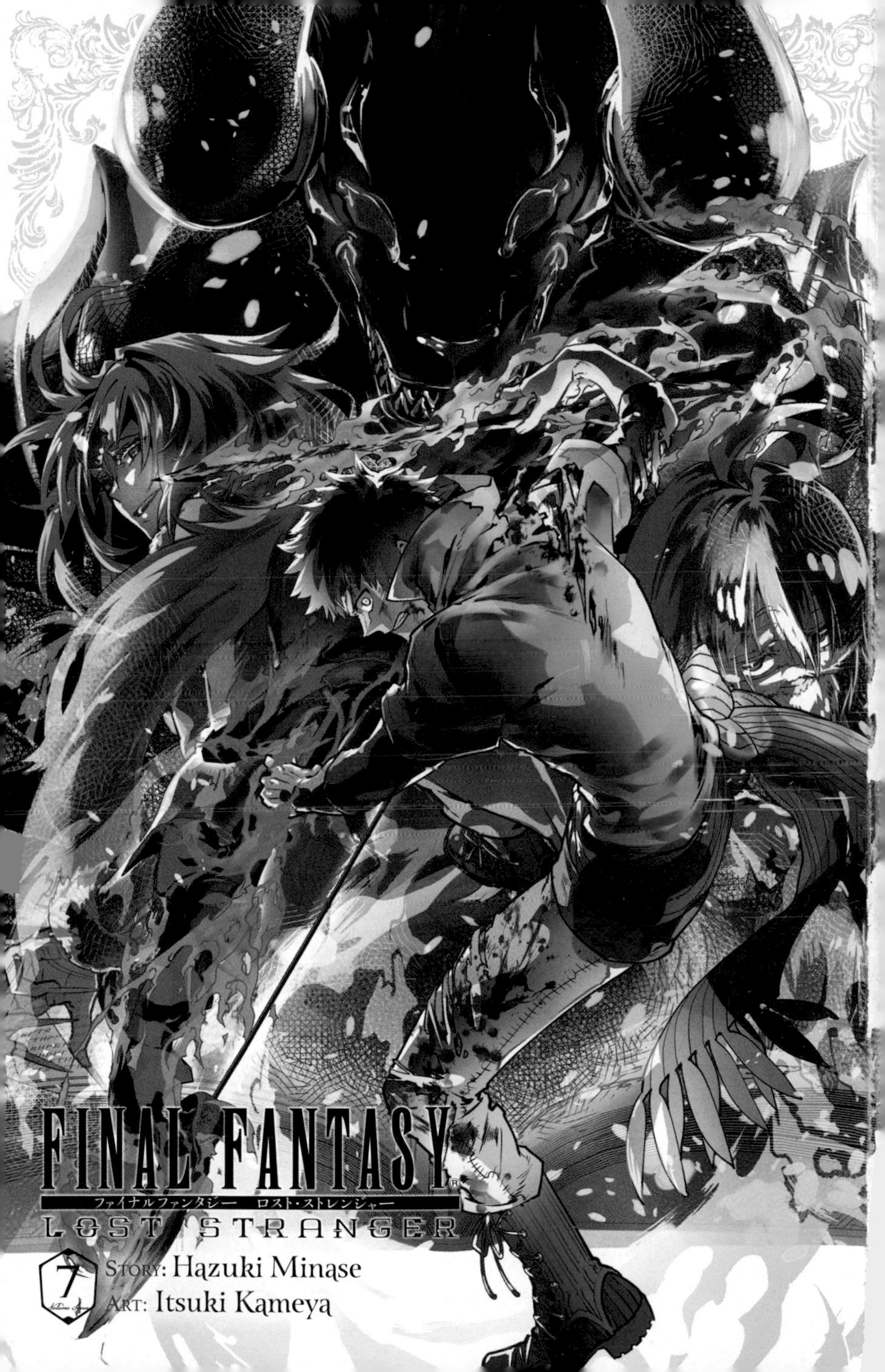
FINAL FANTASY®
ファイナルファンタジー　ロスト・ストレンジャー
LOST STRANGER
7
STORY: Hazuki Minase
ART: Itsuki Kameya

# Contents

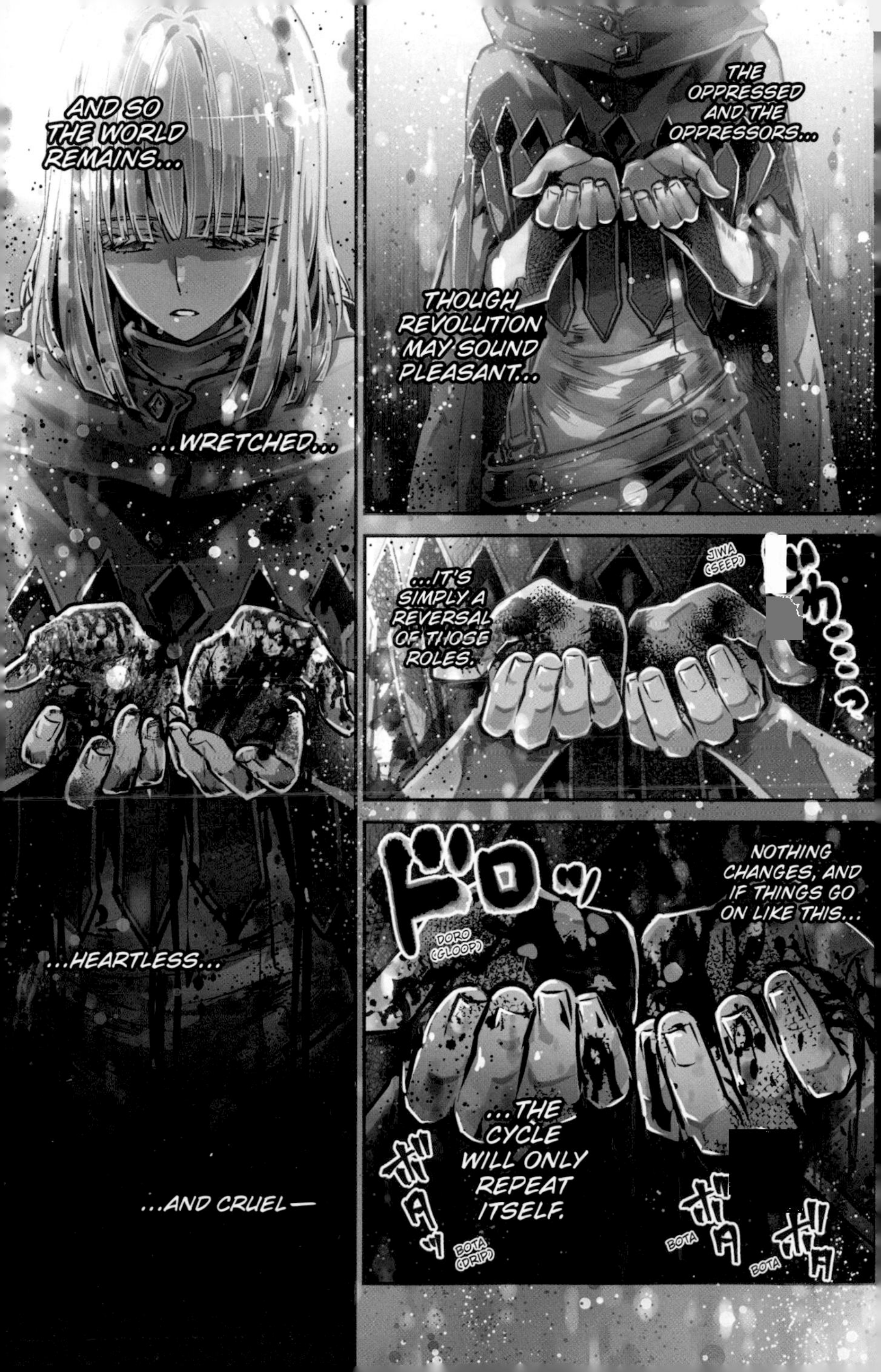
THE OPPRESSED AND THE OPPRESSORS...
THOUGH REVOLUTION MAY SOUND PLEASANT...
JIWA (SEEP)
...IT'S SIMPLY A REVERSAL OF THOSE ROLES.
NOTHING CHANGES, AND IF THINGS GO ON LIKE THIS...
ドロ…
DORO (GLOOP)
...THE CYCLE WILL ONLY REPEAT ITSELF.
[redacted]
ボタ
BOTA
ボタ
BOTA
ボタ
BOTA (DRIP)
AND SO THE WORLD REMAINS...
...WRETCHED...
...HEARTLESS...
...AND CRUEL—

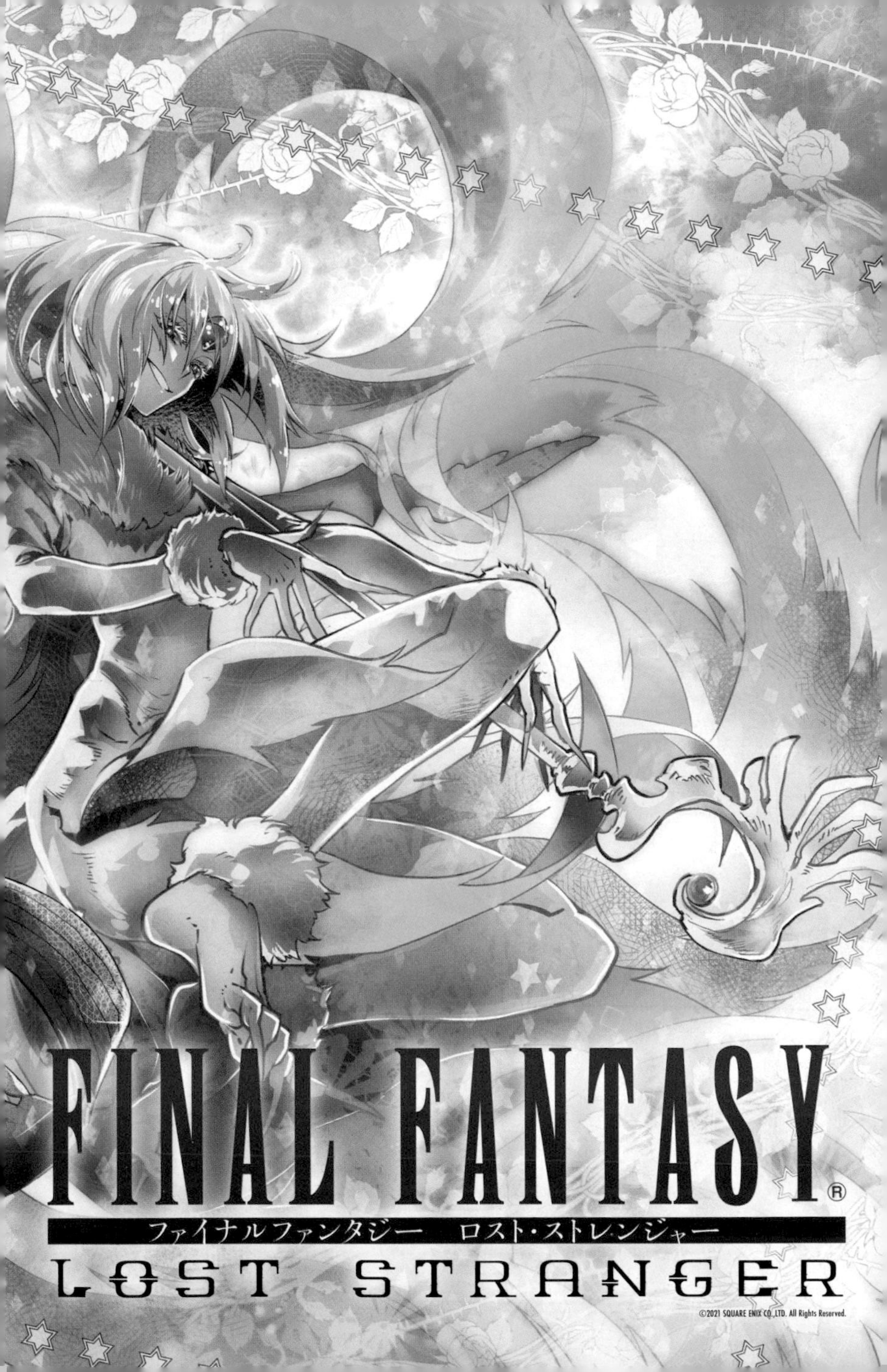
FINAL FANTASY®
ファイナルファンタジー　ロスト・ストレンジャー
LOST STRANGER
©2021 SQUARE ENIX CO., LTD. All Rights Reserved.

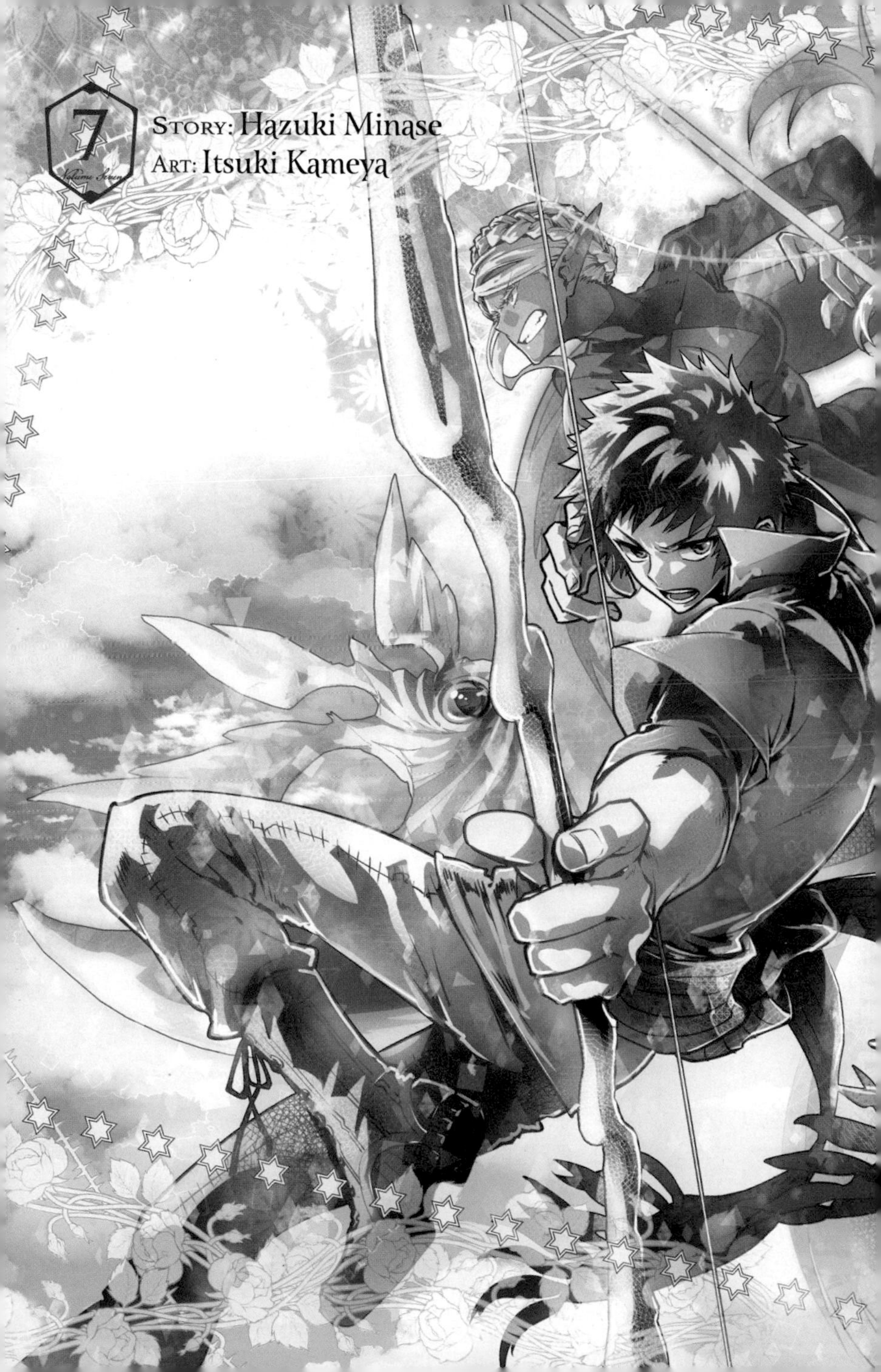
7
Volume Seven
STORY: Hazuki Minase
ART: Itsuki Kameya

# FINAL FANTASY®

ファイナルファンタジー　ロスト・ストレンジャー

LOST STRANGER

## STORY & CHARACTERS

Shogo and his little sister Yuko are SE employees. After awakening from their run-in with a truck, they found themselves in the *FF* world they'd always longed for...! Much like in the games, Shogo and Yuko had fun exploring the area, but tragedy would soon befall them. The ultimate fantasy awaits—a forbidden tale of reincarnation in another world with an *FF* twist!!

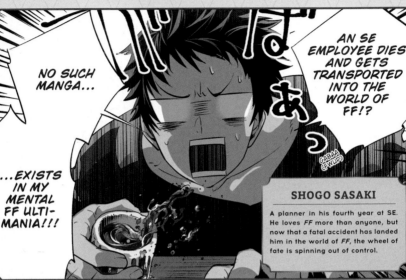

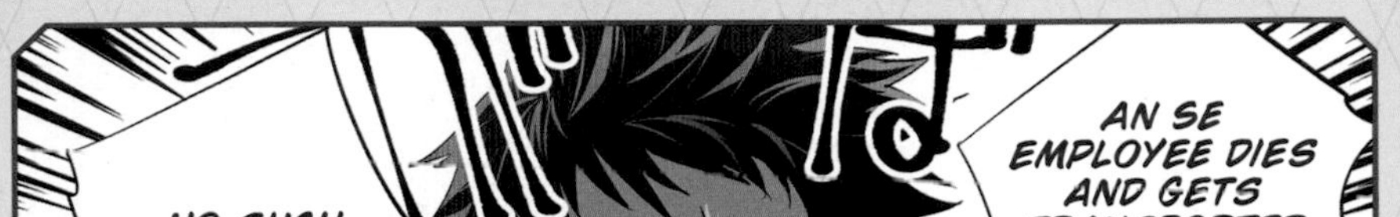
AN SE EMPLOYEE DIES AND GETS TRANSPORTED INTO THE WORLD OF FF!?
GABAA (FWUP)
NO SUCH MANGA...
...EXISTS IN MY MENTAL FF ULTI-MANIA!!!

### SHOGO SASAKI

A planner in his fourth year at SE. He loves *FF* more than anyone, but now that a fatal accident has landed him in the world of *FF*, the wheel of fate is spinning out of control.

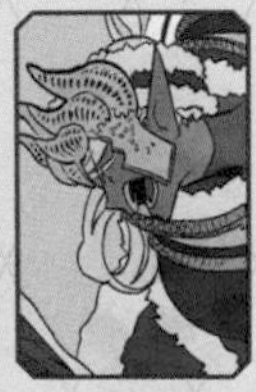

### REI HAGAKURE

An Elrein Warrior who is loyal to Sharu to a fault.

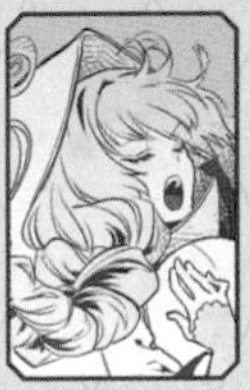

### SHARURU LINKINGFEATHER

A kindhearted White Mage who eagerly treats all who are injured.

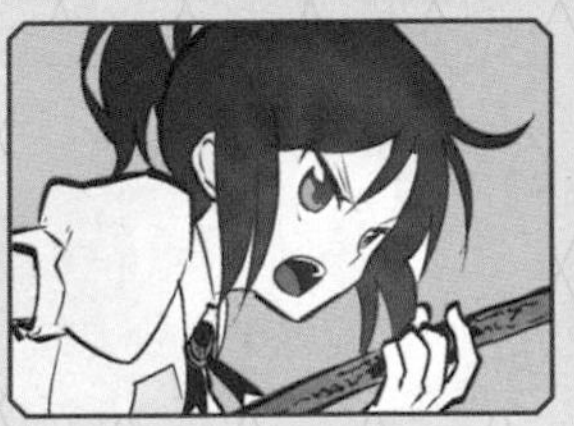

### YUKO SASAKI

A second-year sales department employee at SE. She was transported alongside her brother Shogo but was killed saving a little girl from a dragon. Her soul was turned into a crystal.

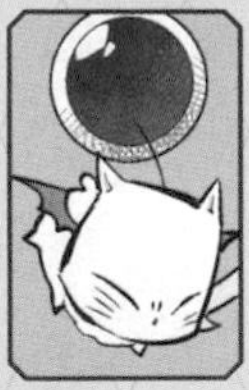

### MOG MOGCAN

A moogle who travels with Sharuru's party.

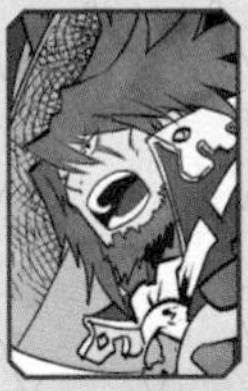

### DUSTON VOLTA

A burly Black Mage of the Hyuuj race who also cooks.

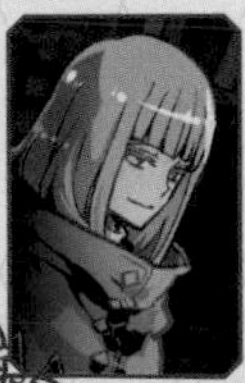

### ALUS

A young man with blond hair and aquamarine eyes. Wields powerful spells such as "Reflect."

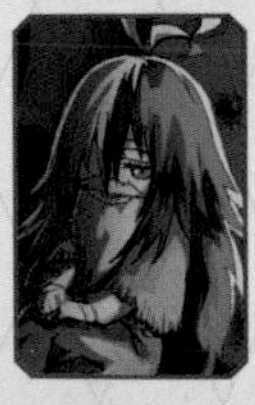

### G-SENPAI

A mysterious elderly man the party met in the Great Library. Well versed in the library's secrets.

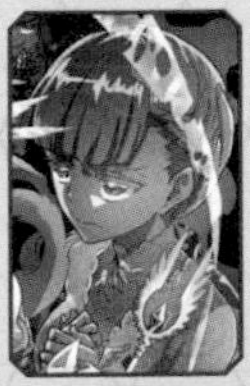

### SARA MYSIDIAN

Princess of the Mysidian Kingdom. Concerned for her nation's future, she teams up with Shogo and company.

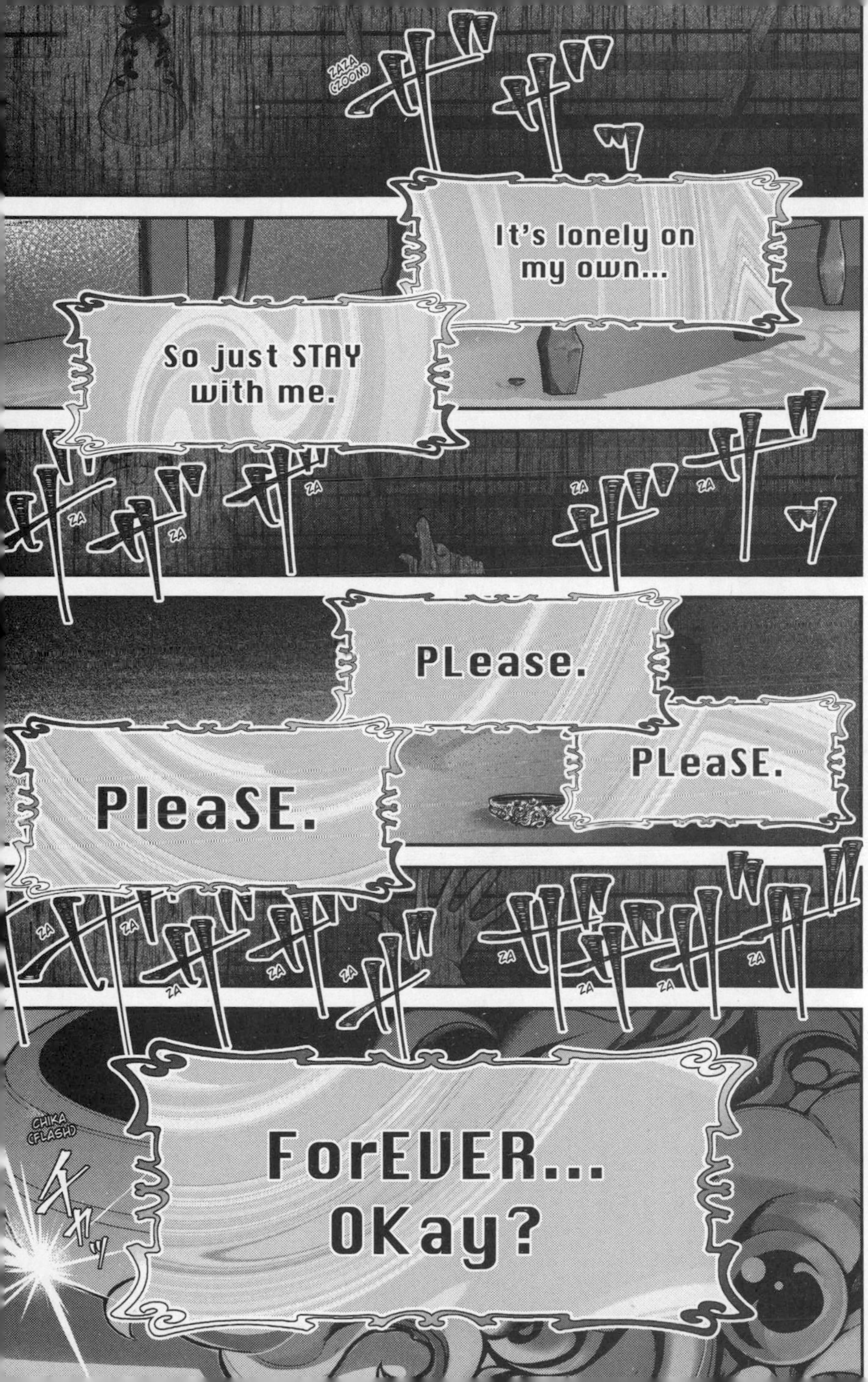
ZAZA (ZOOM)
It's lonely on my own...
So just STAY with me.
ZA
ZA
ZA
ZA
ZA
PLease.
PLeaSE.
PleaSE.
ZA
ZA
ZA
ZA
ZA
ZA
ZA
ZA
ZA
ZA
ForEVER... OKay?
CHIKA (FLASH)

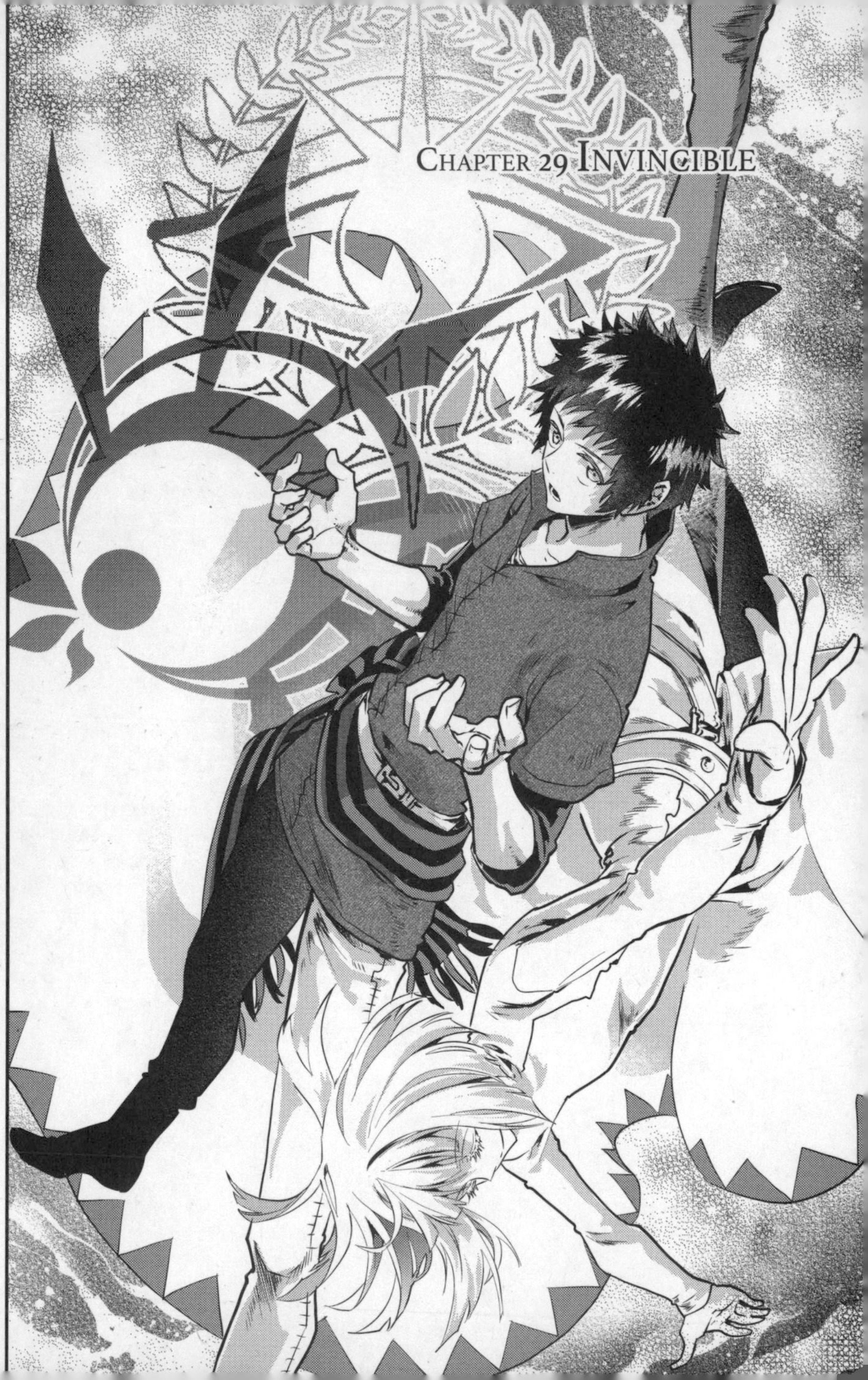
Chapter 29 Invincible

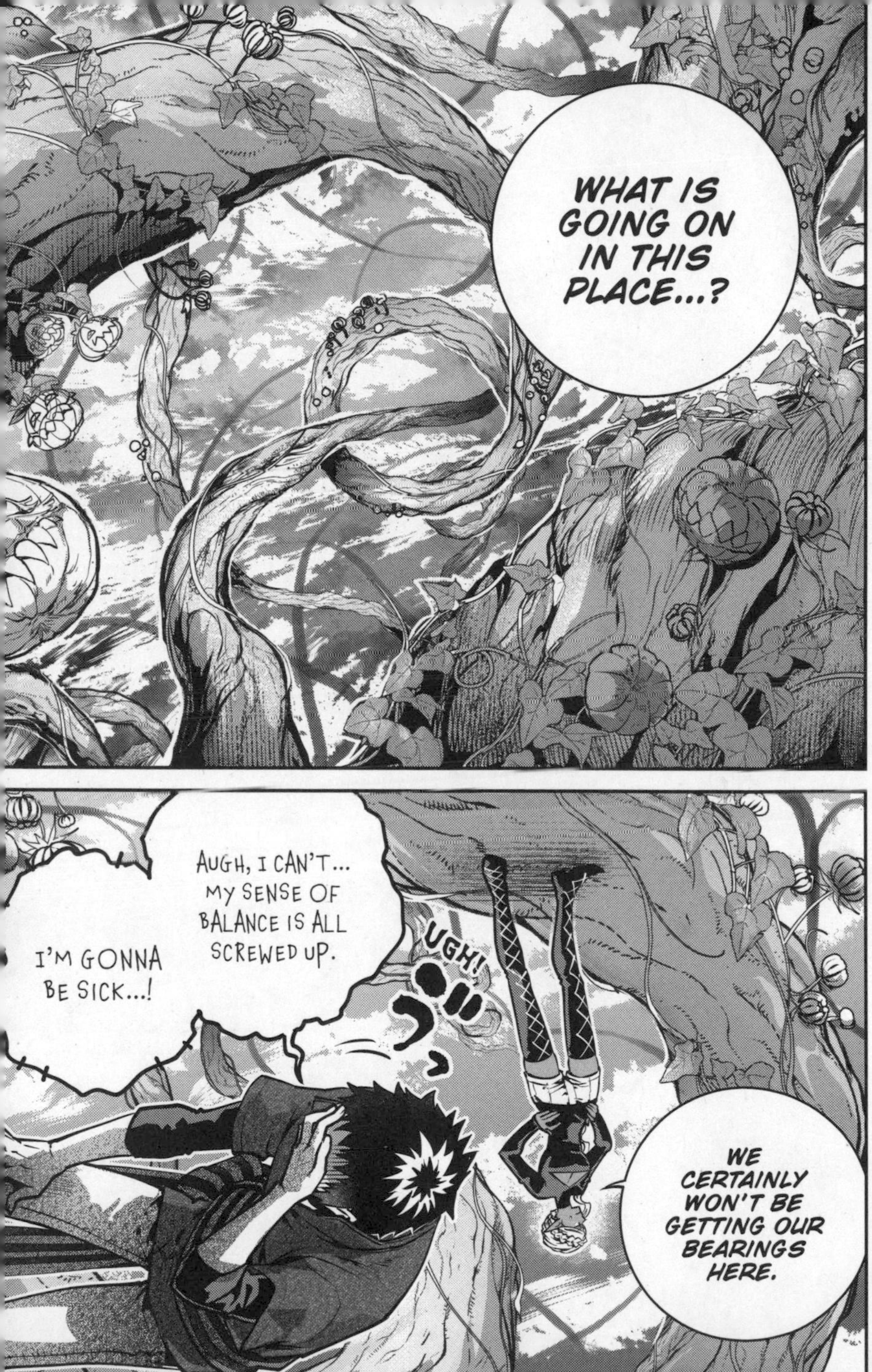
WHAT IS GOING ON IN THIS PLACE...?
WE CERTAINLY WON'T BE GETTING OUR BEARINGS HERE.
UGH!
AUGH, I CAN'T... MY SENSE OF BALANCE IS ALL SCREWED UP.
I'M GONNA BE SICK...!

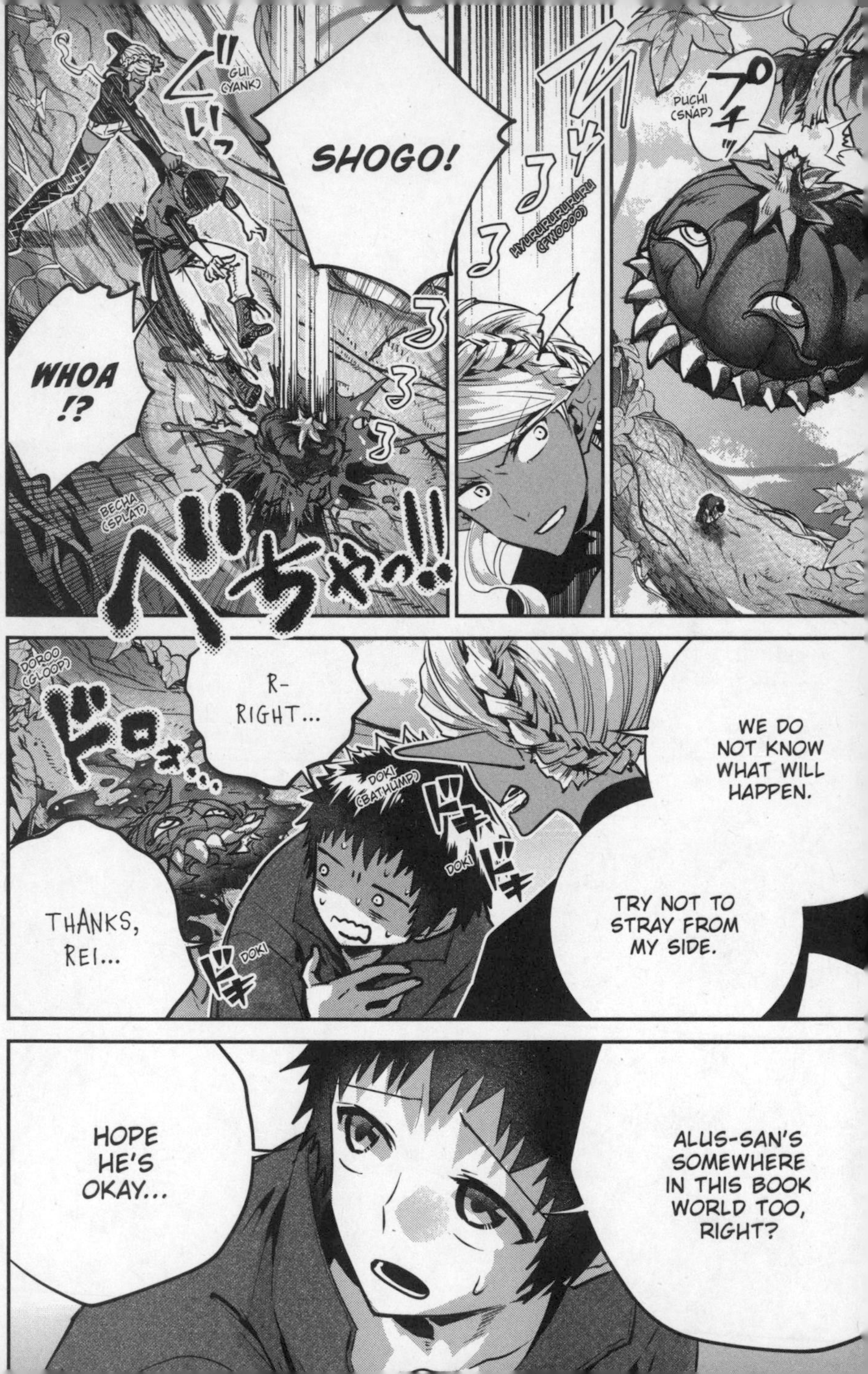
PUCHI (SNAP)
HYURURURURU (FWOOOO)
SHOGO!
GUI (YANK)
WHOA!?
BECHA (SPLAT)
WE DO NOT KNOW WHAT WILL HAPPEN.
TRY NOT TO STRAY FROM MY SIDE.
DOKI (BATHUMP)
DOKI
DOKI
R-RIGHT...
THANKS, REI...
DOROO (GLOOP)
ALUS-SAN'S SOMEWHERE IN THIS BOOK WORLD TOO, RIGHT?
HOPE HE'S OKAY...

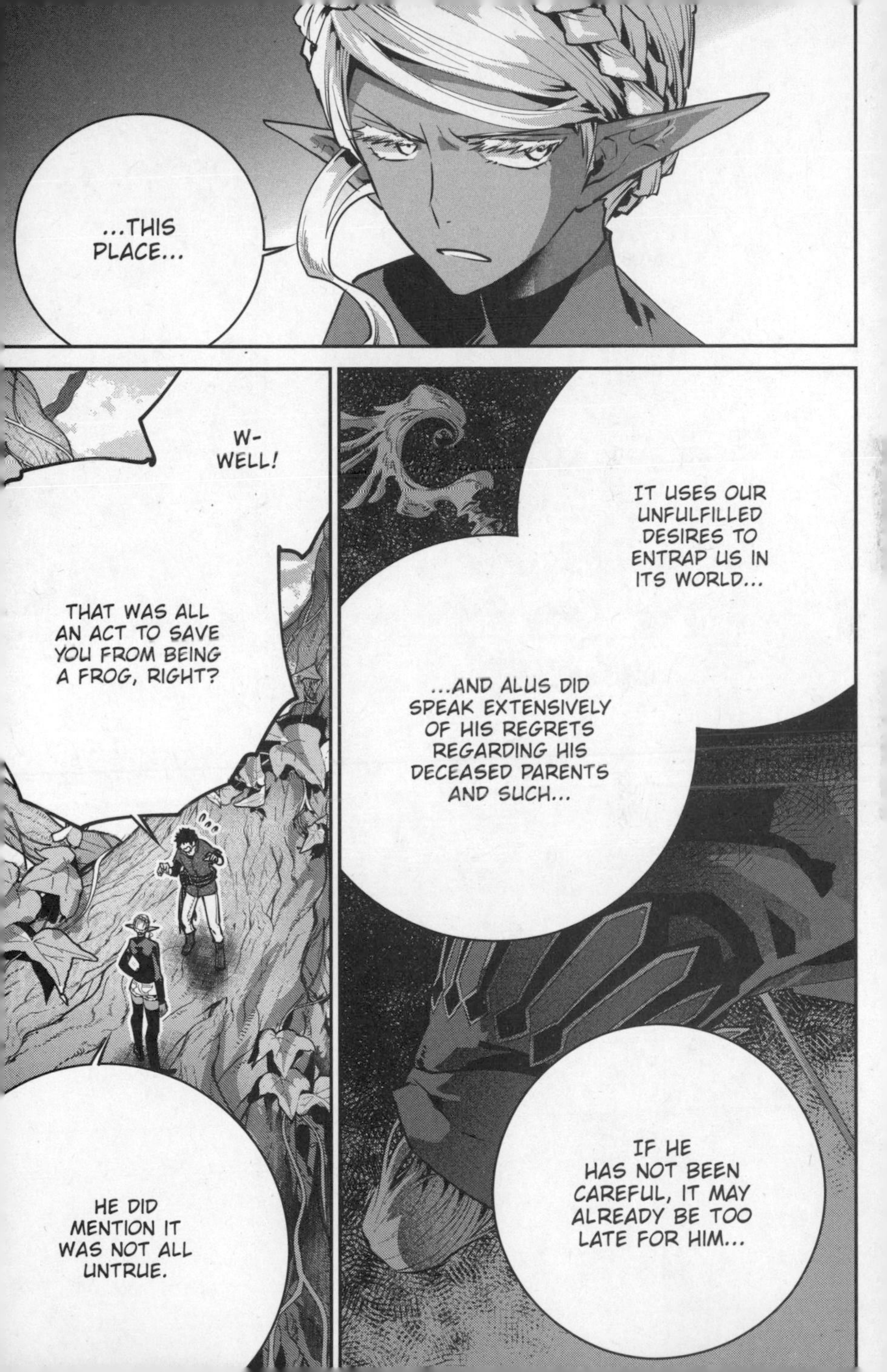
...THIS PLACE...
IT USES OUR UNFULFILLED DESIRES TO ENTRAP US IN ITS WORLD...
...AND ALUS DID SPEAK EXTENSIVELY OF HIS REGRETS REGARDING HIS DECEASED PARENTS AND SUCH...
IF HE HAS NOT BEEN CAREFUL, IT MAY ALREADY BE TOO LATE FOR HIM...
W-WELL!
THAT WAS ALL AN ACT TO SAVE YOU FROM BEING A FROG, RIGHT?
HE DID MENTION IT WAS NOT ALL UNTRUE.

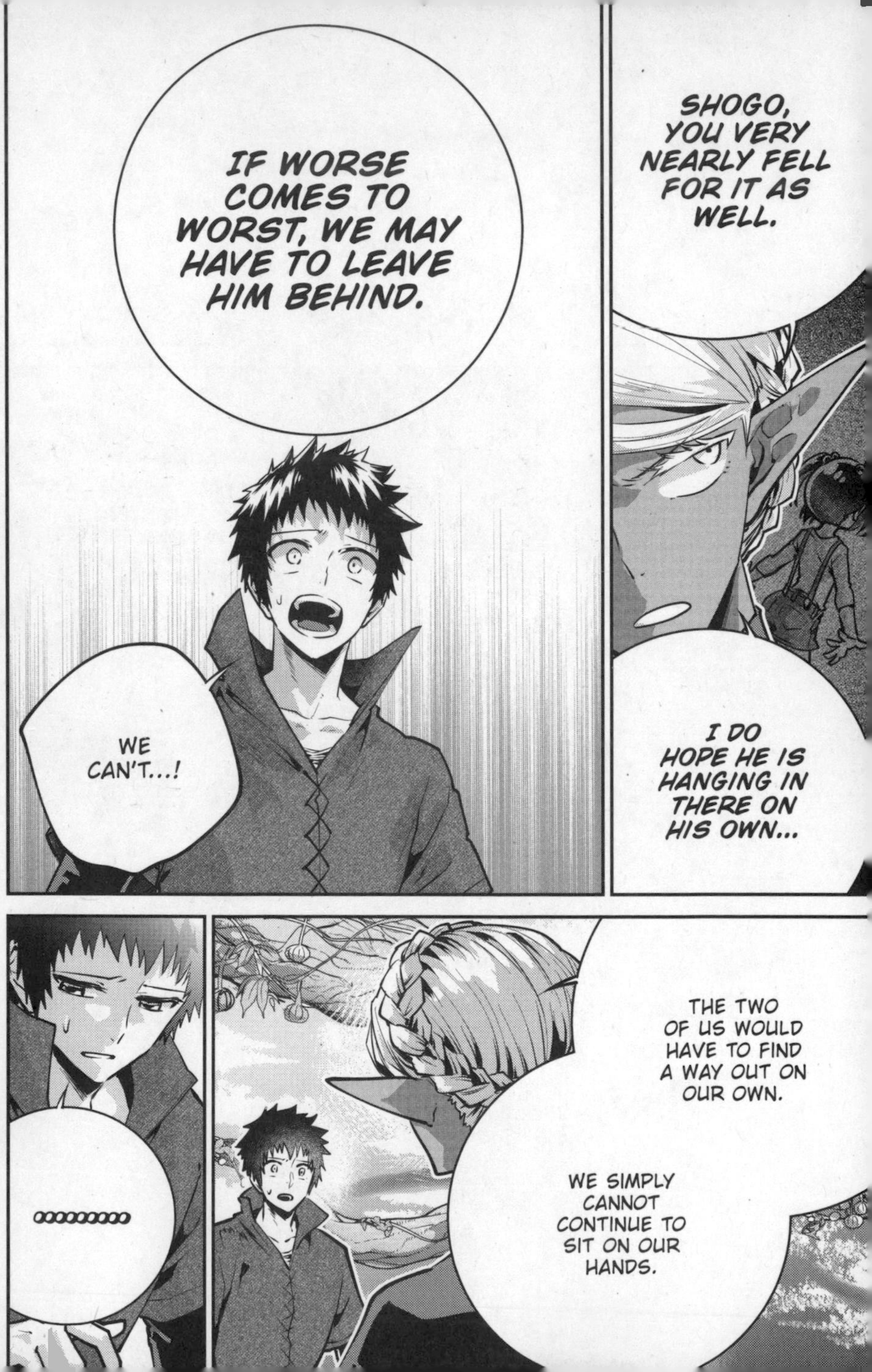
SHOGO, YOU VERY NEARLY FELL FOR IT AS WELL.
I DO HOPE HE IS HANGING IN THERE ON HIS OWN...
IF WORSE COMES TO WORST, WE MAY HAVE TO LEAVE HIM BEHIND.
WE CAN'T...!
THE TWO OF US WOULD HAVE TO FIND A WAY OUT ON OUR OWN.
WE SIMPLY CANNOT CONTINUE TO SIT ON OUR HANDS.
.........

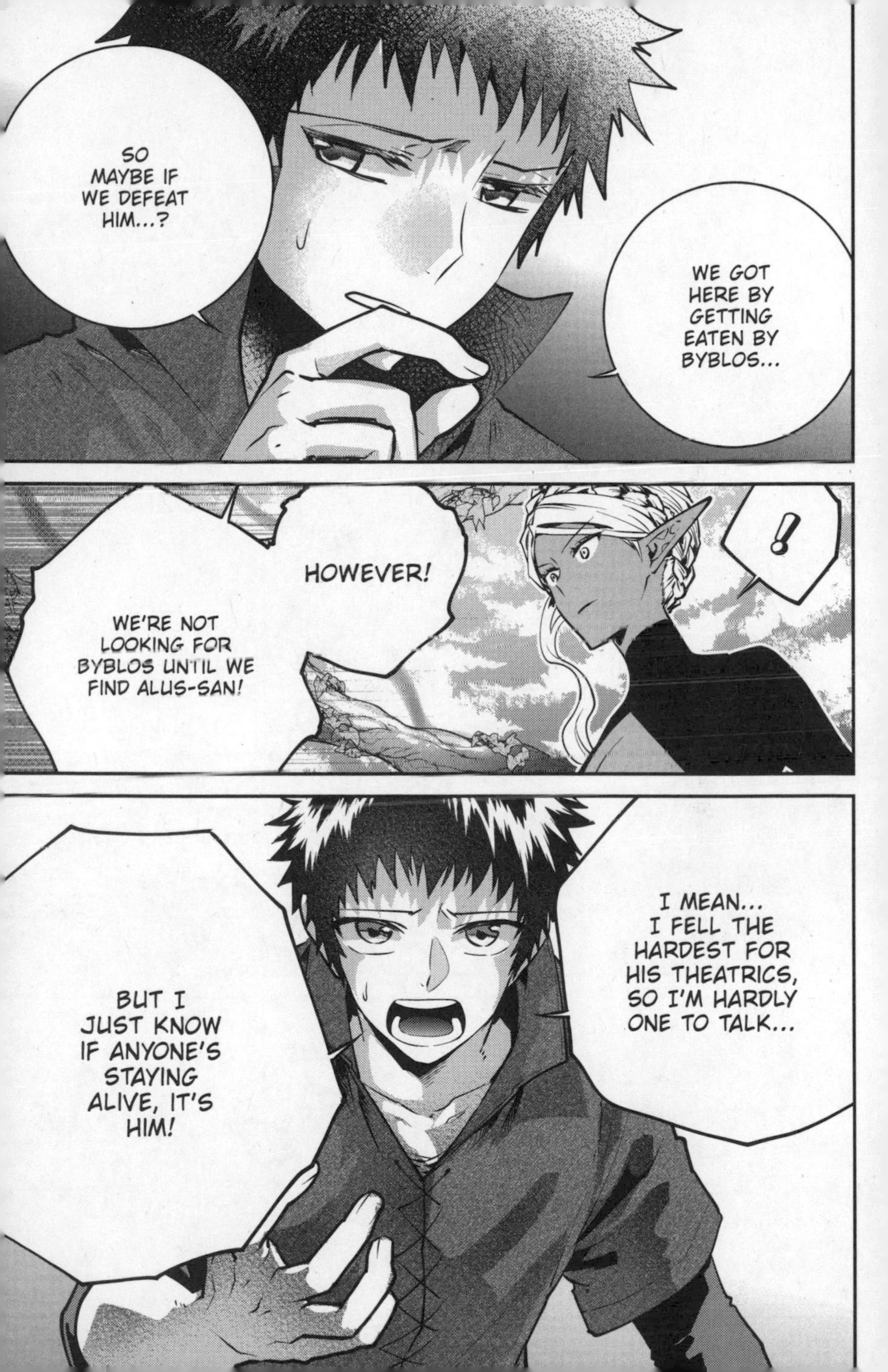
WE GOT HERE BY GETTING EATEN BY BYBLOS...
SO MAYBE IF WE DEFEAT HIM...?
!
HOWEVER!
WE'RE NOT LOOKING FOR BYBLOS UNTIL WE FIND ALUS-SAN!
I MEAN... I FELL THE HARDEST FOR HIS THEATRICS, SO I'M HARDLY ONE TO TALK...
BUT I JUST KNOW IF ANYONE'S STAYING ALIVE, IT'S HIM!

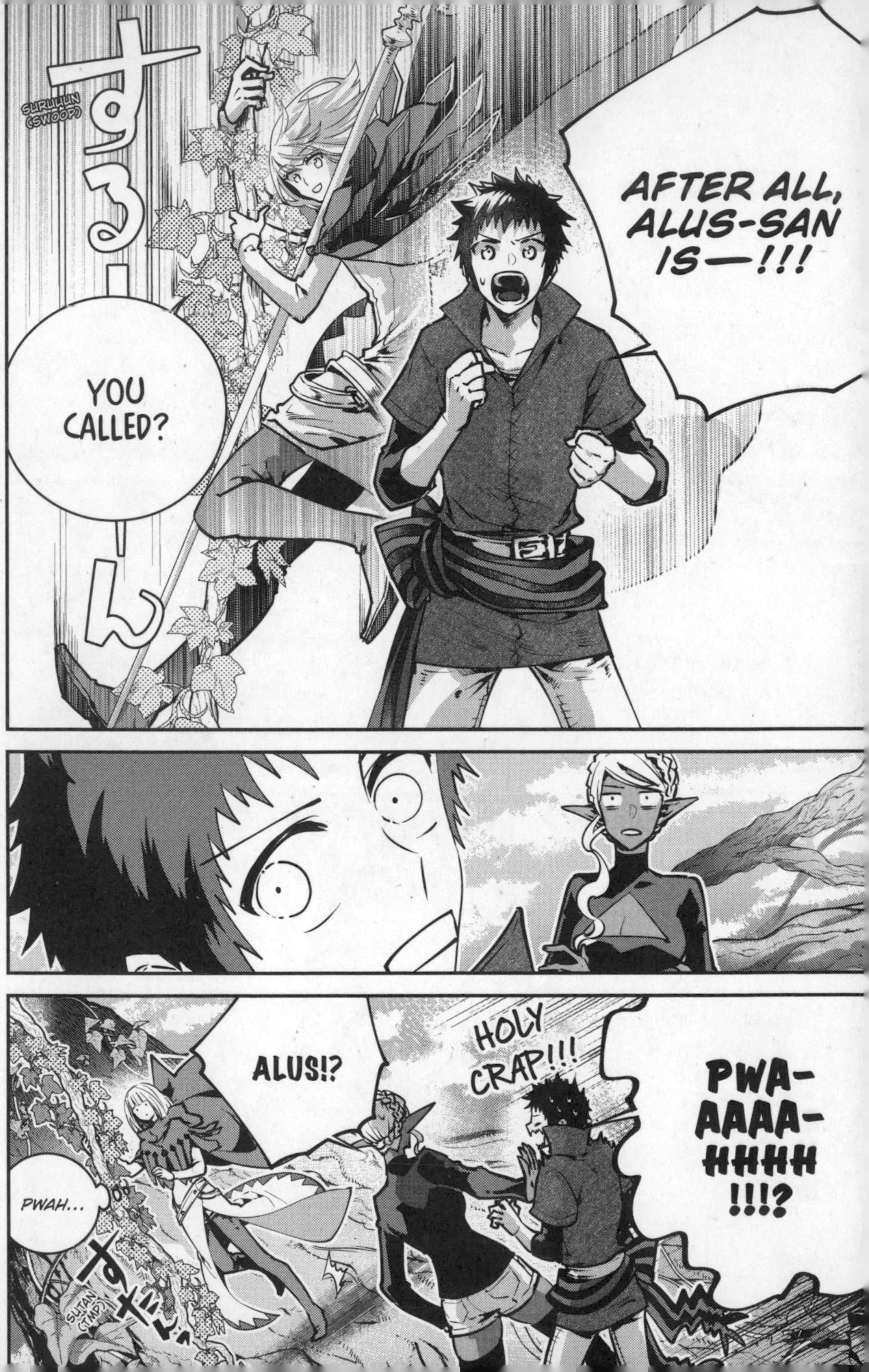
AFTER ALL, ALUS-SAN IS—!!!
YOU CALLED?
するーん
SURUUUN (SWOOP)
PWA-AAAA-HHHH!!!?
HOLY CRAP!!!
ALUS!?
PWAH...
すたっ!!
SUTAN (TMP)

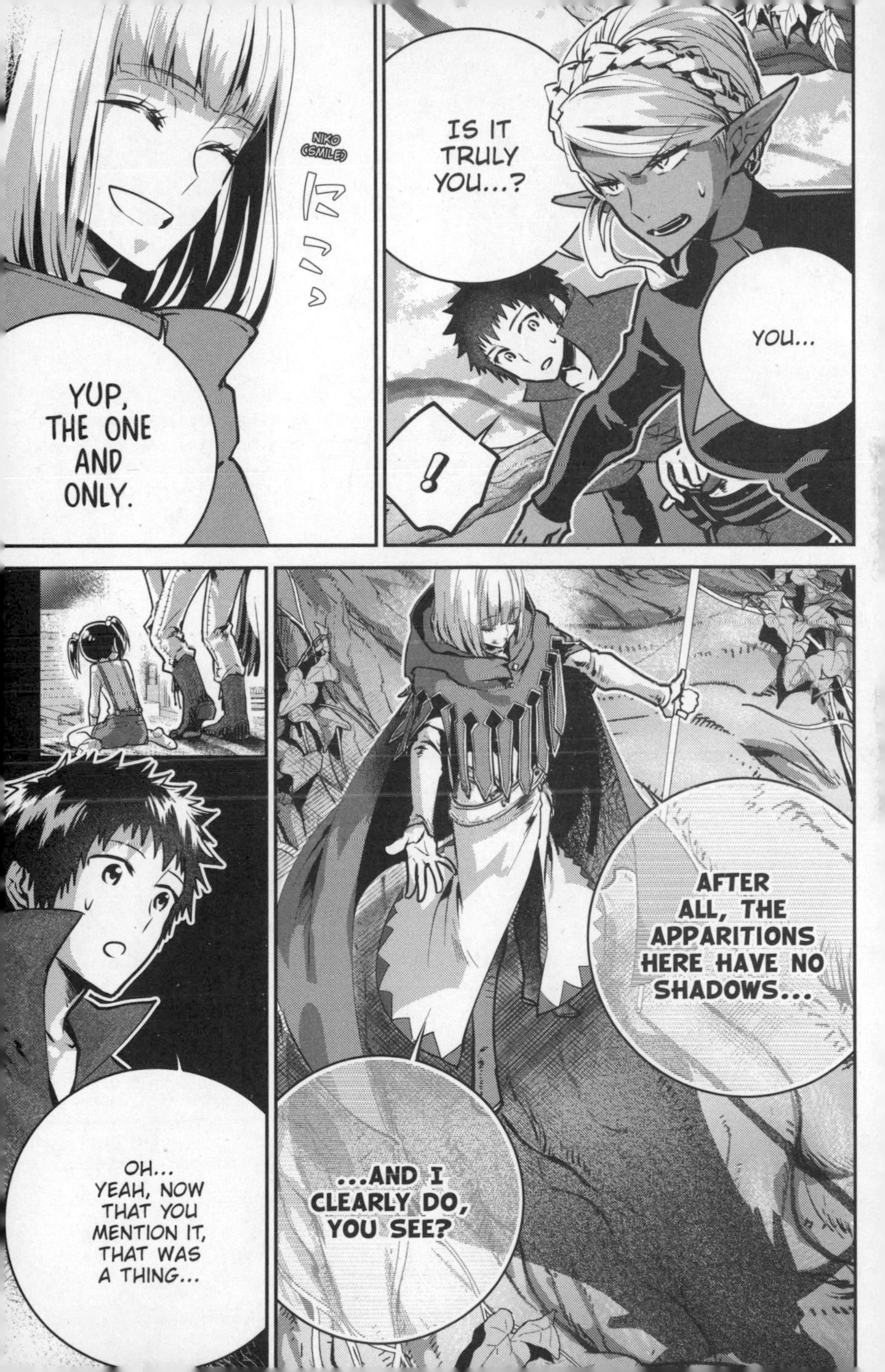
YOU...
IS IT TRULY YOU...?
!
NIKO (SMILE)
にこっ
YUP, THE ONE AND ONLY.
AFTER ALL, THE APPARITIONS HERE HAVE NO SHADOWS...
...AND I CLEARLY DO, YOU SEE?
OH... YEAH, NOW THAT YOU MENTION IT, THAT WAS A THING...

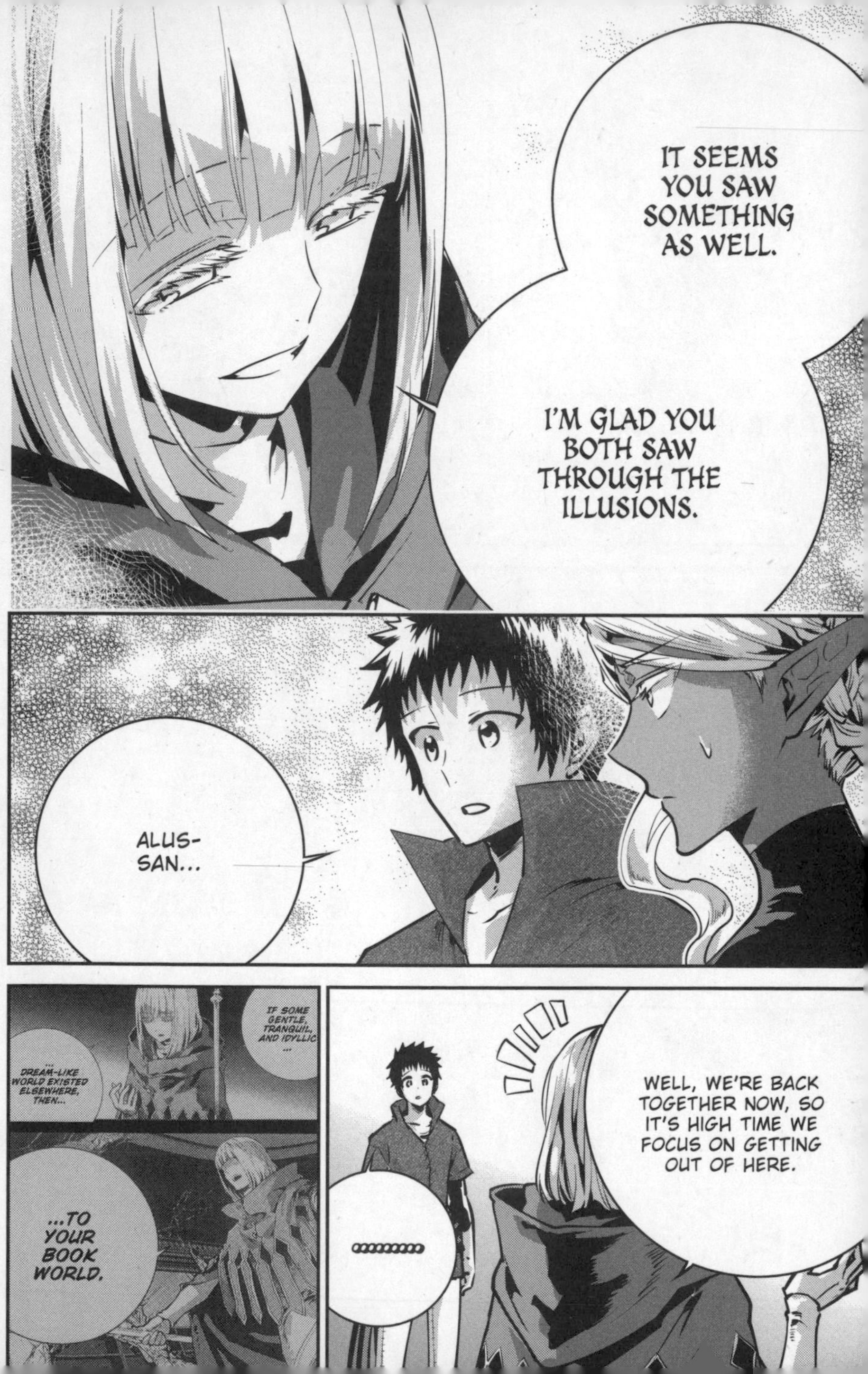
IT SEEMS YOU SAW SOMETHING AS WELL.
I'M GLAD YOU BOTH SAW THROUGH THE ILLUSIONS.
ALUS-SAN...
WELL, WE'RE BACK TOGETHER NOW, SO IT'S HIGH TIME WE FOCUS ON GETTING OUT OF HERE.
……
IF SOME GENTLE, TRANQUIL, AND IDYLLIC...
...DREAM-LIKE WORLD EXISTED ELSEWHERE, THEN...
...TO YOUR BOOK WORLD.

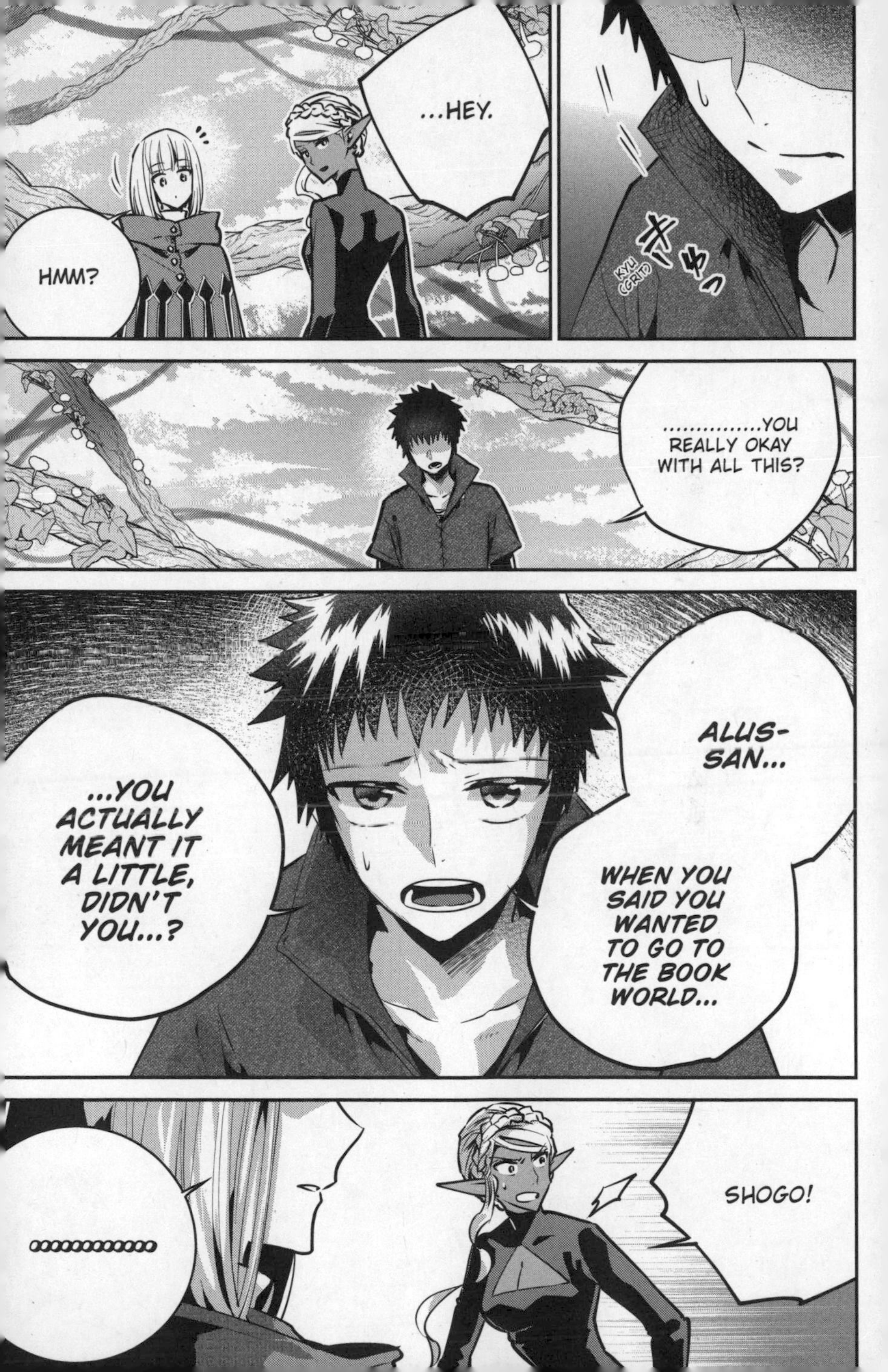
KYU (GRIT)
...HEY.
HMM?
...............YOU REALLY OKAY WITH ALL THIS?
ALUS-SAN...
WHEN YOU SAID YOU WANTED TO GO TO THE BOOK WORLD...
...YOU ACTUALLY MEANT IT A LITTLE, DIDN'T YOU...?
SHOGO!
ooooooooooooo

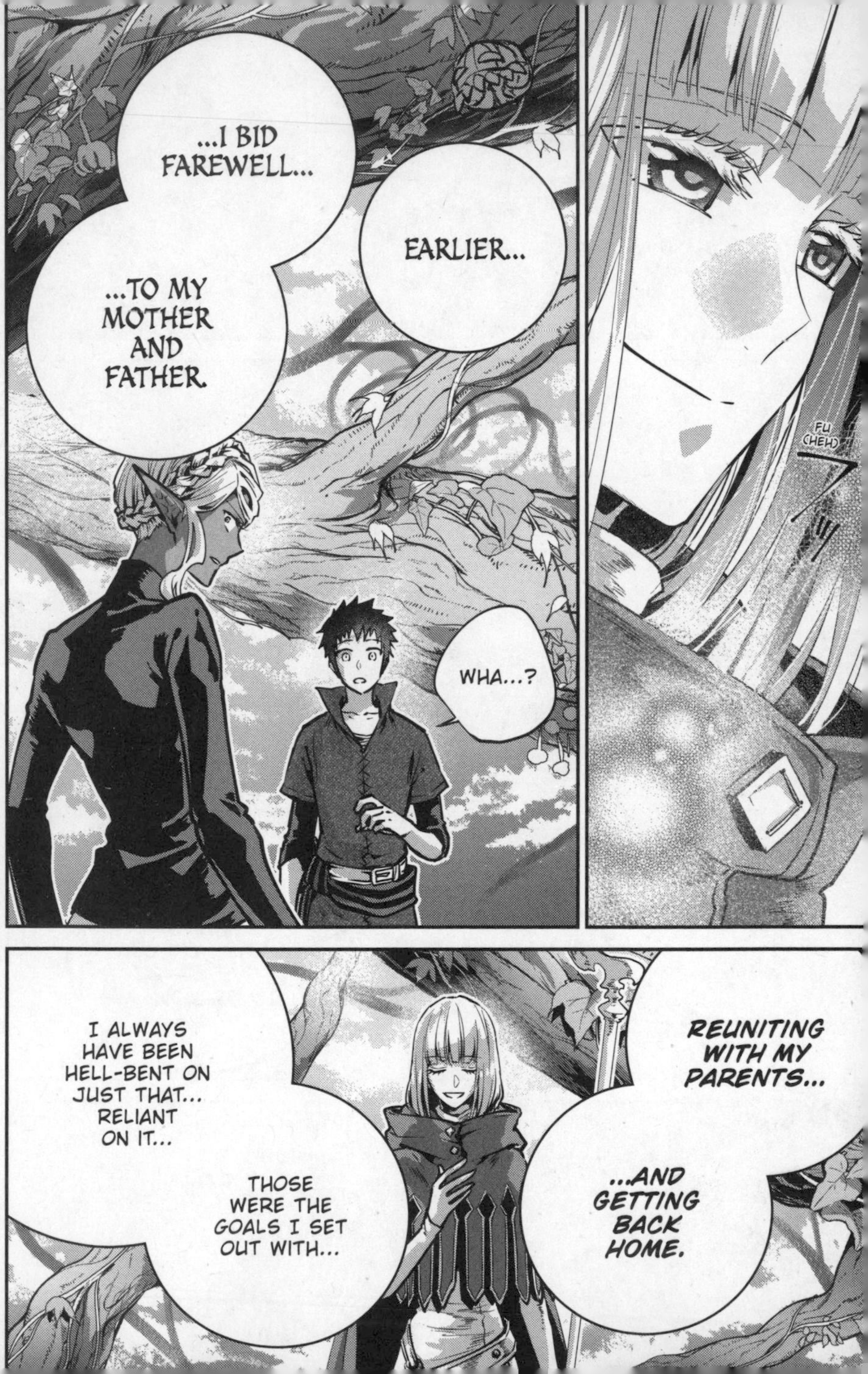
FU (HEH)
EARLIER...
...I BID FAREWELL...
...TO MY MOTHER AND FATHER.
WHA...?
REUNITING WITH MY PARENTS...
...AND GETTING BACK HOME.
THOSE WERE THE GOALS I SET OUT WITH...
I ALWAYS HAVE BEEN HELL-BENT ON JUST THAT... RELIANT ON IT...

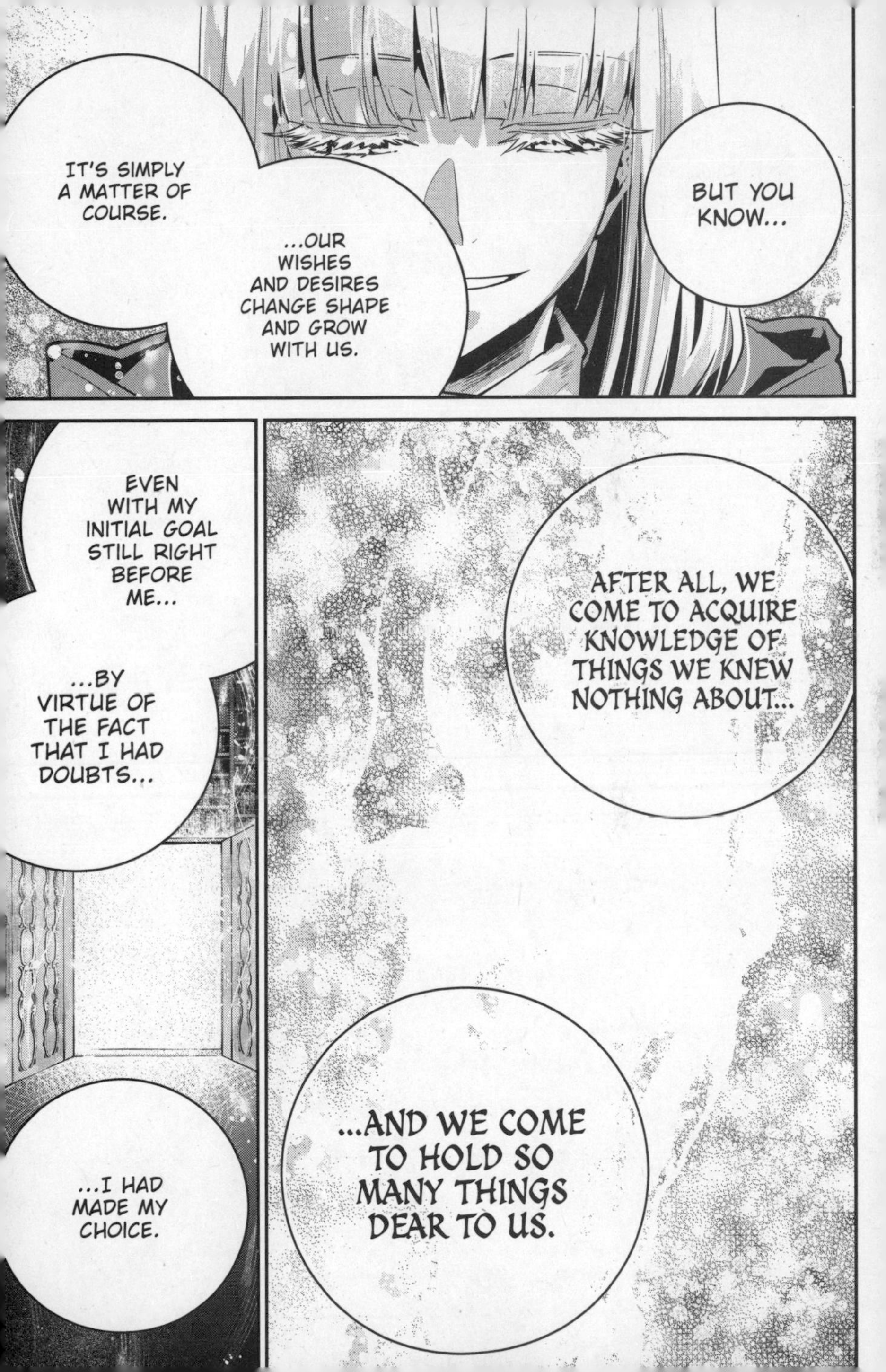
BUT YOU KNOW...
IT'S SIMPLY A MATTER OF COURSE.
...OUR WISHES AND DESIRES CHANGE SHAPE AND GROW WITH US.
AFTER ALL, WE COME TO ACQUIRE KNOWLEDGE OF THINGS WE KNEW NOTHING ABOUT...
...AND WE COME TO HOLD SO MANY THINGS DEAR TO US.
EVEN WITH MY INITIAL GOAL STILL RIGHT BEFORE ME...
...BY VIRTUE OF THE FACT THAT I HAD DOUBTS...
...I HAD MADE MY CHOICE.

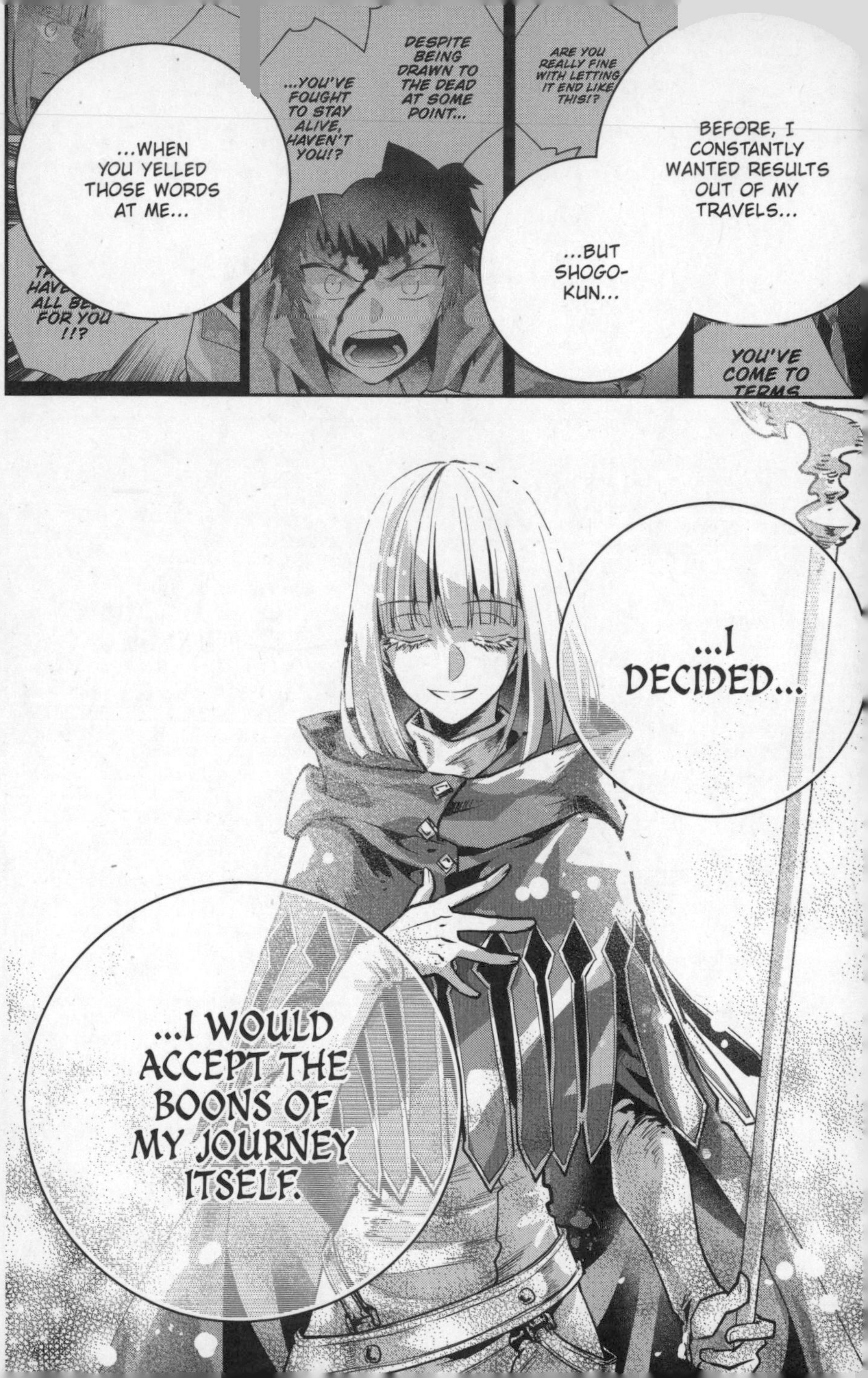
BEFORE, I CONSTANTLY WANTED RESULTS OUT OF MY TRAVELS...
ARE YOU REALLY FINE WITH LETTING IT END LIKE THIS!?
YOU'VE COME TO
...BUT SHOGO-KUN...
DESPITE BEING DRAWN TO THE DEAD AT SOME POINT...
...YOU'VE FOUGHT TO STAY ALIVE, HAVEN'T YOU!?
...WHEN YOU YELLED THOSE WORDS AT ME...
...I DECIDED...
...I WOULD ACCEPT THE BOONS OF MY JOURNEY ITSELF.

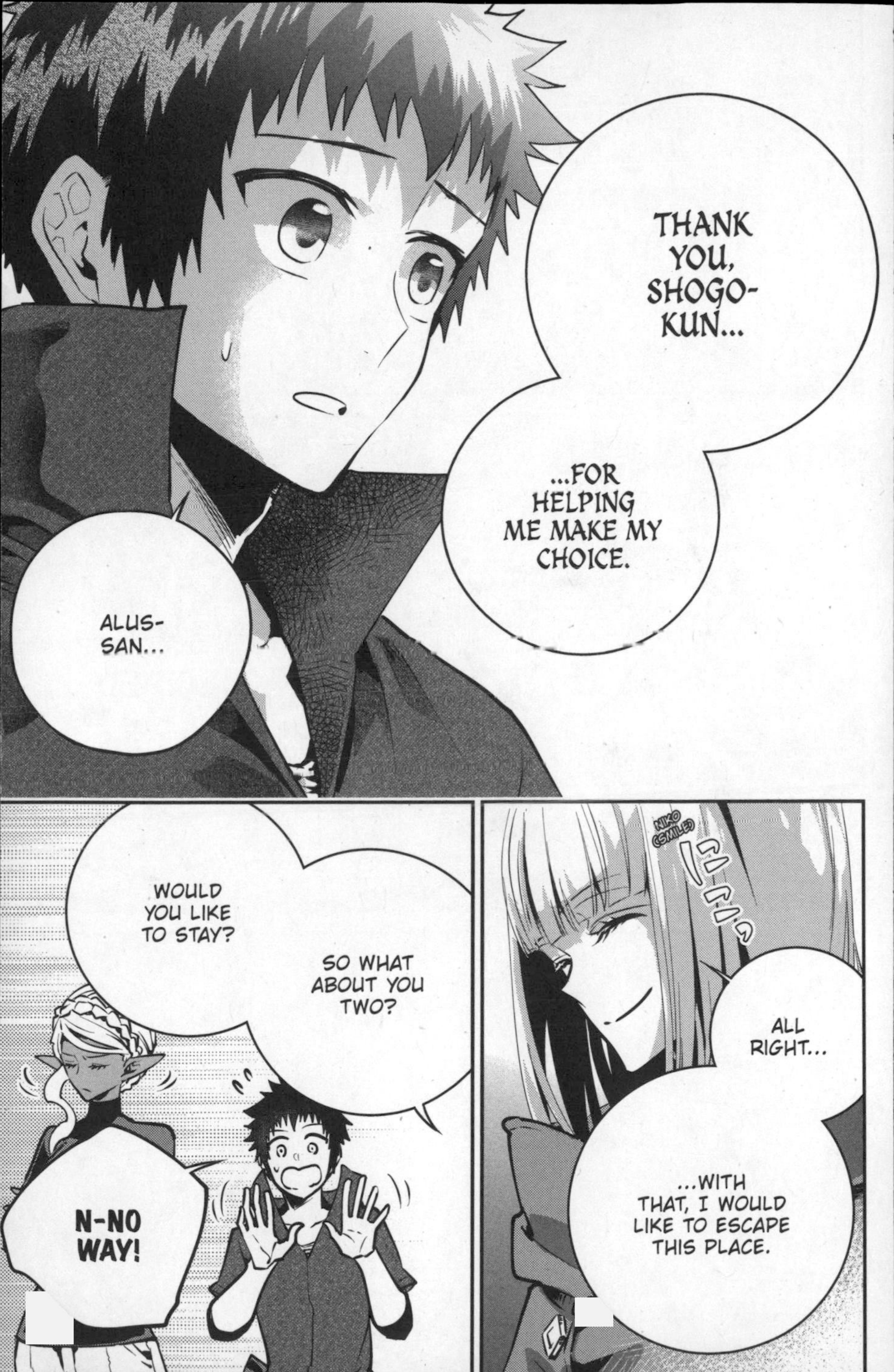
THANK YOU, SHOGO-KUN...
...FOR HELPING ME MAKE MY CHOICE.
ALUS-SAN...
NIKO (SMILE)
ALL RIGHT...
...WITH THAT, I WOULD LIKE TO ESCAPE THIS PLACE.
SO WHAT ABOUT YOU TWO?
WOULD YOU LIKE TO STAY?
N-NO WAY!

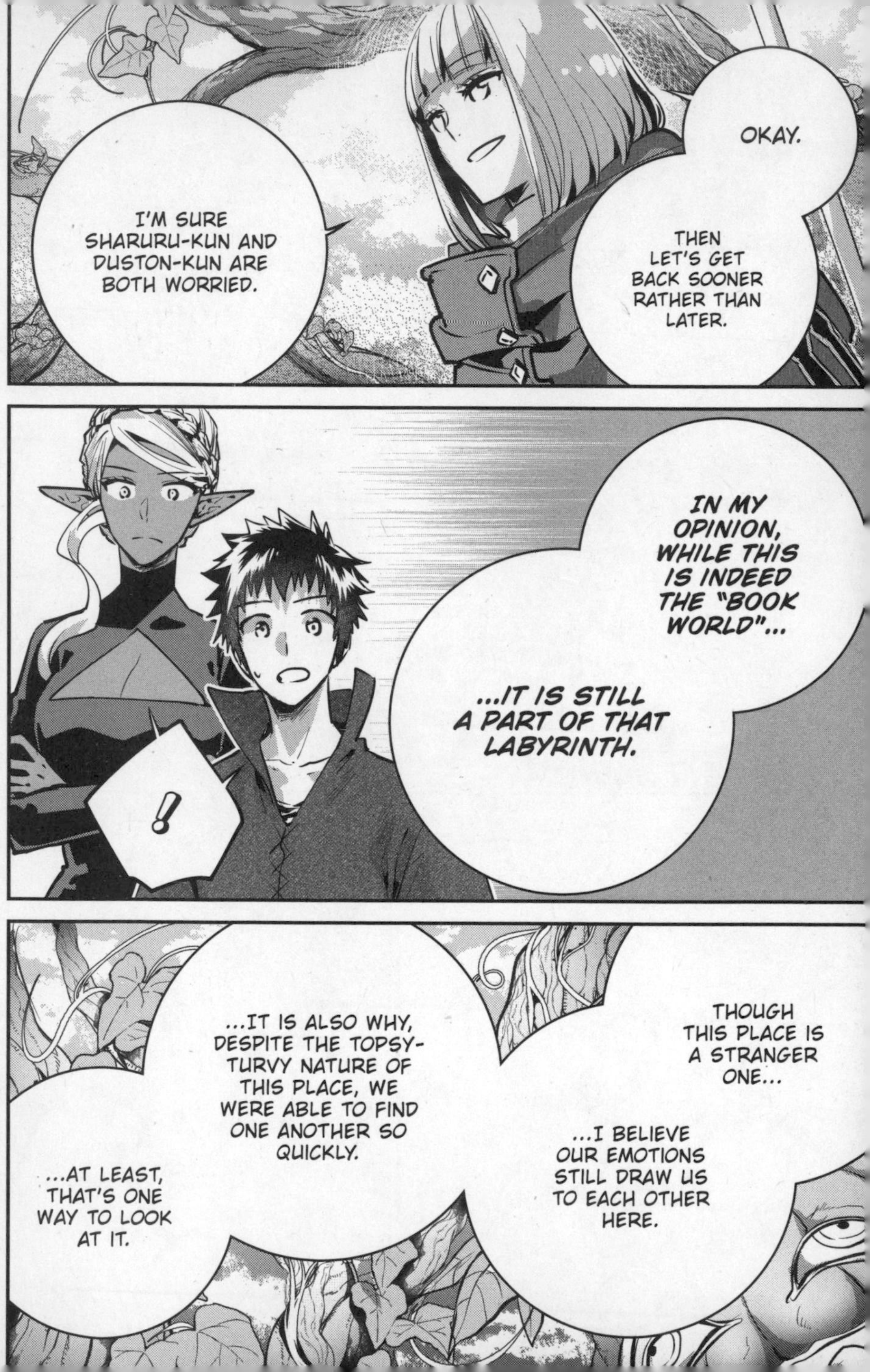
OKAY.
THEN LET'S GET BACK SOONER RATHER THAN LATER.
I'M SURE SHARURU-KUN AND DUSTON-KUN ARE BOTH WORRIED.
IN MY OPINION, WHILE THIS IS INDEED THE "BOOK WORLD"...
...IT IS STILL A PART OF THAT LABYRINTH.
!
THOUGH THIS PLACE IS A STRANGER ONE...
...I BELIEVE OUR EMOTIONS STILL DRAW US TO EACH OTHER HERE.
...IT IS ALSO WHY, DESPITE THE TOPSY-TURVY NATURE OF THIS PLACE, WE WERE ABLE TO FIND ONE ANOTHER SO QUICKLY.
...AT LEAST, THAT'S ONE WAY TO LOOK AT IT.

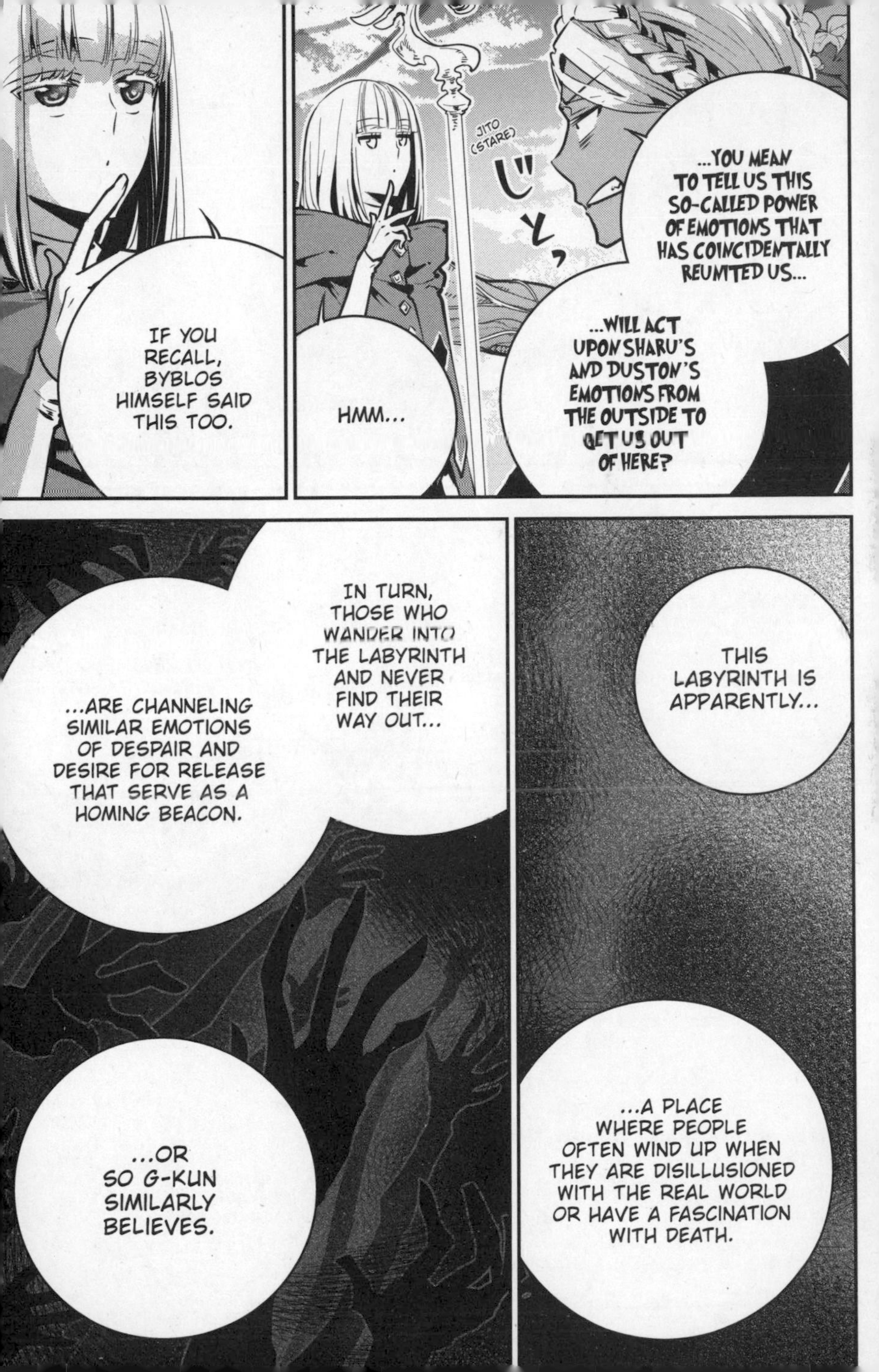
...YOU MEAN TO TELL US THIS SO-CALLED POWER OF EMOTIONS THAT HAS COINCIDENTALLY REUNITED US...
JITO (STARE)
...WILL ACT UPON SHARU'S AND DUSTON'S EMOTIONS FROM THE OUTSIDE TO GET US OUT OF HERE?
HMM...
IF YOU RECALL, BYBLOS HIMSELF SAID THIS TOO.
THIS LABYRINTH IS APPARENTLY...
...A PLACE WHERE PEOPLE OFTEN WIND UP WHEN THEY ARE DISILLUSIONED WITH THE REAL WORLD OR HAVE A FASCINATION WITH DEATH.
IN TURN, THOSE WHO WANDER INTO THE LABYRINTH AND NEVER FIND THEIR WAY OUT...
...ARE CHANNELING SIMILAR EMOTIONS OF DESPAIR AND DESIRE FOR RELEASE THAT SERVE AS A HOMING BEACON.
...OR SO G-KUN SIMILARLY BELIEVES.

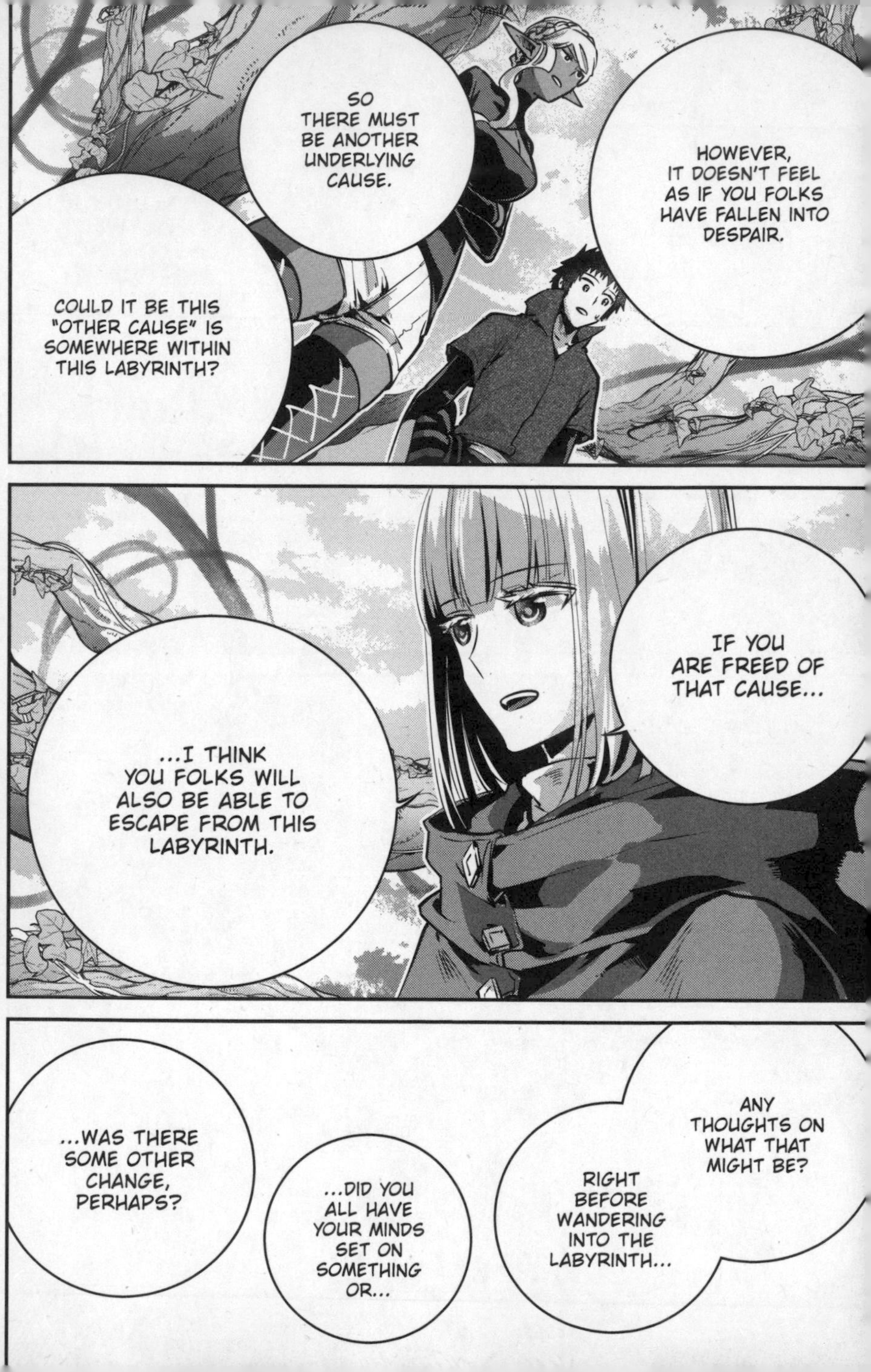
HOWEVER, IT DOESN'T FEEL AS IF YOU FOLKS HAVE FALLEN INTO DESPAIR.
SO THERE MUST BE ANOTHER UNDERLYING CAUSE.
COULD IT BE THIS "OTHER CAUSE" IS SOMEWHERE WITHIN THIS LABYRINTH?
IF YOU ARE FREED OF THAT CAUSE...
...I THINK YOU FOLKS WILL ALSO BE ABLE TO ESCAPE FROM THIS LABYRINTH.
ANY THOUGHTS ON WHAT THAT MIGHT BE?
RIGHT BEFORE WANDERING INTO THE LABYRINTH...
...DID YOU ALL HAVE YOUR MINDS SET ON SOMETHING OR...
...WAS THERE SOME OTHER CHANGE, PERHAPS?

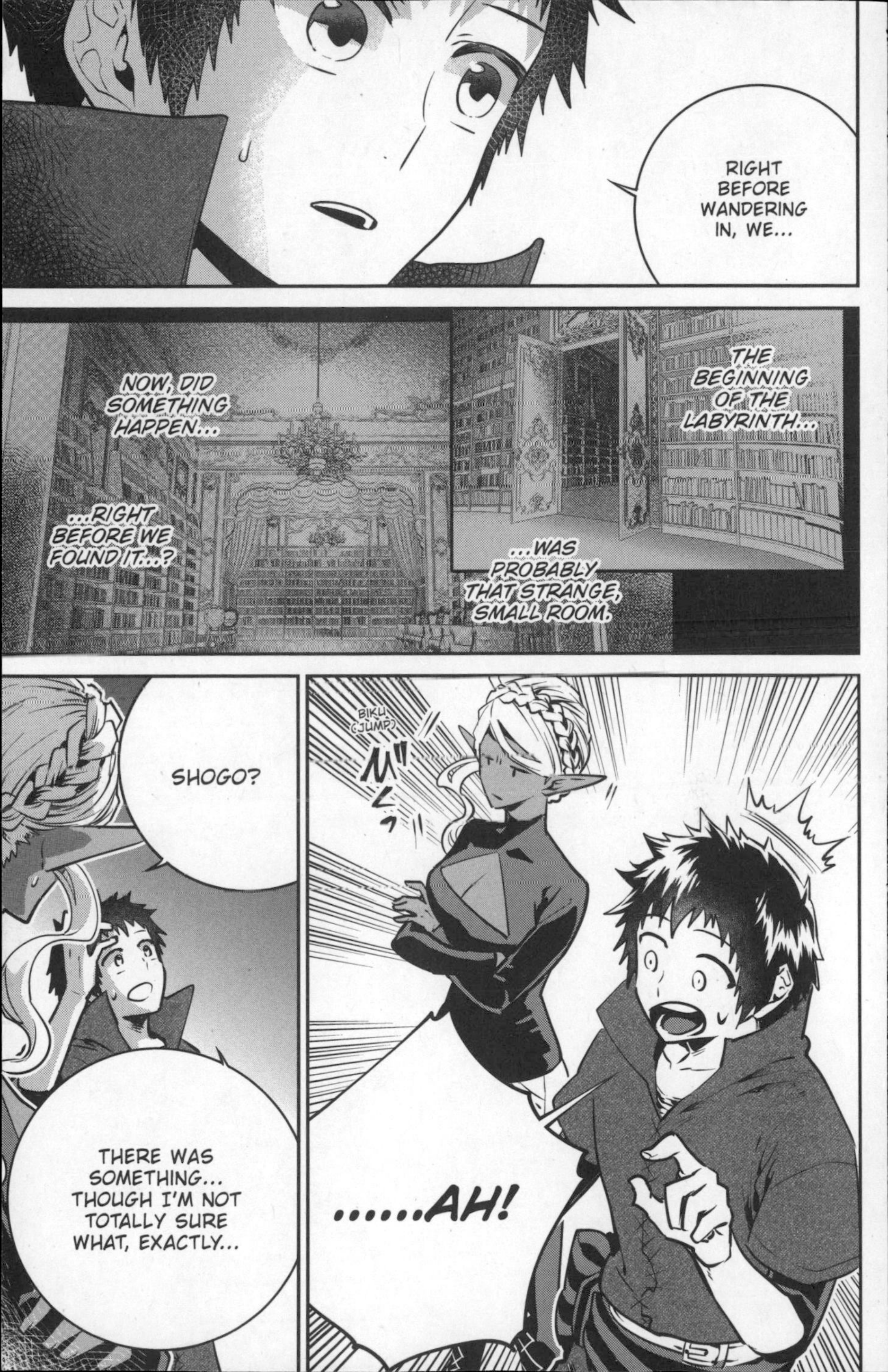
RIGHT BEFORE WANDERING IN, WE...
THE BEGINNING OF THE LABYRINTH...
...WAS PROBABLY THAT STRANGE, SMALL ROOM.
NOW, DID SOMETHING HAPPEN...
...RIGHT BEFORE WE FOUND IT...?
BIKU (JUMP)
......AH!
SHOGO?
THERE WAS SOMETHING... THOUGH I'M NOT TOTALLY SURE WHAT, EXACTLY...

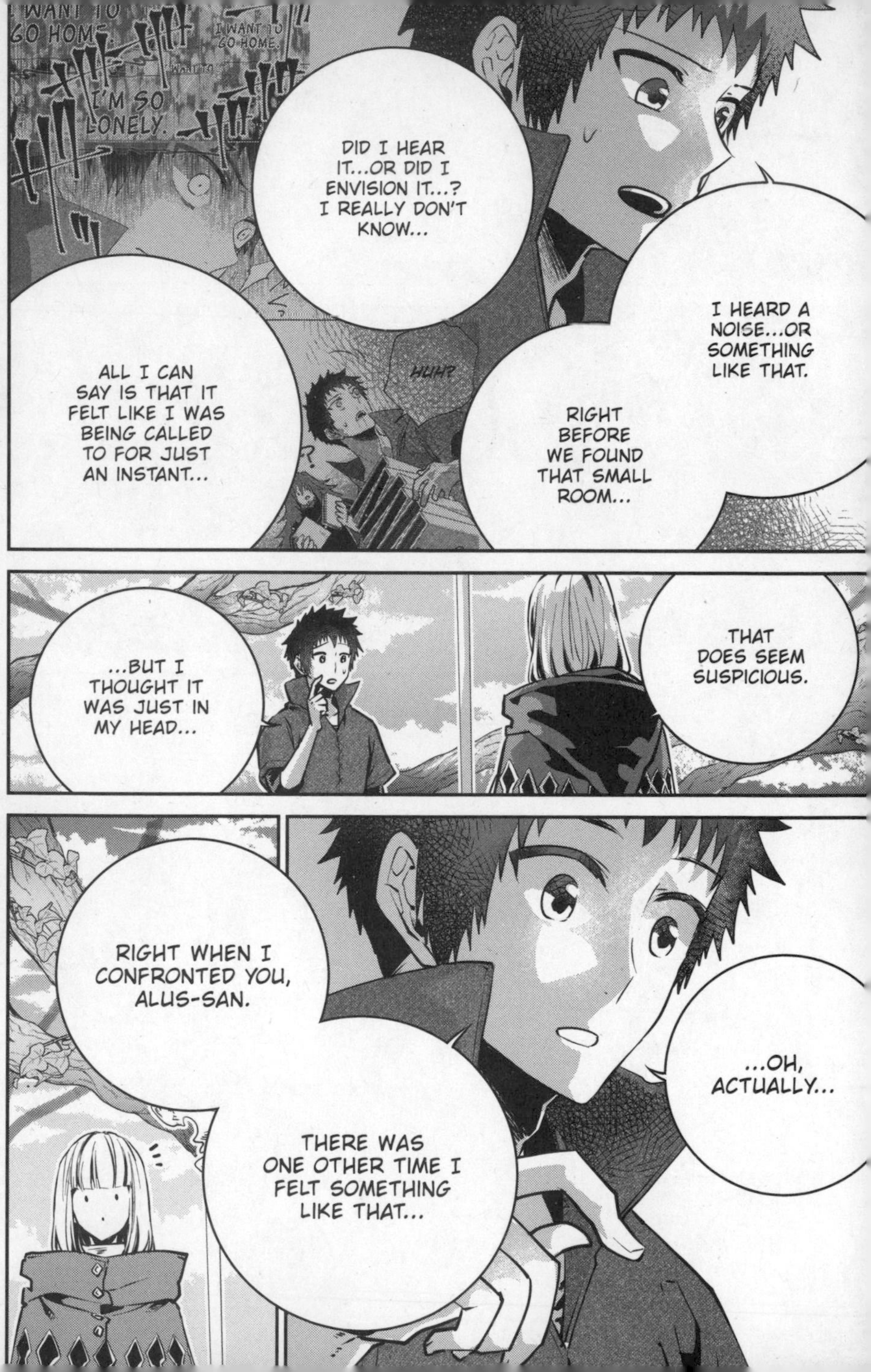
I HEARD A NOISE...OR SOMETHING LIKE THAT.
RIGHT BEFORE WE FOUND THAT SMALL ROOM...
DID I HEAR IT...OR DID I ENVISION IT...? I REALLY DON'T KNOW...
I WANT TO GO HOME.
I WANT TO GO HOME
I'M SO LONELY.
HUH?
ALL I CAN SAY IS THAT IT FELT LIKE I WAS BEING CALLED TO FOR JUST AN INSTANT...
THAT DOES SEEM SUSPICIOUS.
...BUT I THOUGHT IT WAS JUST IN MY HEAD...
...OH, ACTUALLY...
RIGHT WHEN I CONFRONTED YOU, ALUS-SAN.
THERE WAS ONE OTHER TIME I FELT SOMETHING LIKE THAT...

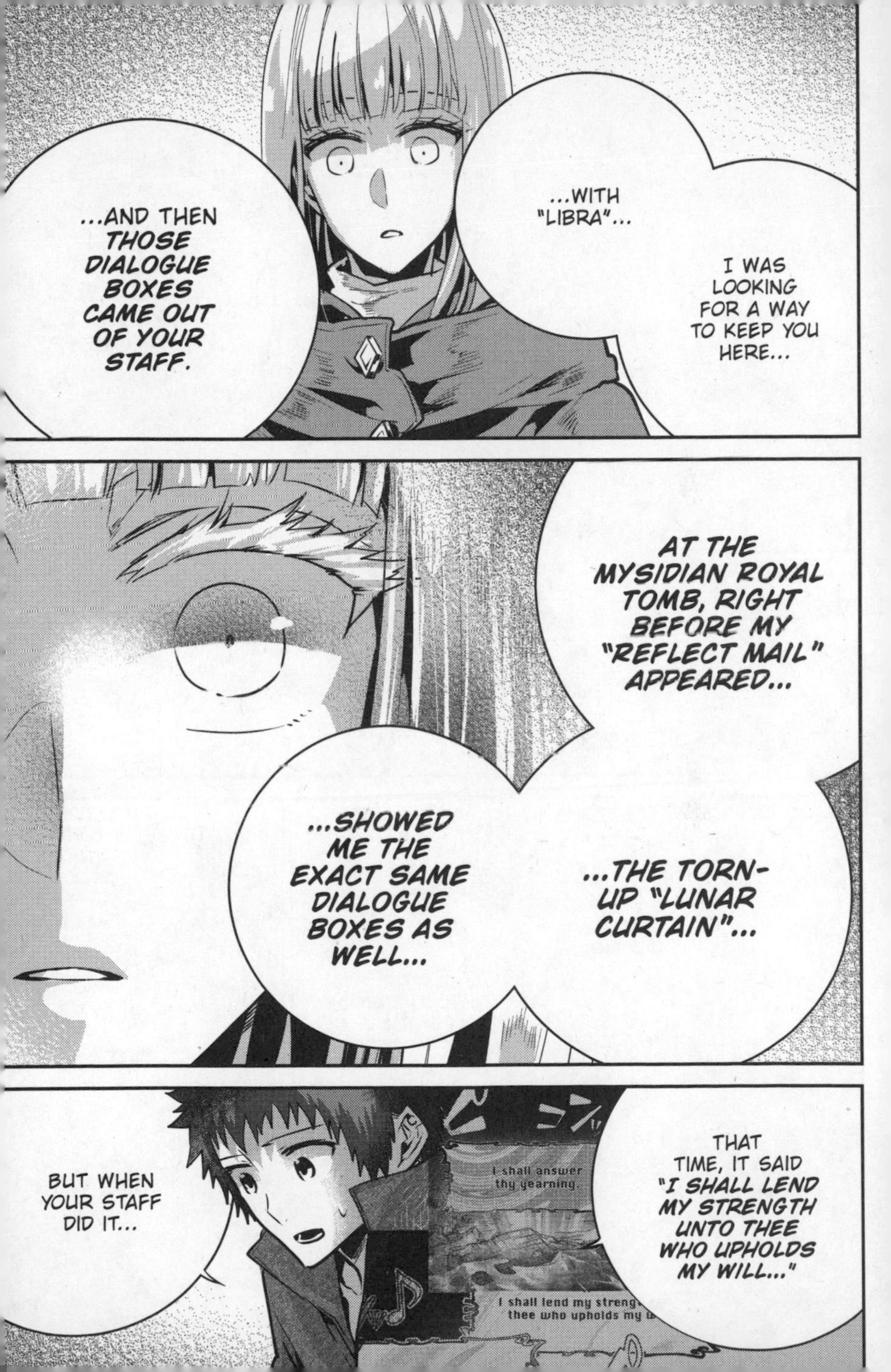
...WITH "LIBRA"...
I WAS LOOKING FOR A WAY TO KEEP YOU HERE...
...AND THEN THOSE DIALOGUE BOXES CAME OUT OF YOUR STAFF.
AT THE MYSIDIAN ROYAL TOMB, RIGHT BEFORE MY "REFLECT MAIL" APPEARED...
...THE TORN-UP "LUNAR CURTAIN"...
...SHOWED ME THE EXACT SAME DIALOGUE BOXES AS WELL...
THAT TIME, IT SAID "I SHALL LEND MY STRENGTH UNTO THEE WHO UPHOLDS MY WILL..."
I shall answer thy yearning.
BUT WHEN YOUR STAFF DID IT...

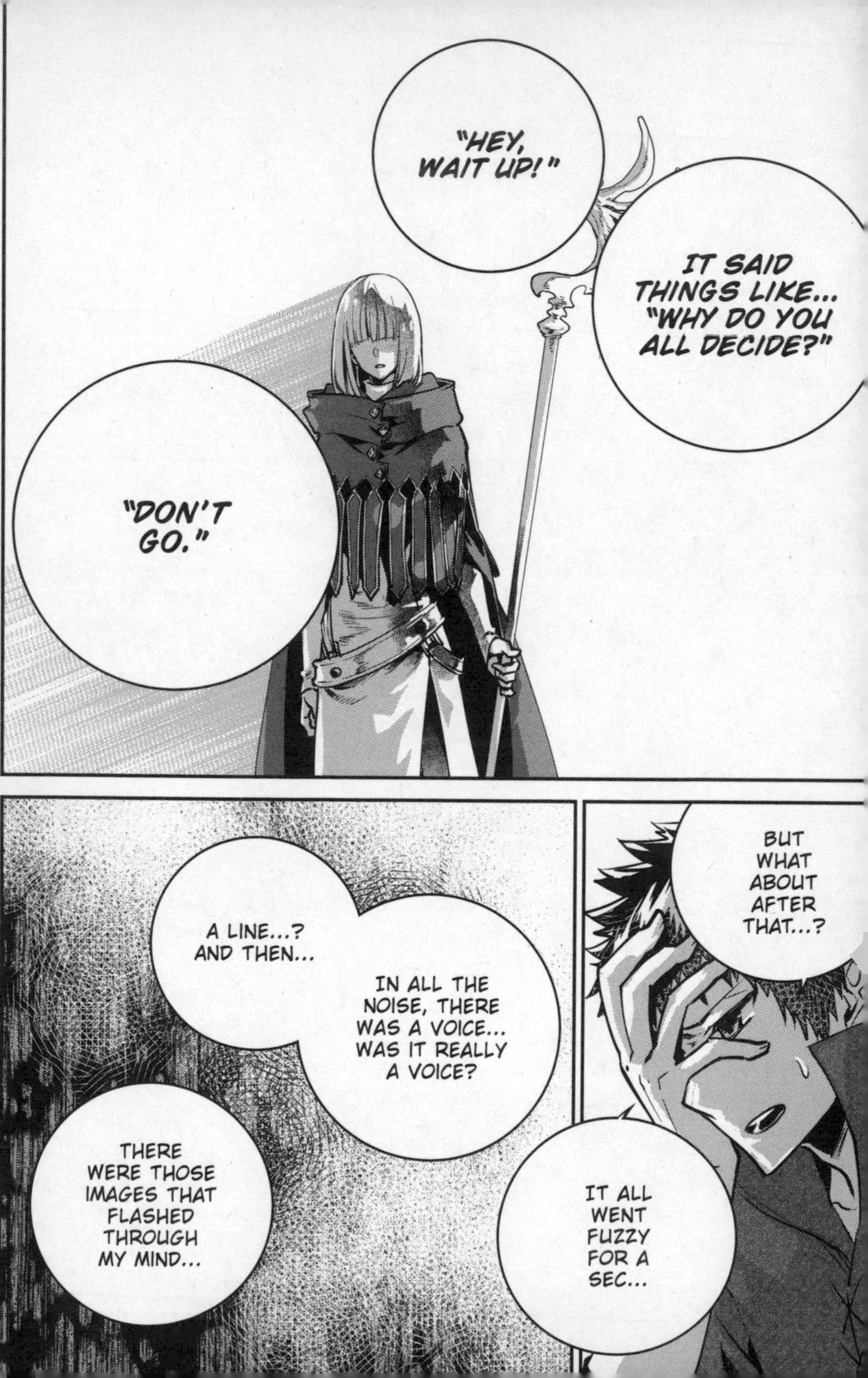
IT SAID THINGS LIKE... "WHY DO YOU ALL DECIDE?"
"HEY, WAIT UP!"
"DON'T GO."
BUT WHAT ABOUT AFTER THAT...?
IT ALL WENT FUZZY FOR A SEC...
IN ALL THE NOISE, THERE WAS A VOICE... WAS IT REALLY A VOICE?
A LINE...? AND THEN...
THERE WERE THOSE IMAGES THAT FLASHED THROUGH MY MIND...

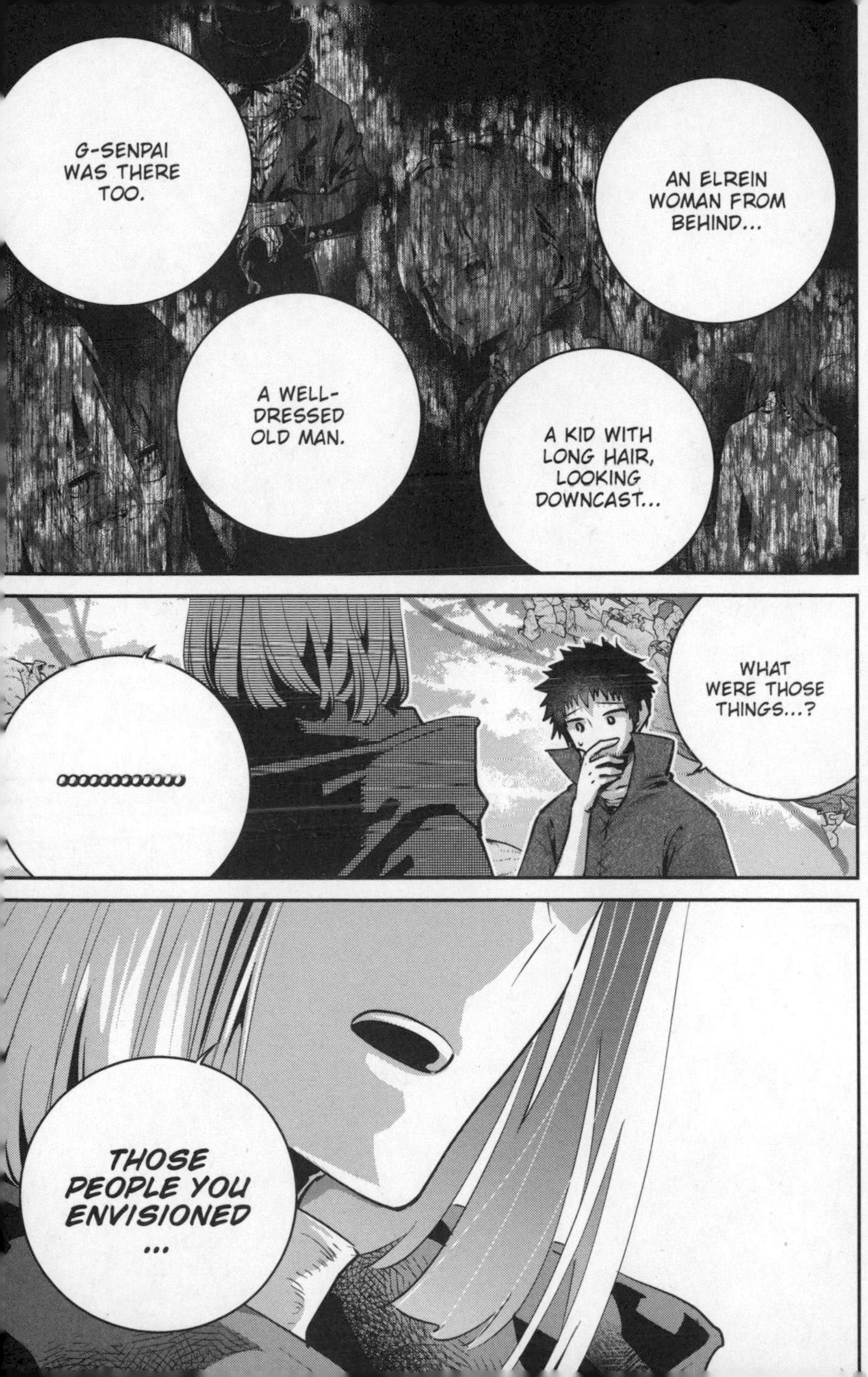
AN ELREIN WOMAN FROM BEHIND...
G-SENPAI WAS THERE TOO.
A KID WITH LONG HAIR, LOOKING DOWNCAST...
A WELL-DRESSED OLD MAN.
WHAT WERE THOSE THINGS...?
............
THOSE PEOPLE YOU ENVISIONED ...

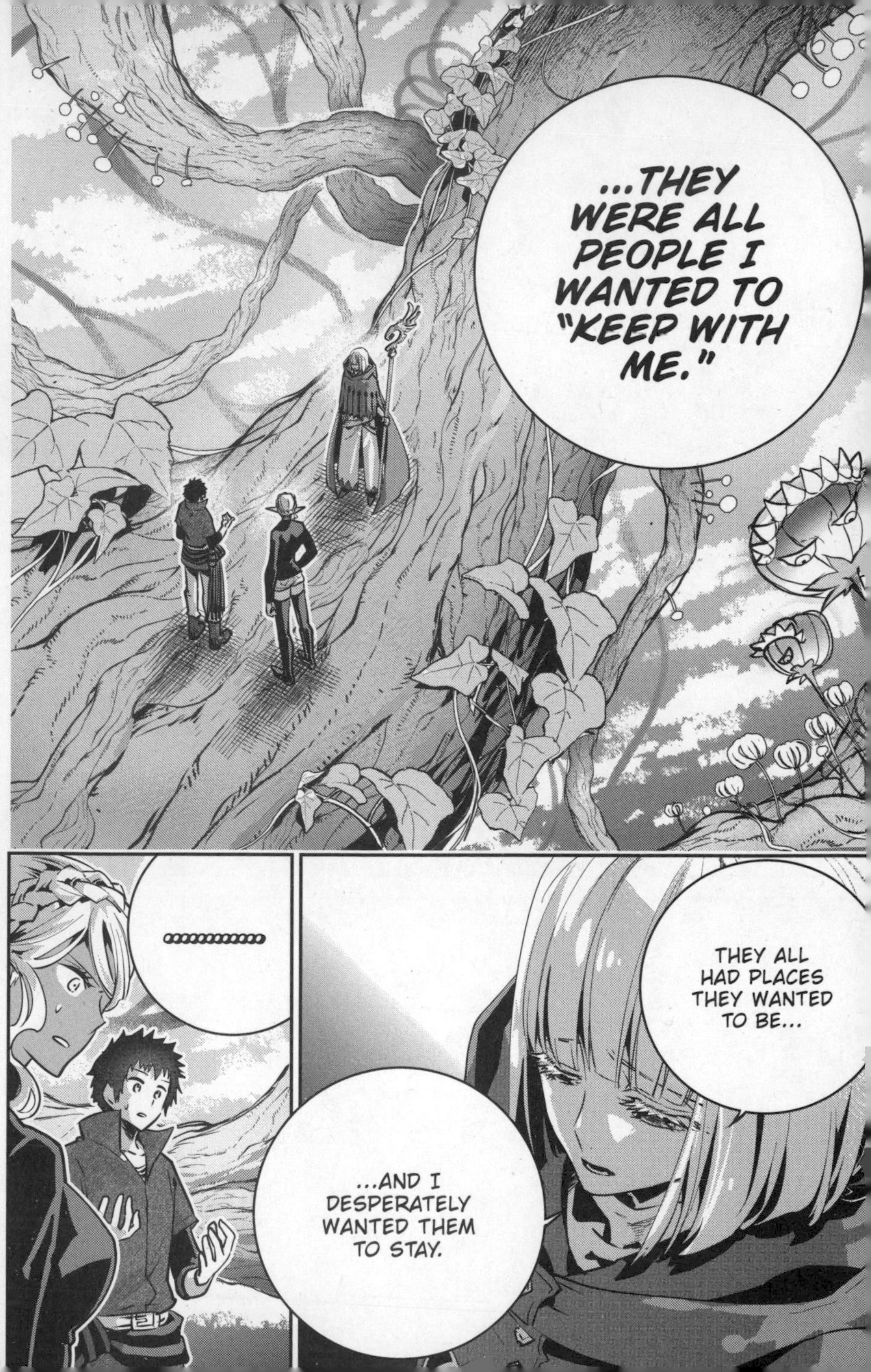
...THEY WERE ALL PEOPLE I WANTED TO "KEEP WITH ME."
THEY ALL HAD PLACES THEY WANTED TO BE...
...AND I DESPERATELY WANTED THEM TO STAY.
............

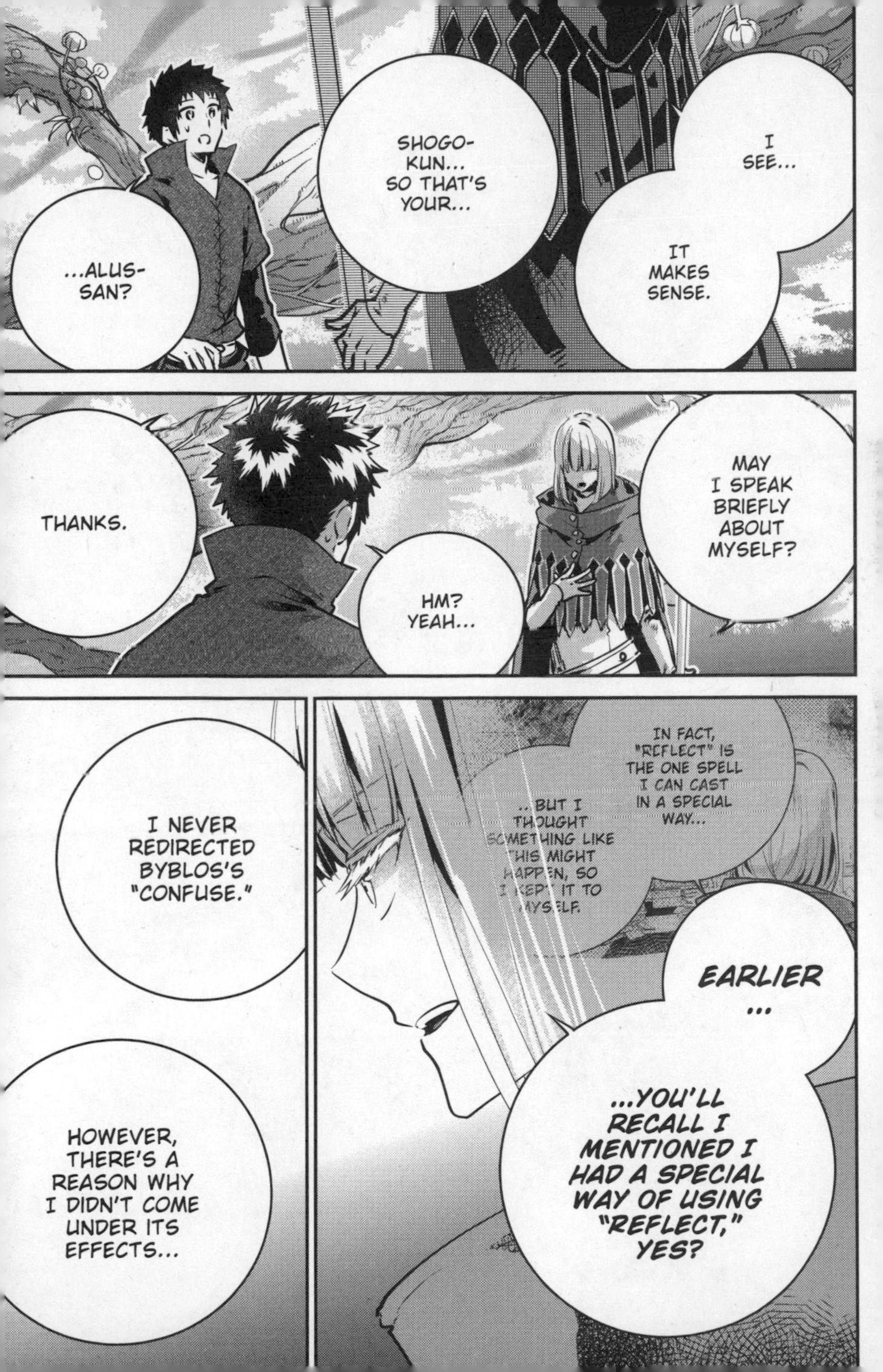
I SEE...
IT MAKES SENSE.
SHOGO-KUN... SO THAT'S YOUR...
...ALUS-SAN?
MAY I SPEAK BRIEFLY ABOUT MYSELF?
THANKS.
HM? YEAH...
IN FACT, "REFLECT" IS THE ONE SPELL I CAN CAST IN A SPECIAL WAY...
.. BUT I THOUGHT SOMETHING LIKE THIS MIGHT HAPPEN, SO I KEPT IT TO MYSELF.
EARLIER ...
...YOU'LL RECALL I MENTIONED I HAD A SPECIAL WAY OF USING "REFLECT," YES?
I NEVER REDIRECTED BYBLOS'S "CONFUSE."
HOWEVER, THERE'S A REASON WHY I DIDN'T COME UNDER ITS EFFECTS...

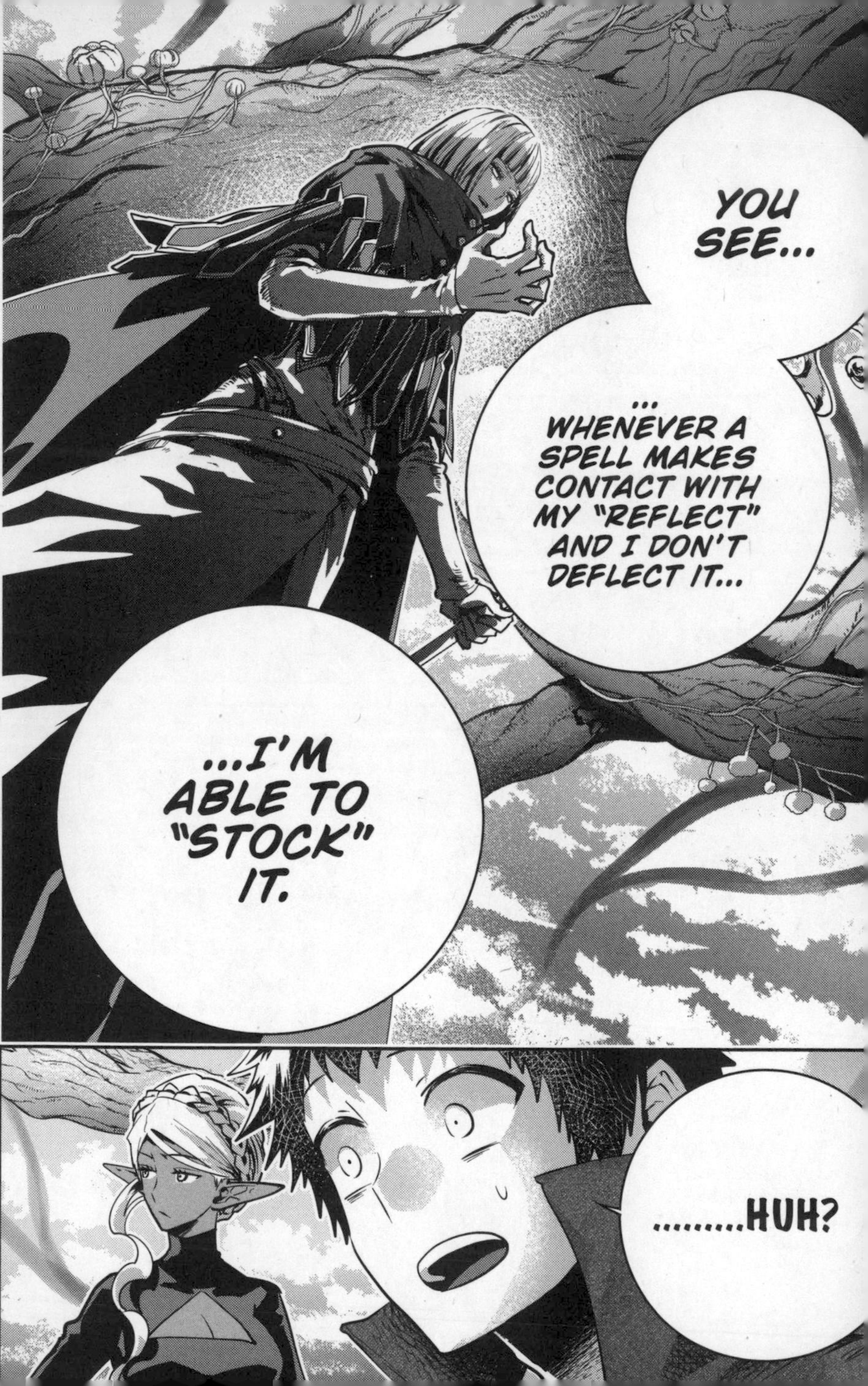
YOU SEE...
...WHENEVER A SPELL MAKES CONTACT WITH MY "REFLECT" AND I DON'T DEFLECT IT...
...I'M ABLE TO "STOCK" IT.
.........HUH?

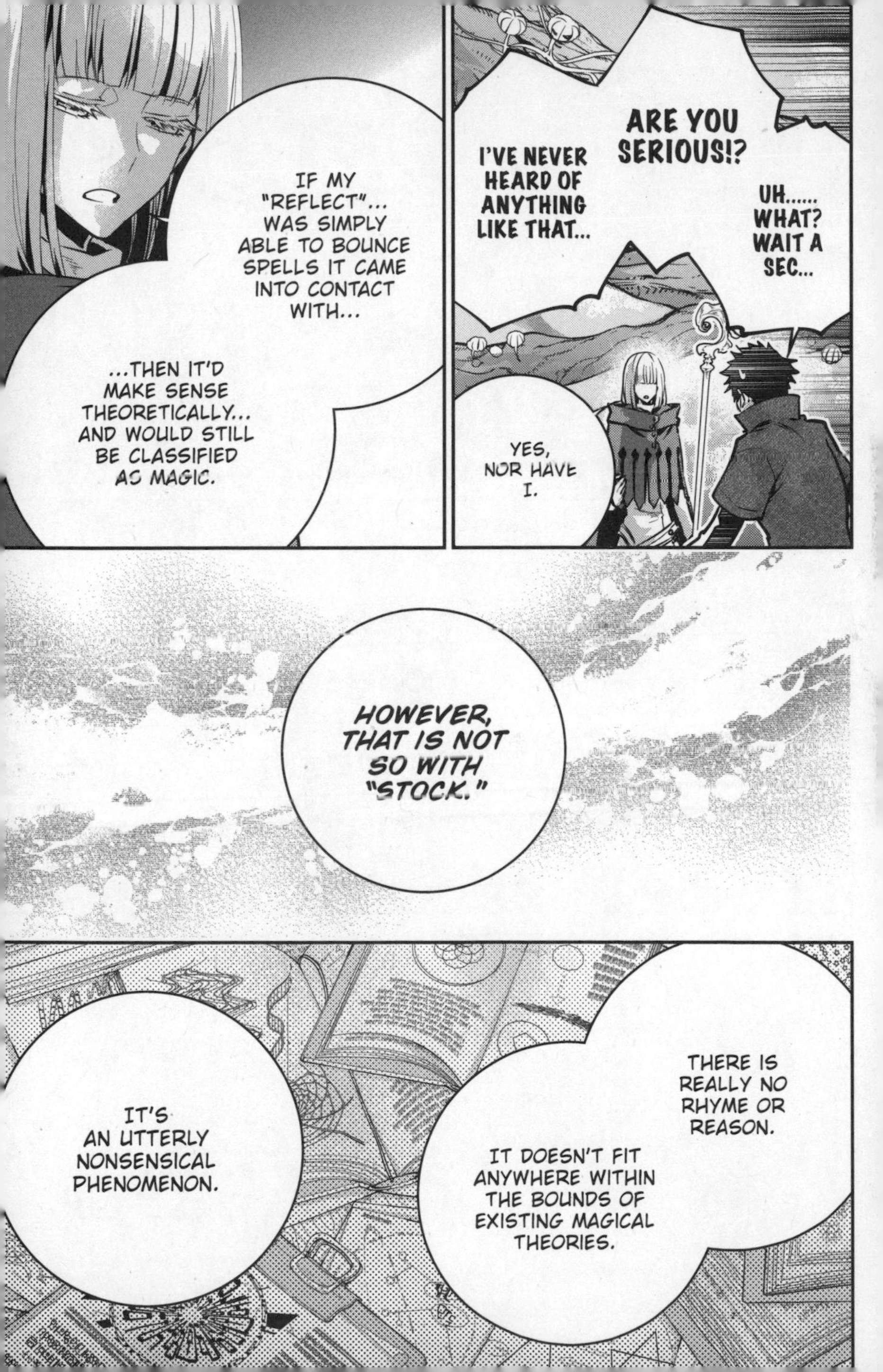
UH...... WHAT? WAIT A SEC...
ARE YOU SERIOUS!?
I'VE NEVER HEARD OF ANYTHING LIKE THAT...
YES, NOR HAVE I.
IF MY "REFLECT"... WAS SIMPLY ABLE TO BOUNCE SPELLS IT CAME INTO CONTACT WITH...
...THEN IT'D MAKE SENSE THEORETICALLY... AND WOULD STILL BE CLASSIFIED AS MAGIC.
HOWEVER, THAT IS NOT SO WITH "STOCK."
THERE IS REALLY NO RHYME OR REASON.
IT DOESN'T FIT ANYWHERE WITHIN THE BOUNDS OF EXISTING MAGICAL THEORIES.
IT'S AN UTTERLY NONSENSICAL PHENOMENON.

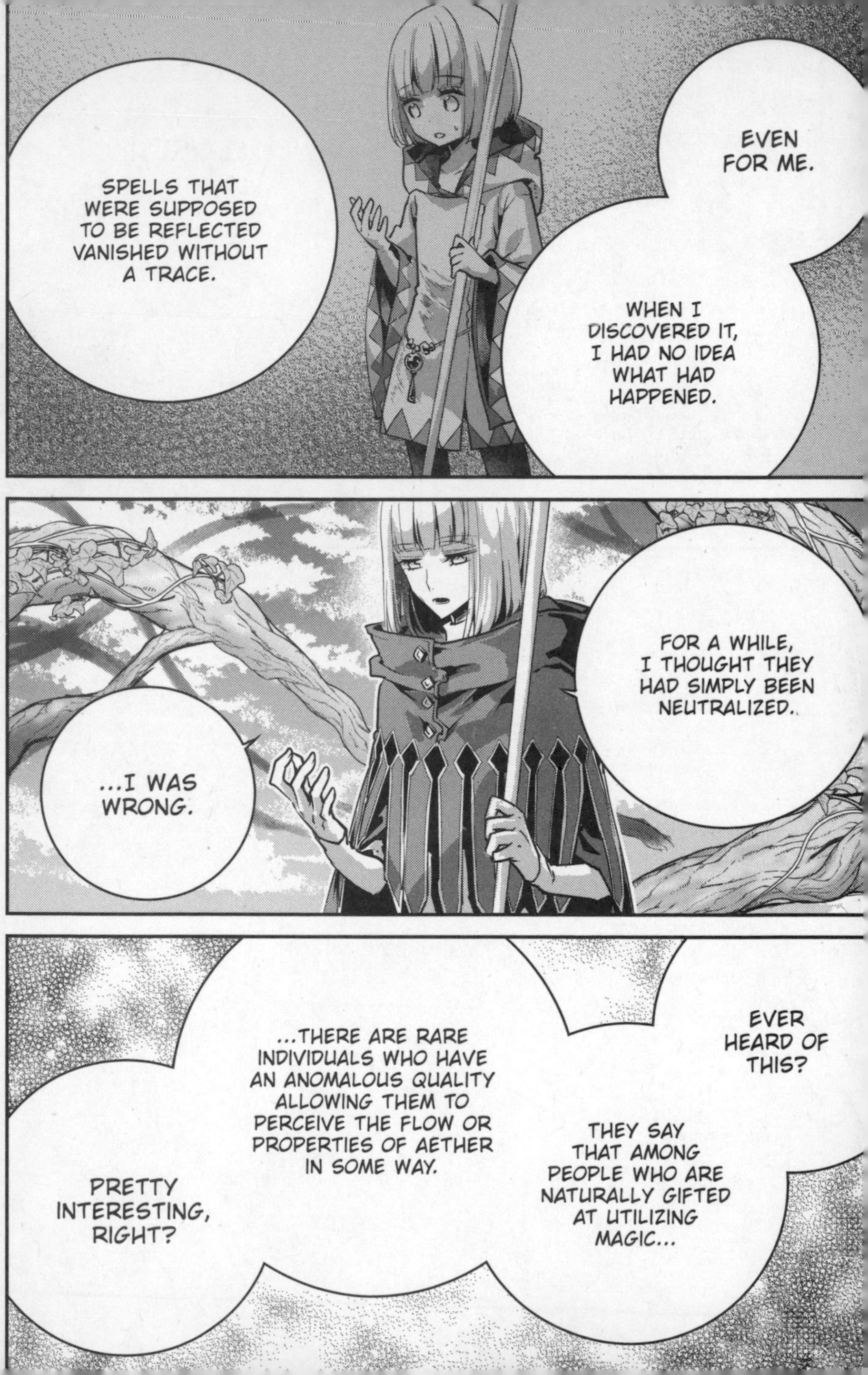
EVEN FOR ME.
WHEN I DISCOVERED IT, I HAD NO IDEA WHAT HAD HAPPENED.
SPELLS THAT WERE SUPPOSED TO BE REFLECTED VANISHED WITHOUT A TRACE.
FOR A WHILE, I THOUGHT THEY HAD SIMPLY BEEN NEUTRALIZED.
...I WAS WRONG.
EVER HEARD OF THIS?
THEY SAY THAT AMONG PEOPLE WHO ARE NATURALLY GIFTED AT UTILIZING MAGIC...
...THERE ARE RARE INDIVIDUALS WHO HAVE AN ANOMALOUS QUALITY ALLOWING THEM TO PERCEIVE THE FLOW OR PROPERTIES OF AETHER IN SOME WAY.
PRETTY INTERESTING, RIGHT?

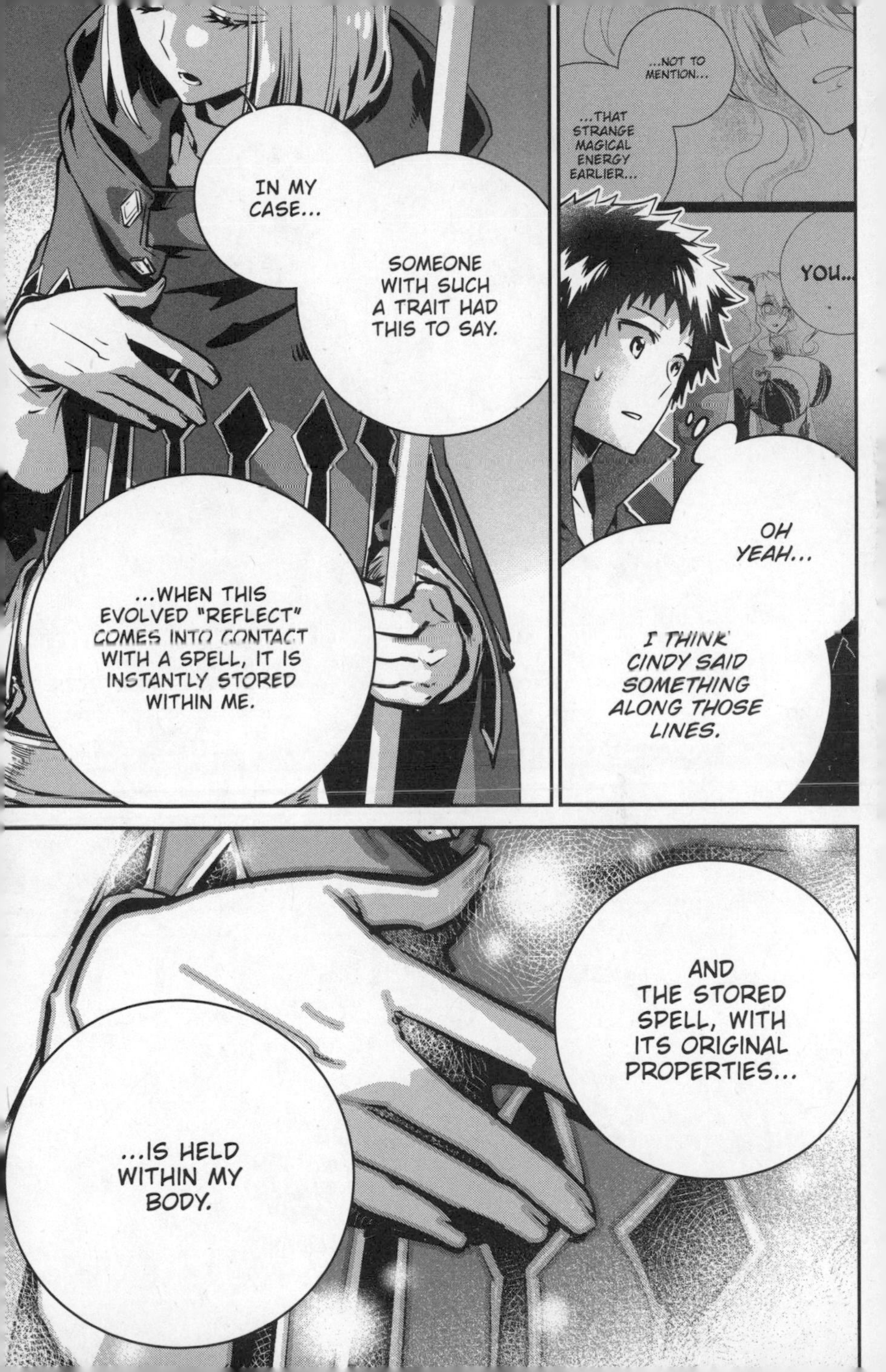
...NOT TO MENTION...
...THAT STRANGE MAGICAL ENERGY EARLIER...
YOU...
OH YEAH...
I THINK CINDY SAID SOMETHING ALONG THOSE LINES.
IN MY CASE...
SOMEONE WITH SUCH A TRAIT HAD THIS TO SAY.
...WHEN THIS EVOLVED "REFLECT" COMES INTO CONTACT WITH A SPELL, IT IS INSTANTLY STORED WITHIN ME.
AND THE STORED SPELL, WITH ITS ORIGINAL PROPERTIES...
...IS HELD WITHIN MY BODY.

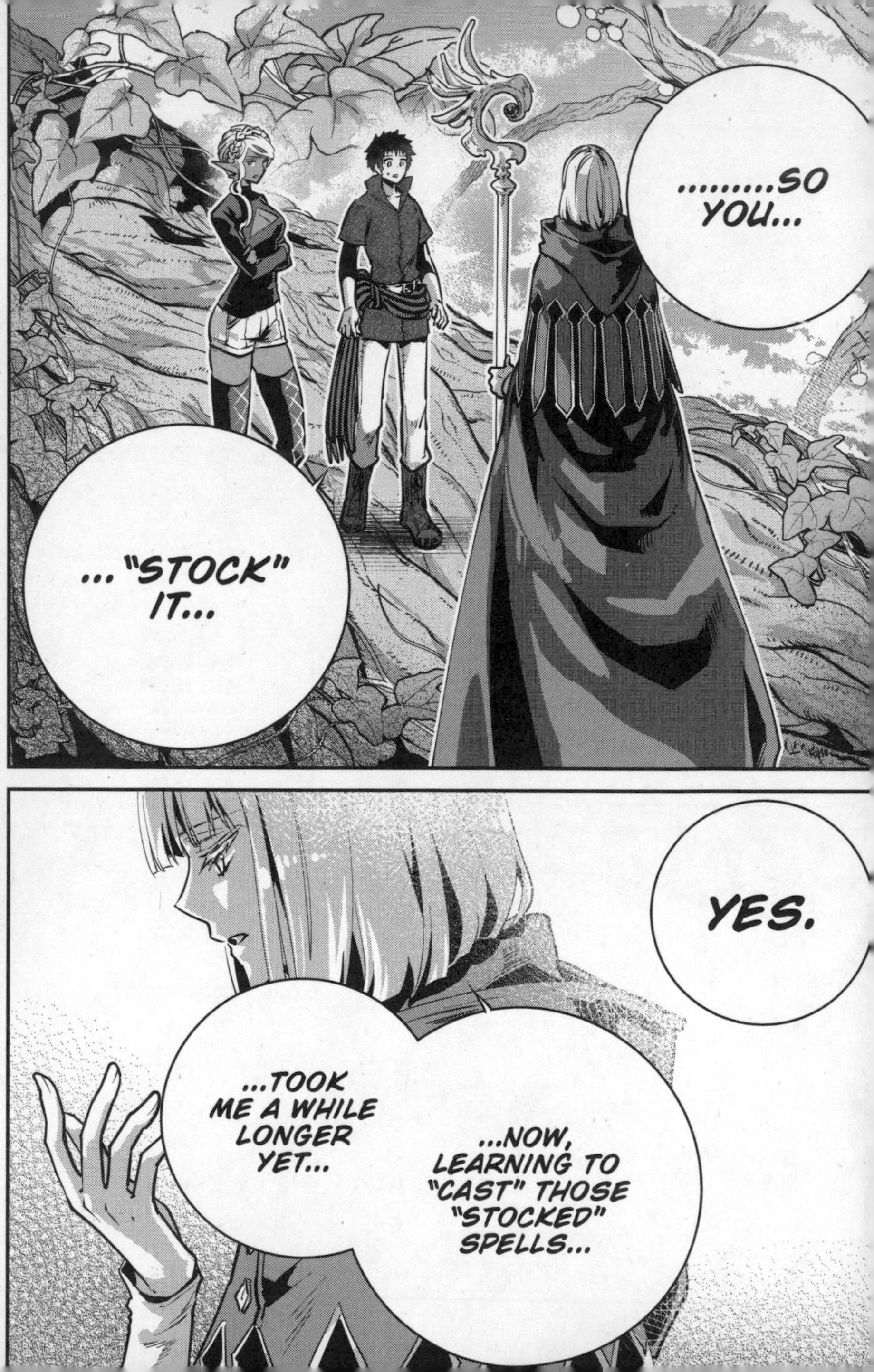
........SO YOU...
..."STOCK" IT...
YES.
...NOW, LEARNING TO "CAST" THOSE "STOCKED" SPELLS...
...TOOK ME A WHILE LONGER YET...

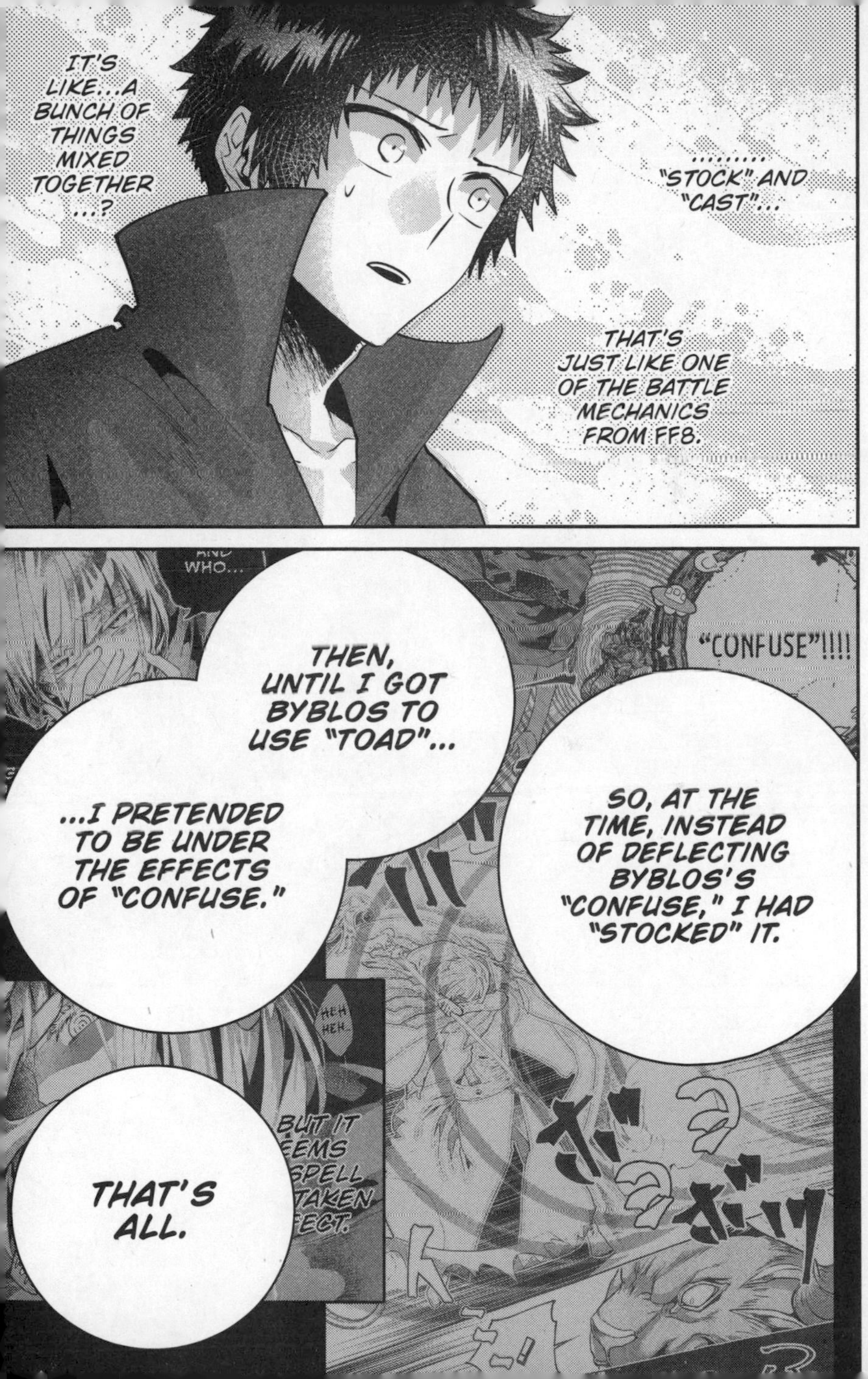
IT'S LIKE...A BUNCH OF THINGS MIXED TOGETHER ...?
........ "STOCK" AND "CAST"...
THAT'S JUST LIKE ONE OF THE BATTLE MECHANICS FROM FF8.
"CONFUSE"!!!!
AND WHO...
SO, AT THE TIME, INSTEAD OF DEFLECTING BYBLOS'S "CONFUSE," I HAD "STOCKED" IT.
THEN, UNTIL I GOT BYBLOS TO USE "TOAD"...
...I PRETENDED TO BE UNDER THE EFFECTS OF "CONFUSE."
HEH HEH
THAT'S ALL.

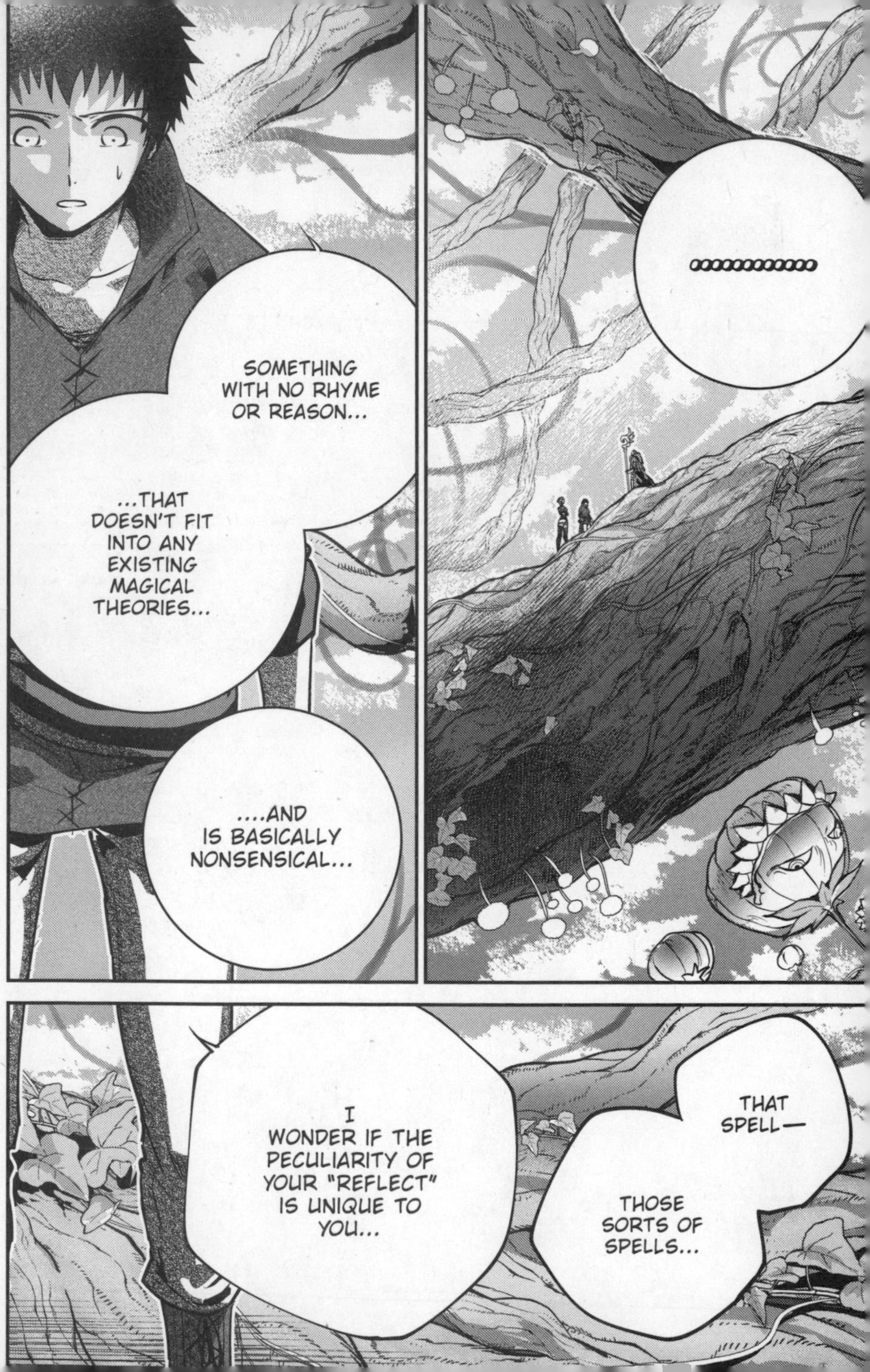
oooooooooooo
SOMETHING WITH NO RHYME OR REASON...
...THAT DOESN'T FIT INTO ANY EXISTING MAGICAL THEORIES...
....AND IS BASICALLY NONSENSICAL...
THAT SPELL—
THOSE SORTS OF SPELLS...
I WONDER IF THE PECULIARITY OF YOUR "REFLECT" IS UNIQUE TO YOU...

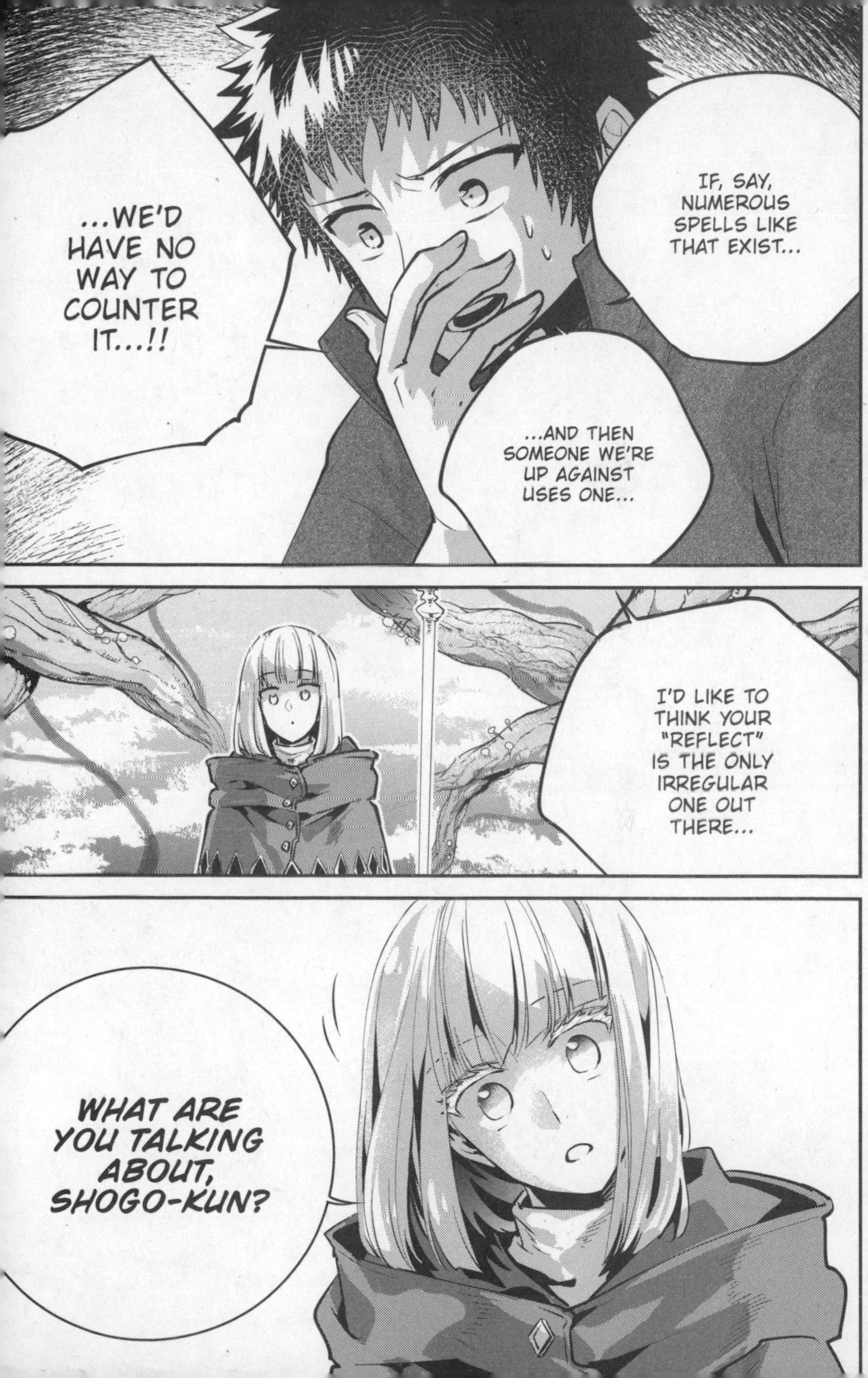
IF, SAY, NUMEROUS SPELLS LIKE THAT EXIST...
...AND THEN SOMEONE WE'RE UP AGAINST USES ONE...
...WE'D HAVE NO WAY TO COUNTER IT...!!
I'D LIKE TO THINK YOUR "REFLECT" IS THE ONLY IRREGULAR ONE OUT THERE...
WHAT ARE YOU TALKING ABOUT, SHOGO-KUN?

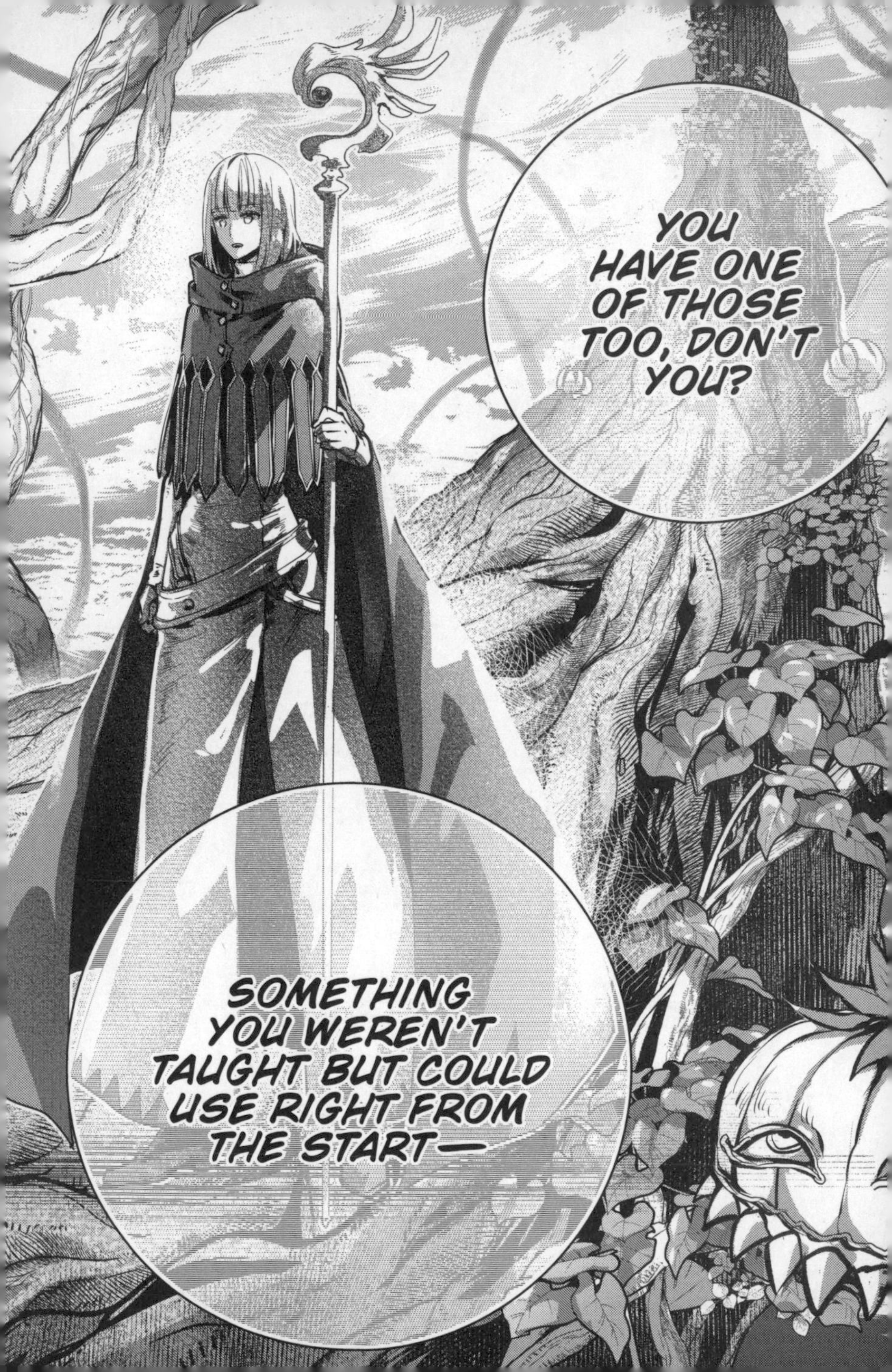
YOU HAVE ONE OF THOSE TOO, DON'T YOU?
SOMETHING YOU WEREN'T TAUGHT BUT COULD USE RIGHT FROM THE START—

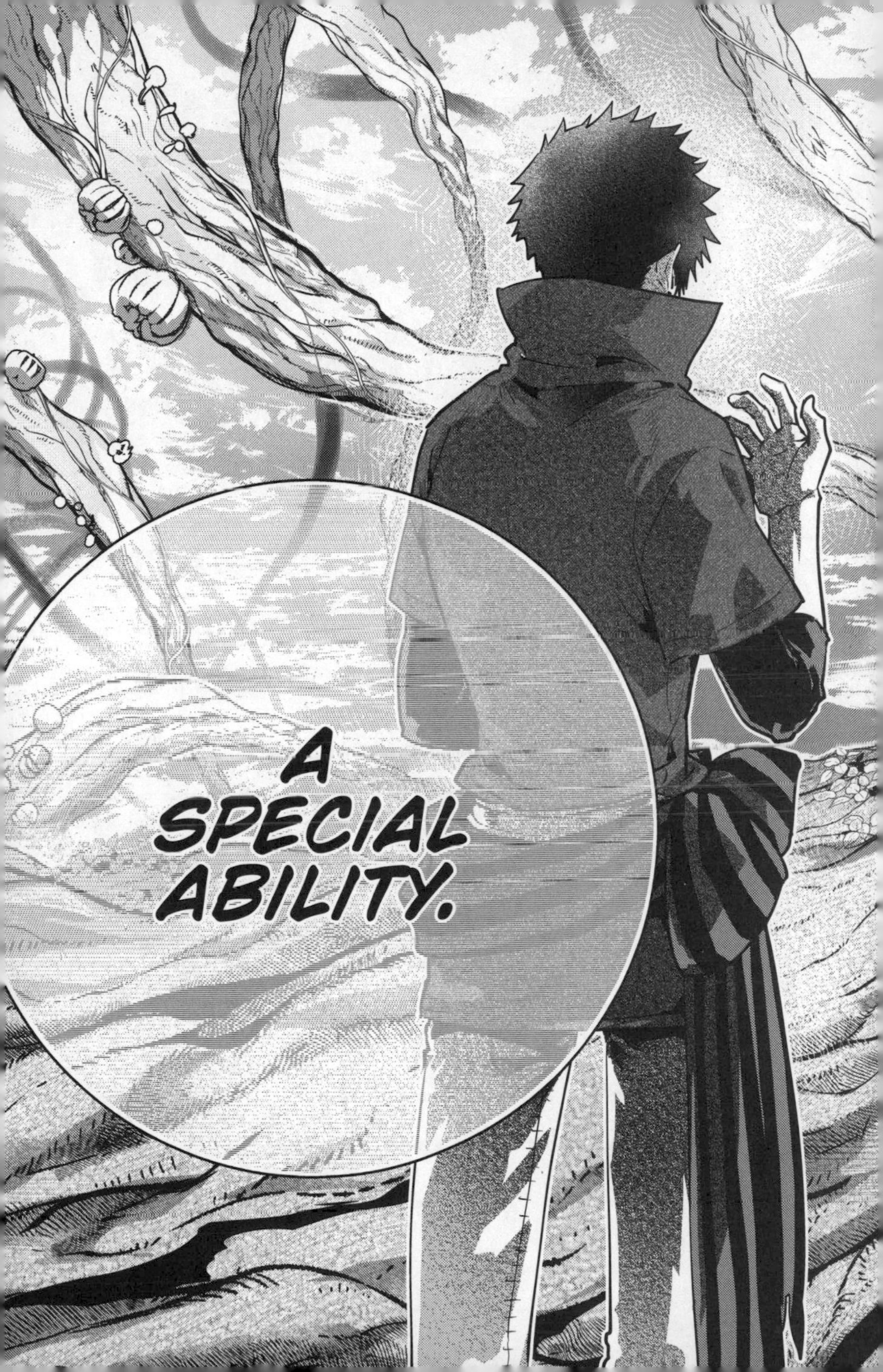
A SPECIAL ABILITY.

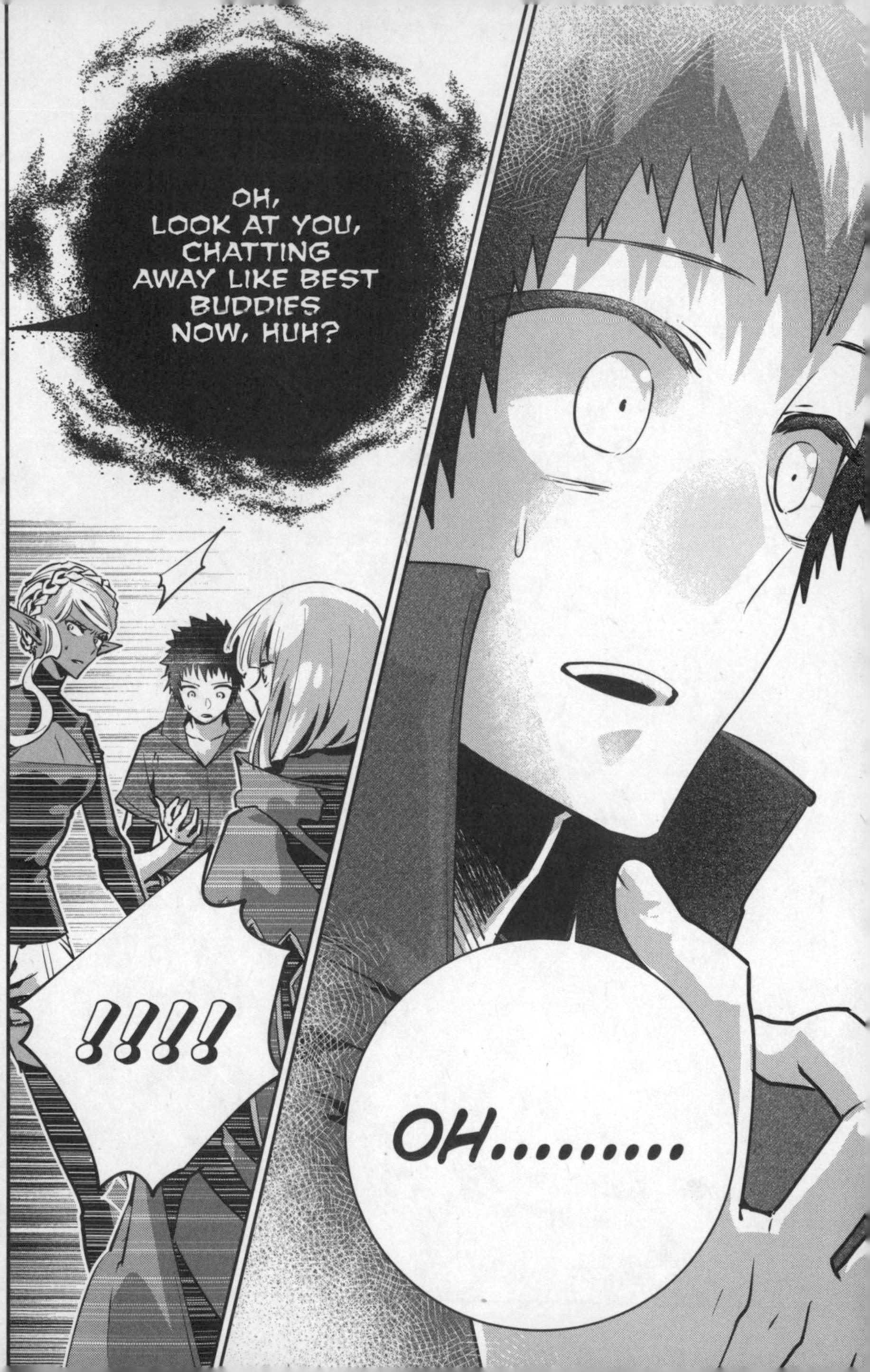
OH, LOOK AT YOU, CHATTING AWAY LIKE BEST BUDDIES NOW, HUH?
!!!!
OH.........

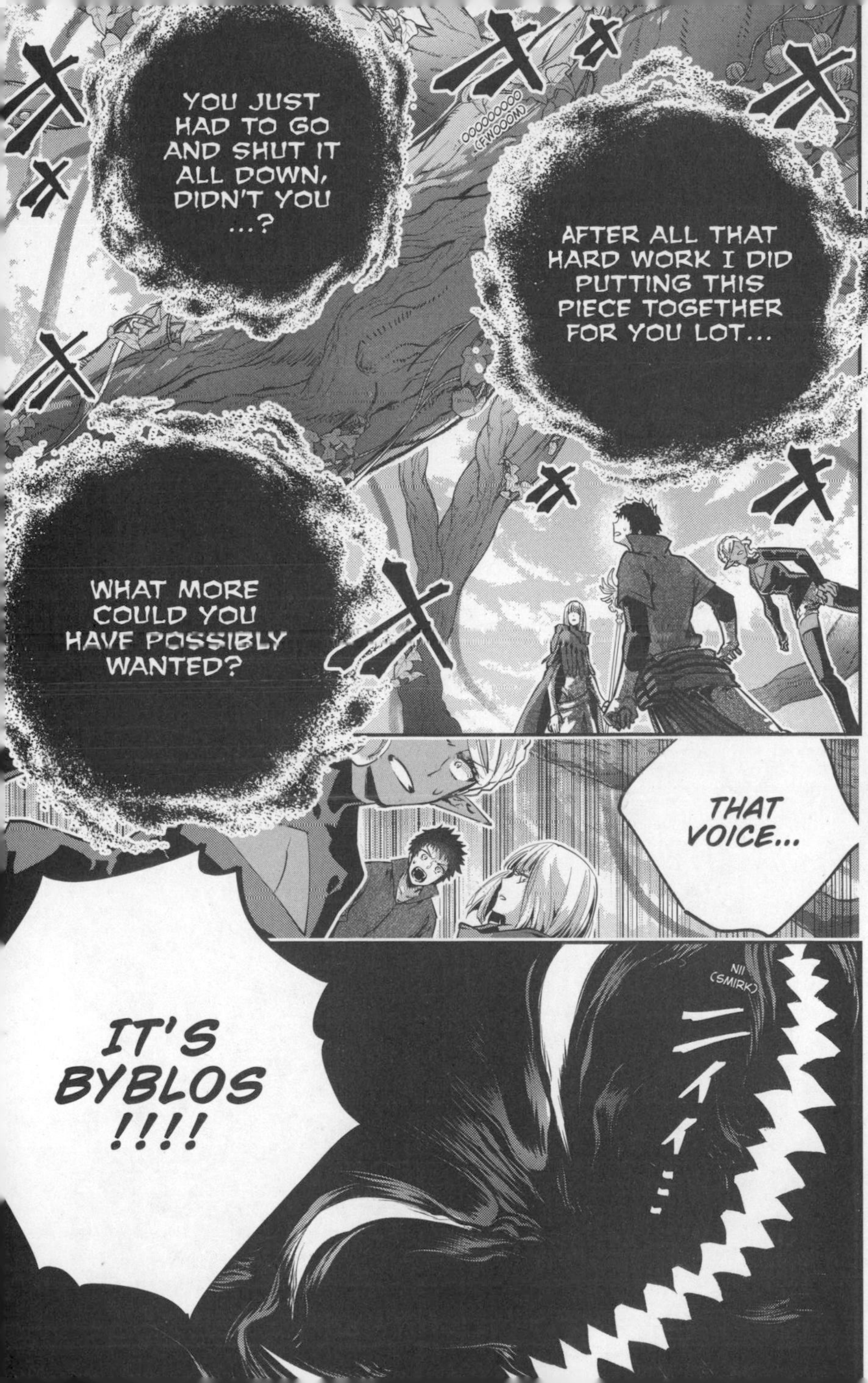
OOOOOOOOO (FWOOOM)
YOU JUST HAD TO GO AND SHUT IT ALL DOWN, DIDN'T YOU ...?
AFTER ALL THAT HARD WORK I DID PUTTING THIS PIECE TOGETHER FOR YOU LOT...
WHAT MORE COULD YOU HAVE POSSIBLY WANTED?
THAT VOICE...
NII (SMIRK)
IT'S BYBLOS !!!!

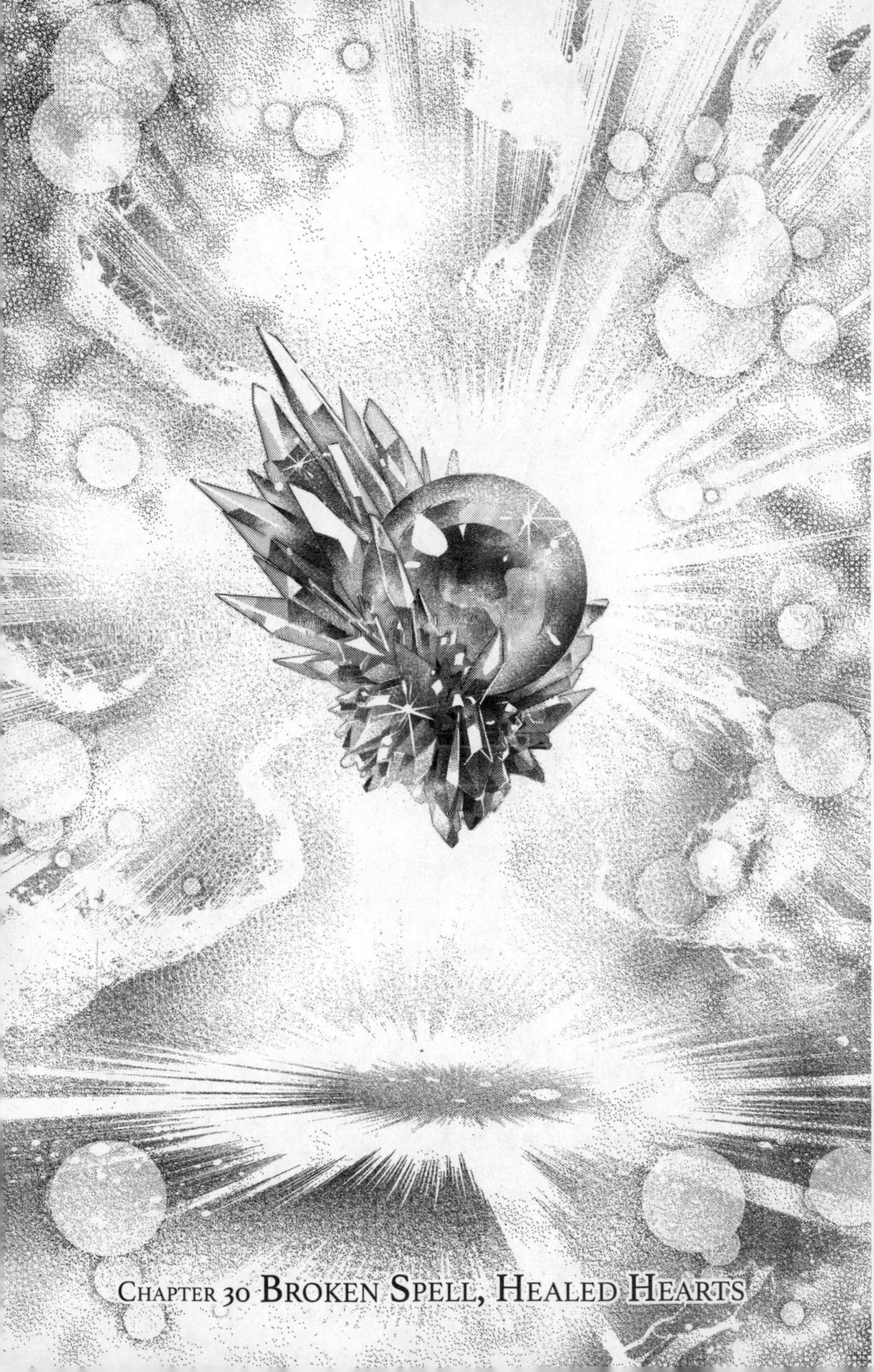

# Chapter 30 Broken Spell, Healed Hearts

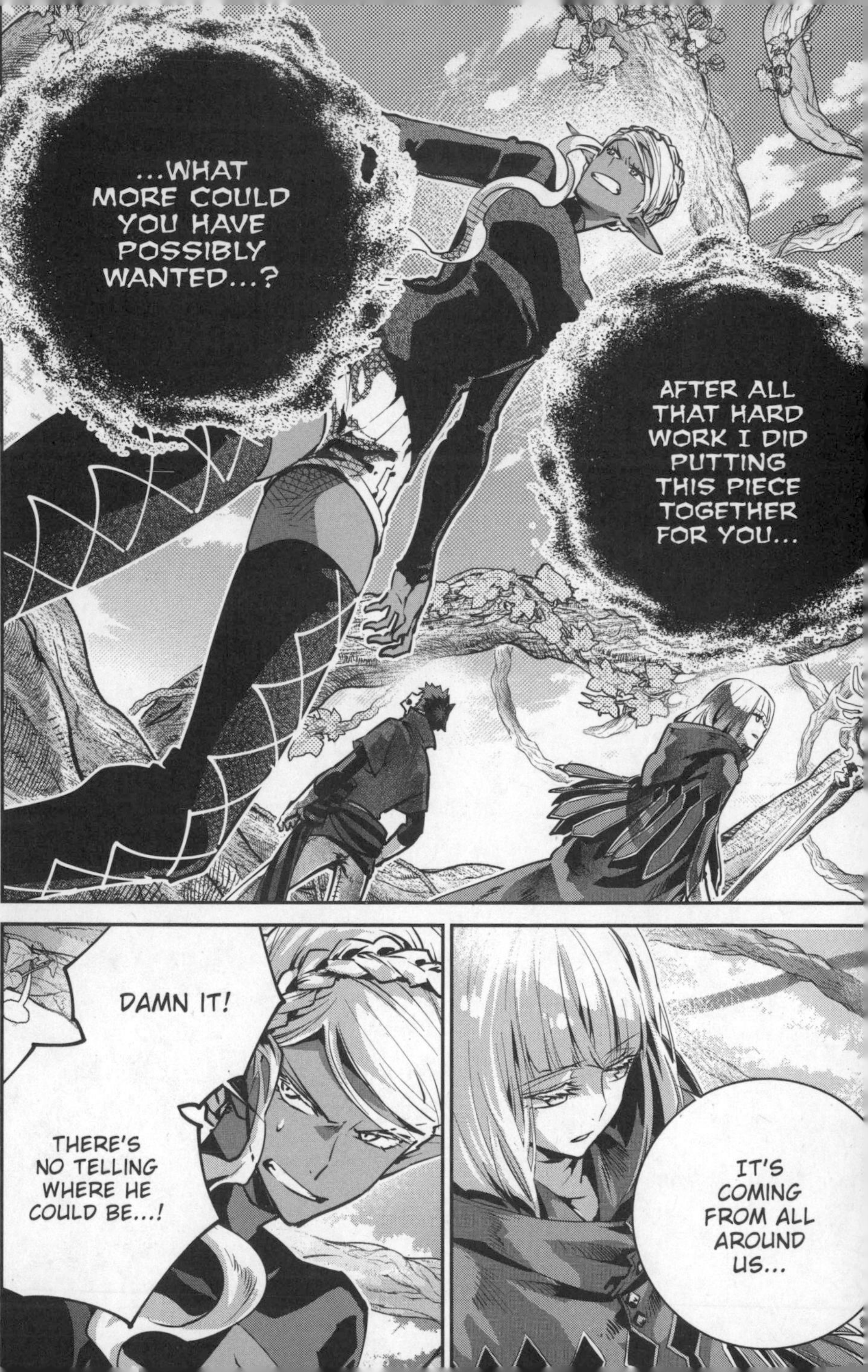
AFTER ALL THAT HARD WORK I DID PUTTING THIS PIECE TOGETHER FOR YOU...
...WHAT MORE COULD YOU HAVE POSSIBLY WANTED...?
IT'S COMING FROM ALL AROUND US...
DAMN IT!
THERE'S NO TELLING WHERE HE COULD BE...!

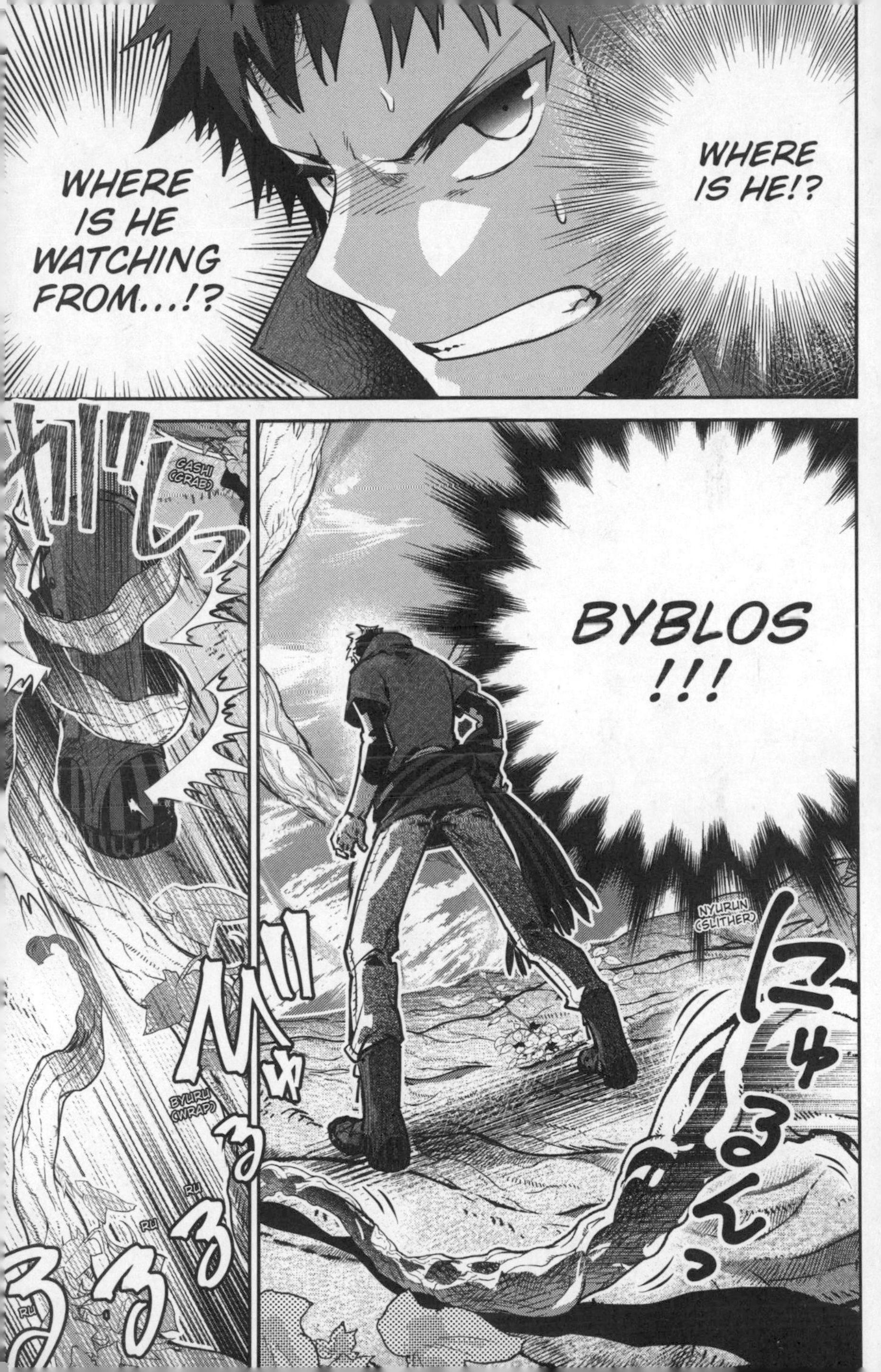
WHERE IS HE!?
WHERE IS HE WATCHING FROM...!?
BYBLOS !!!
NYURUN (SLITHER)
GASHI (GRAB)
BYURU (WRAP)
RU
RU
RU

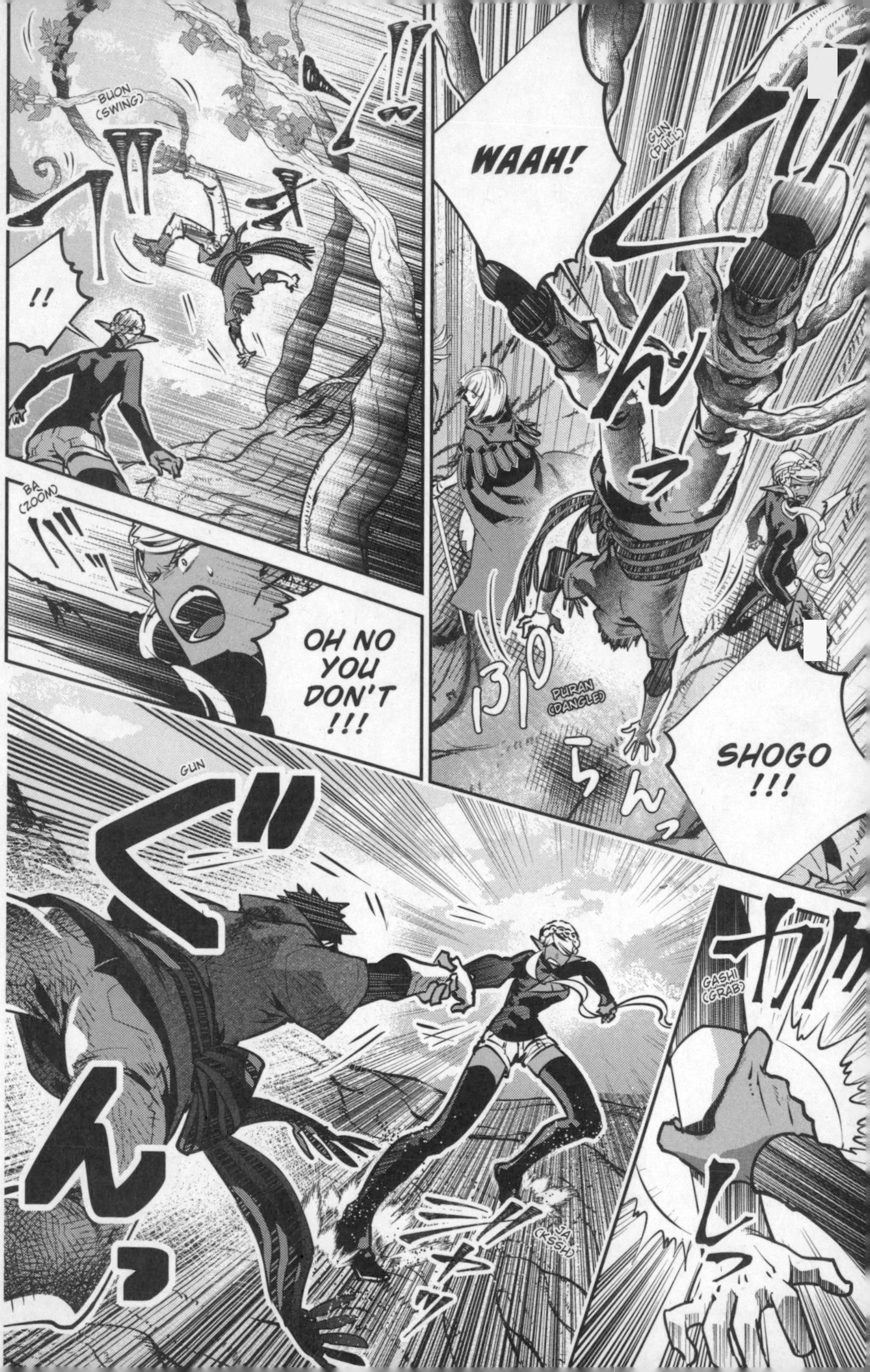
GUN (PULL)
WAAH!
PURAN (DANGLE)
SHOGO !!!
BUON (SWING)
!!
BA (ZOOM)
OH NO YOU DON'T !!!
GASHI (GRAB)
GUN
JA (KSSH)

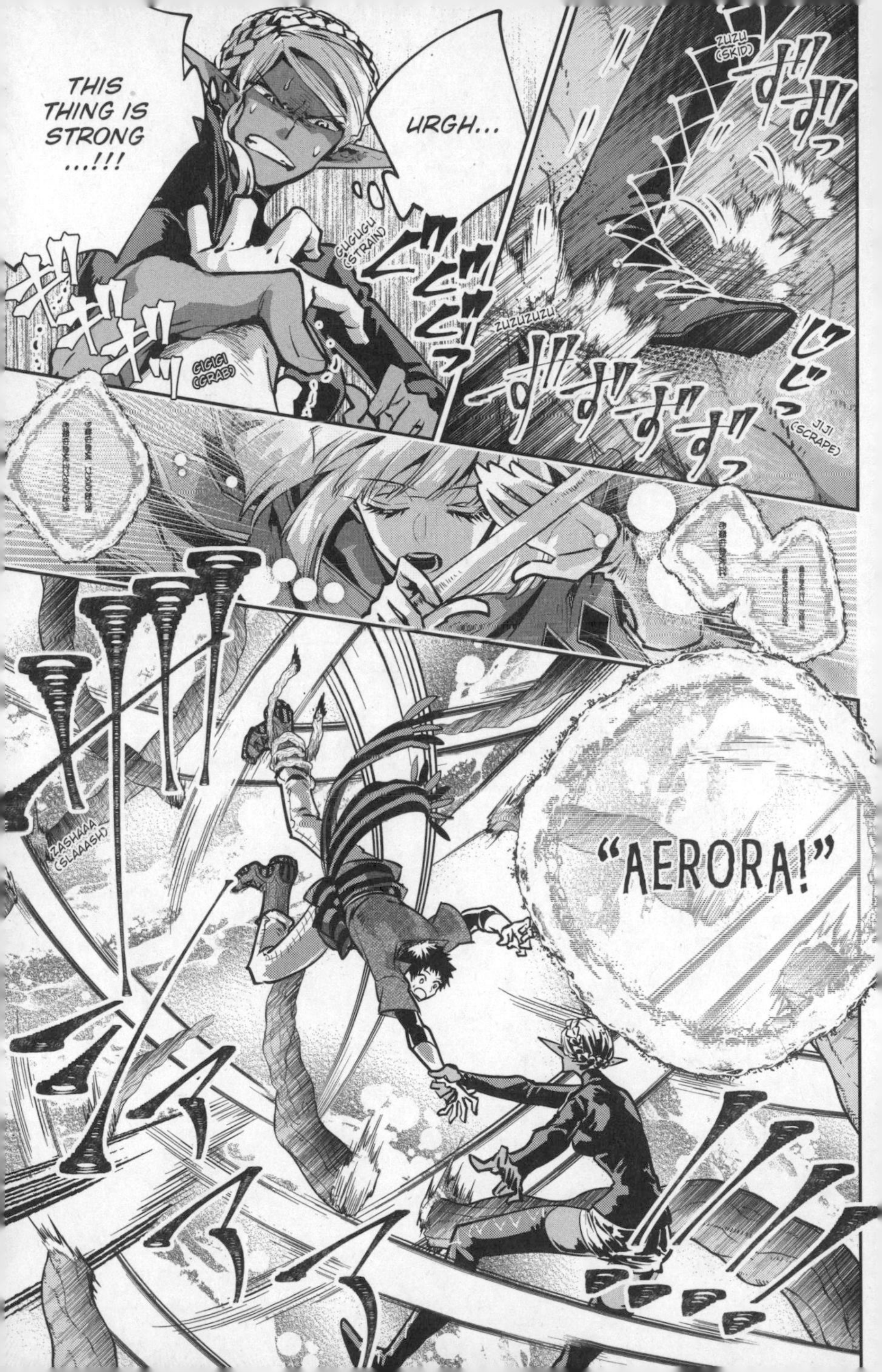
ZUZU (SKID)
ZUZUZUZU
JIJI (SCRAPE)
URGH...
THIS THING IS STRONG ...!!!
GUGUGU (STRAIN)
GIGIGI (GRAB)
"AERORA!"
ZASHAAA (SLAAASH)

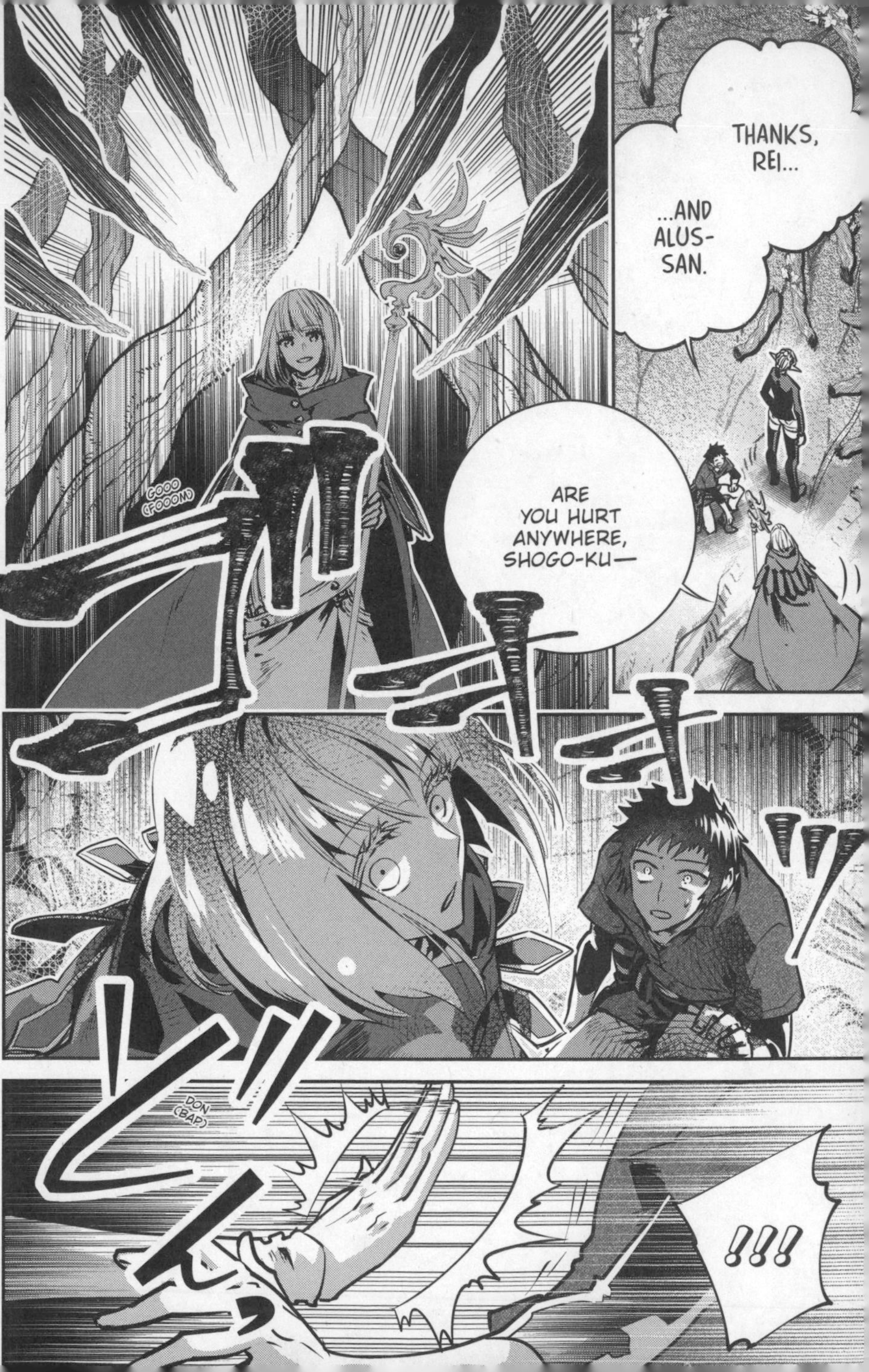
THANKS, REI...
...AND ALUS-SAN.
ARE YOU HURT ANYWHERE, SHOGO-KU—
GOOO (FOOOM)
DON (BAP)
!!!

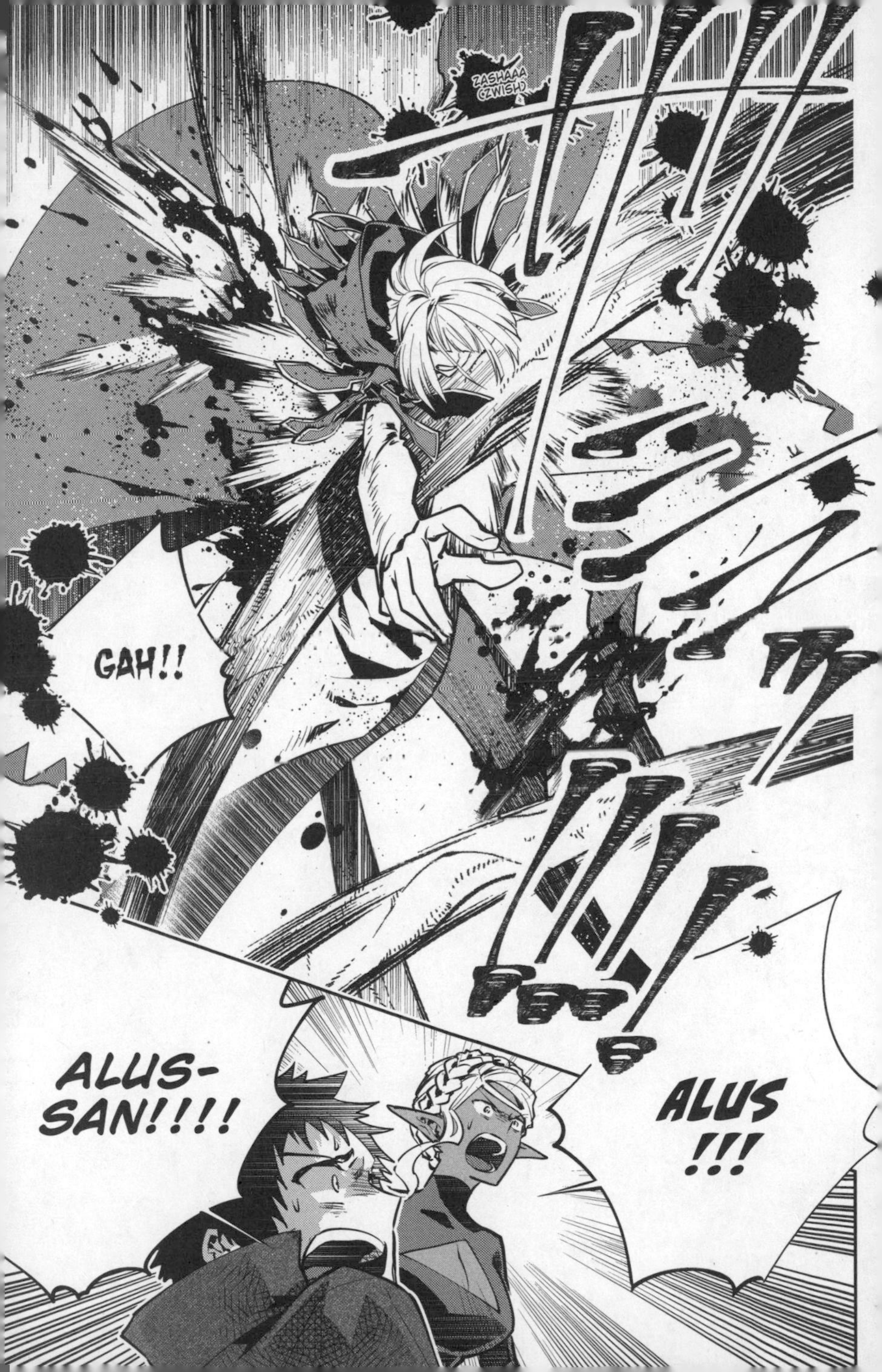
ZASHAAA (ZWISH)
GAH!!
ALUS !!!
ALUS-SAN!!!!

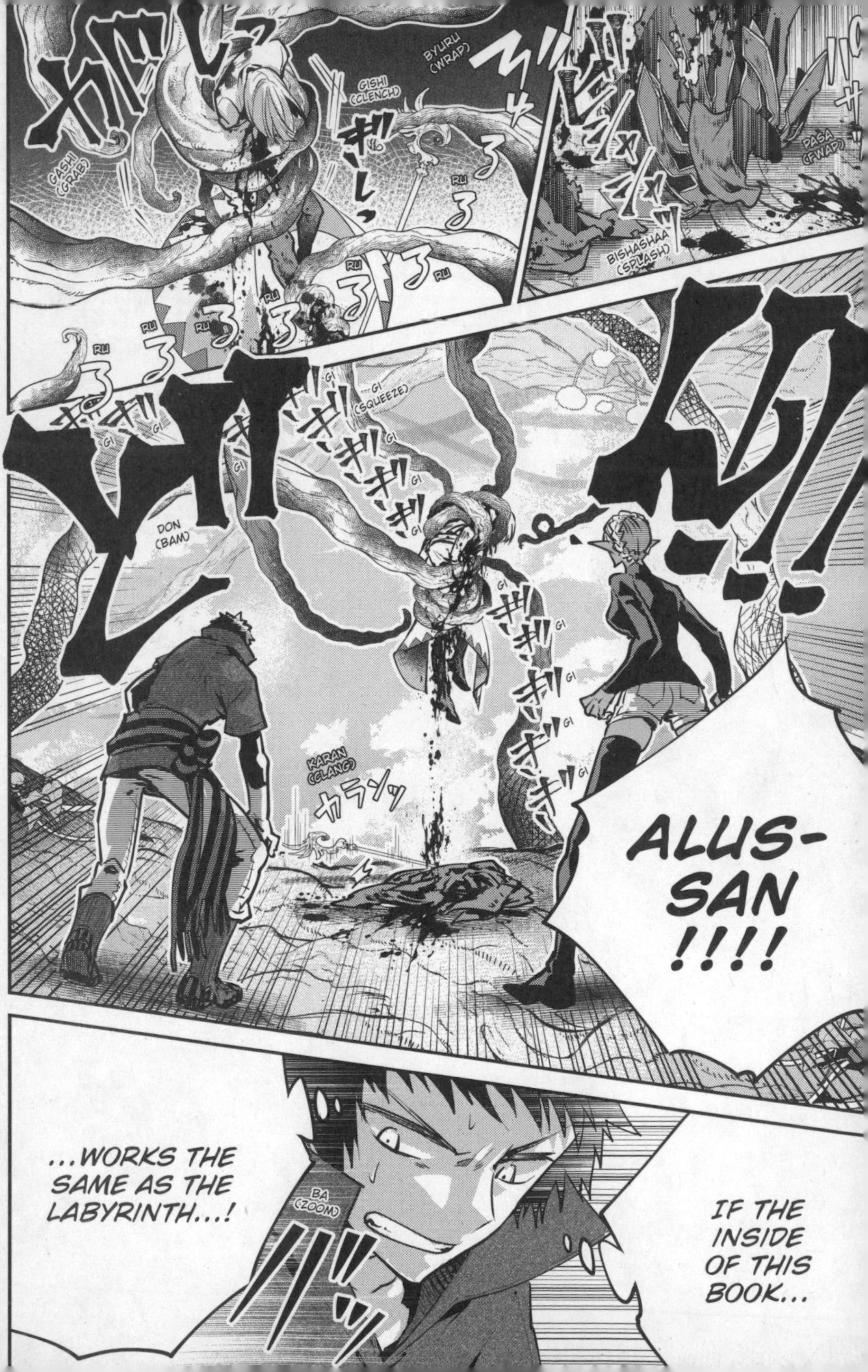

PASA (FWAP)
BISHASHAA (SPLASH)
BYURU (WRAP)
GISHI (CLENCH)
GASHI (GRAB)
RU
GI (SQUEEZE)
DON (BAM)
KARAN (CLANG)
ALUS-SAN!!!!
IF THE INSIDE OF THIS BOOK...
...WORKS THE SAME AS THE LABYRINTH...!
BA (ZOOM)

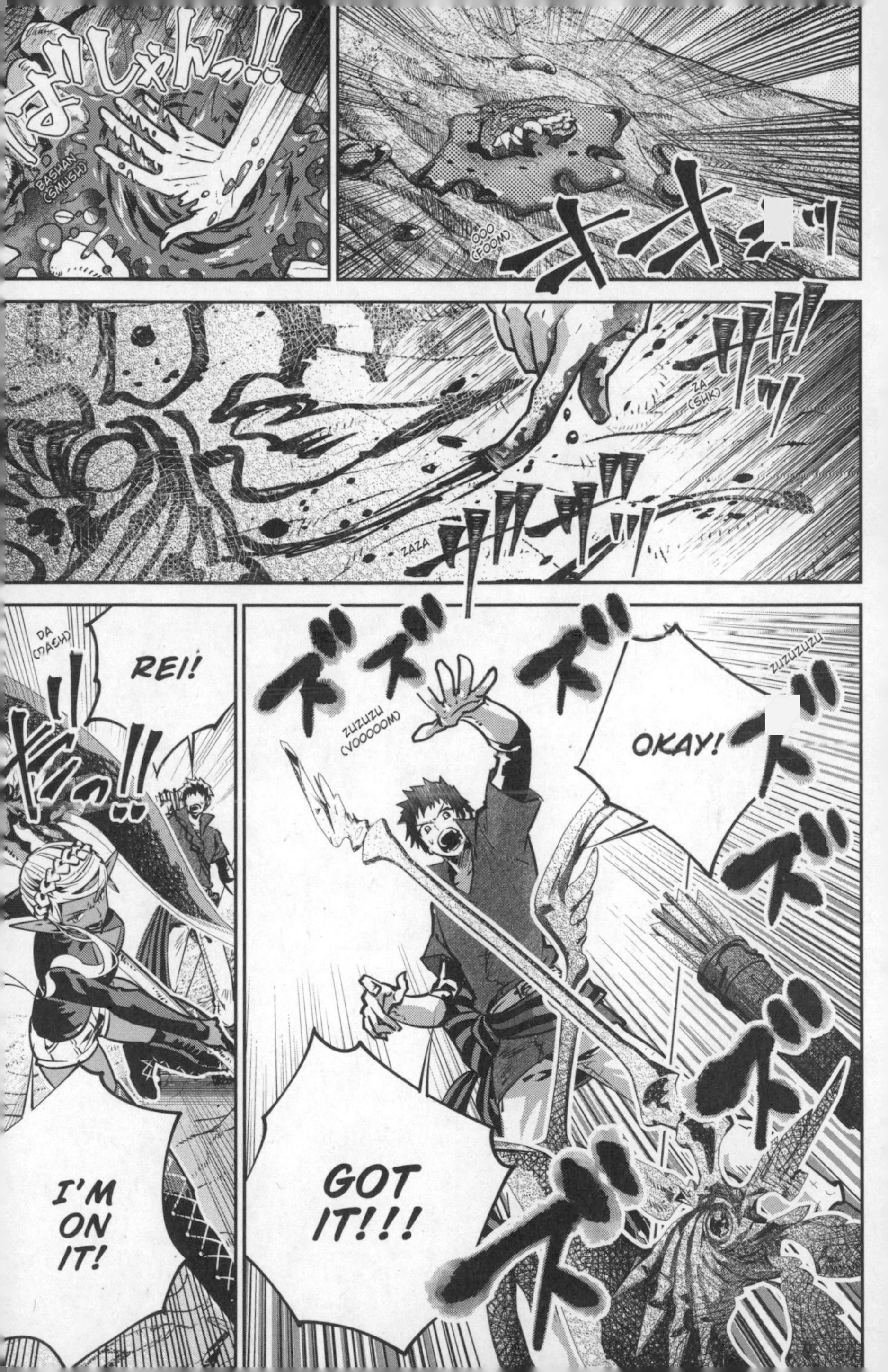
OOO (FOOM)
BASHAN (SMUSH)
ZA (SHK)
ZAZA
ZUZUZUZU
OKAY!
ZUZUZU (VOOOOOM)
GOT IT!!!
DA (DASH)
REI!
I'M ON IT!

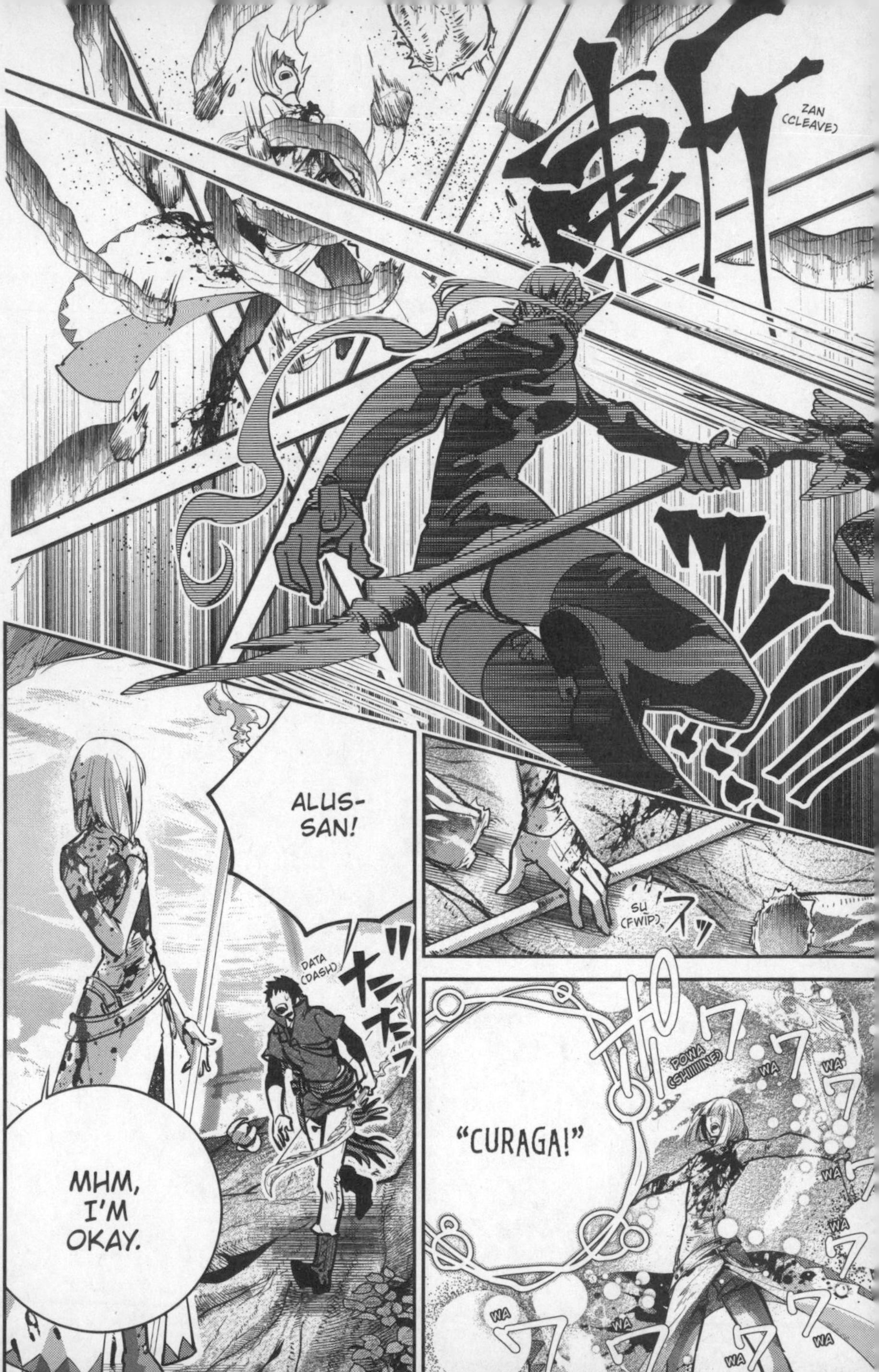

ZAN (CLEAVE)
SU (FWIP)
POWA (SHIIIIINE)
"CURAGA!"
WA
WA
WA
WA
WA
WA
WA
WA
ALUS-SAN!
DATA (DASH)
MHM, I'M OKAY.

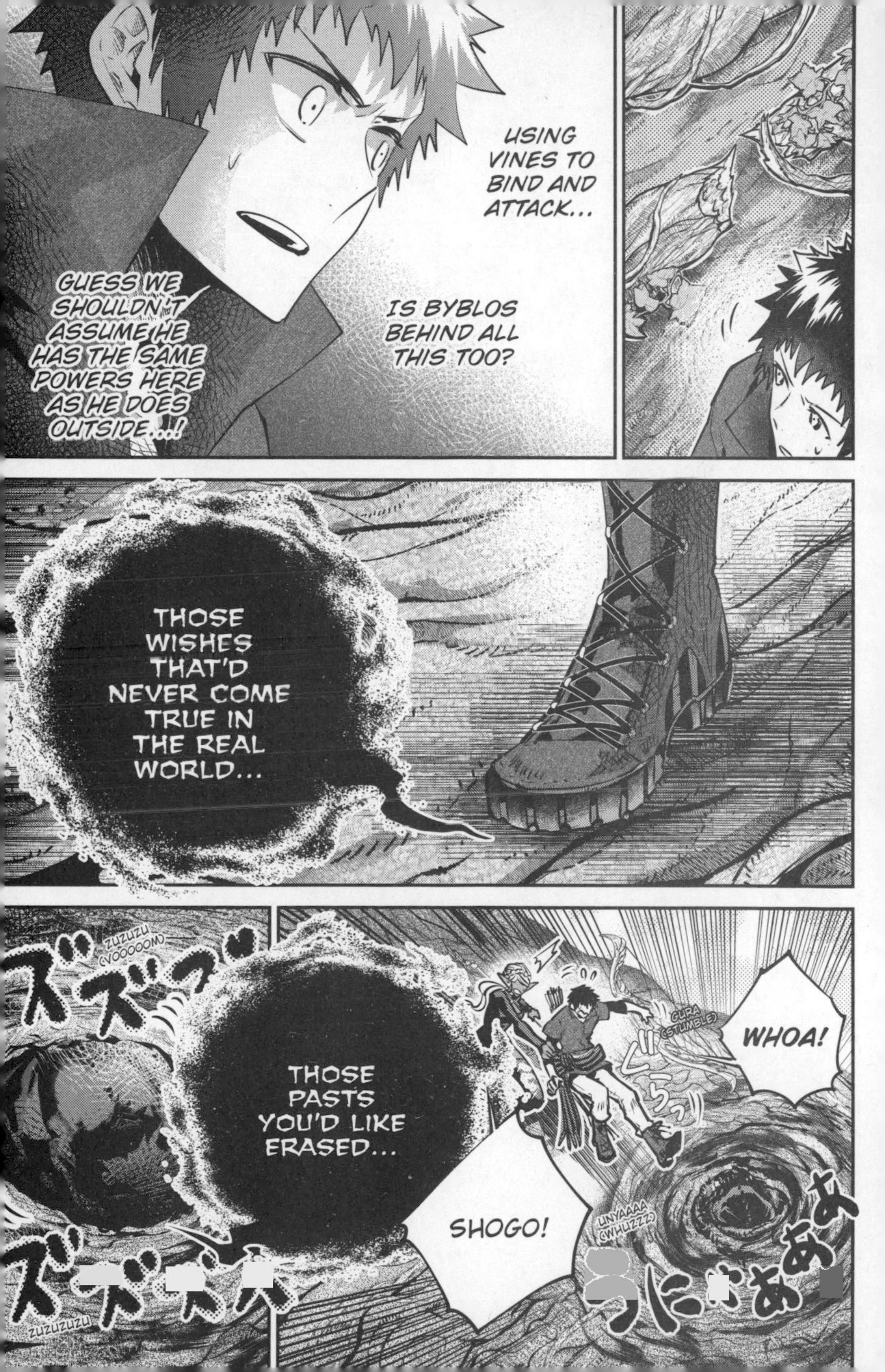
USING VINES TO BIND AND ATTACK...
IS BYBLOS BEHIND ALL THIS TOO?
GUESS WE SHOULDN'T ASSUME HE HAS THE SAME POWERS HERE AS HE DOES OUTSIDE...!
THOSE WISHES THAT'D NEVER COME TRUE IN THE REAL WORLD...
WHOA!
GURA (STUMBLE)
SHOGO!
UNYAAAA (WHUZZZ)
ZUZUZU (VOOOOOM)
THOSE PASTS YOU'D LIKE ERASED...
ZUZUZUZU

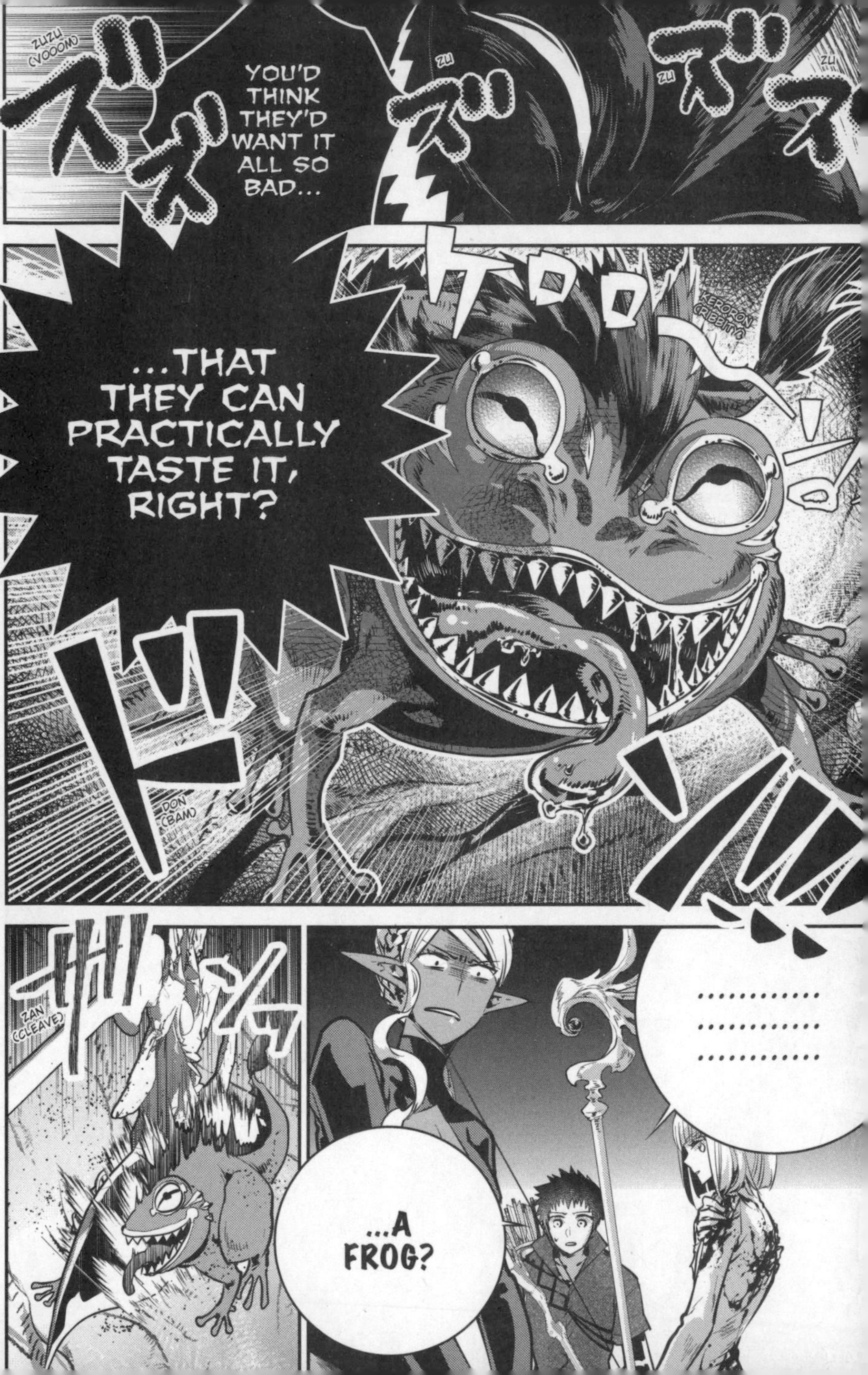
ZU
ZU
ZU
YOU'D THINK THEY'D WANT IT ALL SO BAD...
ZUZU (VOOOM)
KERORON (RIBBIT)
...THAT THEY CAN PRACTICALLY TASTE IT, RIGHT?
DON (BAM)
............
............
............
...A FROG?
ZAN (CLEAVE)

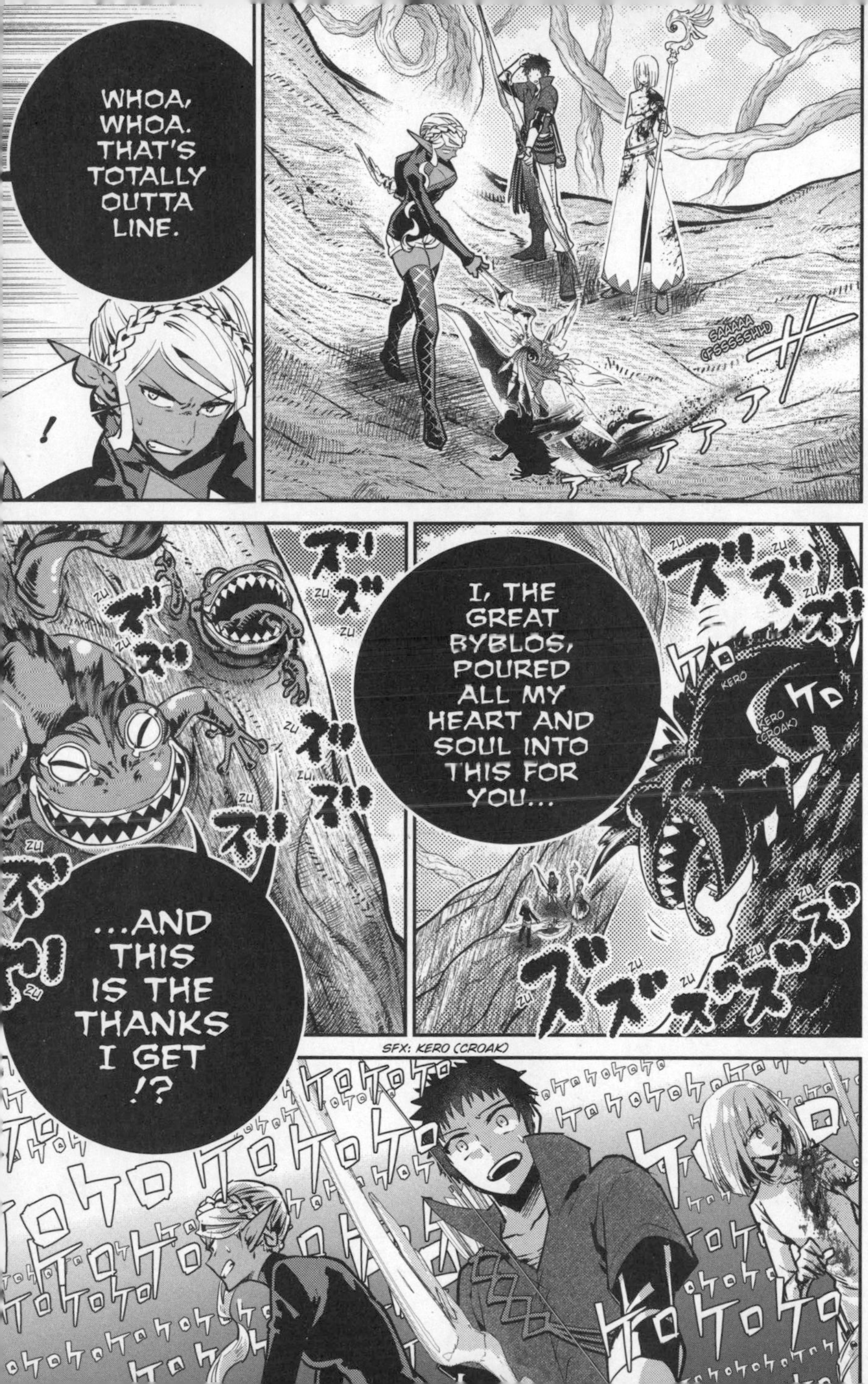
SAAAAA (PSSSSSHH)
WHOA, WHOA. THAT'S TOTALLY OUTTA LINE.
!
KERO
KERO (CROAK)
I, THE GREAT BYBLOS, POURED ALL MY HEART AND SOUL INTO THIS FOR YOU...
...AND THIS IS THE THANKS I GET!?
SFX: KERO (CROAK)

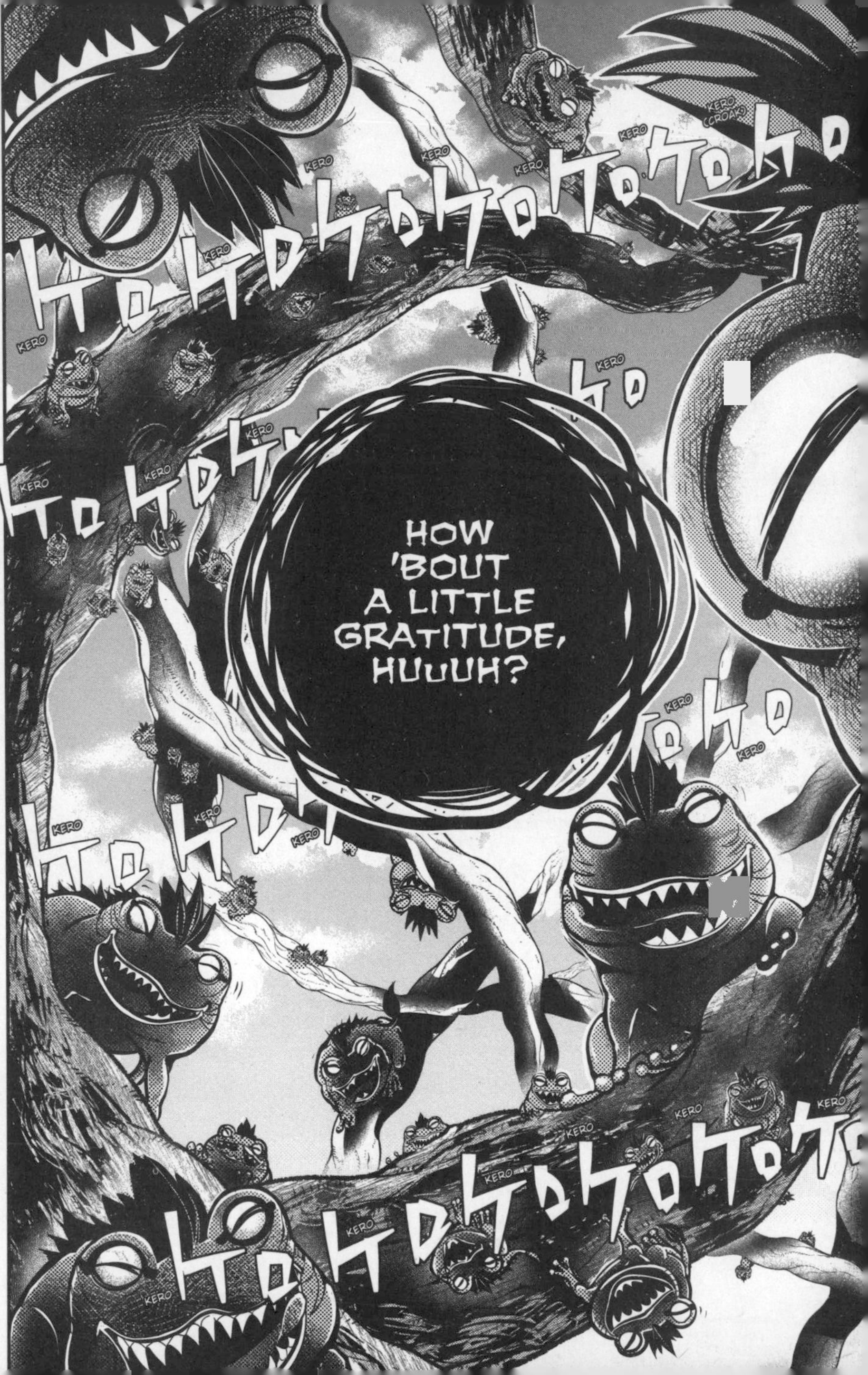
KERO (CROAK)
HOW 'BOUT A LITTLE GRATITUDE, HUUUH?

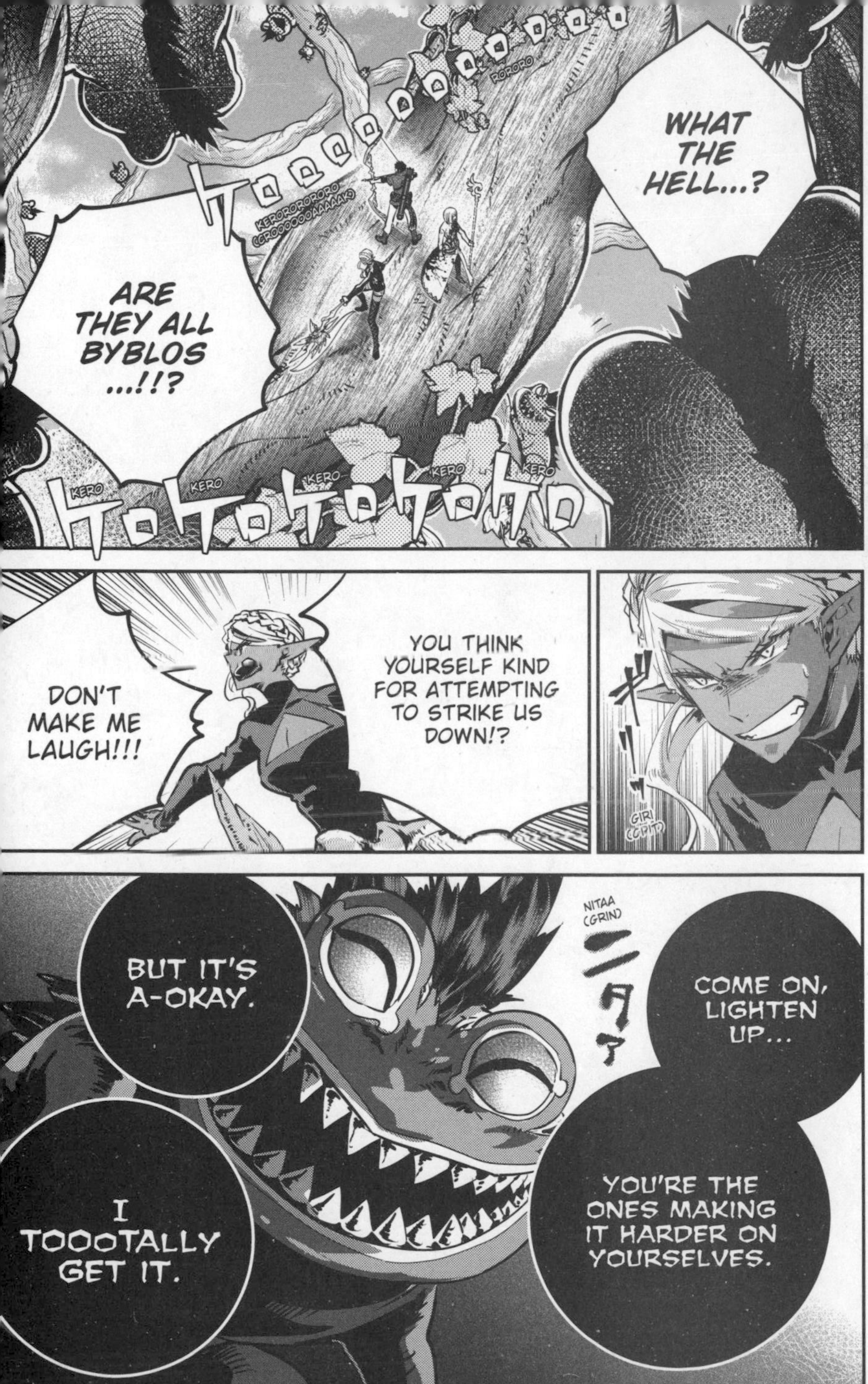
RORORO
KEROROROROROR
(CROOOOOOAAAAAK)
WHAT THE HELL...?
ARE THEY ALL BYBLOS ...!!?
KERO
KERO
KERO
KERO
KERO
GIRI (GRIT)
YOU THINK YOURSELF KIND FOR ATTEMPTING TO STRIKE US DOWN!?
DON'T MAKE ME LAUGH!!!
NITAA (GRIN)
COME ON, LIGHTEN UP...
BUT IT'S A-OKAY.
YOU'RE THE ONES MAKING IT HARDER ON YOURSELVES.
I TOOOTALLY GET IT.

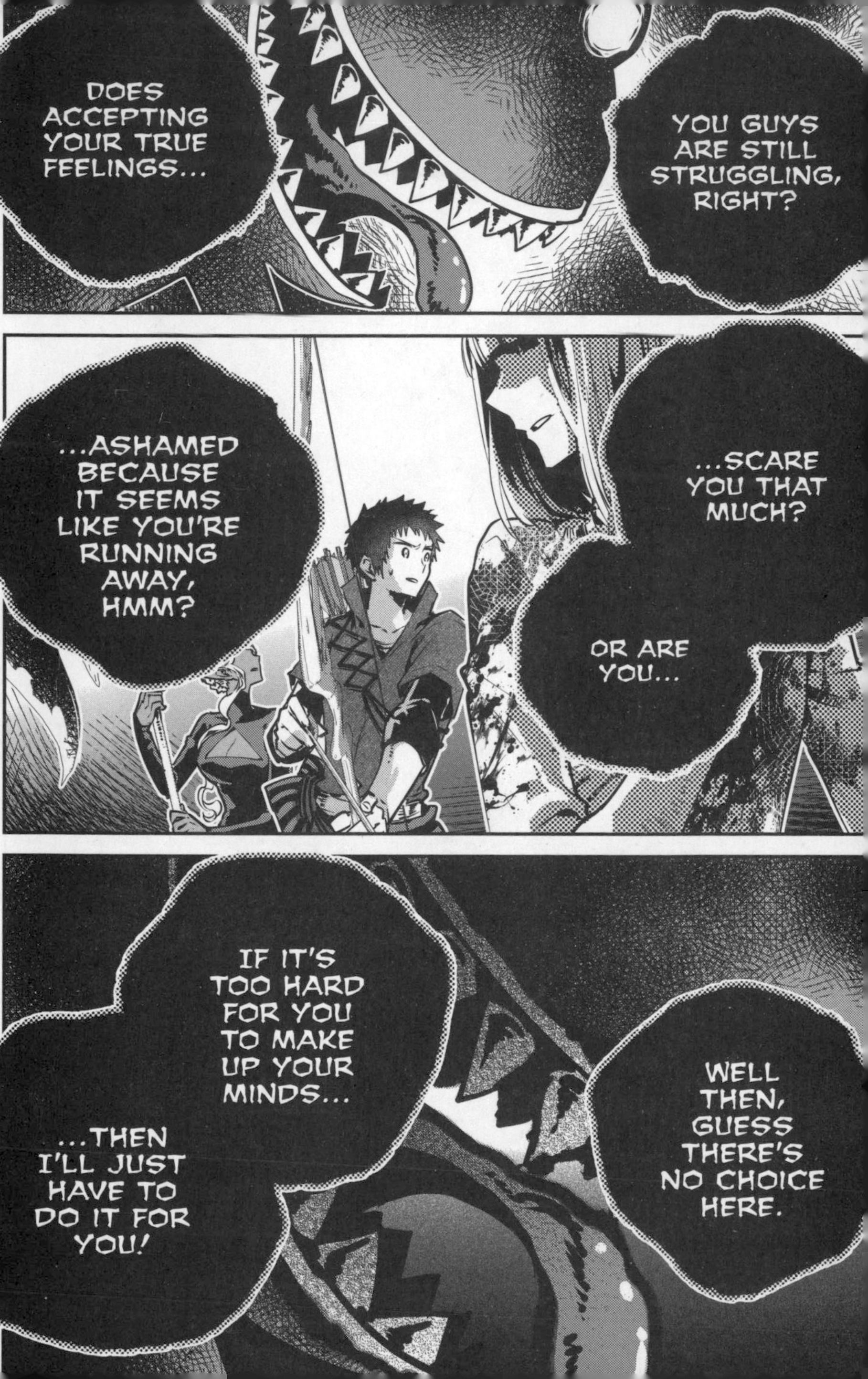
YOU GUYS ARE STILL STRUGGLING, RIGHT?
DOES ACCEPTING YOUR TRUE FEELINGS...
...SCARE YOU THAT MUCH?
OR ARE YOU...
...ASHAMED BECAUSE IT SEEMS LIKE YOU'RE RUNNING AWAY, HMM?
WELL THEN, GUESS THERE'S NO CHOICE HERE.
IF IT'S TOO HARD FOR YOU TO MAKE UP YOUR MINDS...
...THEN I'LL JUST HAVE TO DO IT FOR YOU!

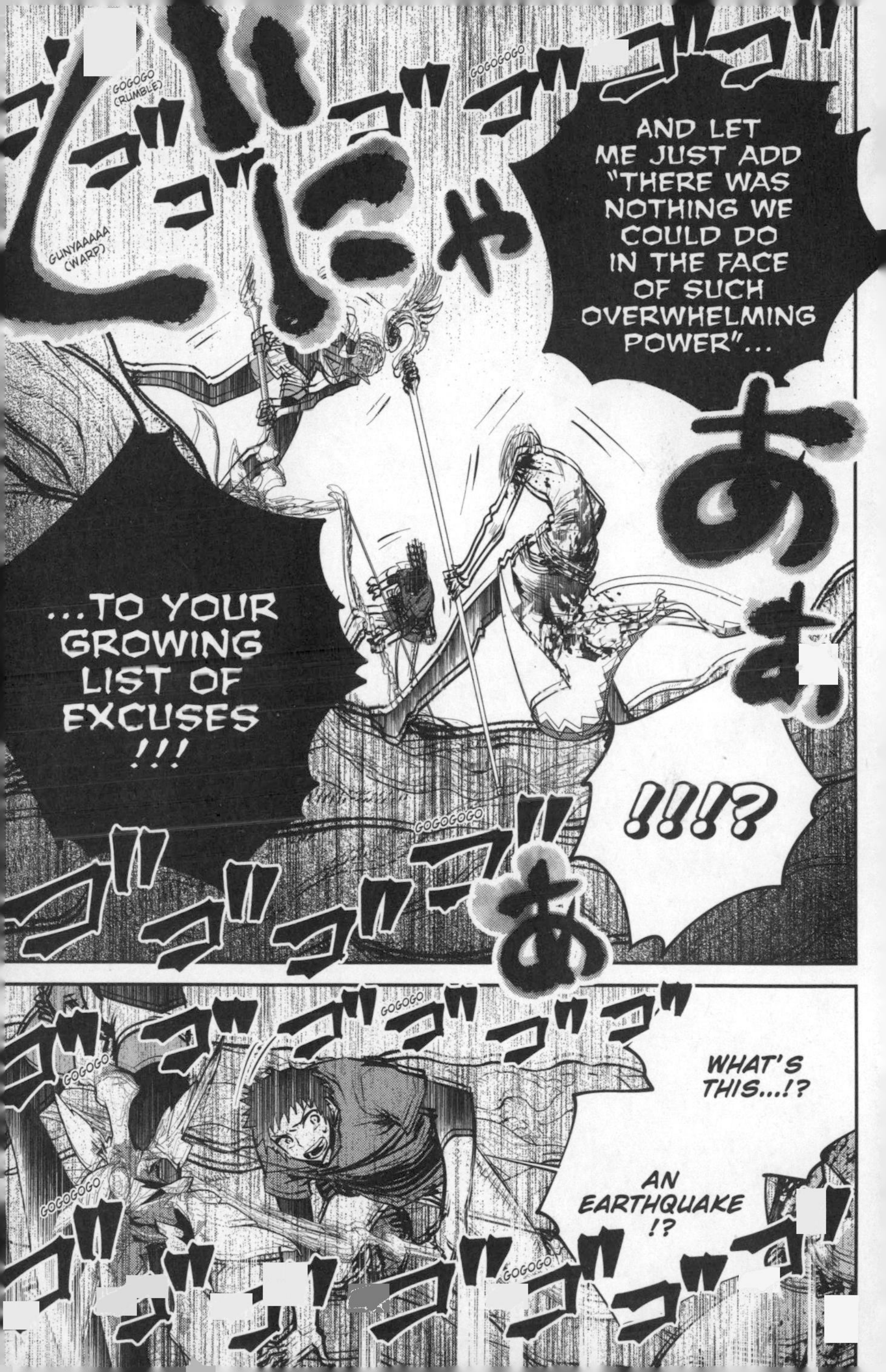
GOGOGOGO
AND LET ME JUST ADD "THERE WAS NOTHING WE COULD DO IN THE FACE OF SUCH OVERWHELMING POWER"...
GOGOGO (RUMBLE)
GUNYAAAAA (WARP)
!!!?
...TO YOUR GROWING LIST OF EXCUSES!!!
GOGOGOGO
WHAT'S THIS...!?
AN EARTHQUAKE!?
GOGOGO
GOGOGO
GOGOGOGO
GOGOGO

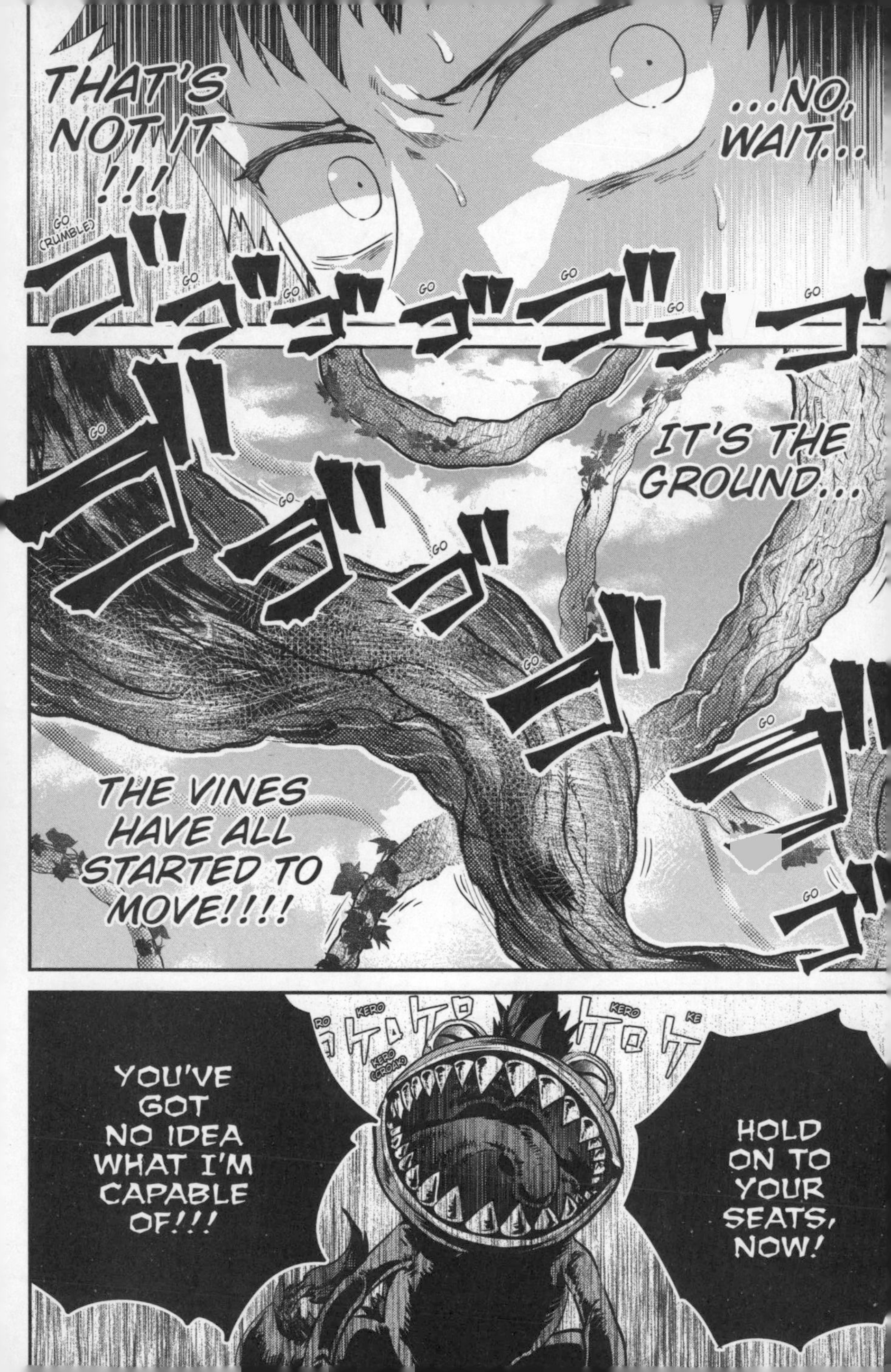
...NO, WAIT...
THAT'S NOT IT!!!
GO (RUMBLE)
GO
GO
IT'S THE GROUND...
THE VINES HAVE ALL STARTED TO MOVE!!!!
KERO (CROAK)
KERO
HOLD ON TO YOUR SEATS, NOW!
YOU'VE GOT NO IDEA WHAT I'M CAPABLE OF!!!

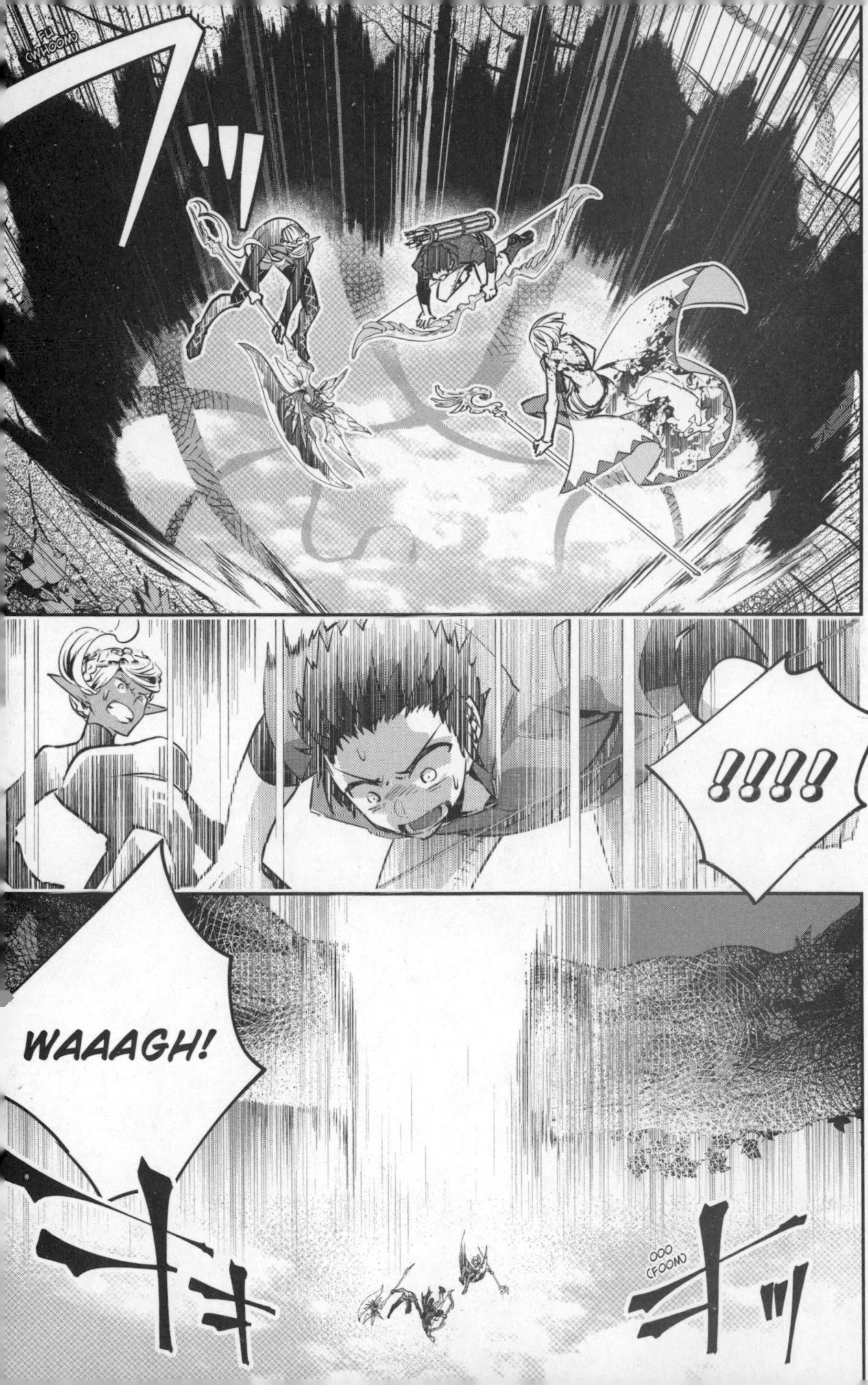
FU
(WHOOMP)
!!!!
WAAAGH!
OOO
(FOOM)

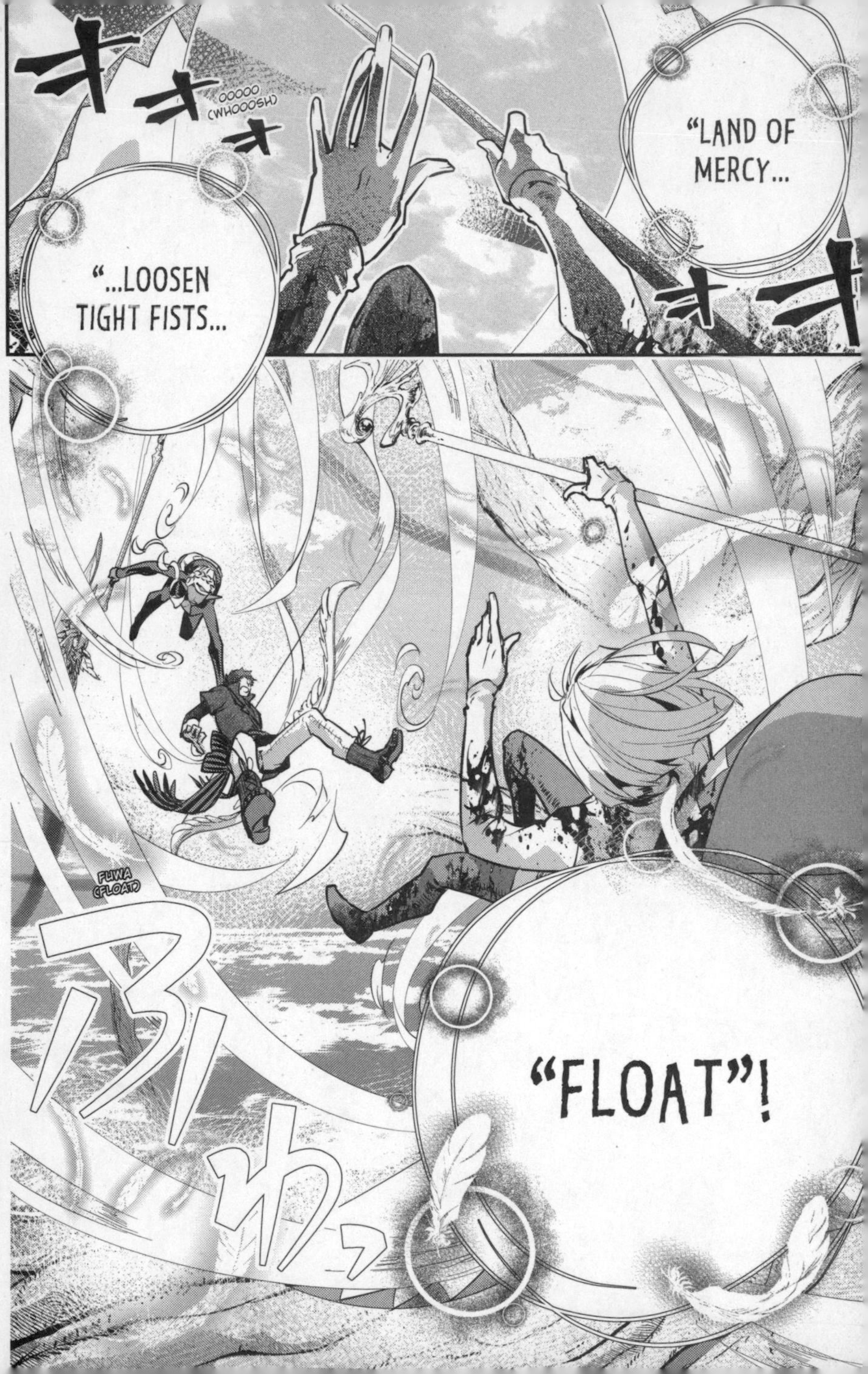
"LAND OF MERCY...
OOOOO (WHOOOSH)
"...LOOSEN TIGHT FISTS...
FUWA (FLOAT)
"FLOAT"!

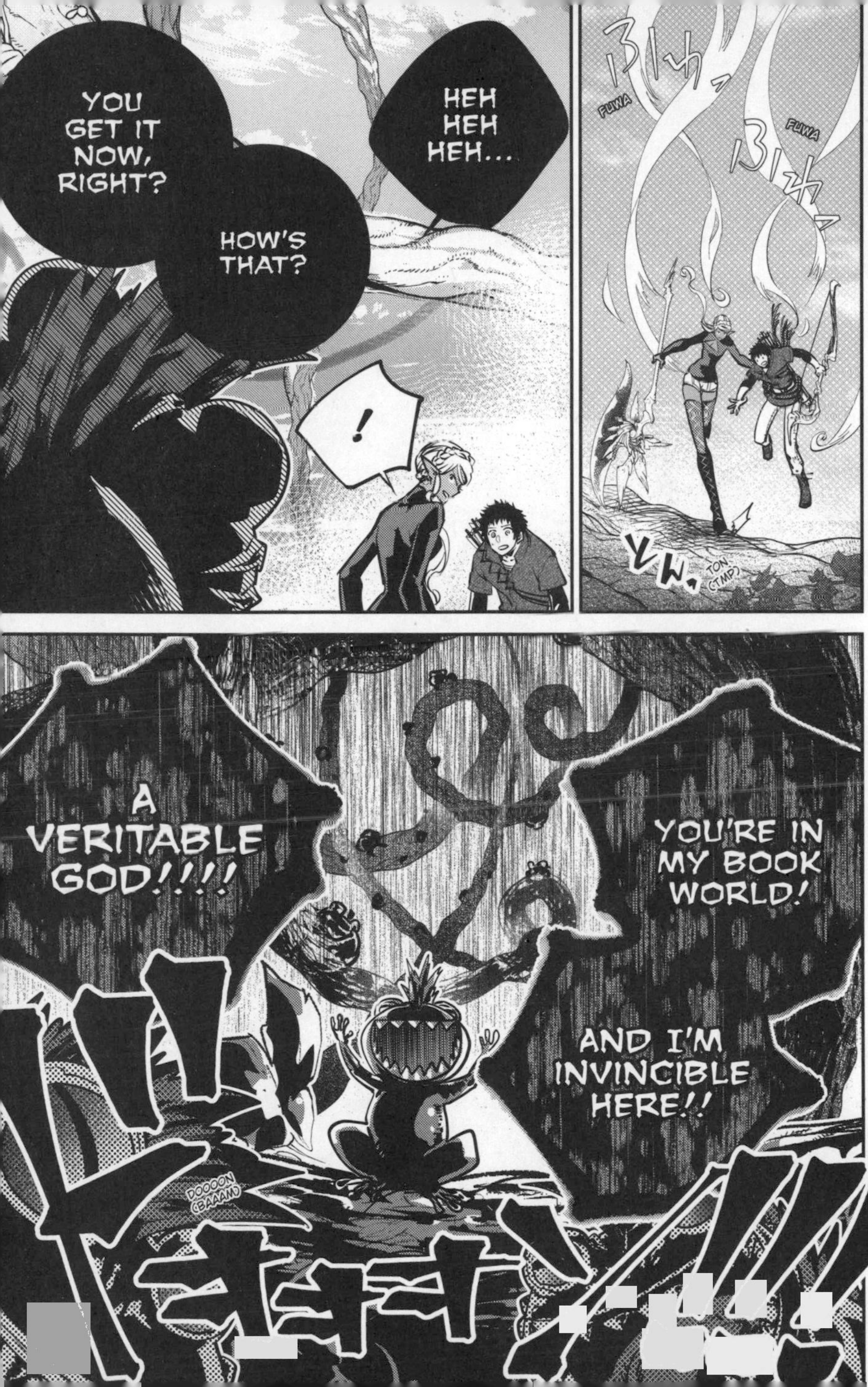
FUWA
FUWA
TON (TMP)
HEH HEH HEH...
YOU GET IT NOW, RIGHT?
HOW'S THAT?
!
YOU'RE IN MY BOOK WORLD!
AND I'M INVINCIBLE HERE!!
A VERITABLE GOD!!!!
DOOOON (BAAAM)

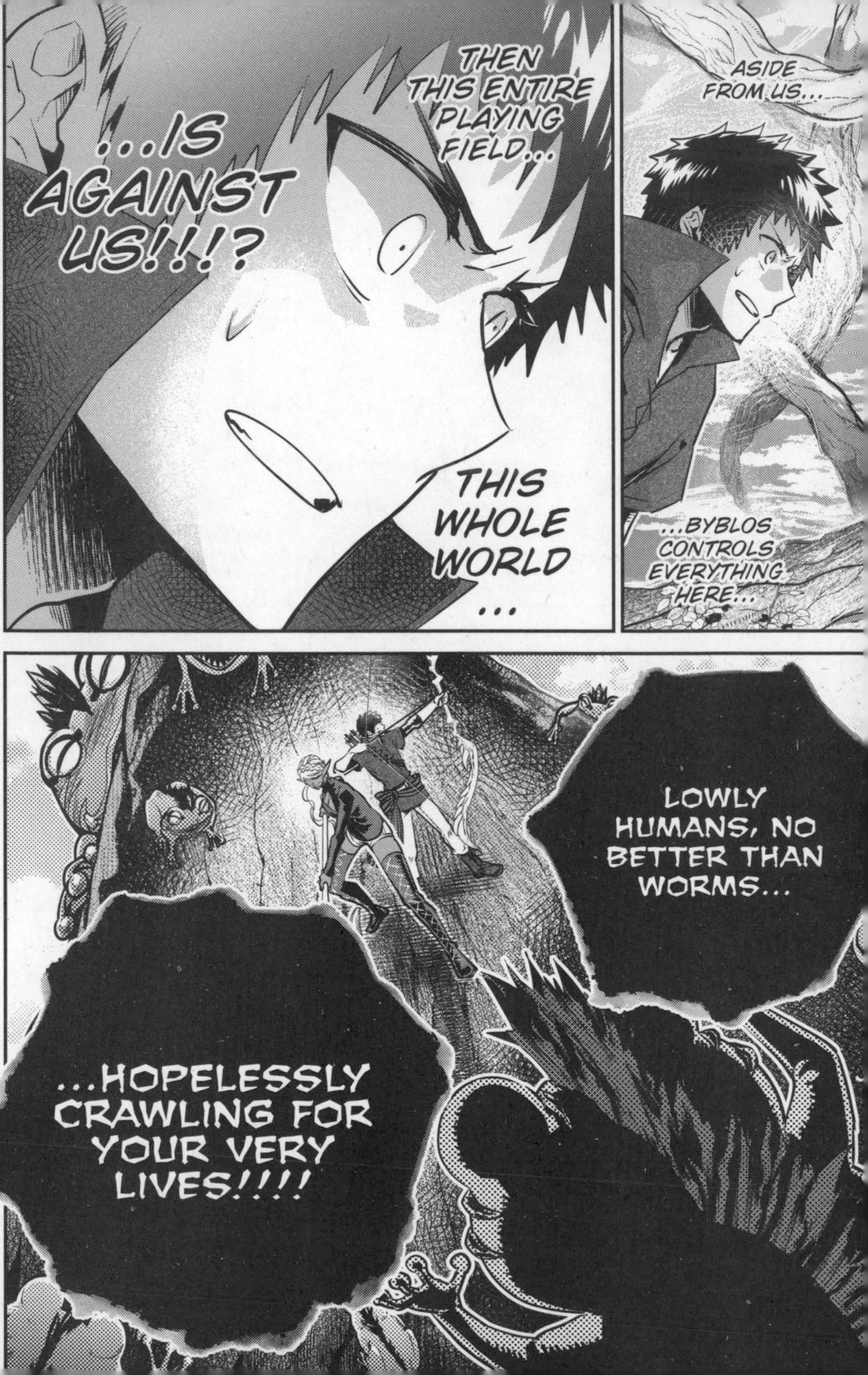
ASIDE FROM US...
...BYBLOS CONTROLS EVERYTHING HERE...
THEN THIS ENTIRE PLAYING FIELD...
THIS WHOLE WORLD ...
...IS AGAINST US!!!?
LOWLY HUMANS, NO BETTER THAN WORMS...
...HOPELESSLY CRAWLING FOR YOUR VERY LIVES!!!!

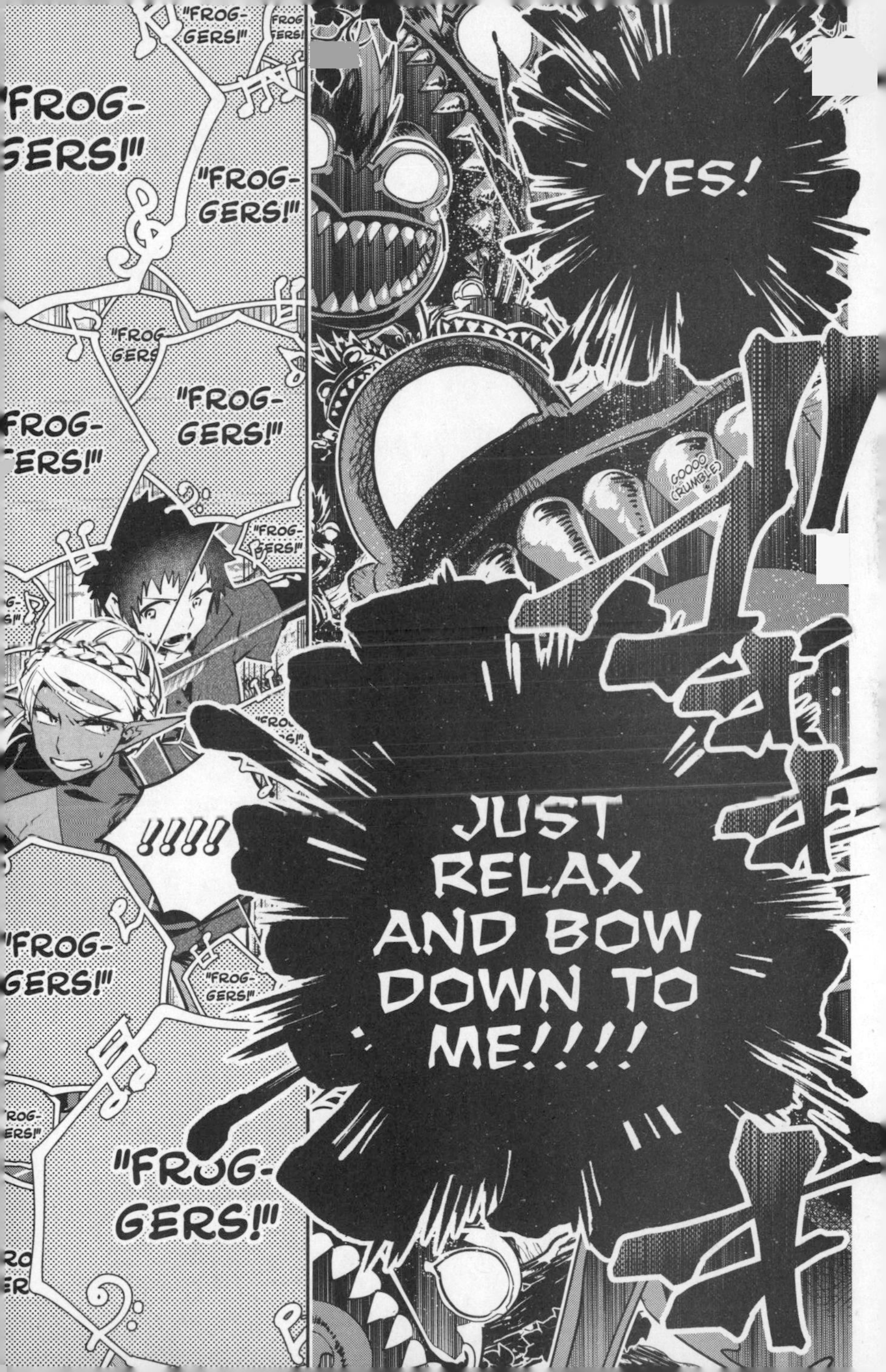
YES!
GOOOO (RUMBLE)
JUST RELAX AND BOW DOWN TO ME!!!!
"FROG-GERS!"
"FROG-GERS!"
"FROG-GERS!"
"FROG-GERS!"
"FROG-GERS!"
"FROG-GERS!"
!!!!
"FROG-GERS!"
"FROG-GERS!"
"FROG-GERS!"

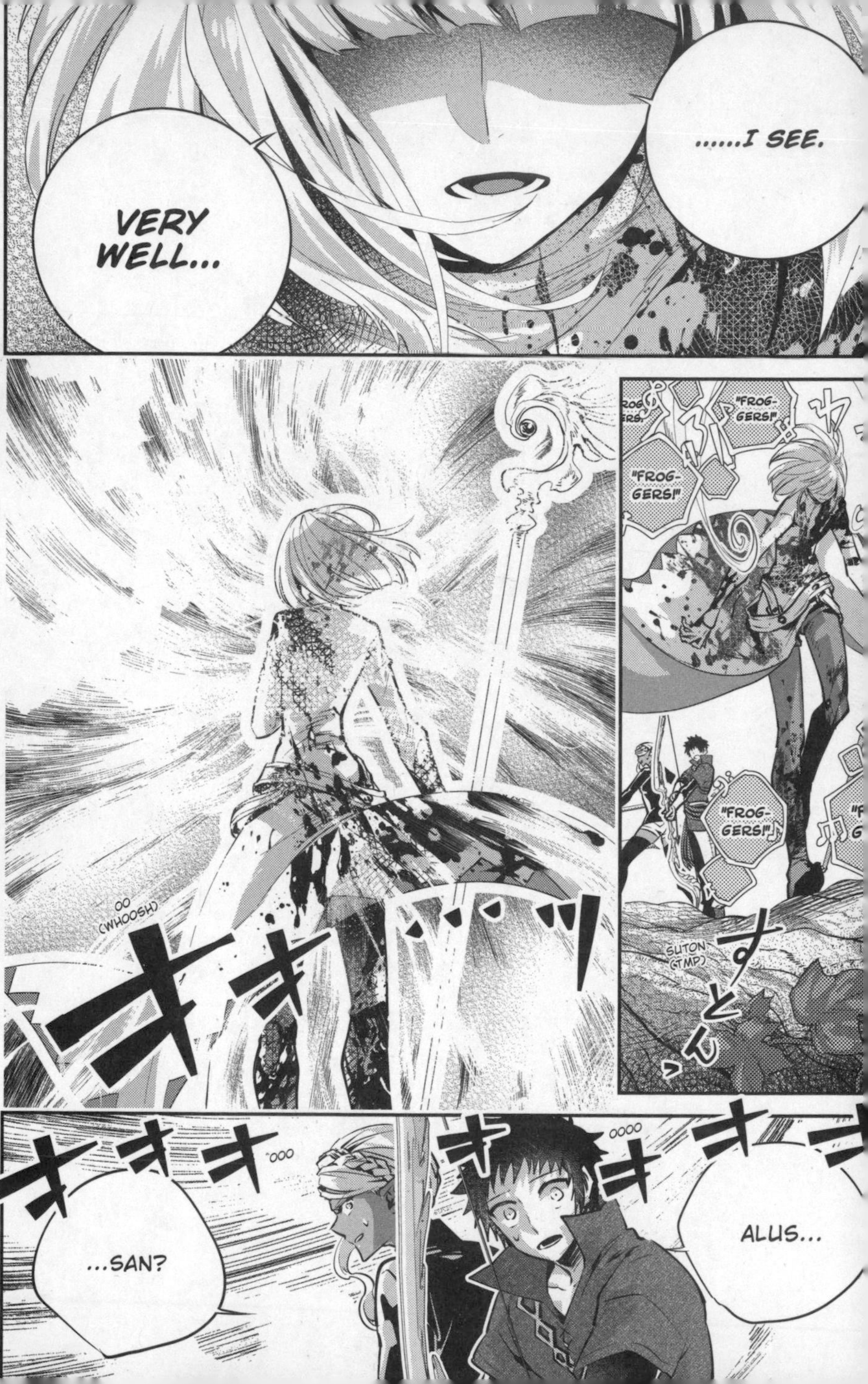

......I SEE.
VERY WELL...
"FROG-GERS!"
"FROG-GERS!"
"FROG-GERS!"
SUTON (TMP)
OO (WHOOSH)
OOOO
ALUS...
OOO
...SAN?

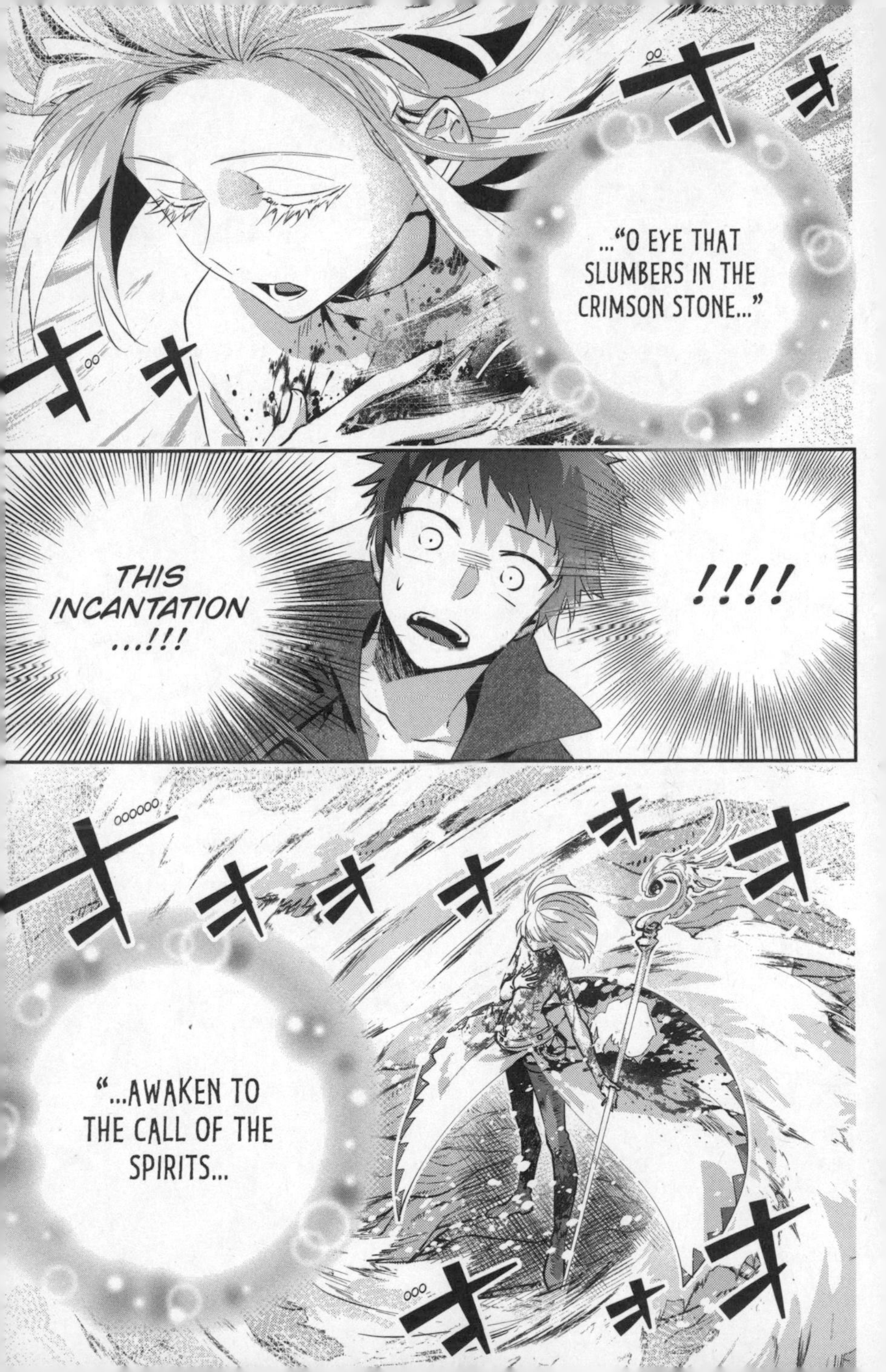
oo
...“O EYE THAT
SLUMBERS IN THE
CRIMSON STONE...”
oo
!!!!
THIS
INCANTATION
...!!!
oooooo
“...AWAKEN TO
THE CALL OF THE
SPIRITS...
ooo

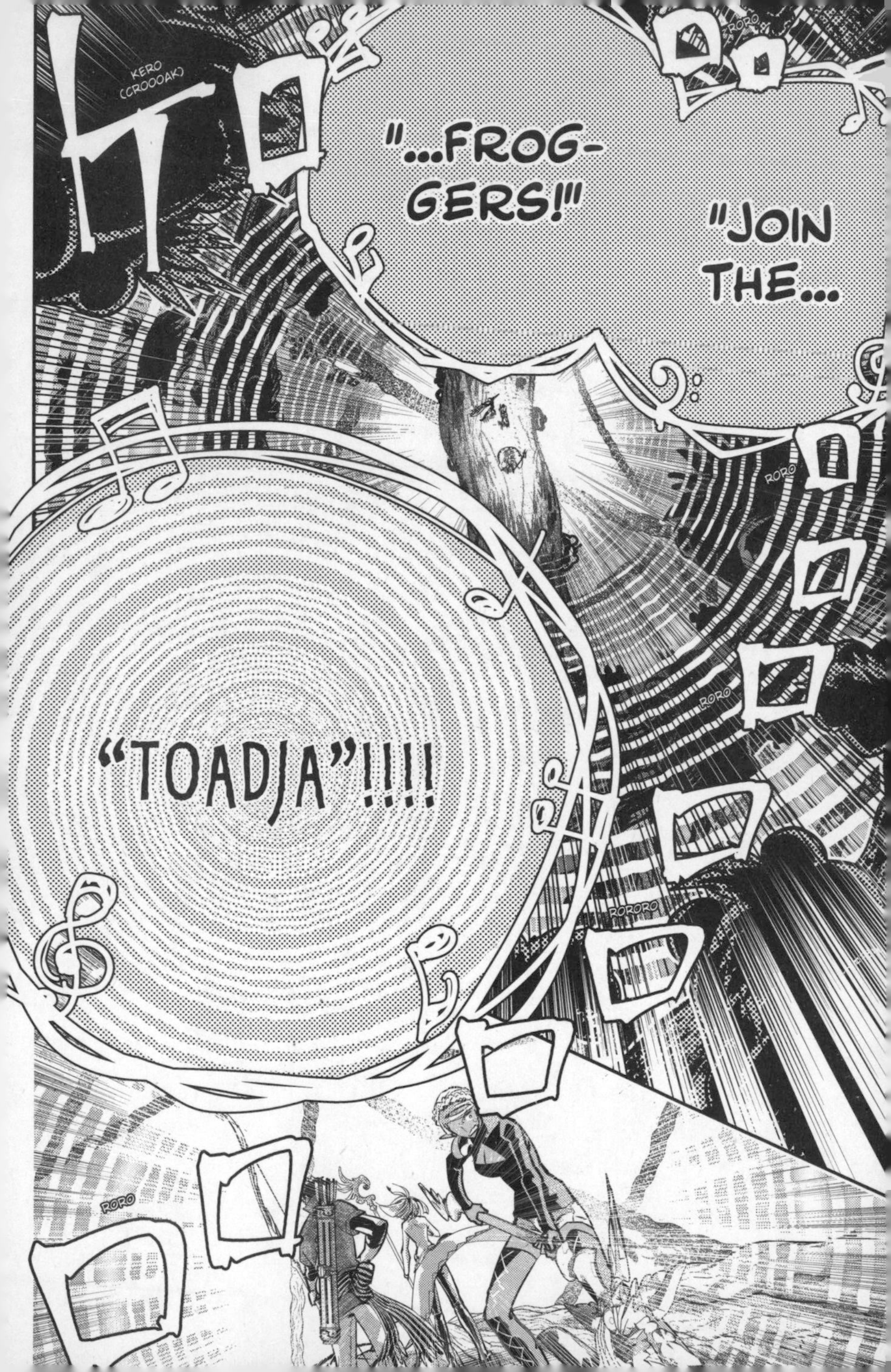
RORO
"JOIN THE...
"...FROG-GERS!"
KERO (CROOOAK)
RORO
RORO
RORORO
"TOADJA"!!!!
RORO

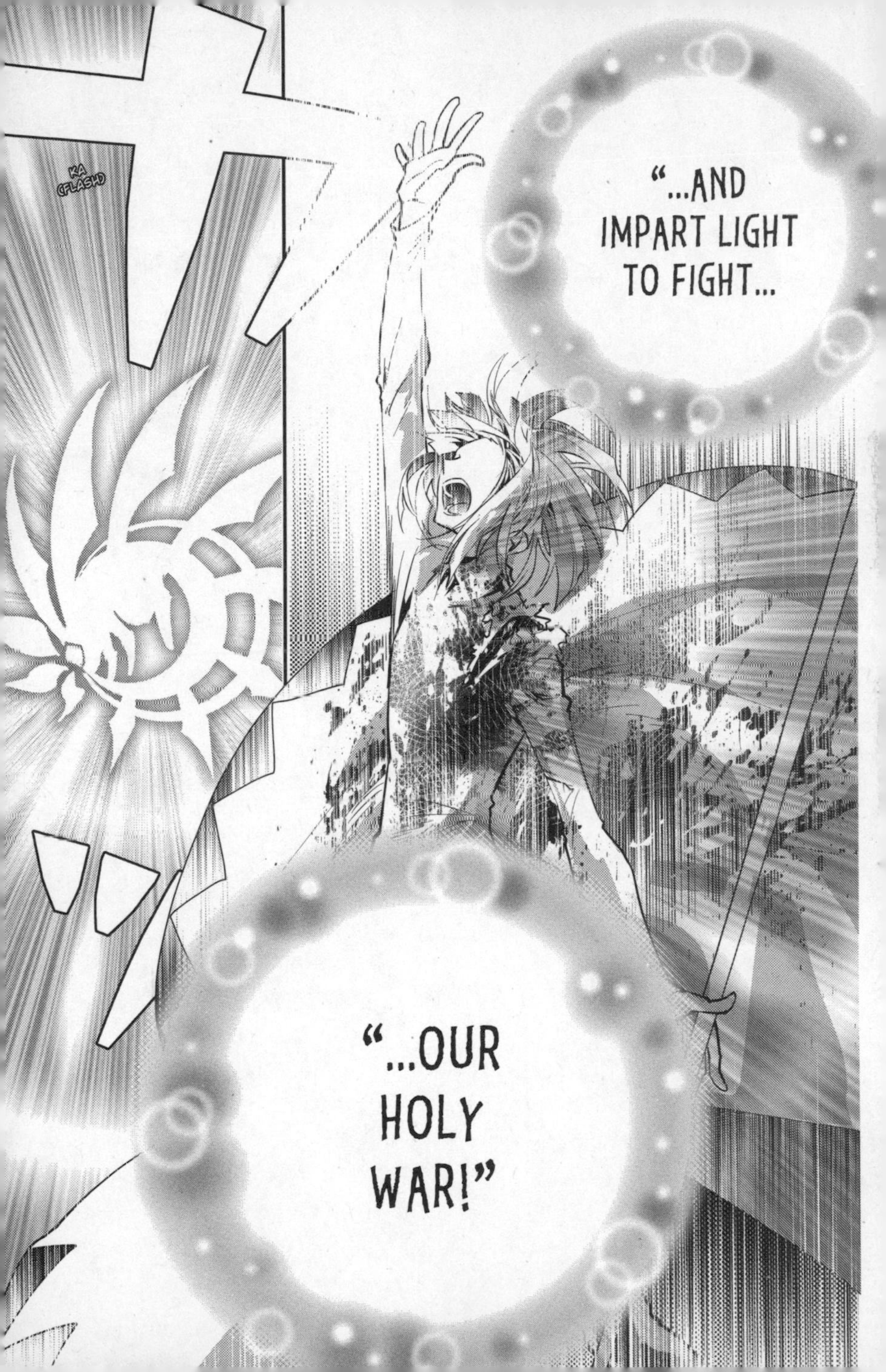
"...AND IMPART LIGHT TO FIGHT...
KA (FLASH)
"...OUR HOLY WAR!"

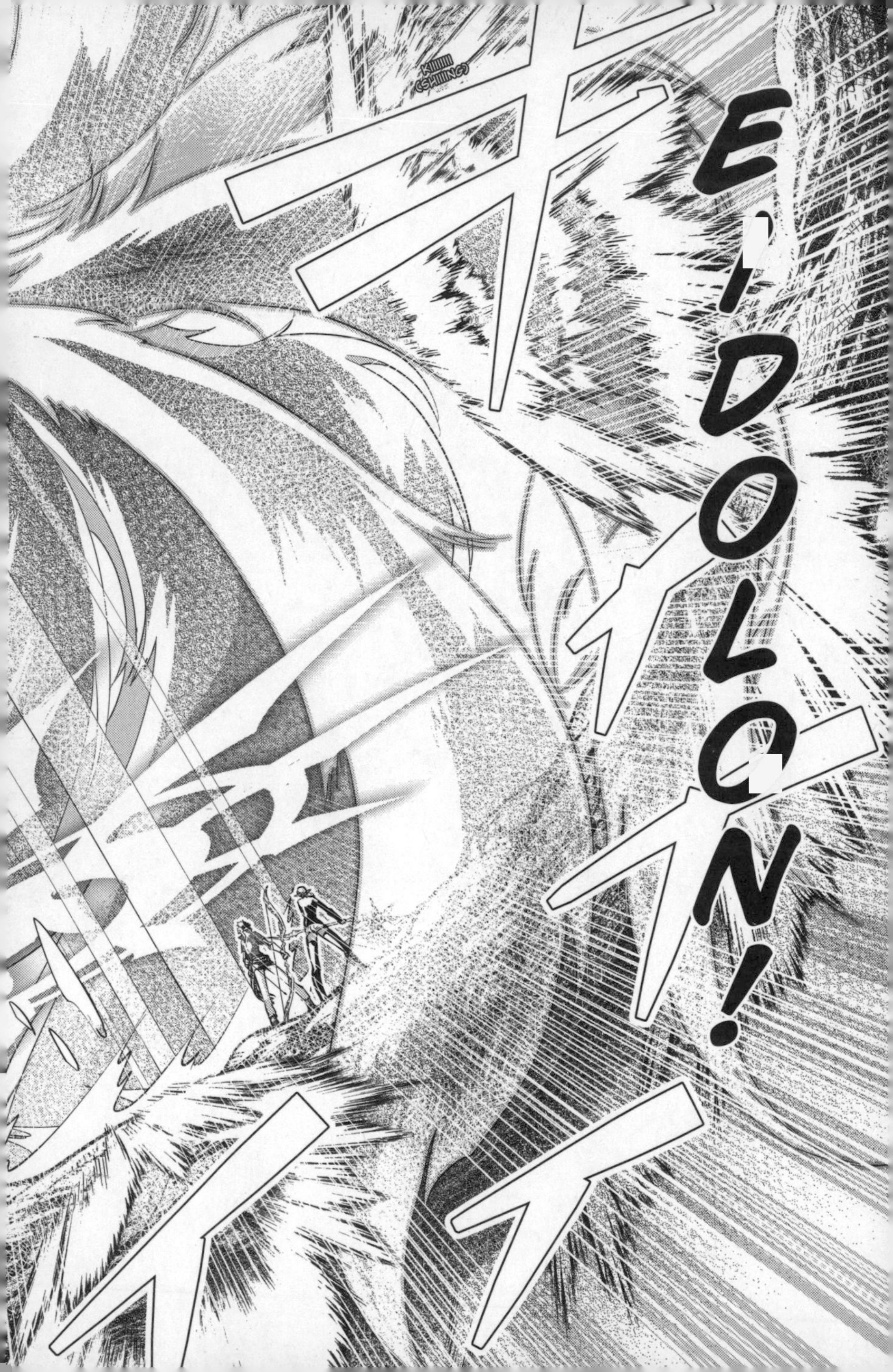
EIDOLON!
KIIIIIIII
(SHIIIING)

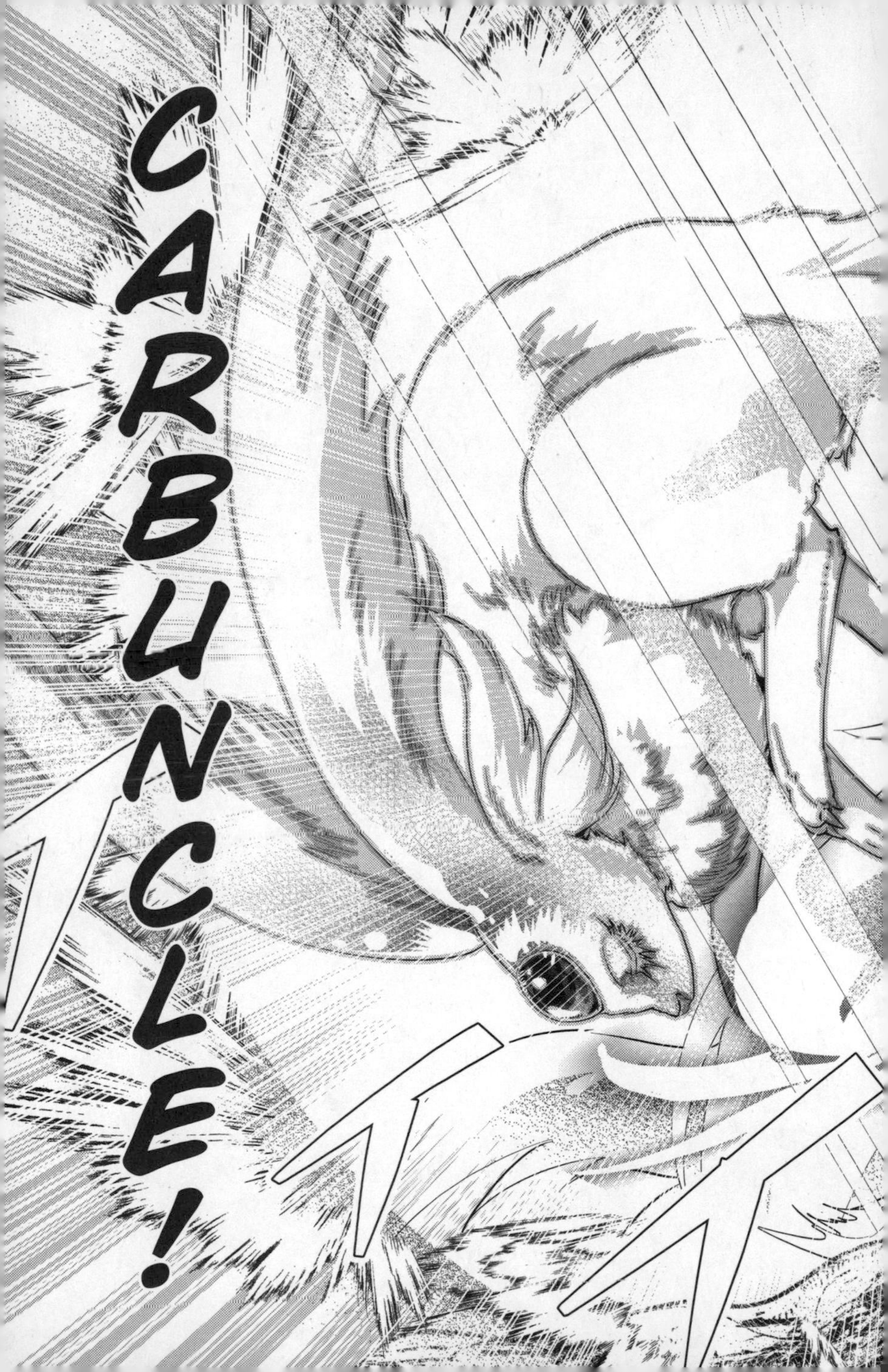
CARBUNCLE!

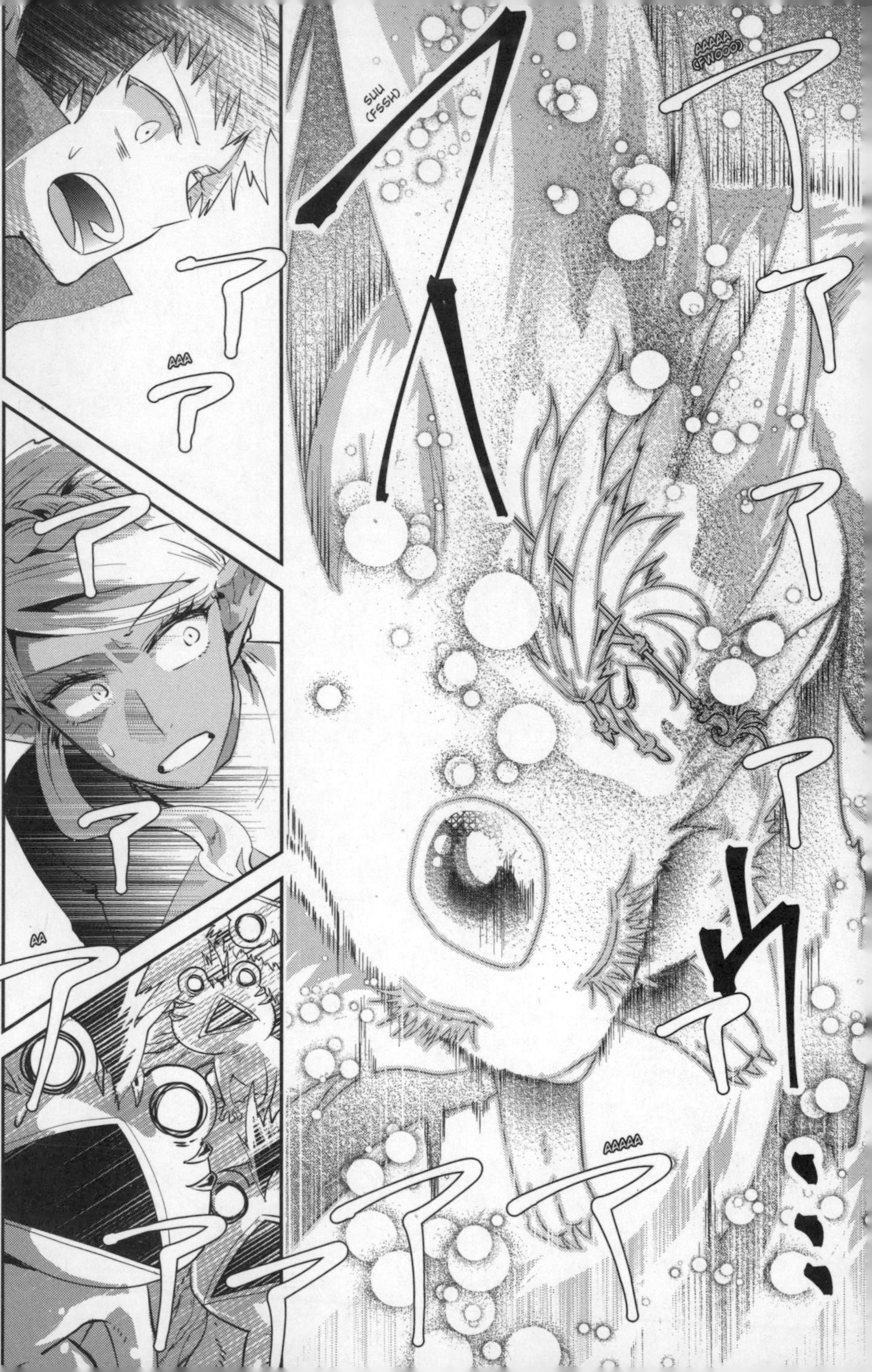
AAAAA (FWOOO)
SUU (FSSH)
AAAAA
AAA
AA

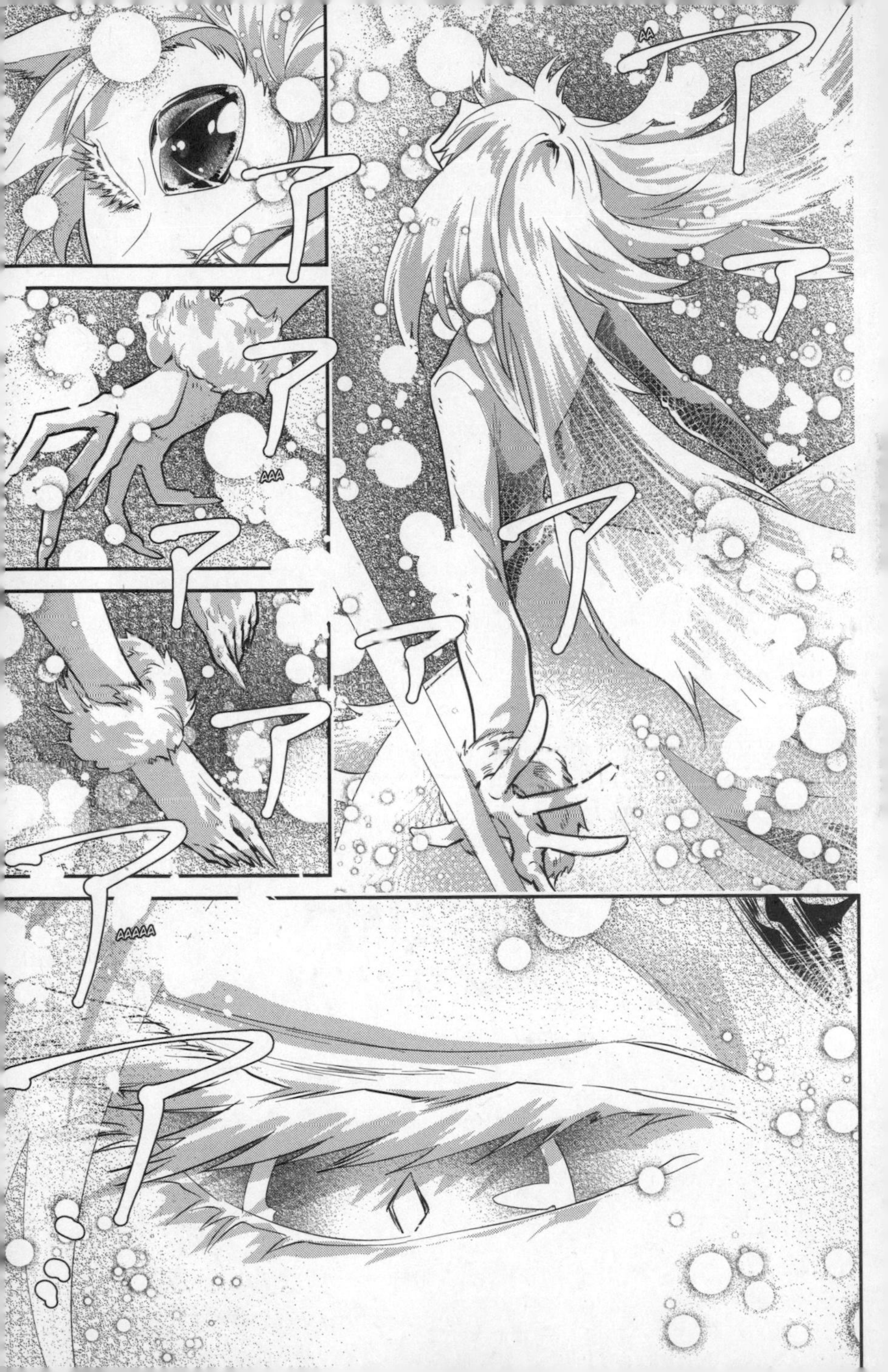
AA
AAA
AAAAA

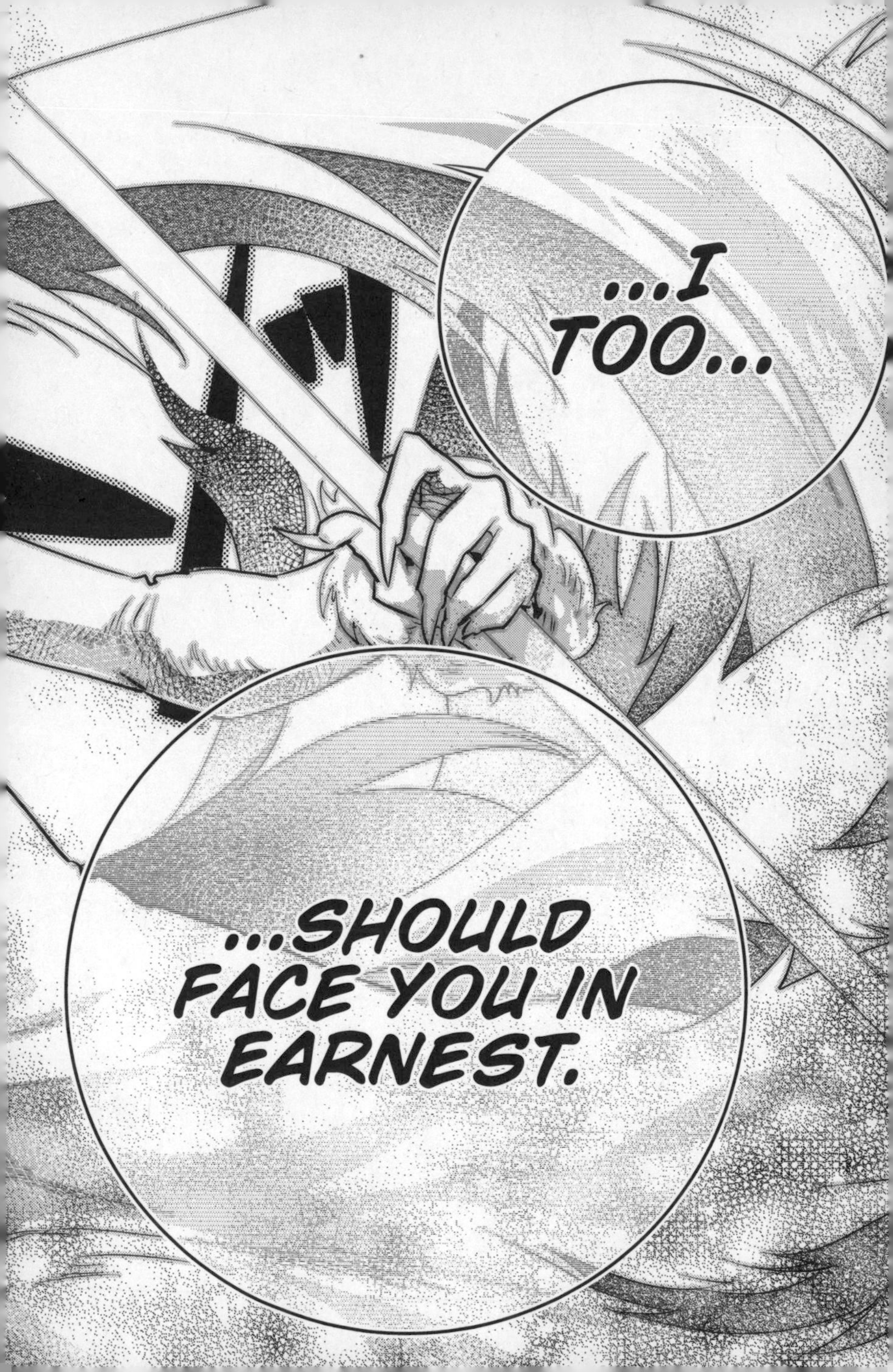
...I TOO...
...SHOULD FACE YOU IN EARNEST.

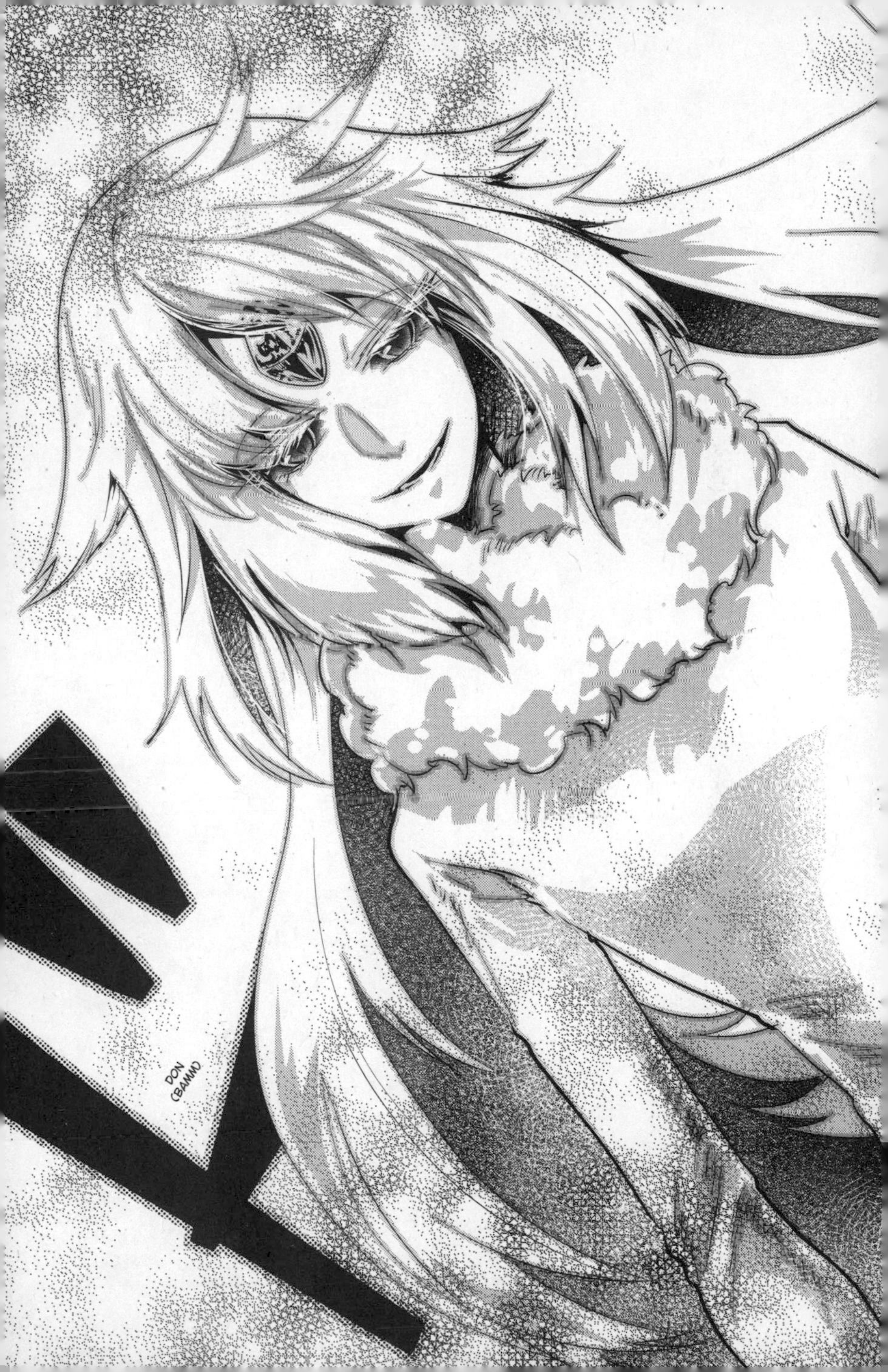
DON (BAMM)

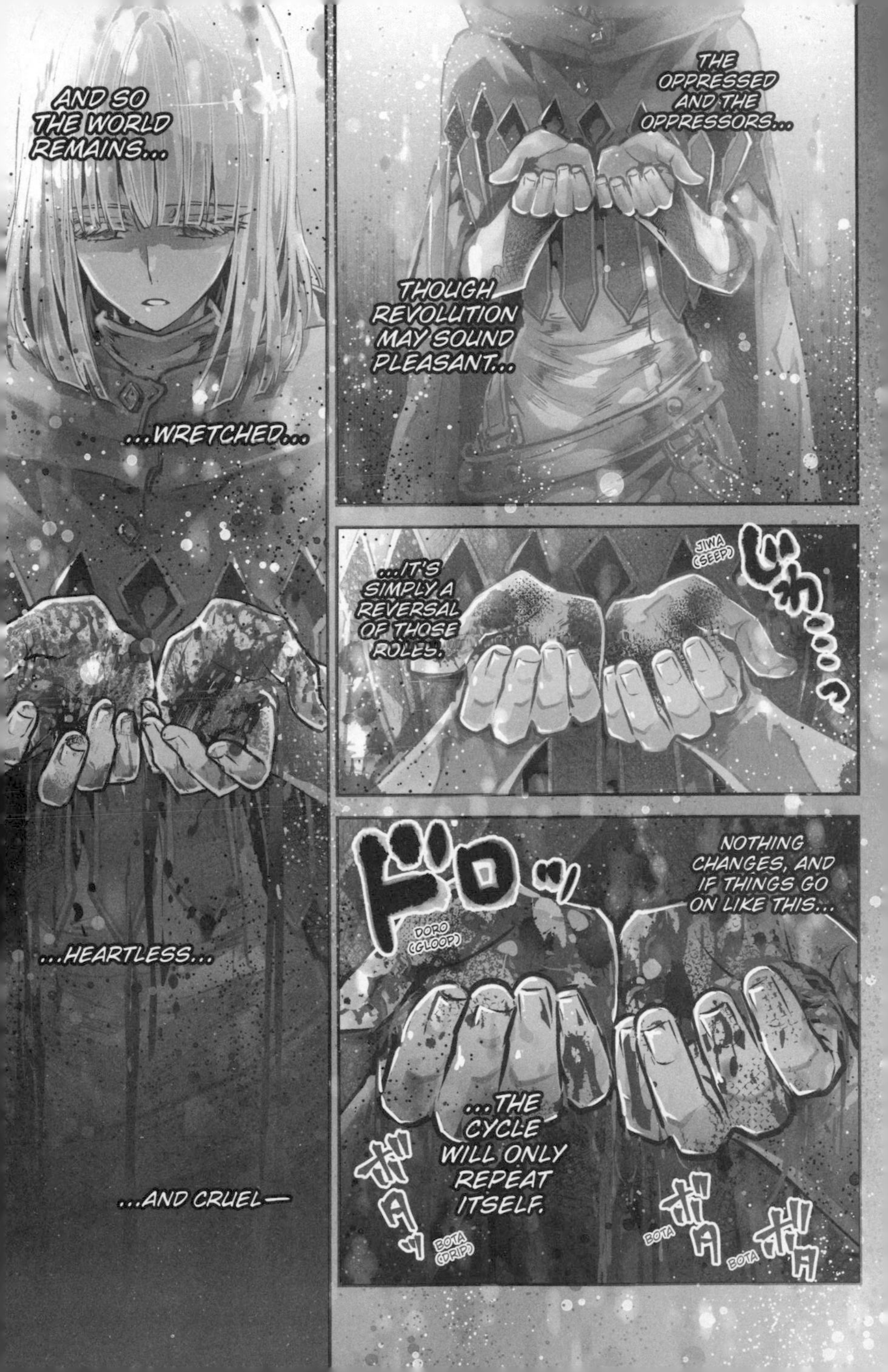
THE OPPRESSED AND THE OPPRESSORS...
THOUGH REVOLUTION MAY SOUND PLEASANT...
JIWA (SEEP)
...IT'S SIMPLY A REVERSAL OF THOSE ROLES.
NOTHING CHANGES, AND IF THINGS GO ON LIKE THIS...
DORO (GLOOP)
...THE CYCLE WILL ONLY REPEAT ITSELF.
BOTA
BOTA
BOTA (DRIP)
AND SO THE WORLD REMAINS...
...WRETCHED...
...HEARTLESS...
...AND CRUEL—

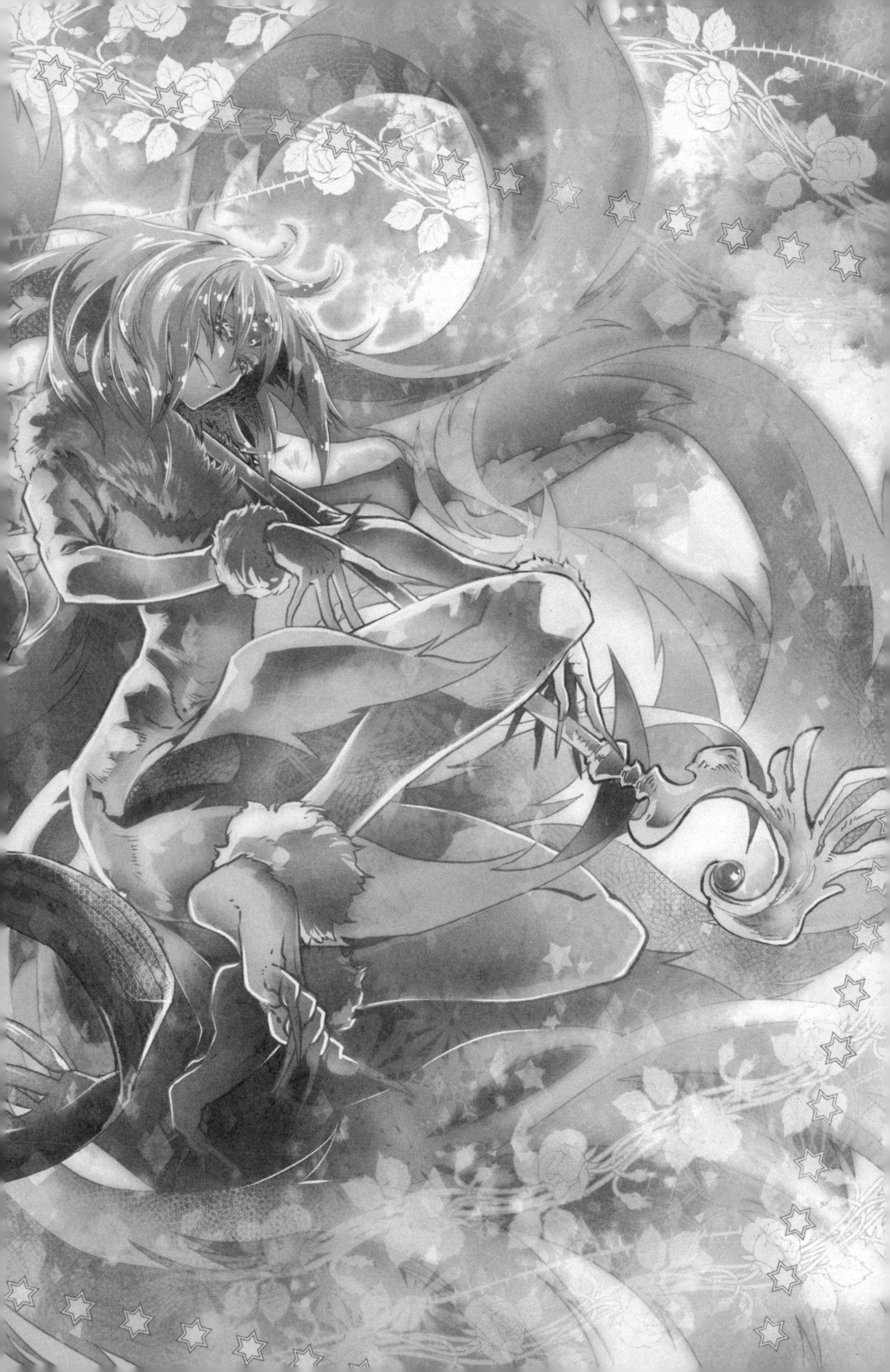

# Chapter 31 Awakening

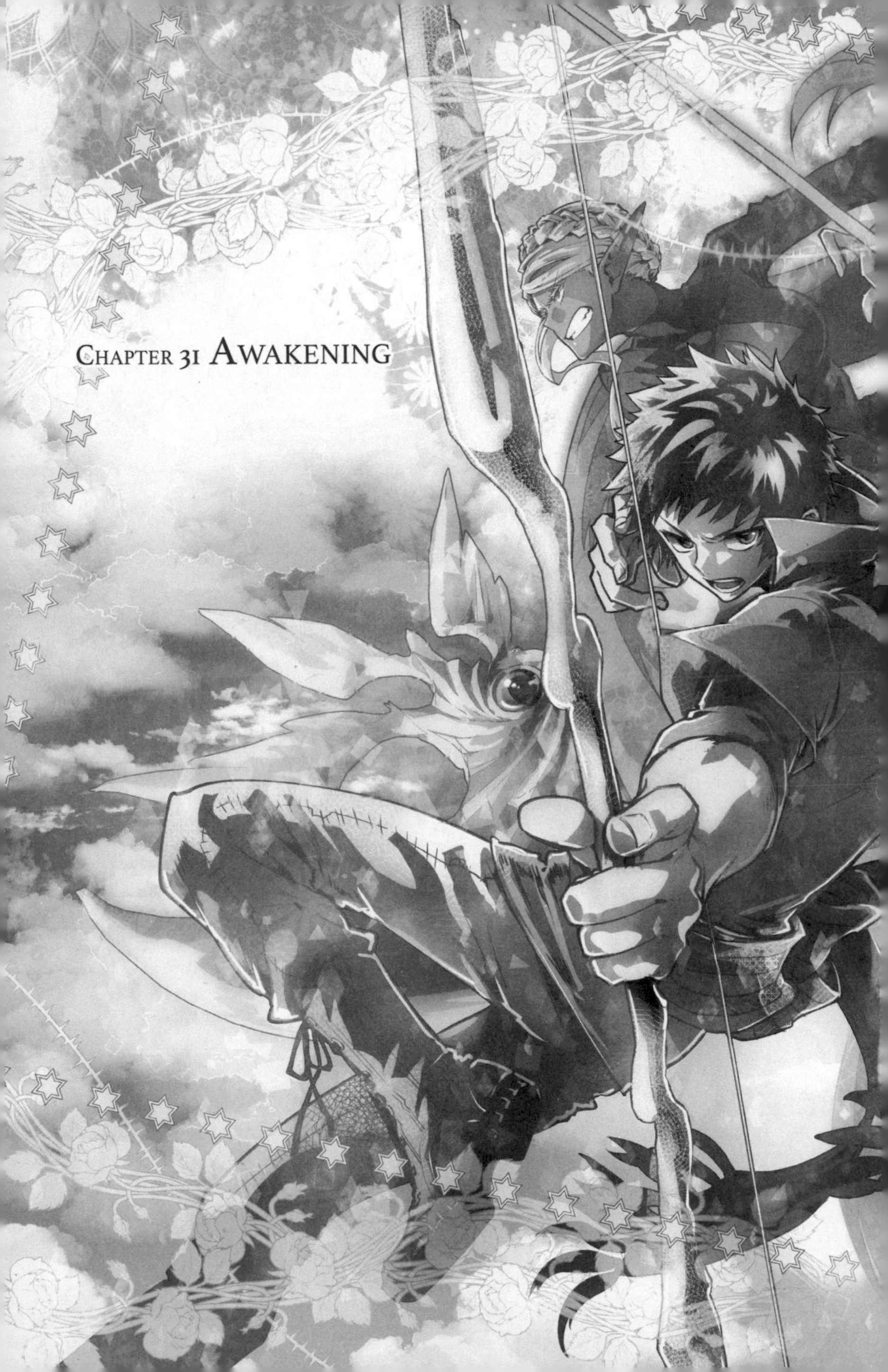

FINAL FANTASY®

ファイナルファンタジー　ロスト・ストレンジャー

LOST STRANGER

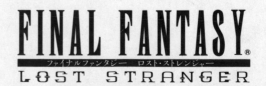

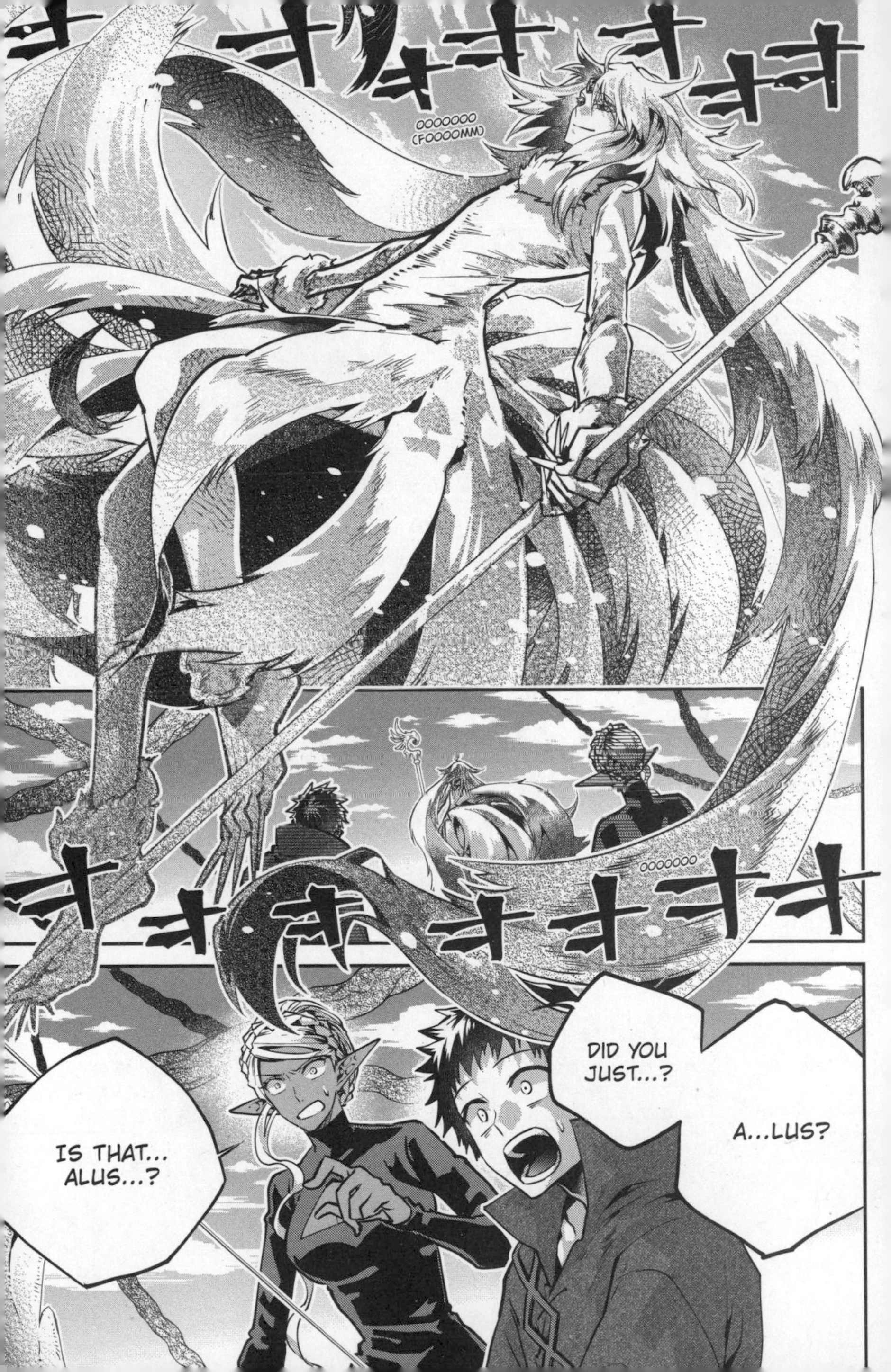
OOOOOOO
(FOOOOMM)
OOOOOOO
DID YOU JUST...?
A...LUS?
IS THAT... ALUS...?

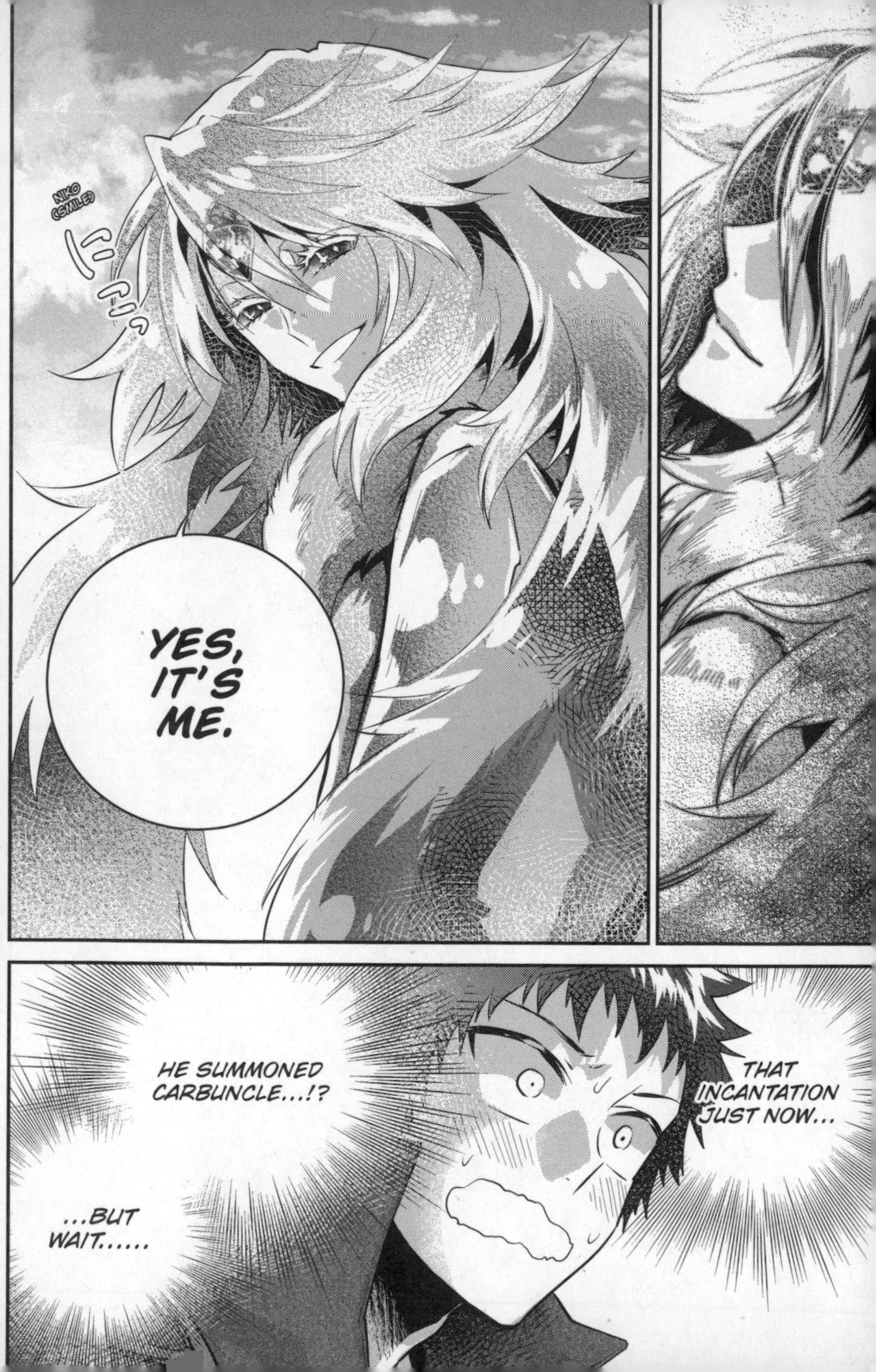
NIKO (SMILE)
YES, IT'S ME.
THAT INCANTATION JUST NOW...
HE SUMMONED CARBUNCLE...!?
...BUT WAIT......

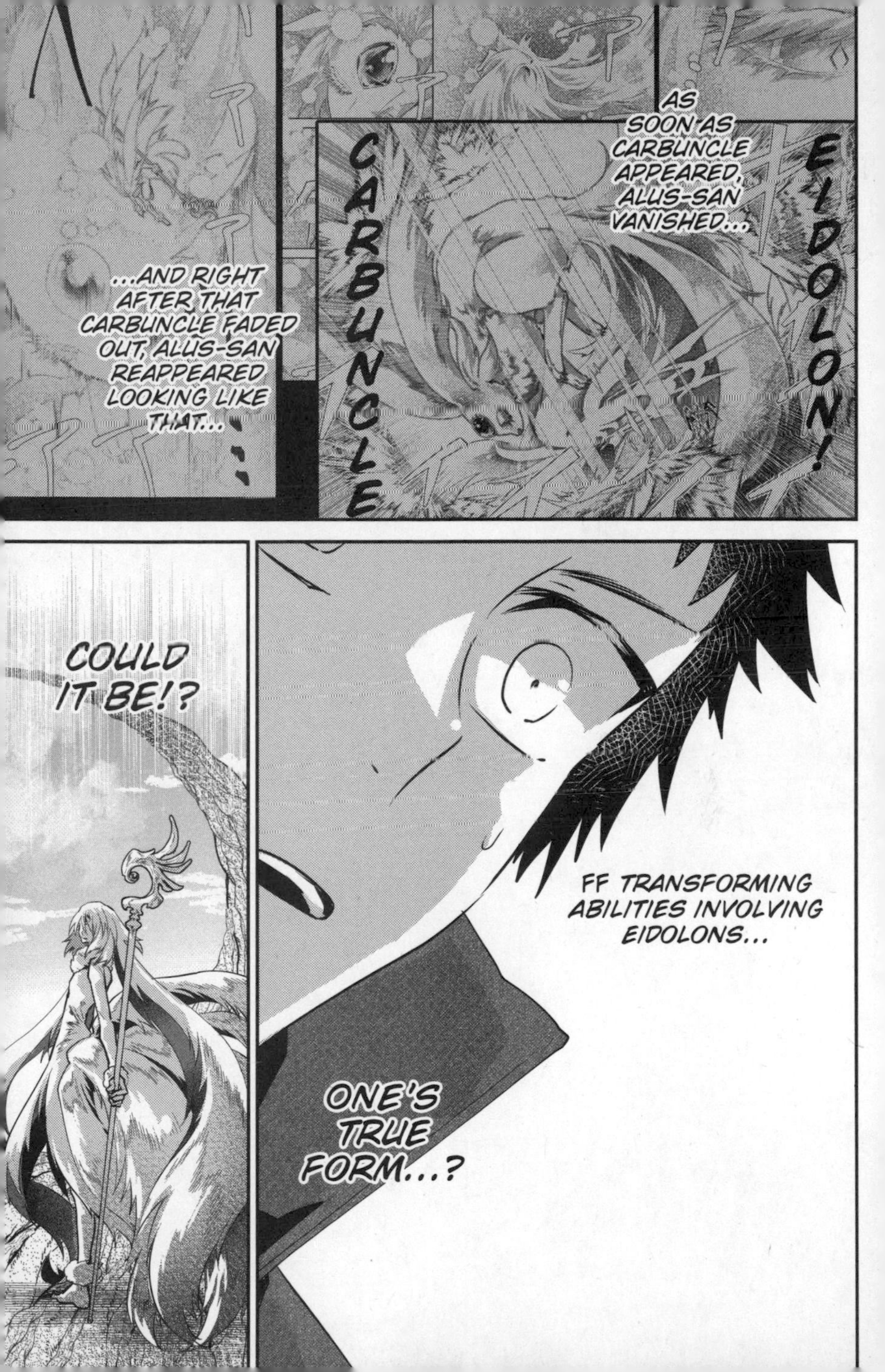
AS SOON AS CARBUNCLE APPEARED, ALUS-SAN VANISHED...
CARBUNCLE
EIDOLON!
...AND RIGHT AFTER THAT CARBUNCLE FADED OUT, ALUS-SAN REAPPEARED LOOKING LIKE THAT...
FF TRANSFORMING ABILITIES INVOLVING EIDOLONS...
ONE'S TRUE FORM...?
COULD IT BE!?

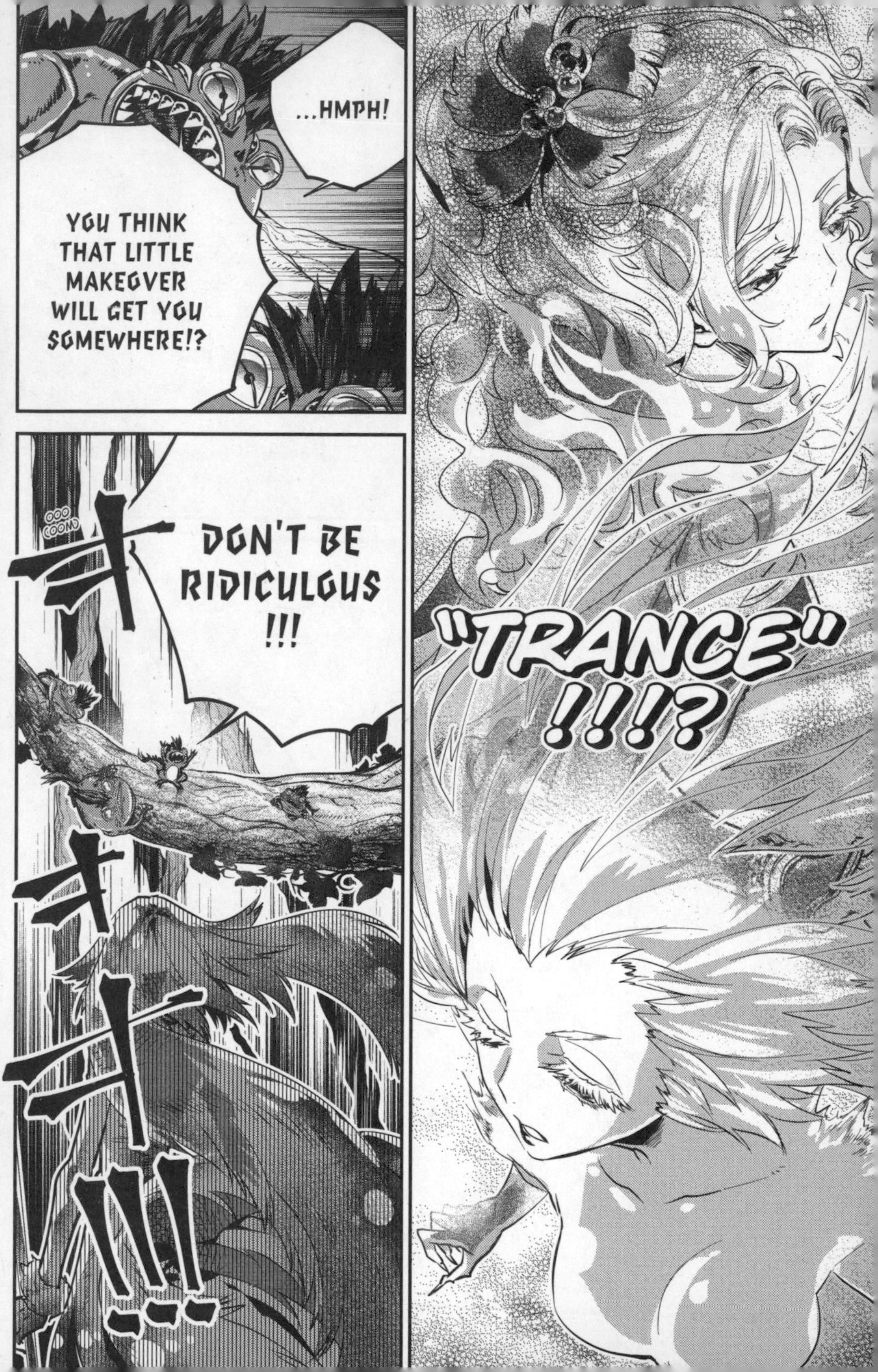
"TRANCE" !!!?
...HMPH!
YOU THINK THAT LITTLE MAKEOVER WILL GET YOU SOMEWHERE!?
DON'T BE RIDICULOUS !!!

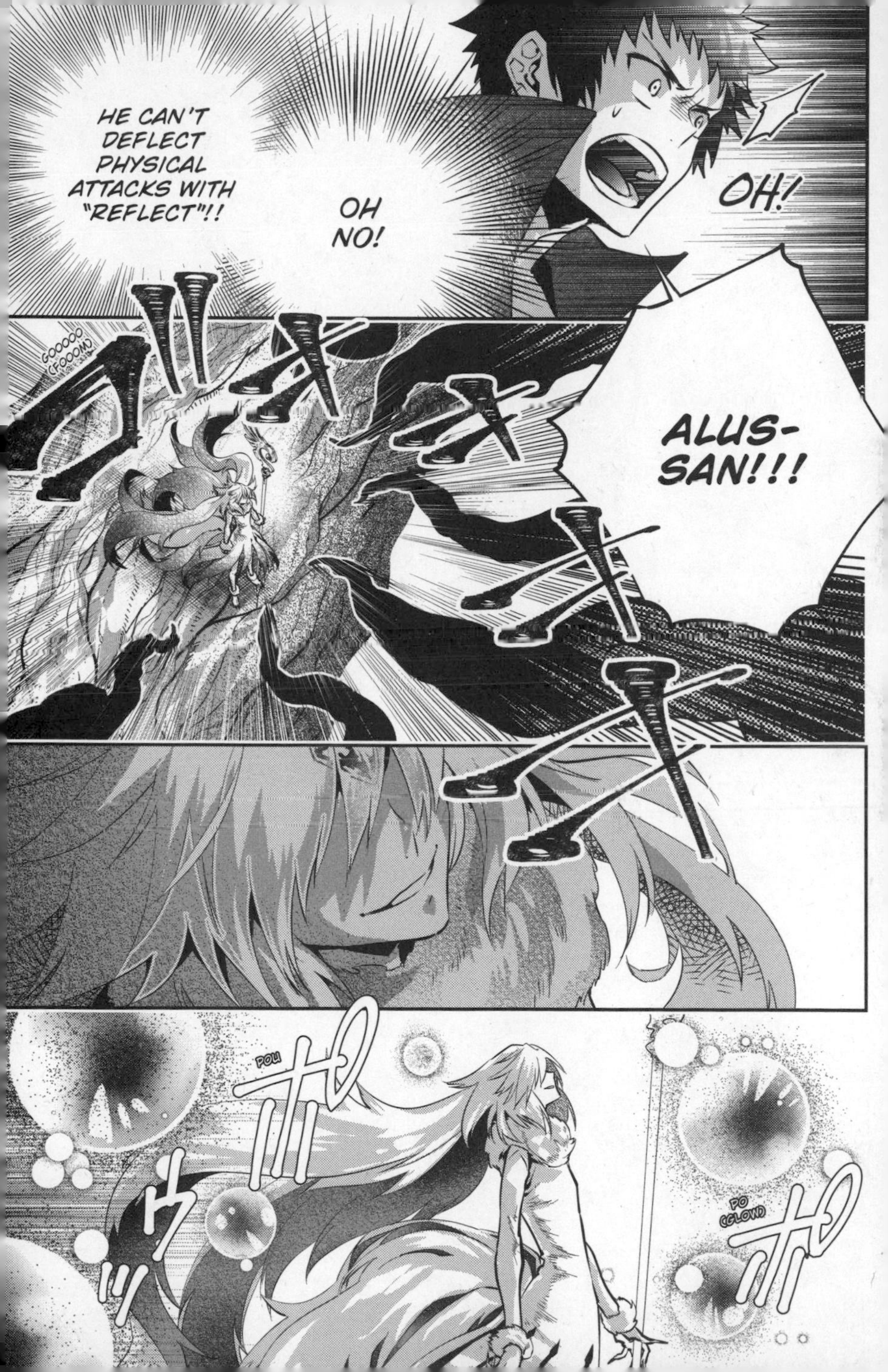
OH!
OH NO!
HE CAN'T DEFLECT PHYSICAL ATTACKS WITH "REFLECT"!!
ALUS-SAN!!!
GOOOOOO (FOOOM)
PO (GLOW)
POU

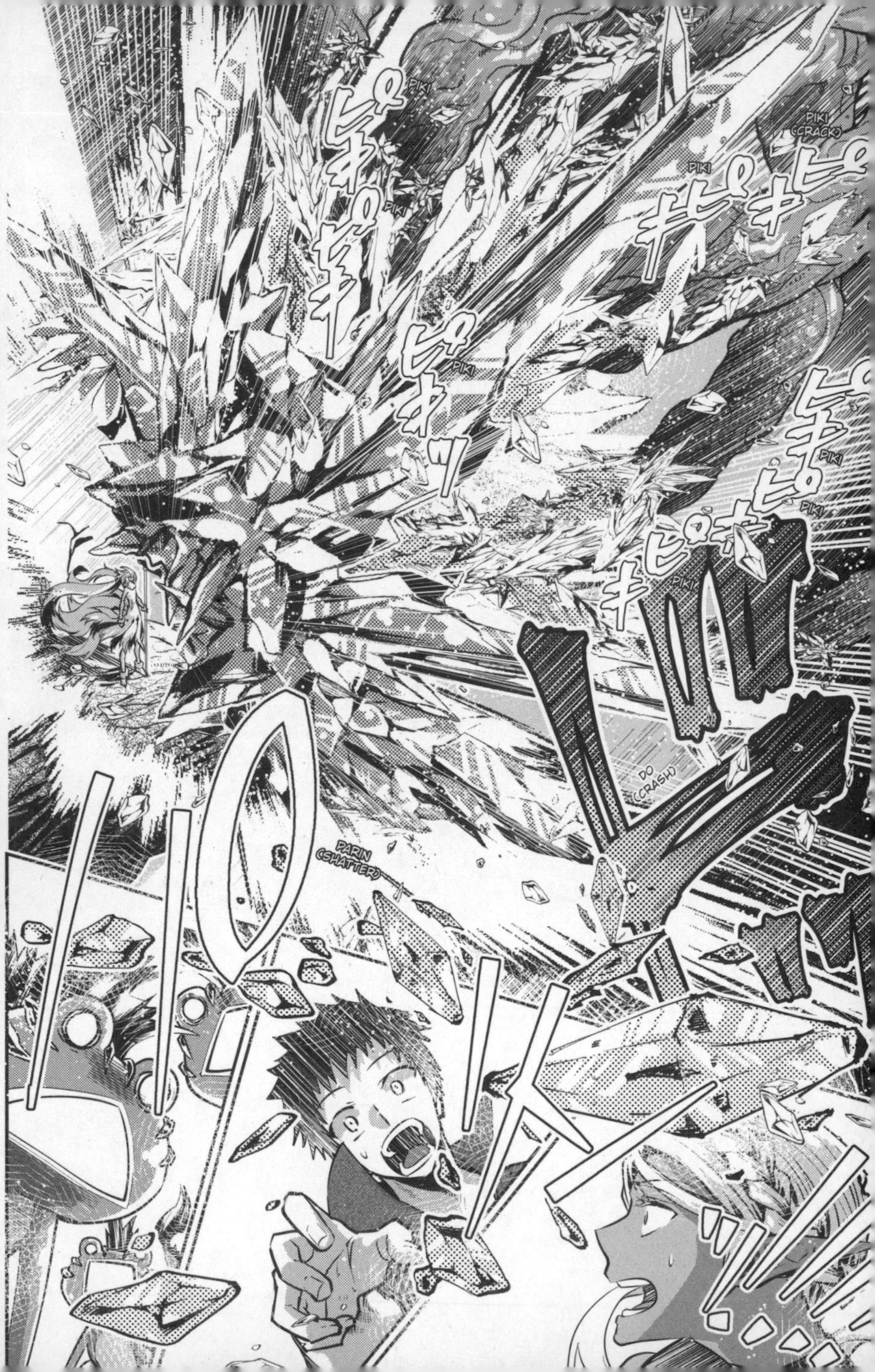
PIKI (CRACK)
PIKI
PIKI
PIKI
PIKI
PIKI
PIKI
PIKI
DO (CRASH)
PARIN (SHATTER)

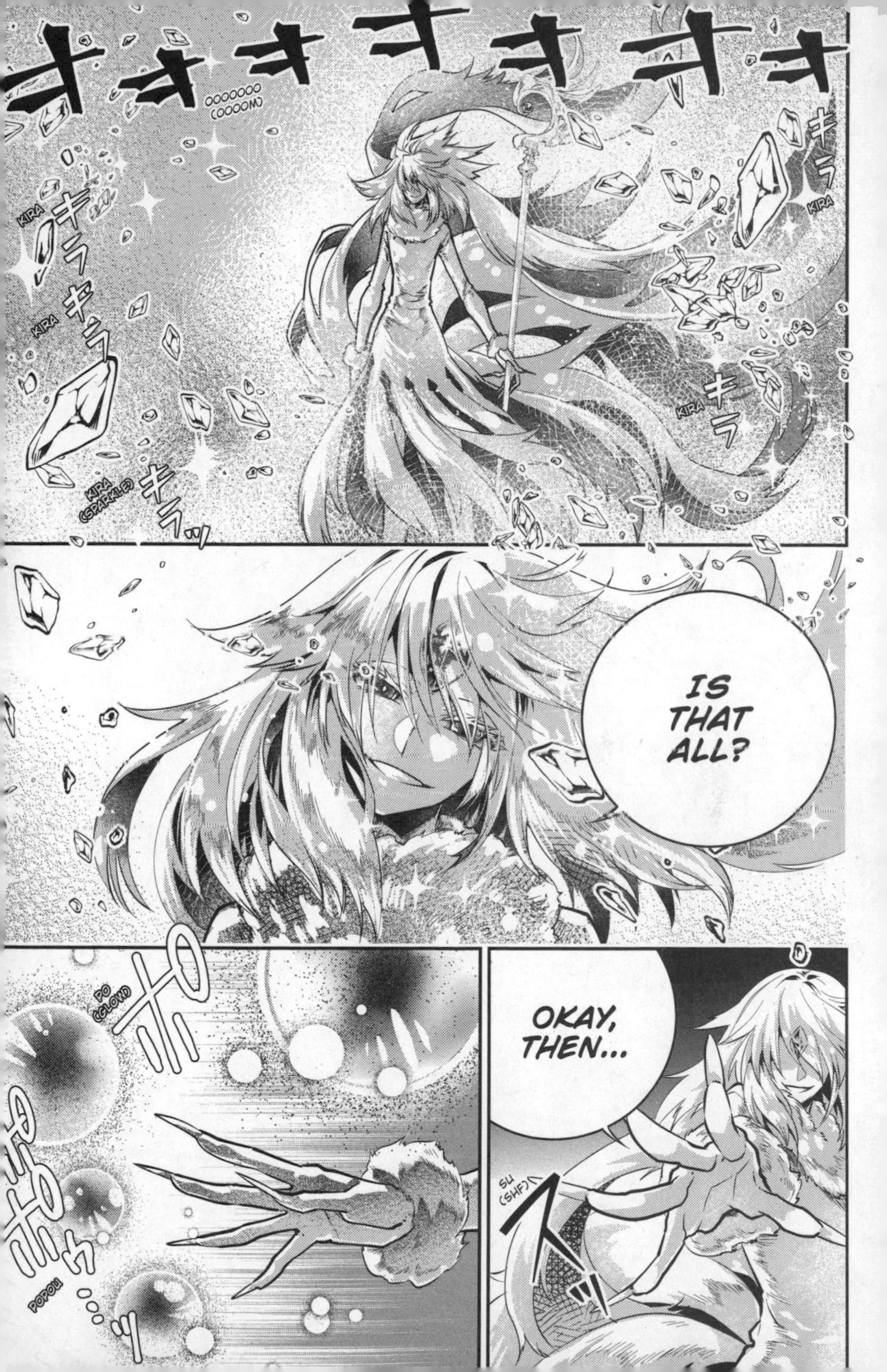

OOOOOOO (OOOOM)
KIRA
KIRA
KIRA
KIRA
KIRA (SPARKLE)
IS THAT ALL?
OKAY, THEN...
SU (SHF)
PO (GLOW)
POPOU

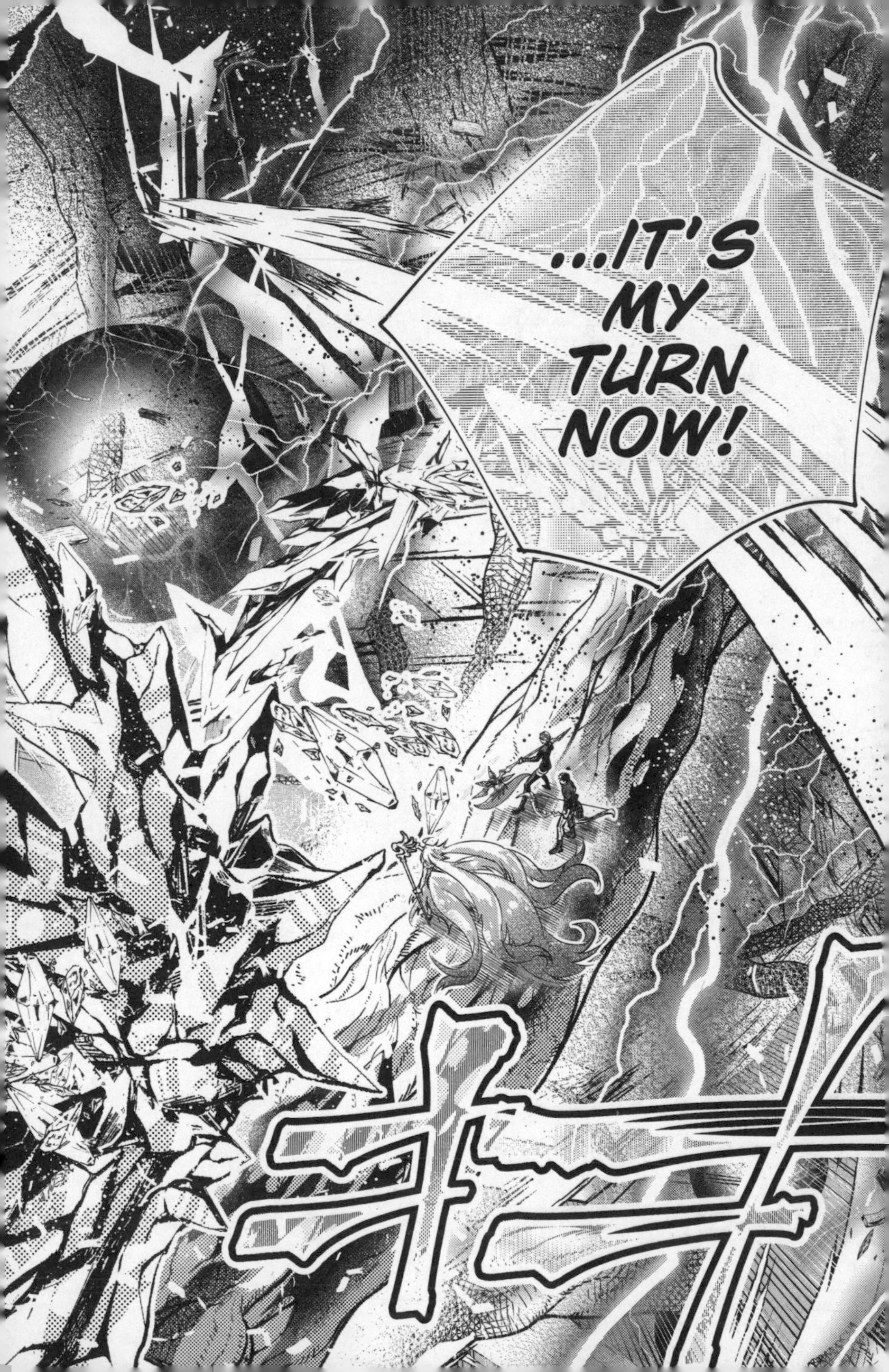
...IT'S MY TURN NOW!

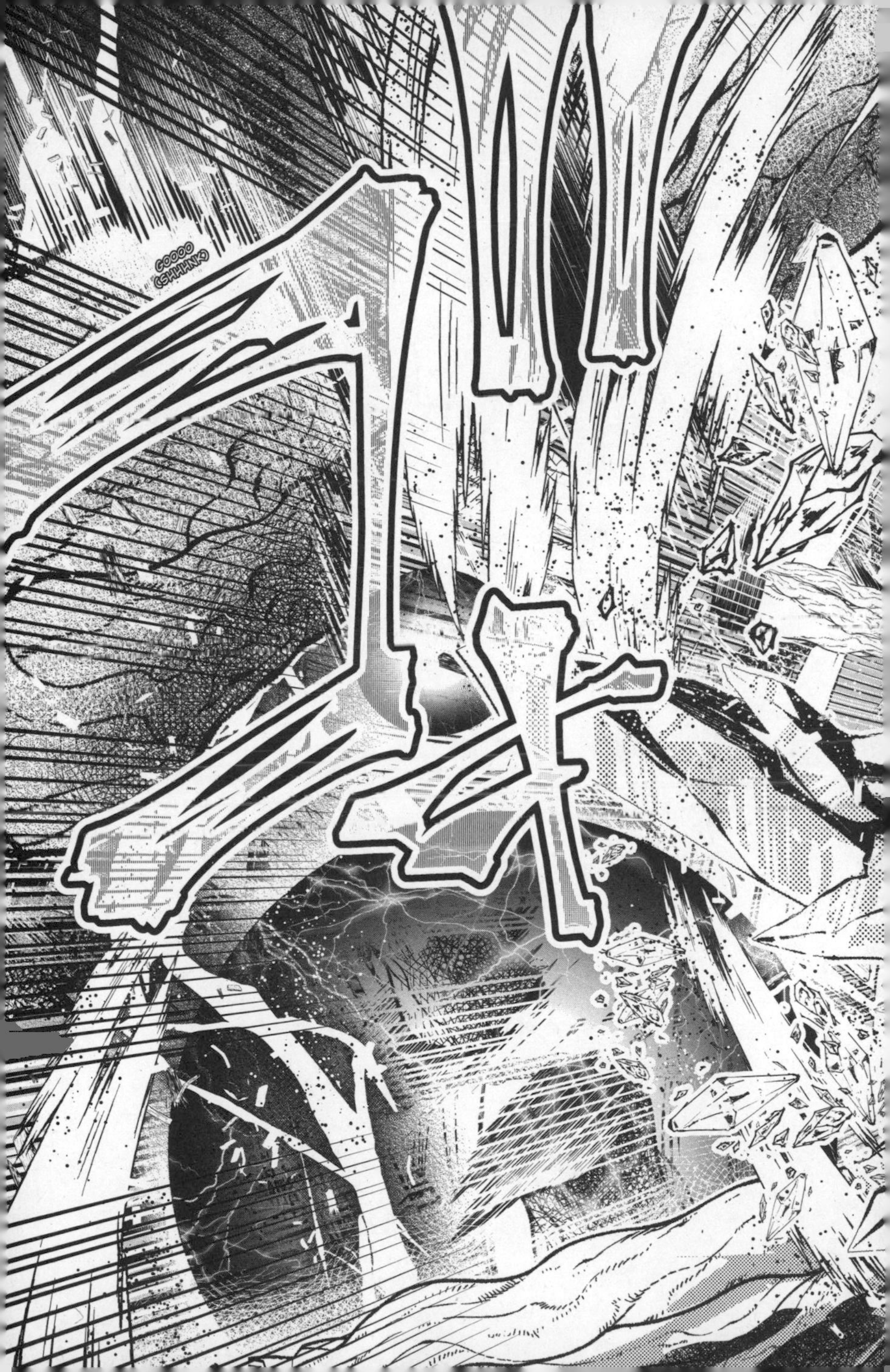
GOOOO
(SHHHNK)

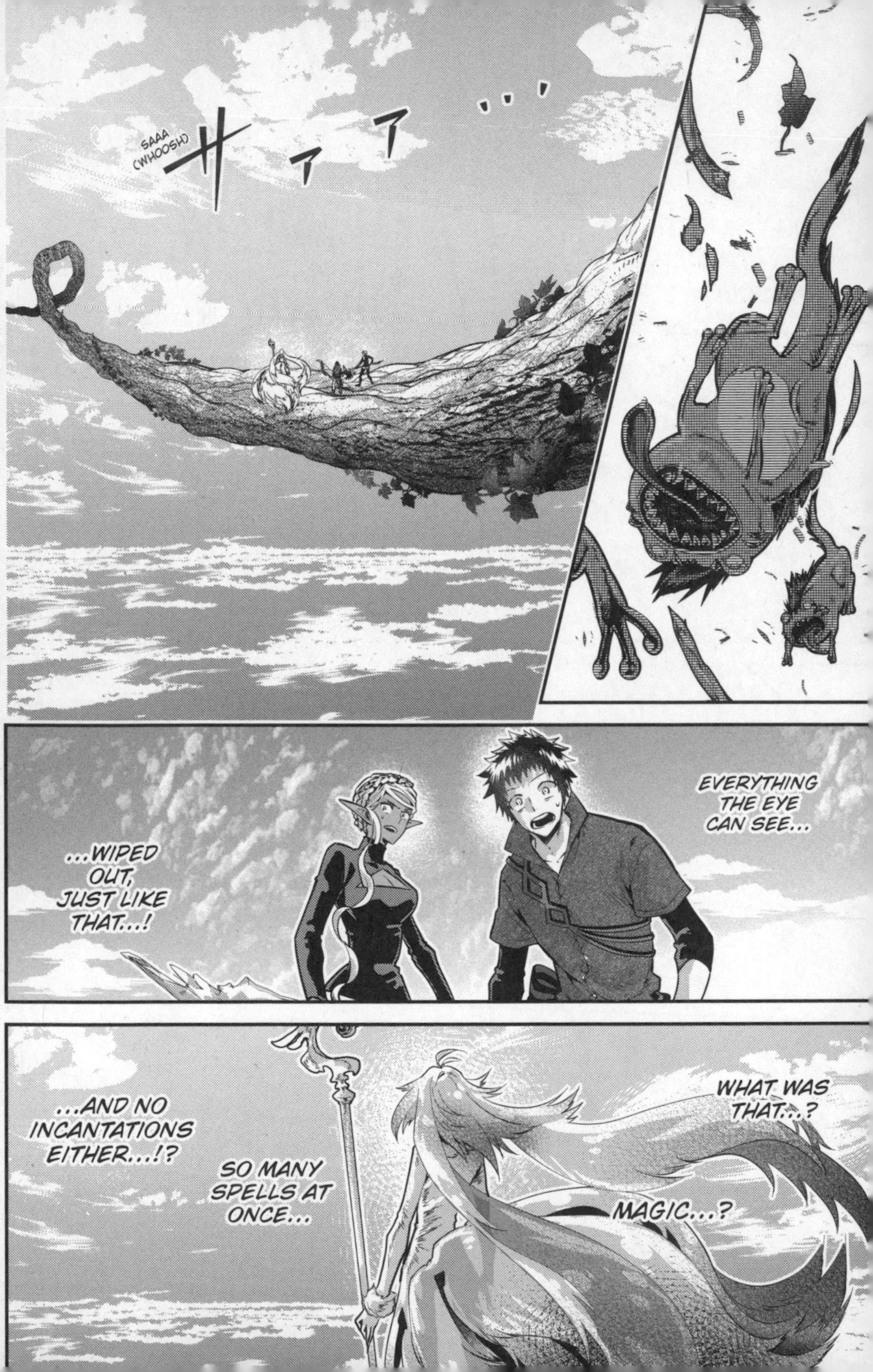
ザァア…
SAAA (WHOOSH)
EVERYTHING THE EYE CAN SEE...
...WIPED OUT, JUST LIKE THAT...!
WHAT WAS THAT...?
MAGIC...?
SO MANY SPELLS AT ONCE...
...AND NO INCANTATIONS EITHER...!?

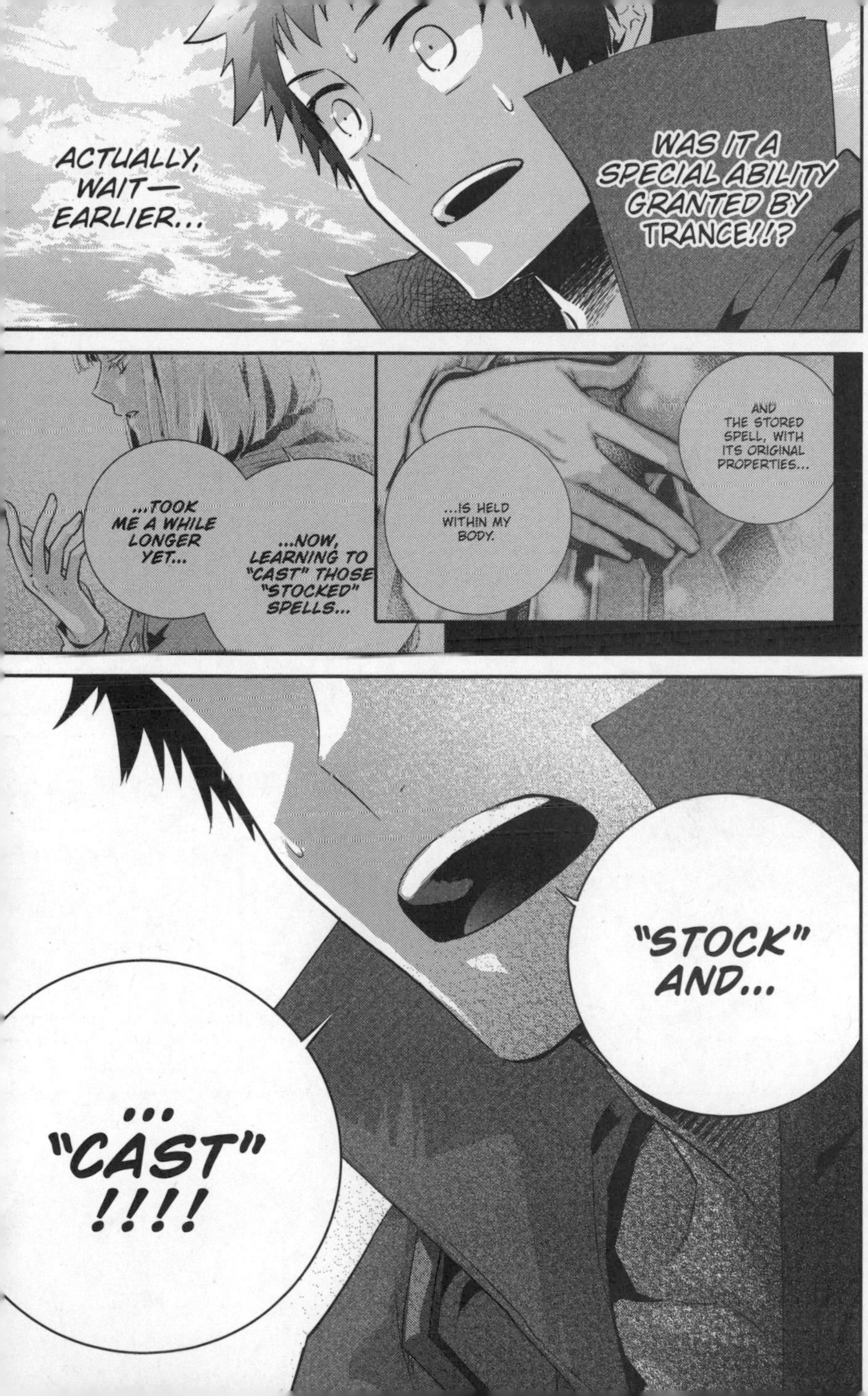
WAS IT A SPECIAL ABILITY GRANTED BY TRANCE!!?
ACTUALLY, WAIT—EARLIER...
AND THE STORED SPELL, WITH ITS ORIGINAL PROPERTIES...
...IS HELD WITHIN MY BODY.
...NOW, LEARNING TO "CAST" THOSE "STOCKED" SPELLS...
...TOOK ME A WHILE LONGER YET...
"STOCK" AND...
..."CAST"!!!!

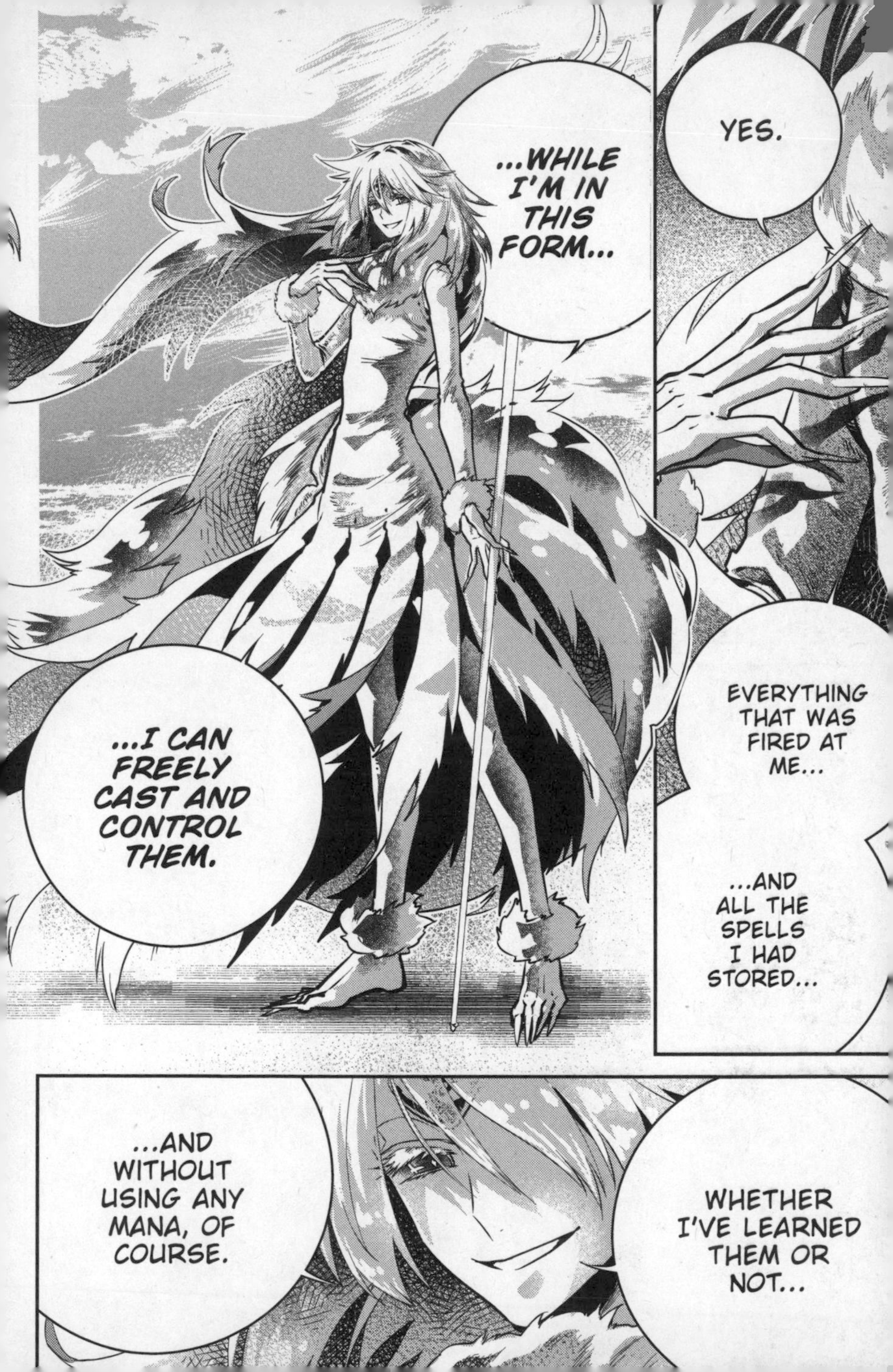
YES.
EVERYTHING THAT WAS FIRED AT ME...
...AND ALL THE SPELLS I HAD STORED...
...WHILE I'M IN THIS FORM...
...I CAN FREELY CAST AND CONTROL THEM.
WHETHER I'VE LEARNED THEM OR NOT...
...AND WITHOUT USING ANY MANA, OF COURSE.

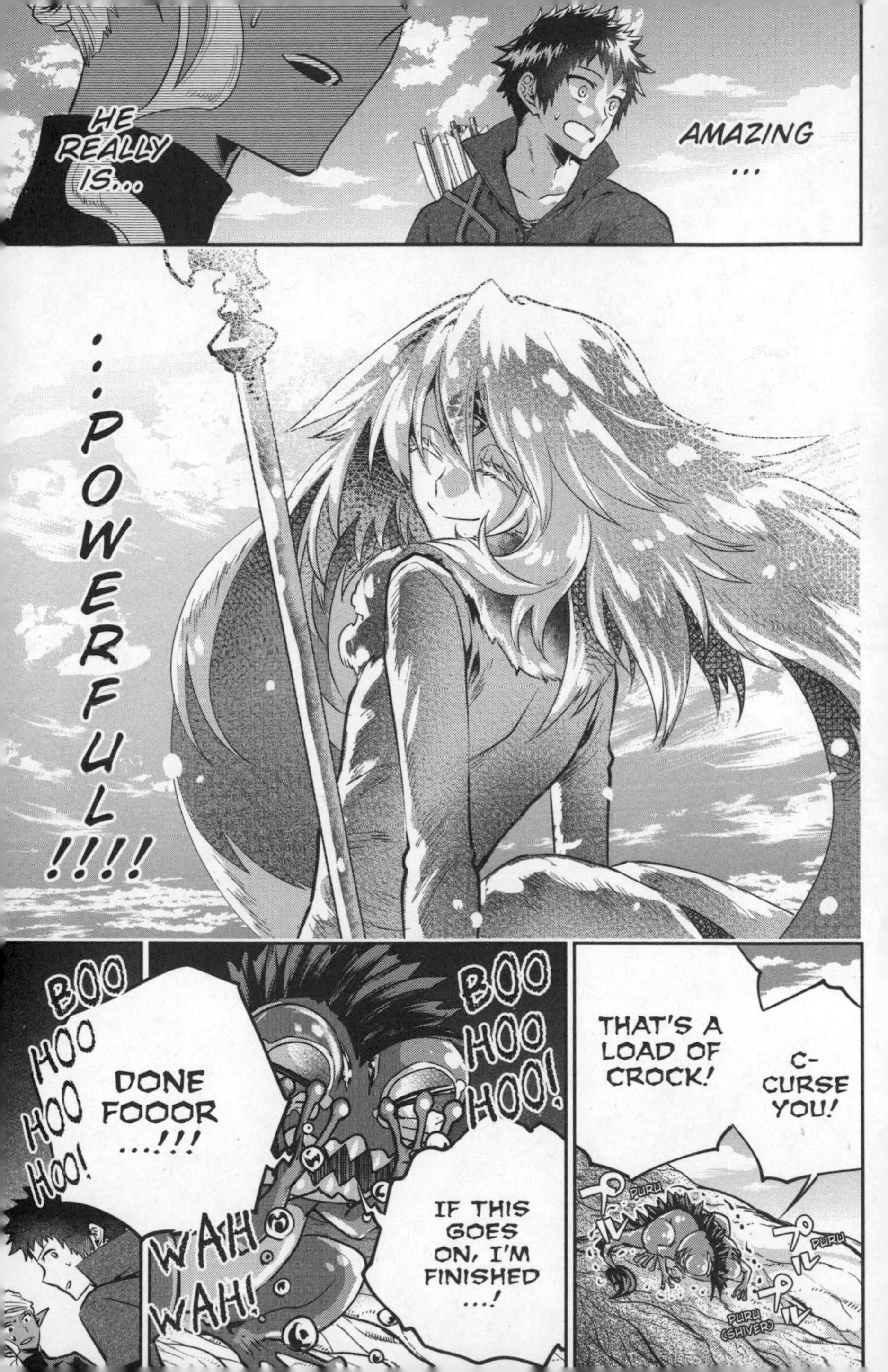

AMAZING ...
HE REALLY IS...
...POWERFUL!!!!
C-CURSE YOU!
THAT'S A LOAD OF CROCK!
PURU
PURU
PURU (SHIVER)
BOO HOO HOO HOO!
IF THIS GOES ON, I'M FINISHED ...!
DONE FOOOR ...!!!
BOO HOO HOO HOO!
WAH WAH!

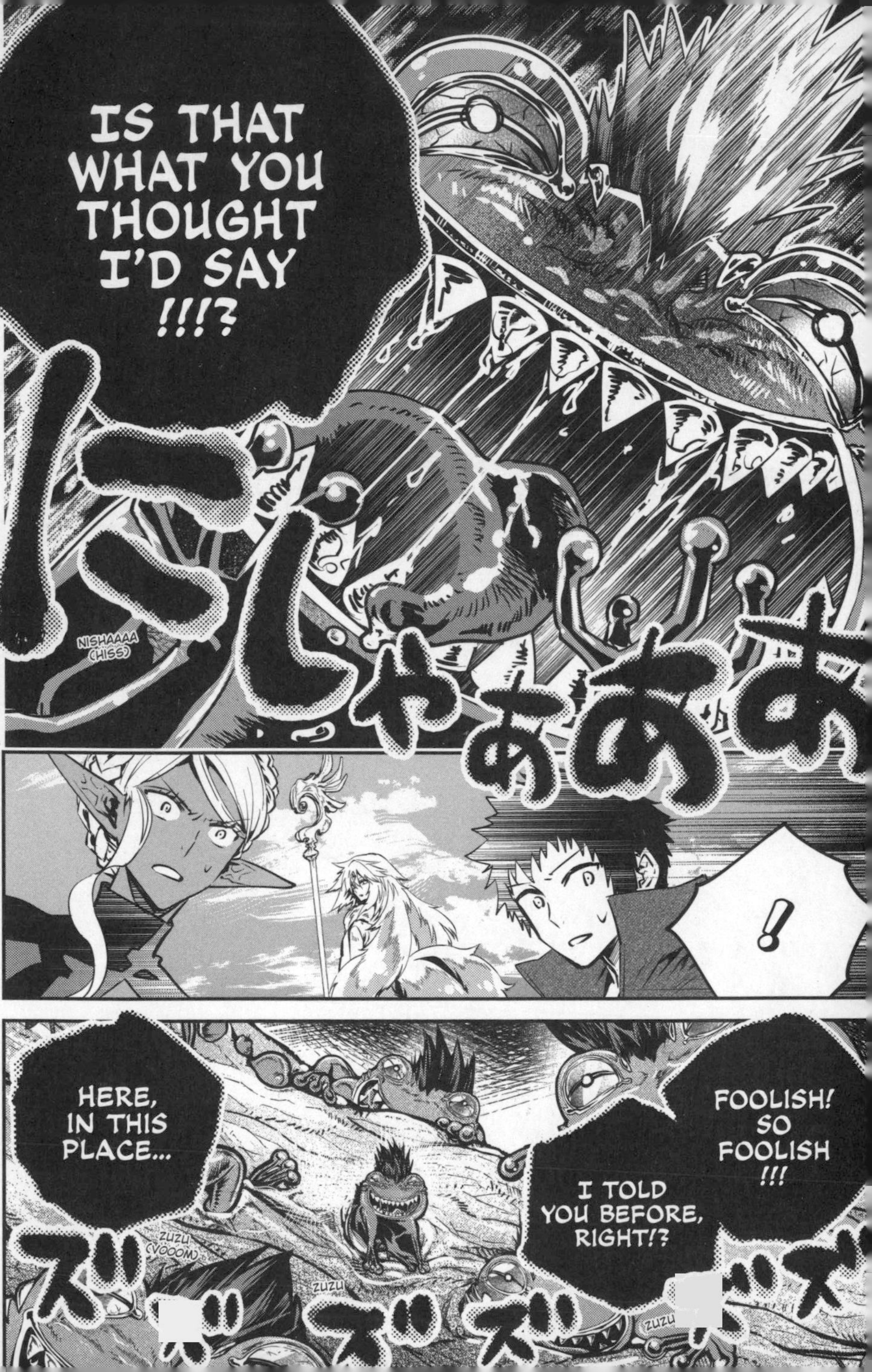
IS THAT WHAT YOU THOUGHT I'D SAY!!!?
NISHAAAA (HISS)
!
FOOLISH! SO FOOLISH!!!
I TOLD YOU BEFORE, RIGHT!?
HERE, IN THIS PLACE...
ZUZU (VOOOM)
ZUZU
ZUZU

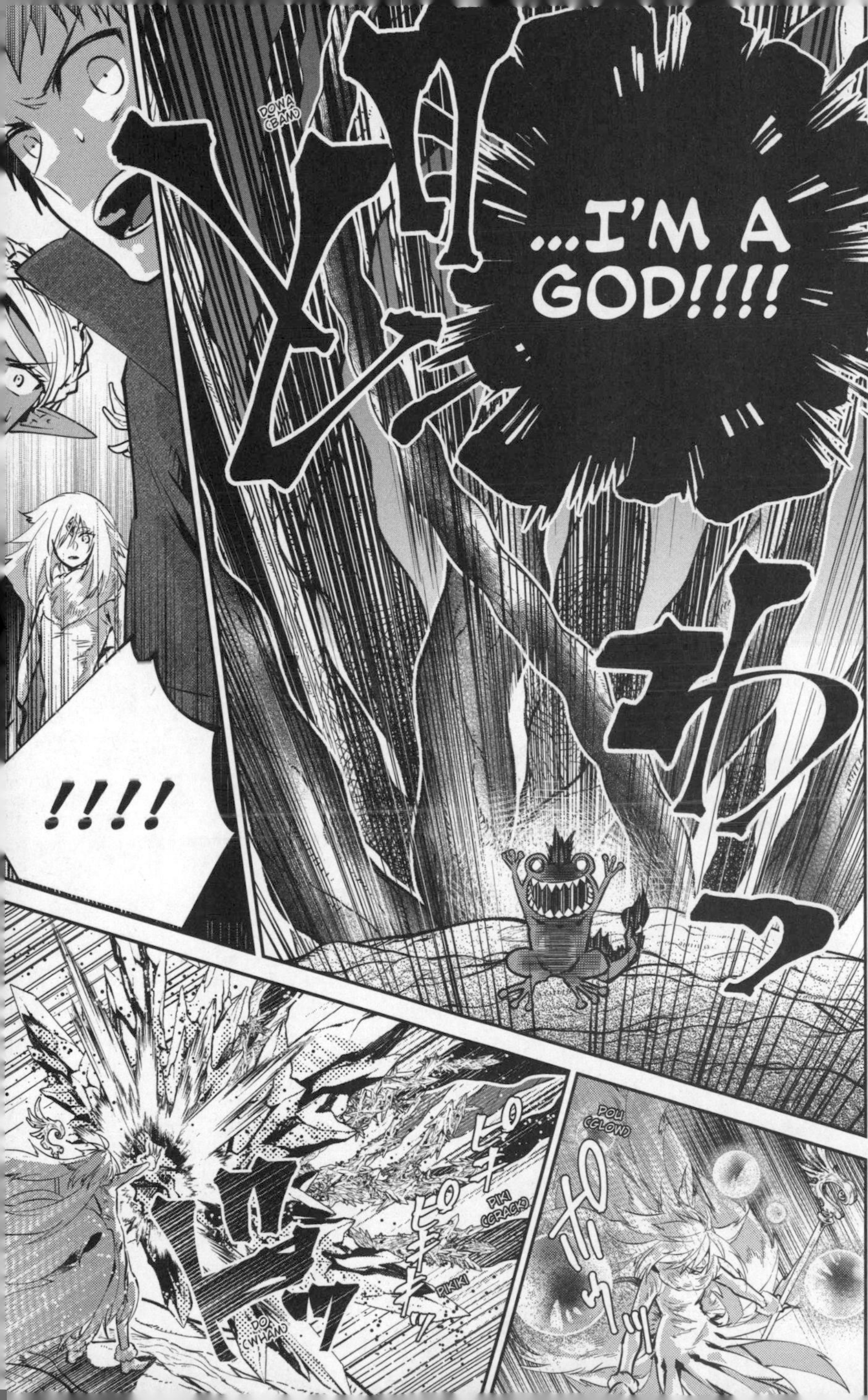
...I'M A GOD!!!!
DOWA (BAM)
!!!!
POU (GLOW)
PIKI (CRACK)
PIKIKI
DO (WHAM)

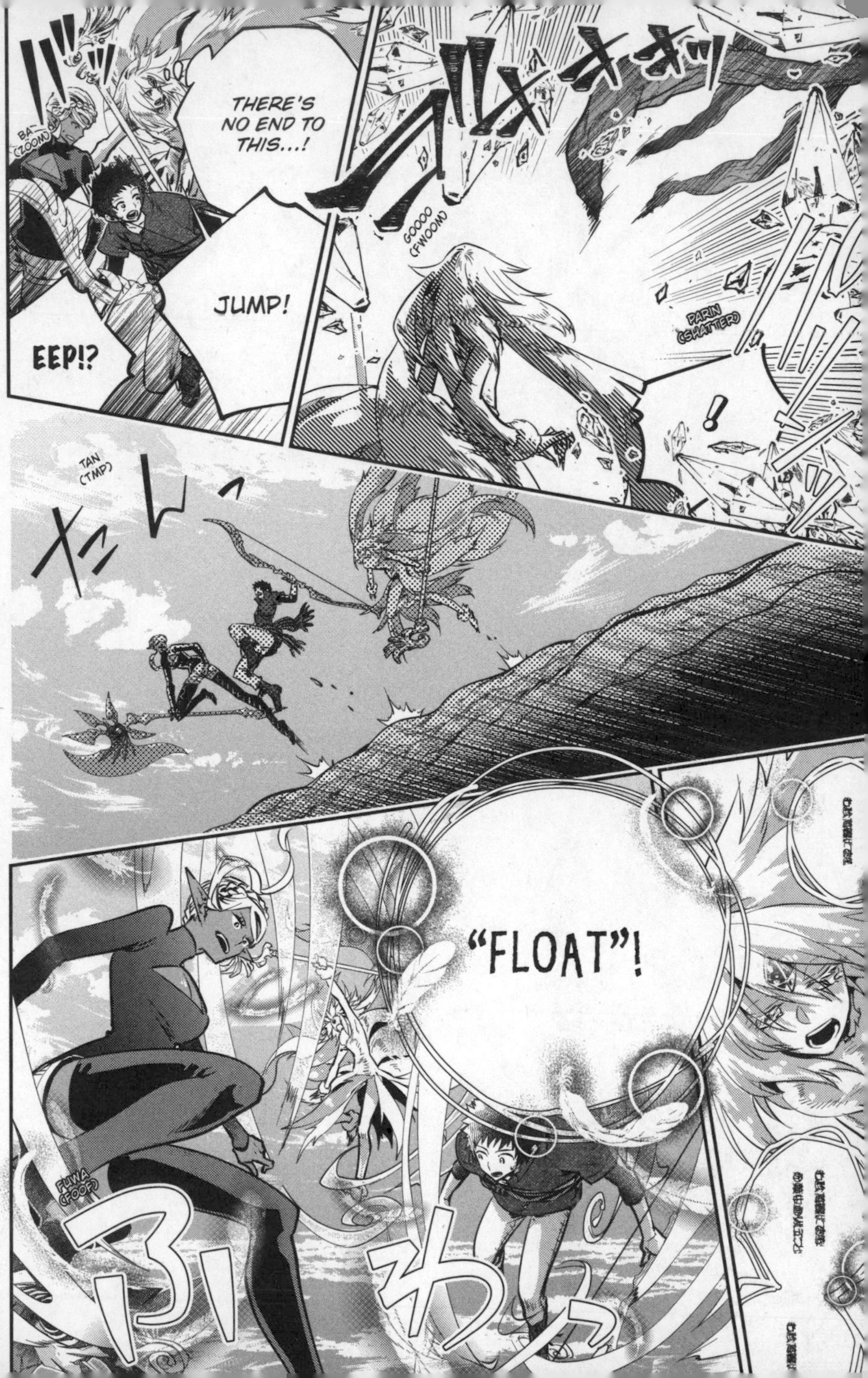
GOOOO (FWOOM)
PARIN (SHATTER)
!
THERE'S NO END TO THIS...!
BA— (ZOOM)
JUMP!
EEP!?
TAN (TMP)
"FLOAT"!
FUWA (FOOP)

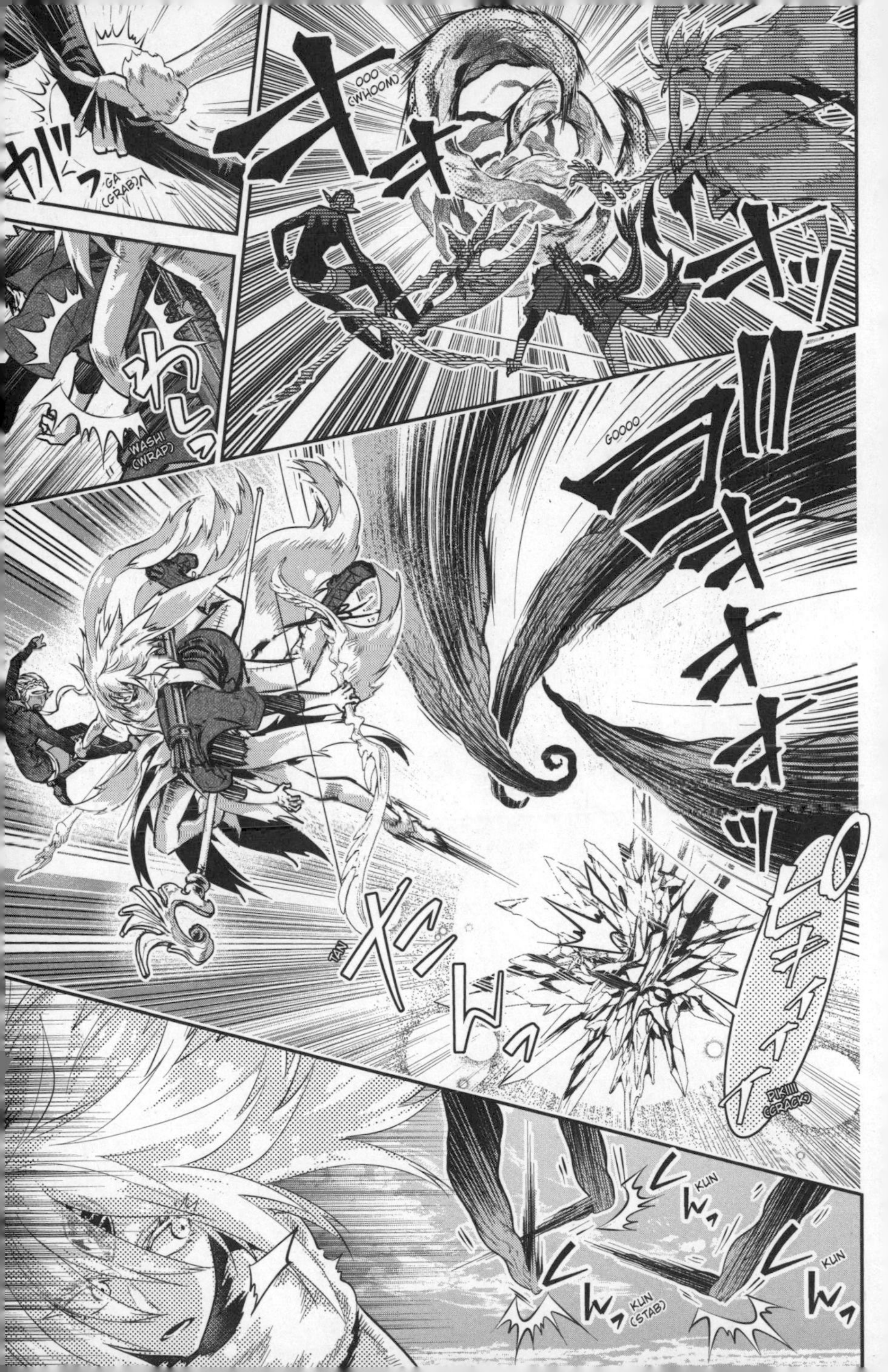
OOO (WHOOM)
GA (GRAB)!
WASHI (WRAP)
GOOOO
PIKIIII (CRACK)
TAN
KUN
KUN
KUN (STAB)

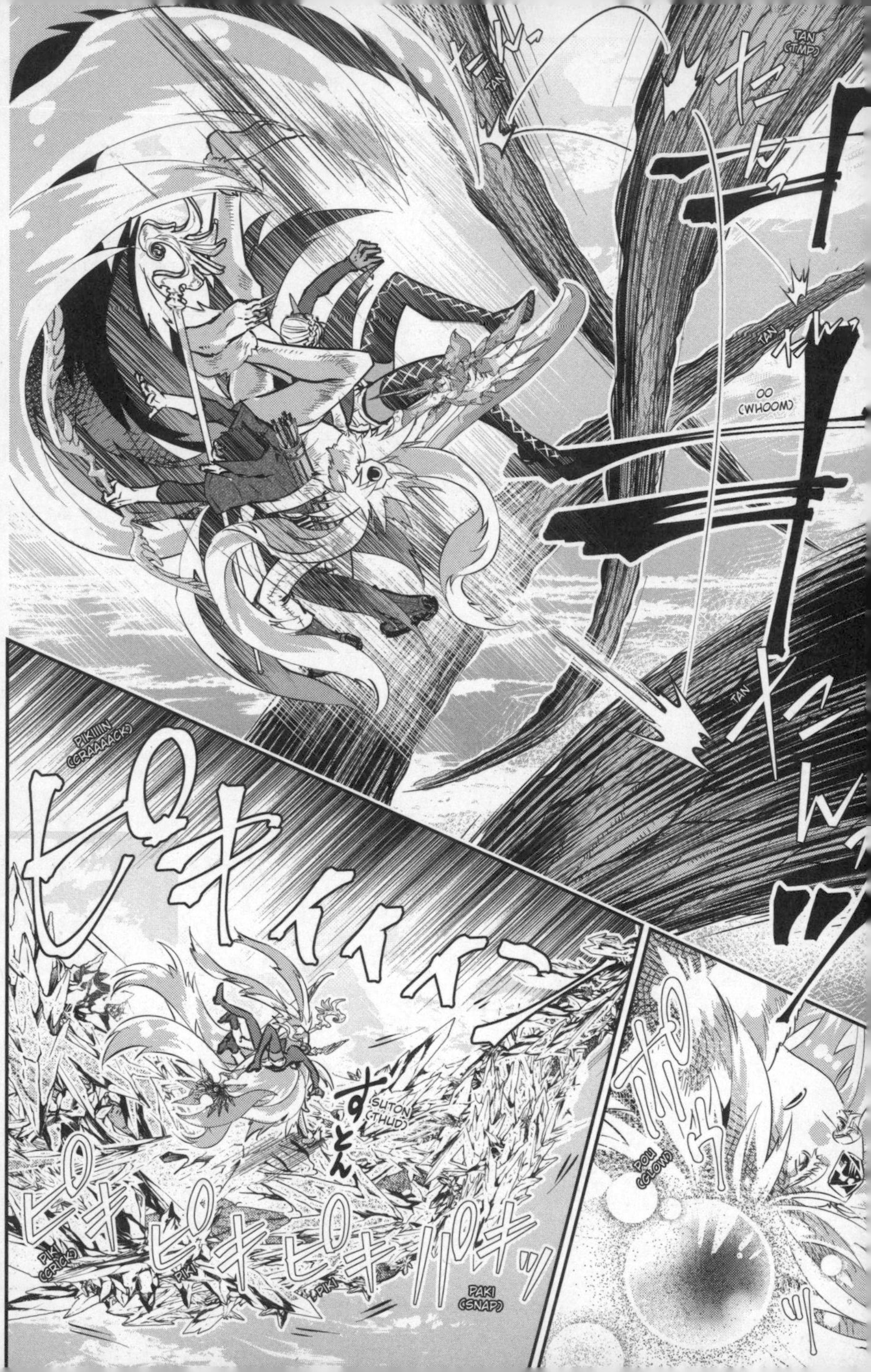
TAN (TMP)
TAN
OO (WHOOM)
TAN
TAN
POU (GLOW)
PIKIIIN (CRAAAACK)
SUTON (THUD)
PAKI (SNAP)
PIKI
PIKI
PI (CRICK)

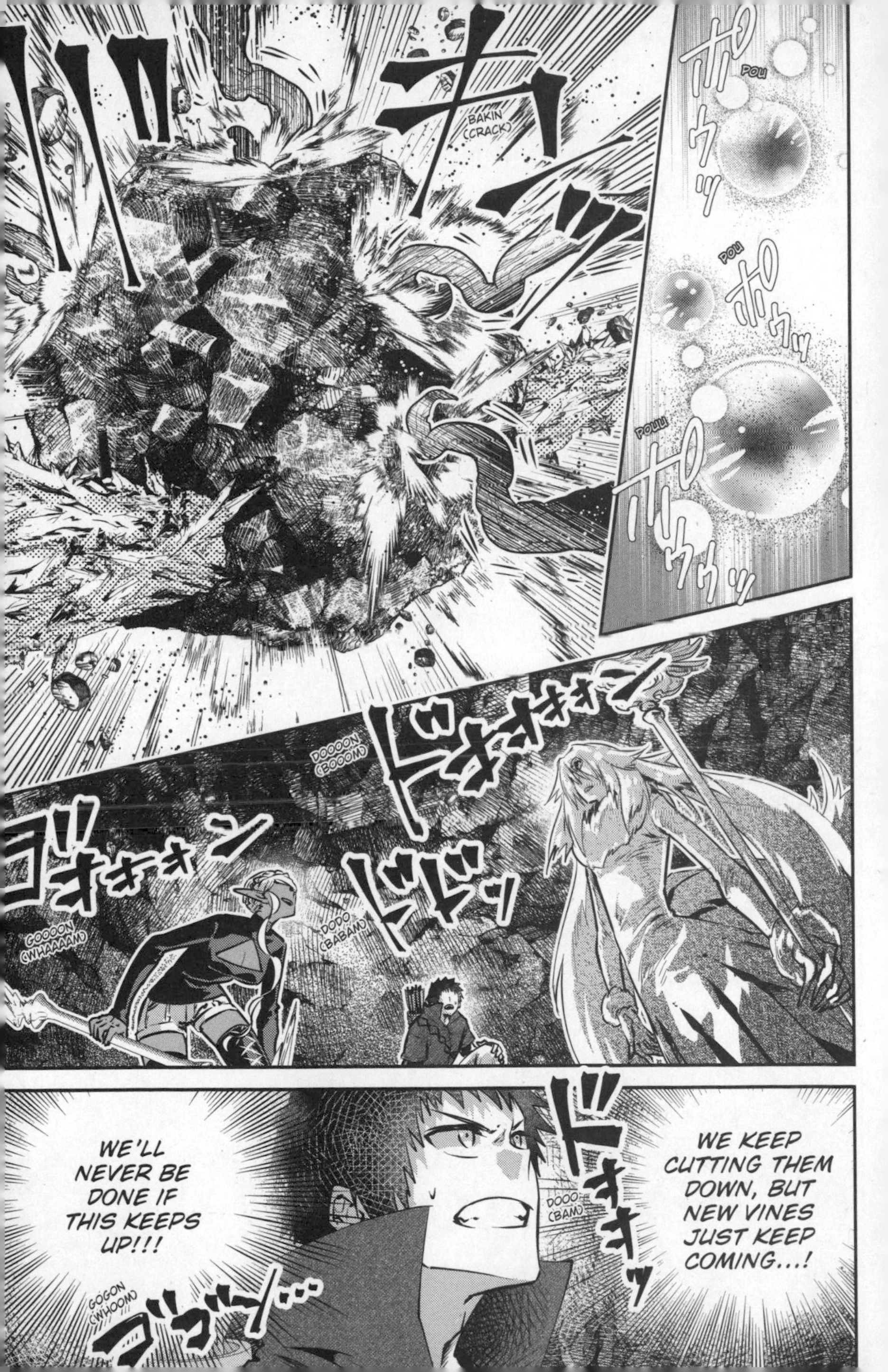
POU
POU
POUU
BAKIN (CRACK)
DOOOON (BOOOM)
DODO (BABAM)
GOOOON (WHAAAAM)
WE KEEP CUTTING THEM DOWN, BUT NEW VINES JUST KEEP COMING...!
DOOO (BAM)
WE'LL NEVER BE DONE IF THIS KEEPS UP!!!
GOGON (WHOOM)

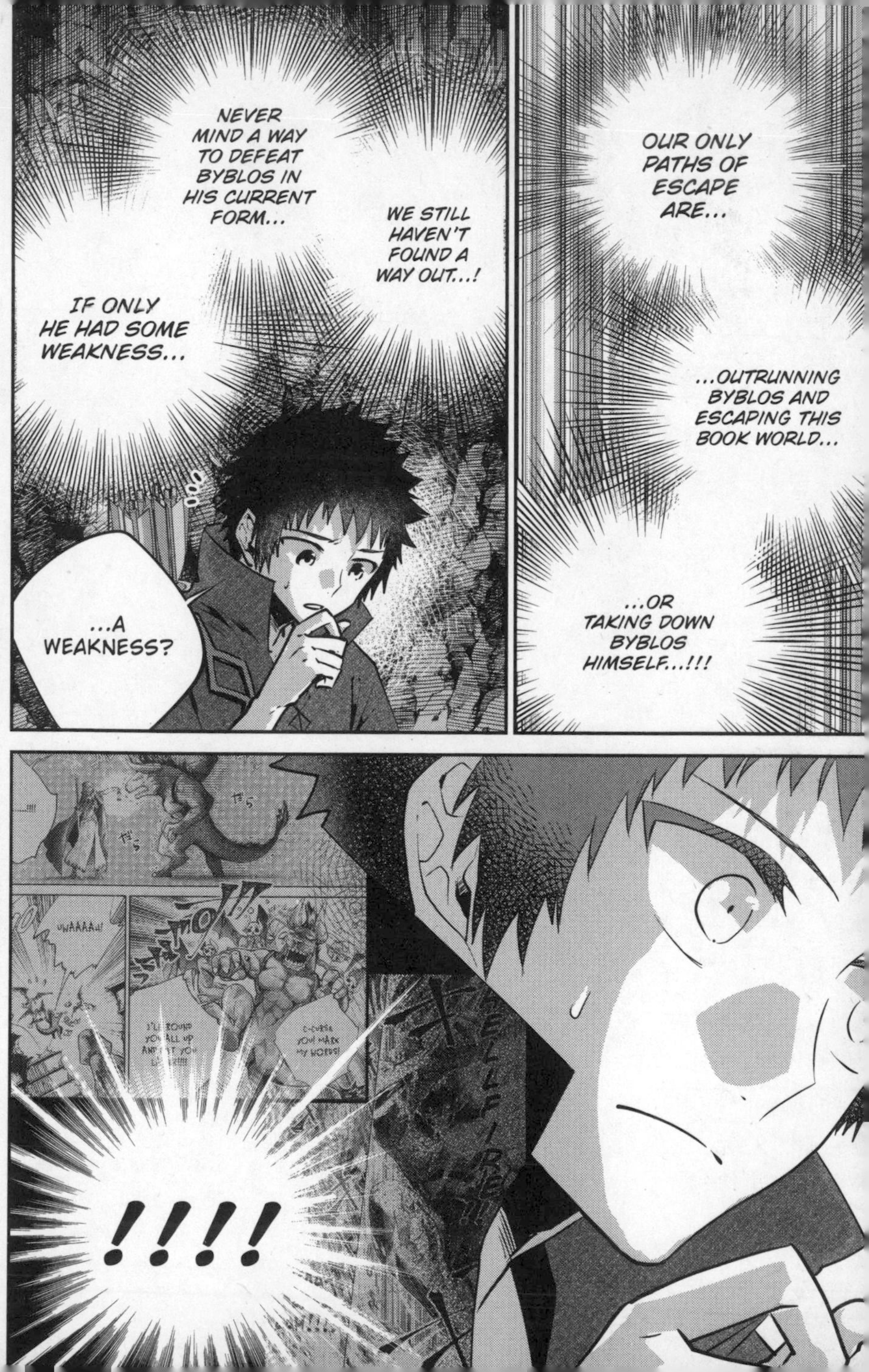
OUR ONLY PATHS OF ESCAPE ARE...
...OUTRUNNING BYBLOS AND ESCAPING THIS BOOK WORLD...
...OR TAKING DOWN BYBLOS HIMSELF...!!!
NEVER MIND A WAY TO DEFEAT BYBLOS IN HIS CURRENT FORM...
WE STILL HAVEN'T FOUND A WAY OUT...!
IF ONLY HE HAD SOME WEAKNESS...
...A WEAKNESS?
!!!!

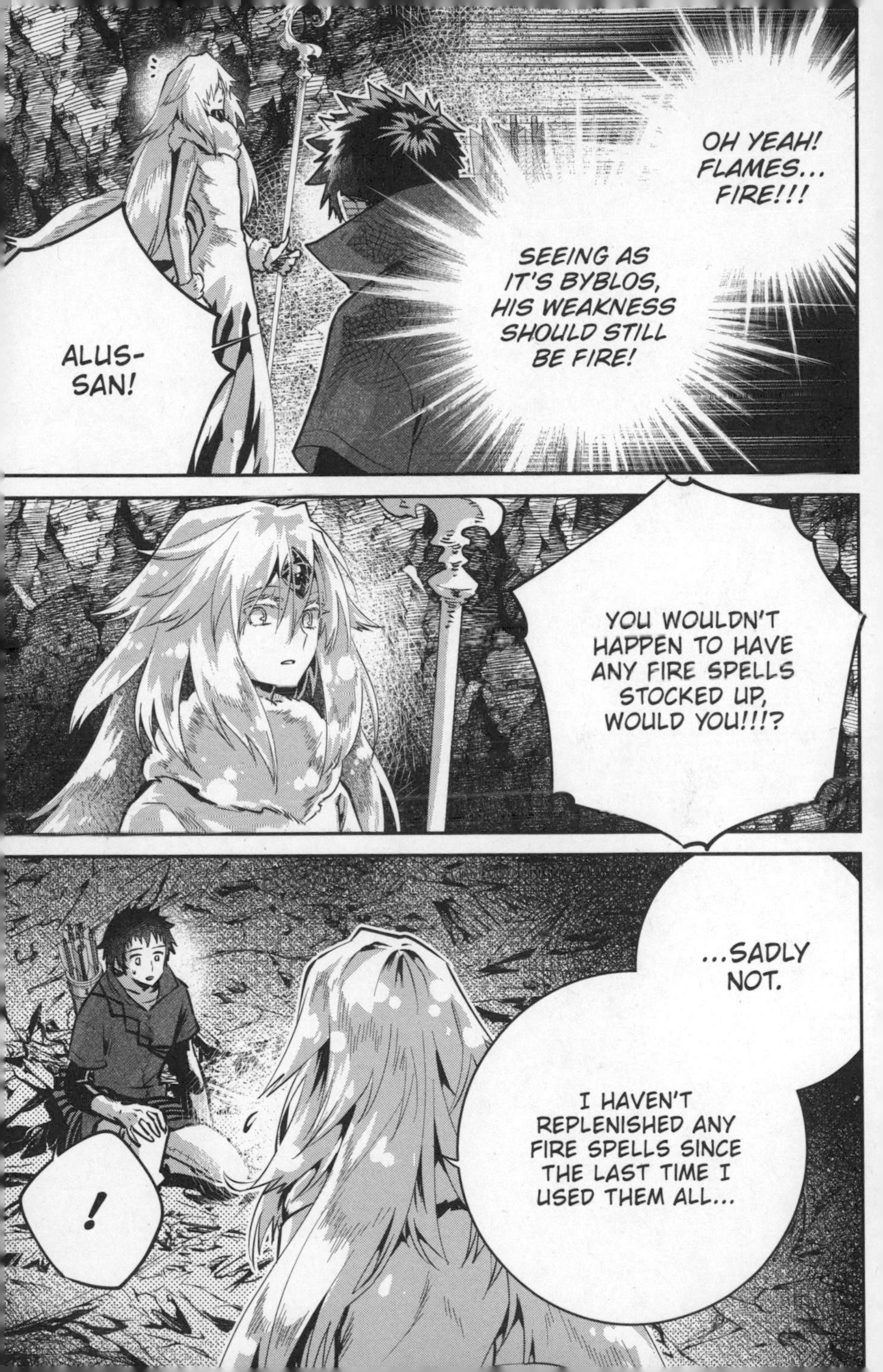
OH YEAH! FLAMES... FIRE!!!
SEEING AS IT'S BYBLOS, HIS WEAKNESS SHOULD STILL BE FIRE!
ALUS-SAN!
YOU WOULDN'T HAPPEN TO HAVE ANY FIRE SPELLS STOCKED UP, WOULD YOU!!!?
...SADLY NOT.
I HAVEN'T REPLENISHED ANY FIRE SPELLS SINCE THE LAST TIME I USED THEM ALL...
!

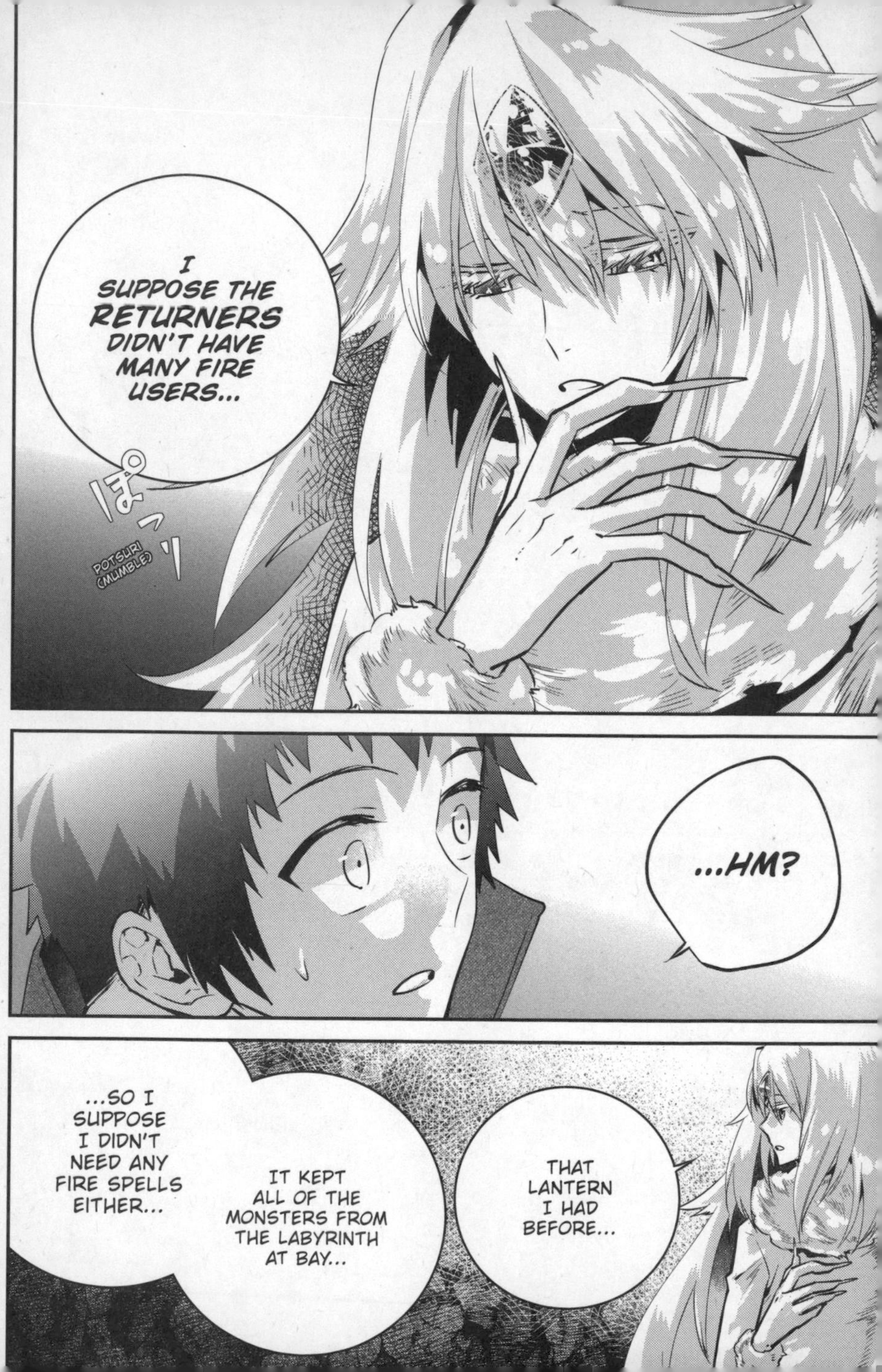
I SUPPOSE THE RETURNERS DIDN'T HAVE MANY FIRE USERS...
ぽつり
POTSURI (MUMBLE)
...HM?
THAT LANTERN I HAD BEFORE...
IT KEPT ALL OF THE MONSTERS FROM THE LABYRINTH AT BAY...
...SO I SUPPOSE I DIDN'T NEED ANY FIRE SPELLS EITHER...

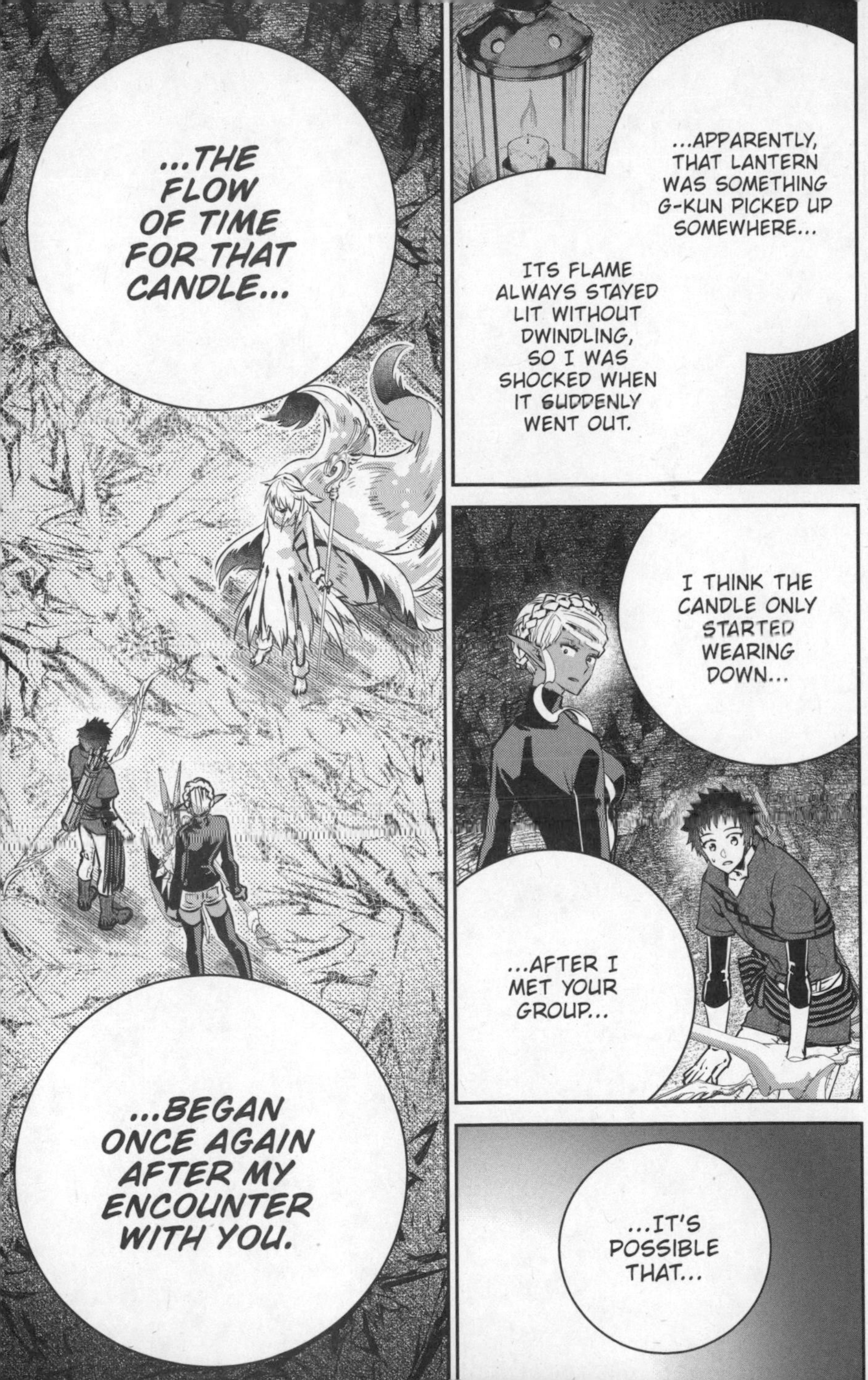
...APPARENTLY, THAT LANTERN WAS SOMETHING G-KUN PICKED UP SOMEWHERE...
ITS FLAME ALWAYS STAYED LIT WITHOUT DWINDLING, SO I WAS SHOCKED WHEN IT SUDDENLY WENT OUT.
I THINK THE CANDLE ONLY STARTED WEARING DOWN...
...AFTER I MET YOUR GROUP...
...IT'S POSSIBLE THAT...
...THE FLOW OF TIME FOR THAT CANDLE...
...BEGAN ONCE AGAIN AFTER MY ENCOUNTER WITH YOU.

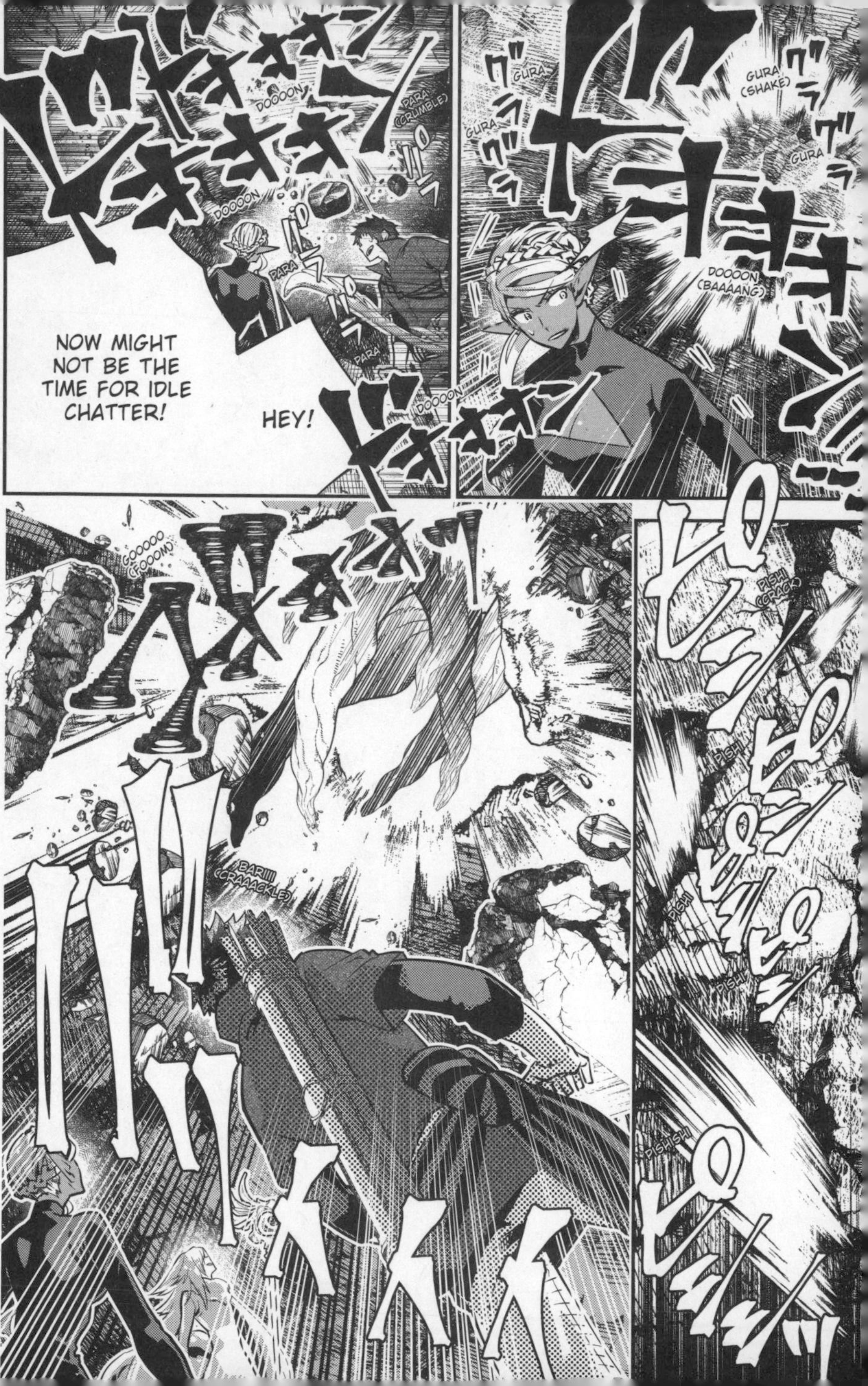
GURA
GURA
GURA (SHAKE)
GURA
DOOOON (BAAAANG)
DOOOON
DOOOON
PARA (CRUMBLE)
DOOOON
PARA
PARA
HEY!
NOW MIGHT NOT BE THE TIME FOR IDLE CHATTER!
PISHI (CRACK)
PISHI
PISHI
PISHI
PISHISHI
GOOOOO (FOOOM)
BARIIII (CRAAACKLE)

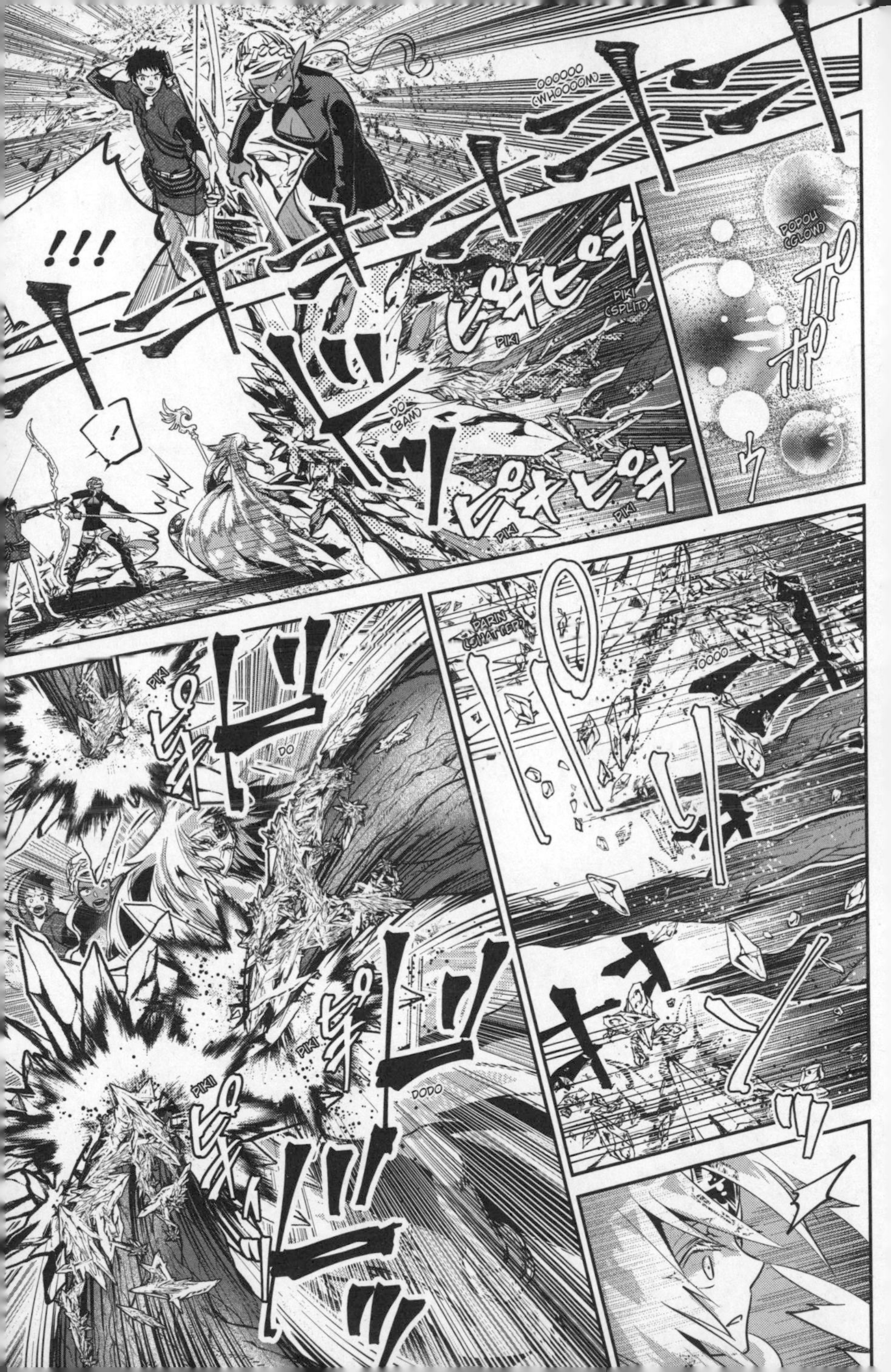
OOOOOO (WHOOOOM)
!!!
!
POPOU (GLOW)
PIKI (SPLIT)
PIKI
DO (BAM)
PIKI
PIKI
PARIN (SHATTER)
OOOO
PIKI
DO
PIKI
PIKII
DODO

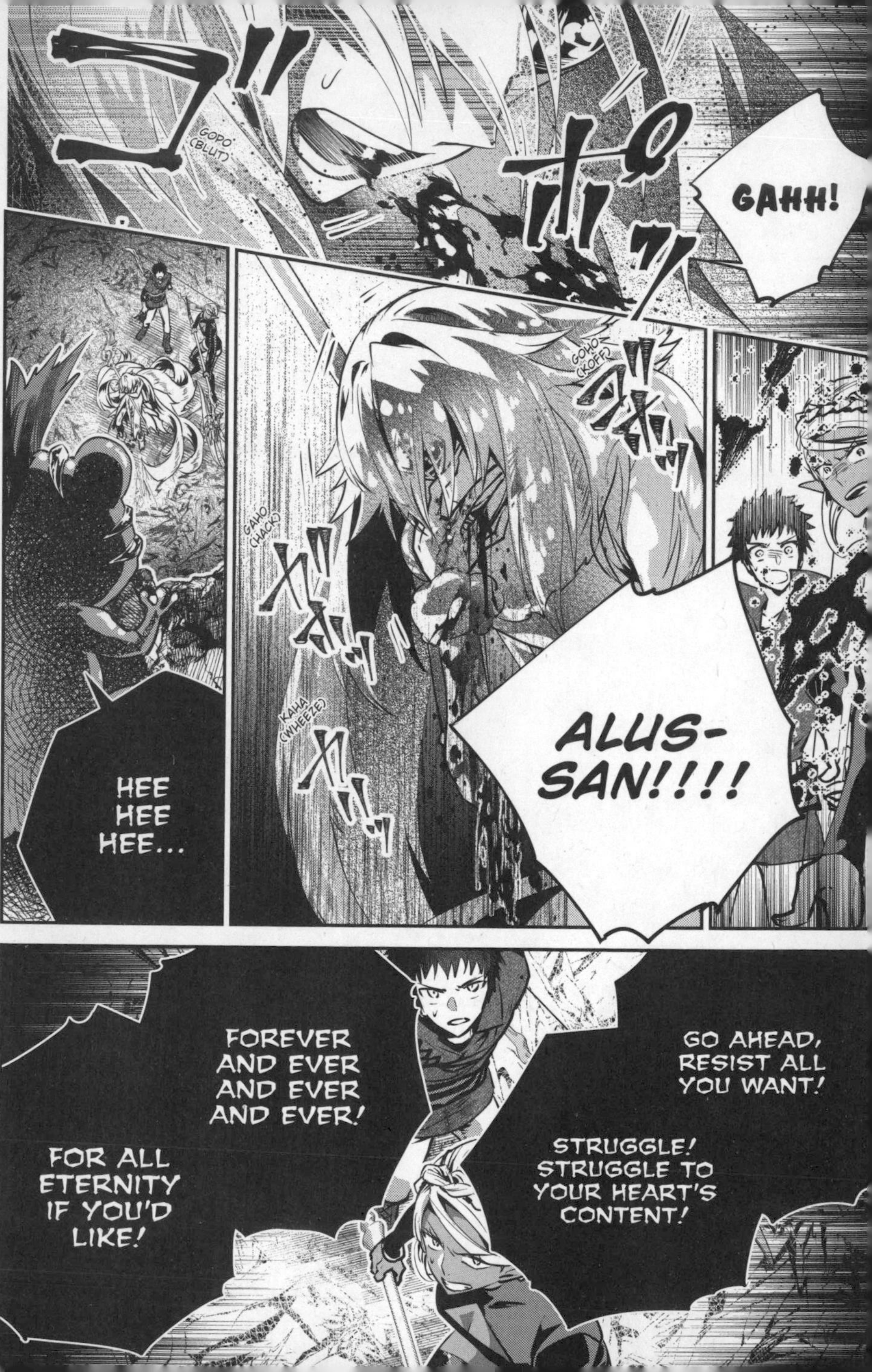
GAHH!
GOPO (BLUT)
ALUS-SAN!!!!
GOHO (KOFF)
GAHO (CHACK)
KAHA (WHEEZE)
HEE HEE HEE...
GO AHEAD, RESIST ALL YOU WANT!
STRUGGLE! STRUGGLE TO YOUR HEART'S CONTENT!
FOREVER AND EVER AND EVER AND EVER!
FOR ALL ETERNITY IF YOU'D LIKE!

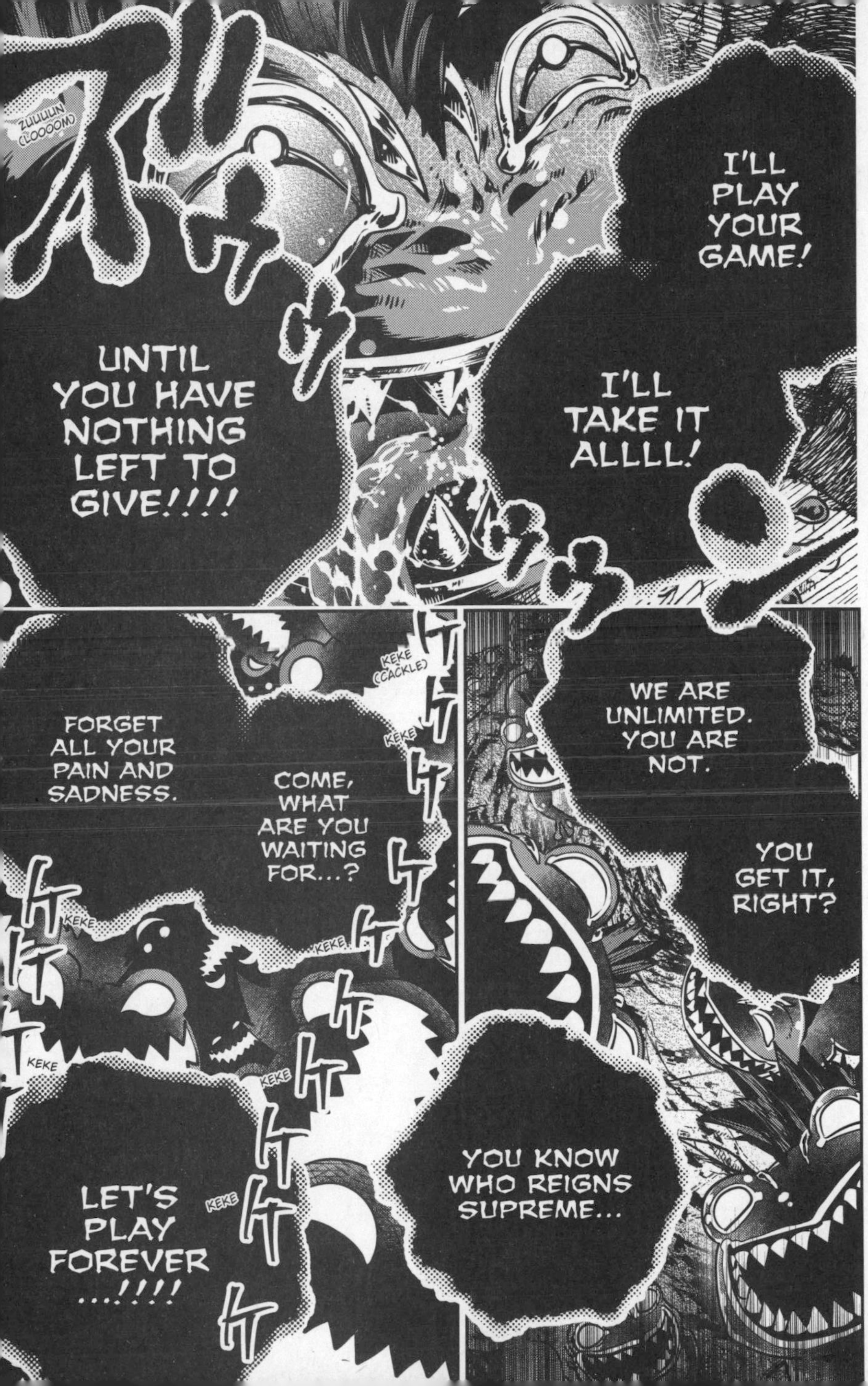
I'LL PLAY YOUR GAME!
I'LL TAKE IT ALLLL!
ZUUUUN (LOOOOM)
UNTIL YOU HAVE NOTHING LEFT TO GIVE!!!!
WE ARE UNLIMITED. YOU ARE NOT.
YOU GET IT, RIGHT?
YOU KNOW WHO REIGNS SUPREME...
KEKE (CACKLE)
FORGET ALL YOUR PAIN AND SADNESS.
KEKE
COME, WHAT ARE YOU WAITING FOR...?
KEKE
KEKE
KEKE
KEKE
KEKE
LET'S PLAY FOREVER ....!!!!

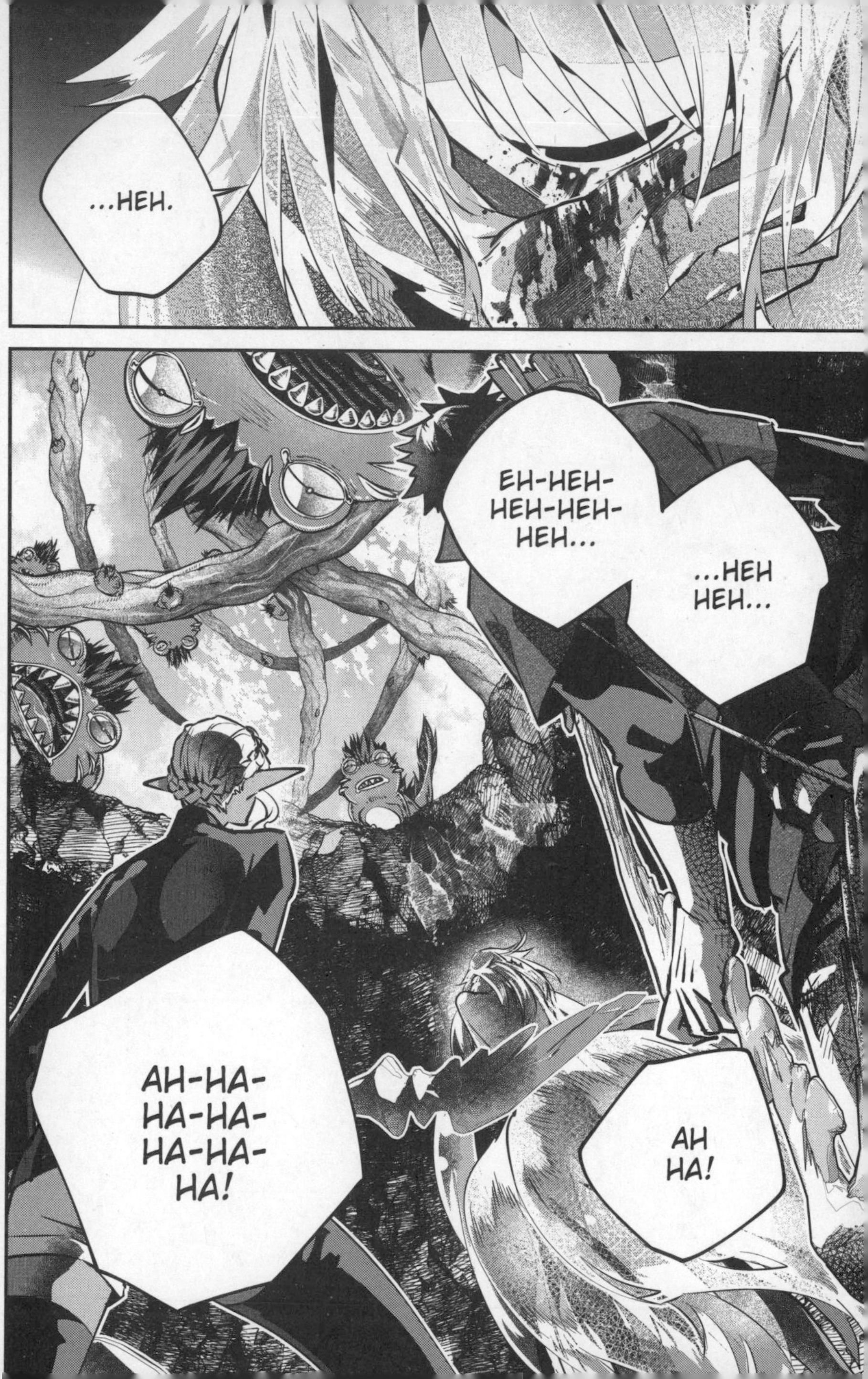
...HEH.
EH-HEH-HEH-HEH-HEH...
...HEH HEH...
AH HA!
AH-HA-HA-HA-HA-HA-HA!

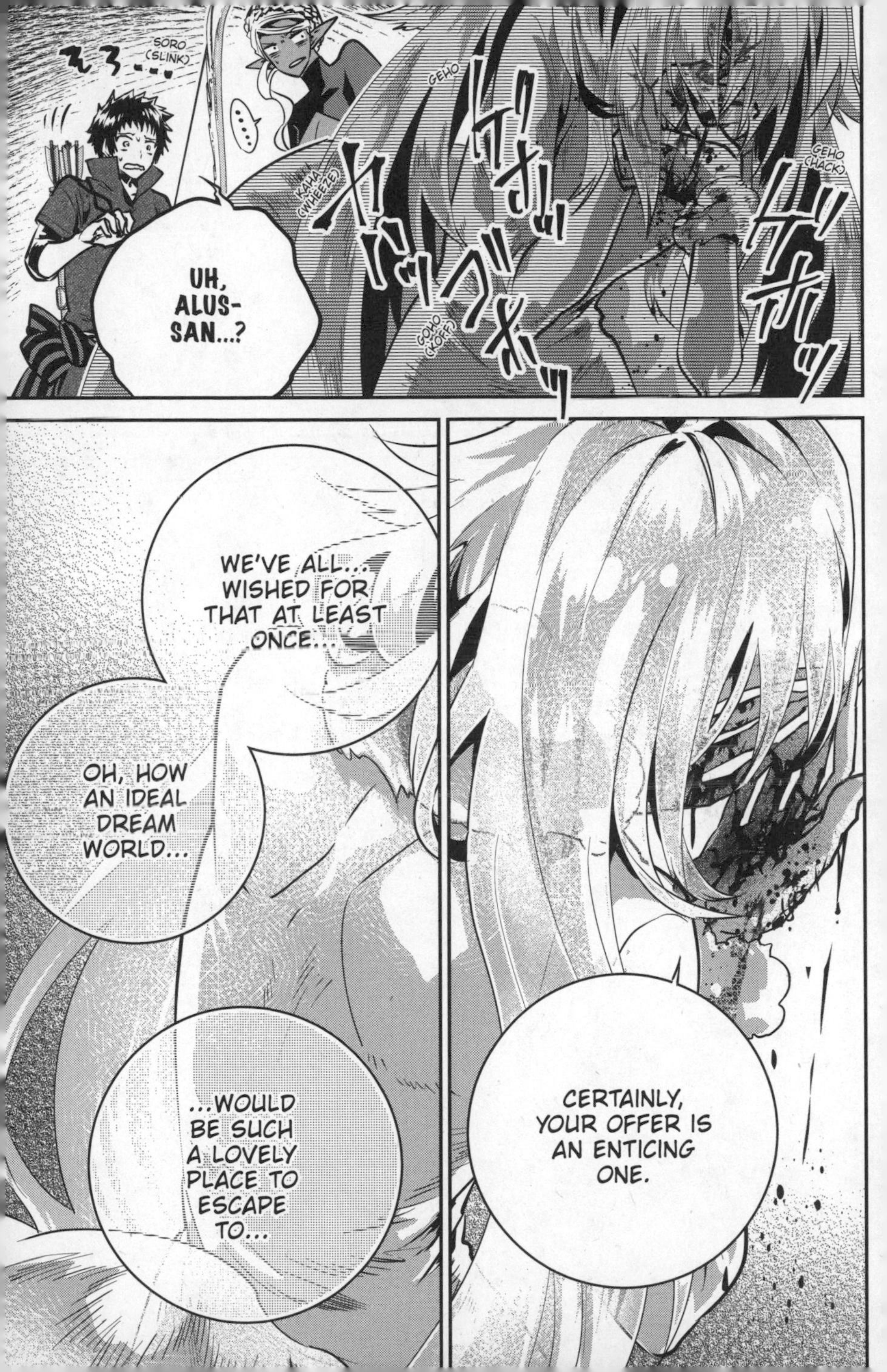
GEHO (HACK)
GEHO
KAHA (WHEEZE)
GOHO (KOFF)
SORO (SLINK)
...
UH, ALUS-SAN...?
CERTAINLY, YOUR OFFER IS AN ENTICING ONE.
WE'VE ALL... WISHED FOR THAT AT LEAST ONCE...
OH, HOW AN IDEAL DREAM WORLD...
...WOULD BE SUCH A LOVELY PLACE TO ESCAPE TO...

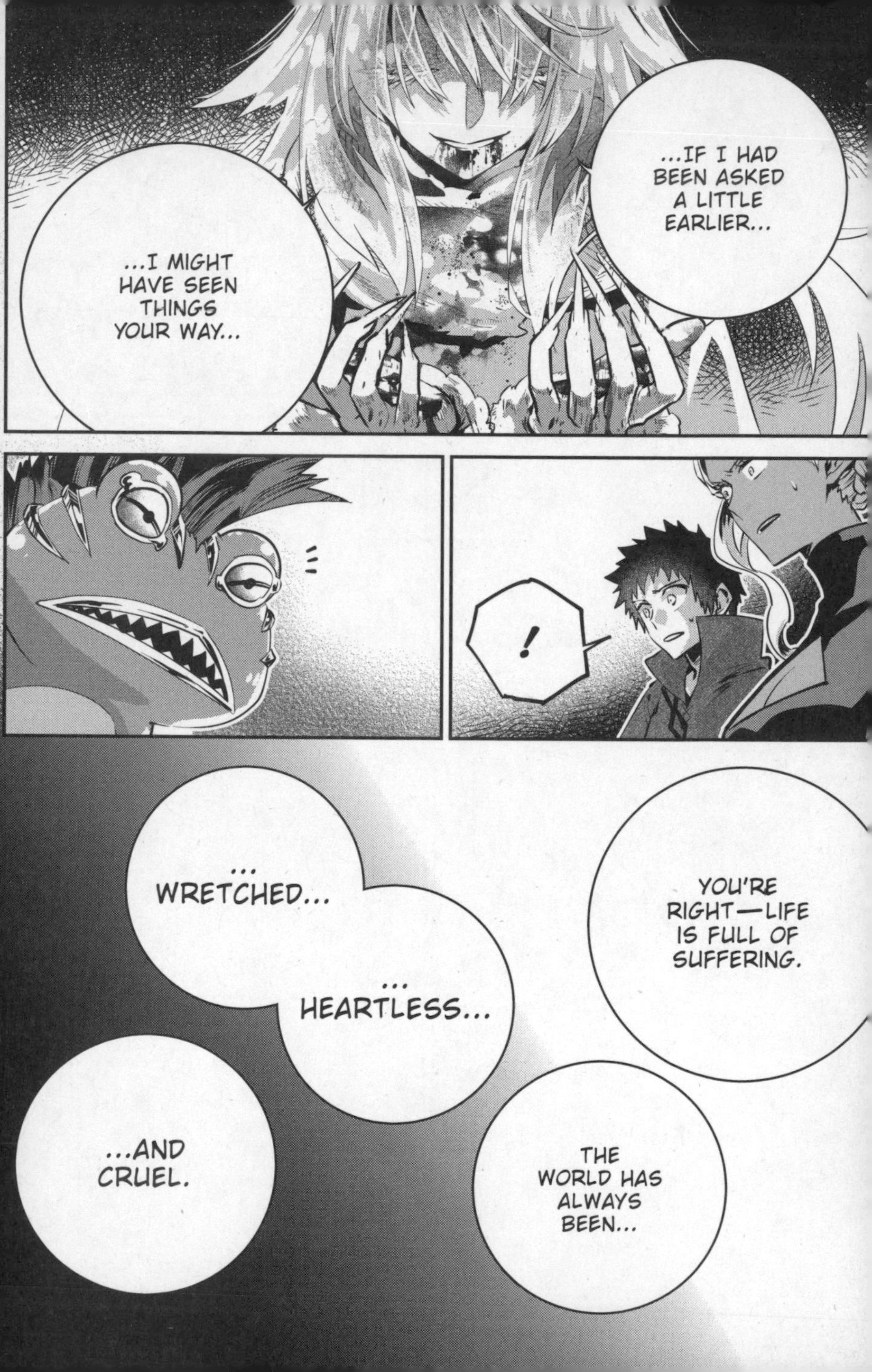
...IF I HAD BEEN ASKED A LITTLE EARLIER...
...I MIGHT HAVE SEEN THINGS YOUR WAY...
!
YOU'RE RIGHT—LIFE IS FULL OF SUFFERING.
THE WORLD HAS ALWAYS BEEN...
...WRETCHED...
...HEARTLESS...
...AND CRUEL.

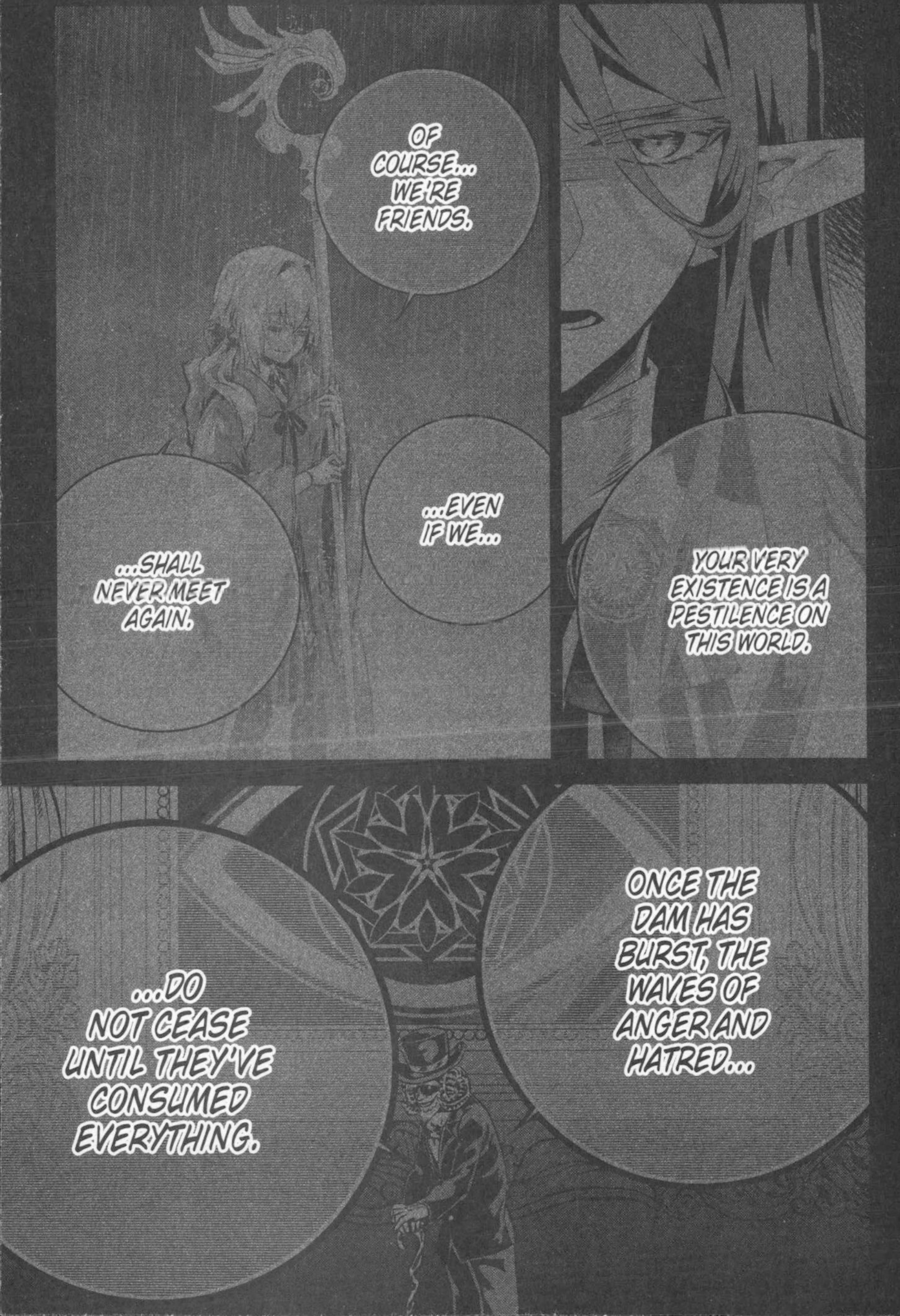
YOUR VERY EXISTENCE IS A PESTILENCE ON THIS WORLD.
OF COURSE... WE'RE FRIENDS.
...EVEN IF WE...
...SHALL NEVER MEET AGAIN.
ONCE THE DAM HAS BURST, THE WAVES OF ANGER AND HATRED...
...DO NOT CEASE UNTIL THEY'VE CONSUMED EVERYTHING.

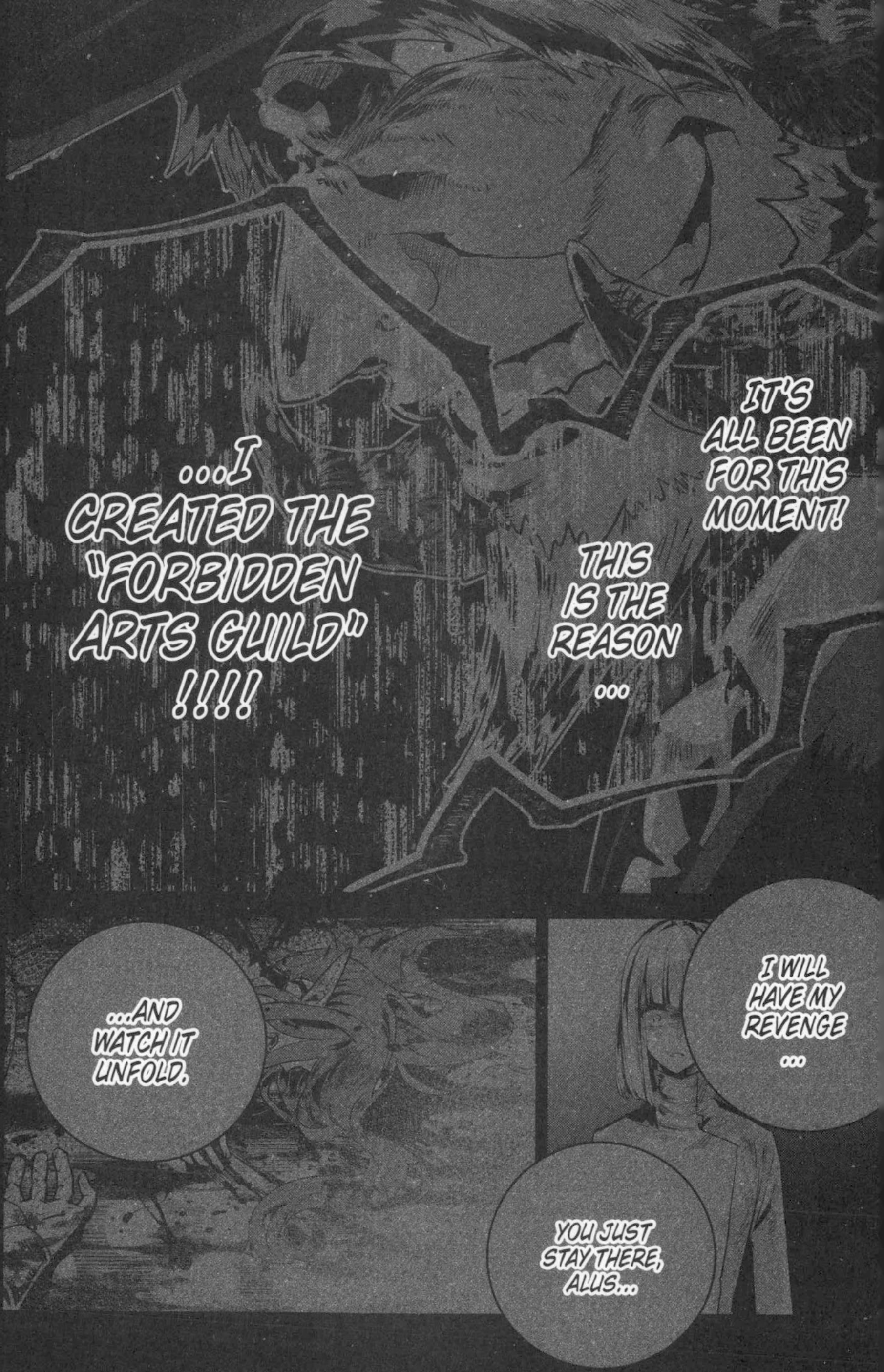
IT'S ALL BEEN FOR THIS MOMENT!
THIS IS THE REASON...
...I CREATED THE "FORBIDDEN ARTS GUILD"!!!!
I WILL HAVE MY REVENGE...
YOU JUST STAY THERE, ALUS...
...AND WATCH IT UNFOLD.

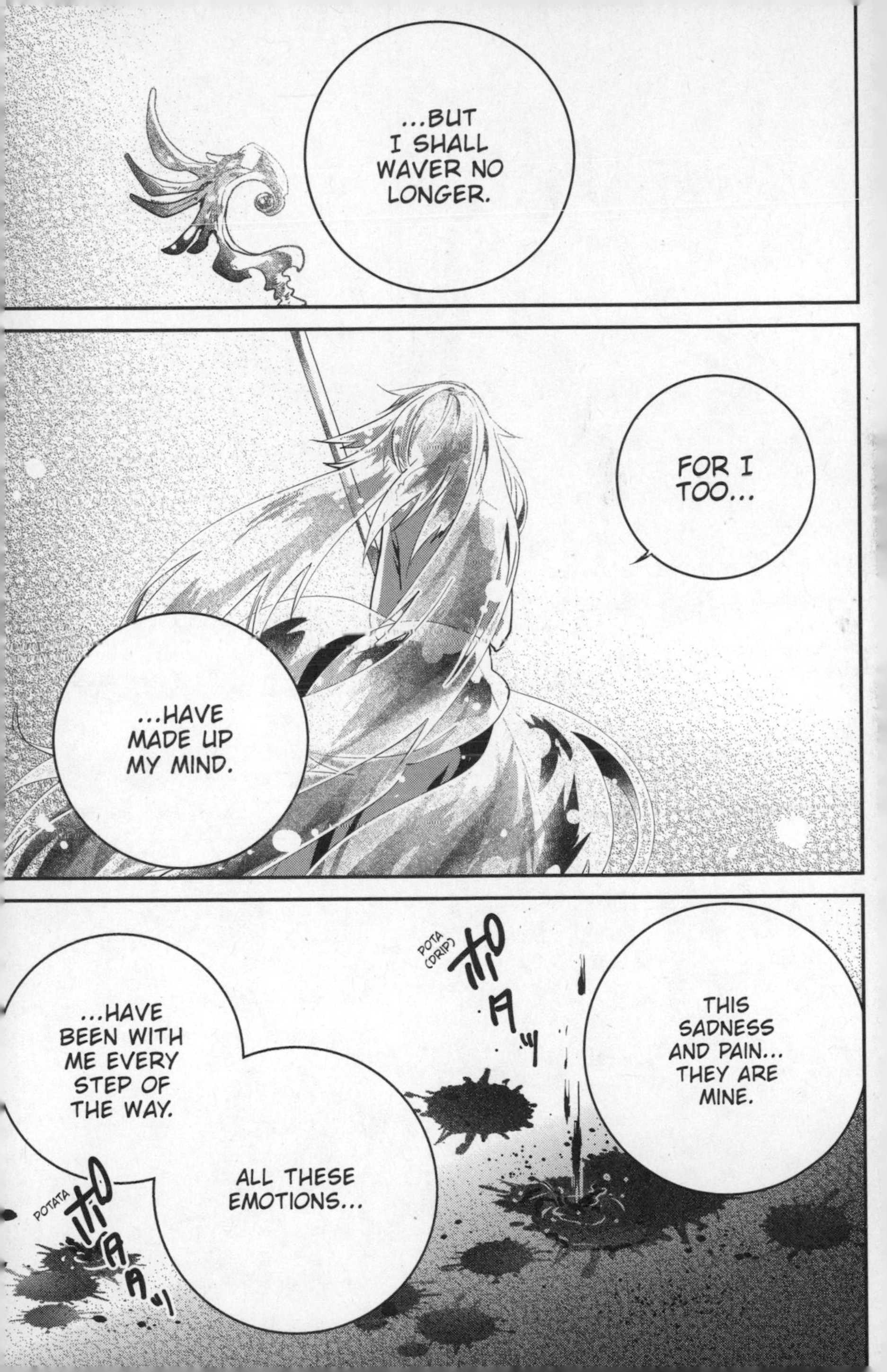
...BUT I SHALL WAVER NO LONGER.
FOR I TOO...
...HAVE MADE UP MY MIND.
THIS SADNESS AND PAIN... THEY ARE MINE.
POTA (DRIP)
ALL THESE EMOTIONS...
...HAVE BEEN WITH ME EVERY STEP OF THE WAY.
POTATA

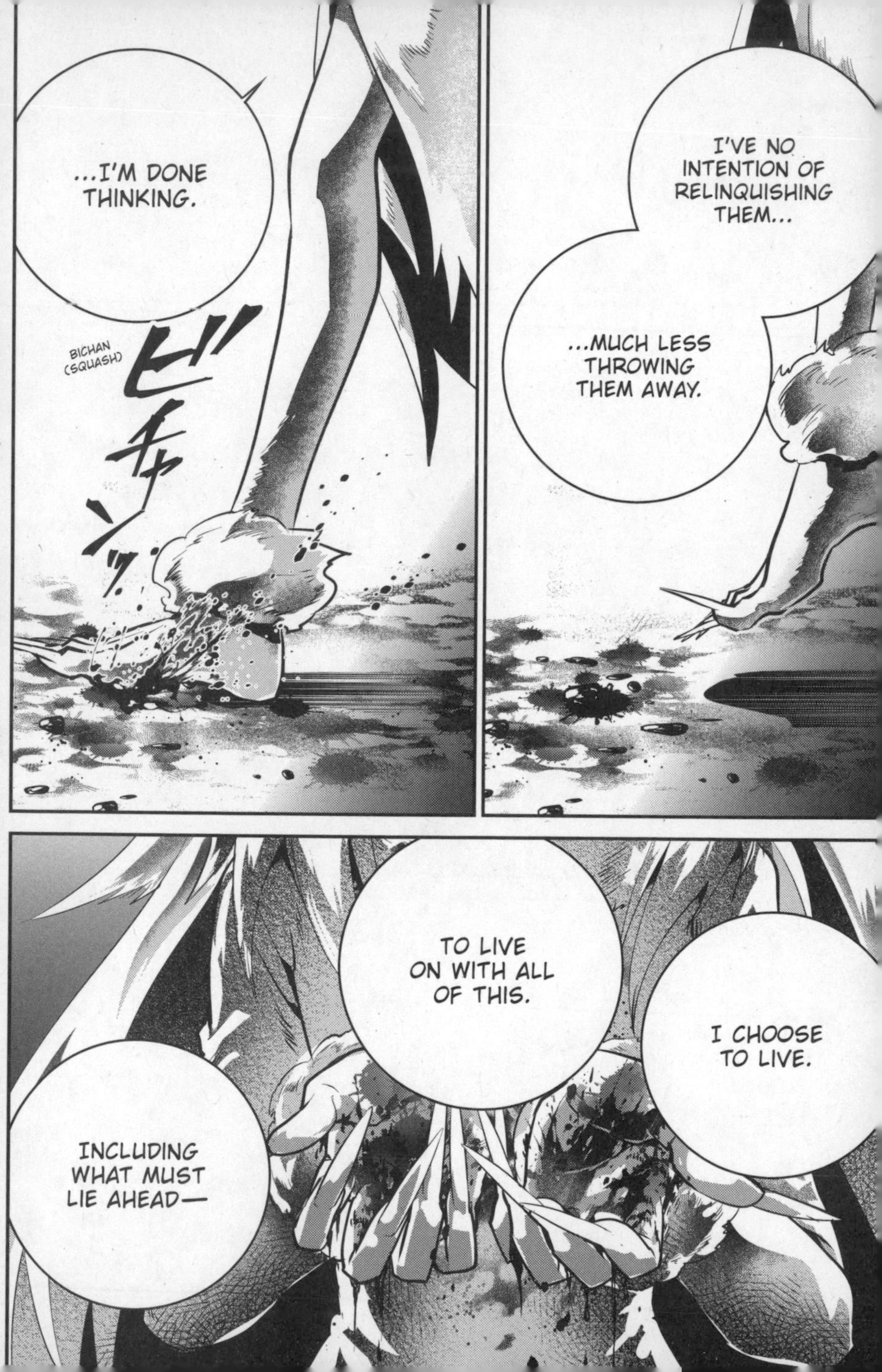
I'VE NO INTENTION OF RELINQUISHING THEM...
...MUCH LESS THROWING THEM AWAY.
...I'M DONE THINKING.
ビチャンッ
BICHAN (SQUASH)
I CHOOSE TO LIVE.
TO LIVE ON WITH ALL OF THIS.
INCLUDING WHAT MUST LIE AHEAD—

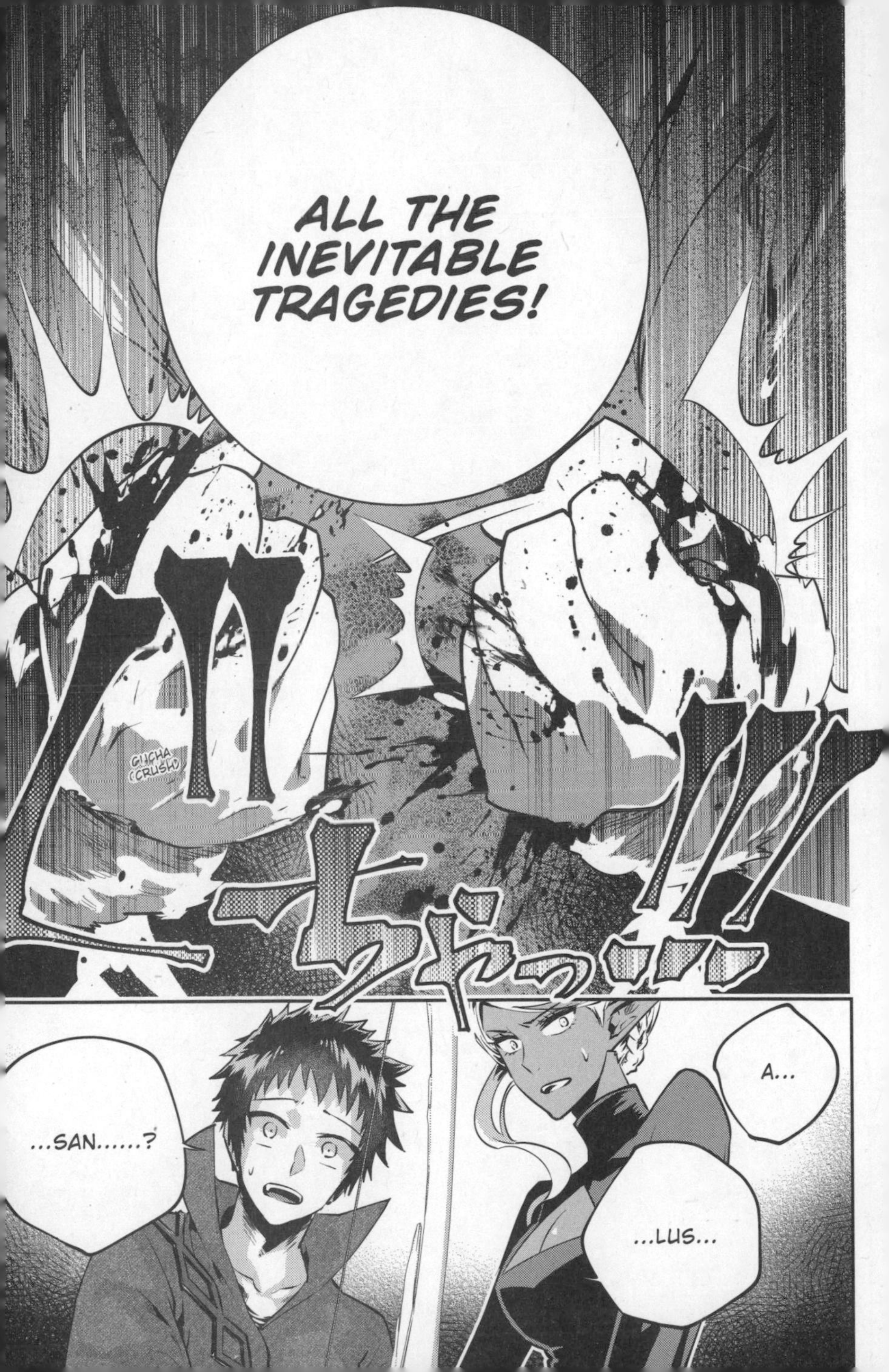
ALL THE INEVITABLE TRAGEDIES!
GUCHA (CRUSH)
A...
...LUS...
...SAN......?

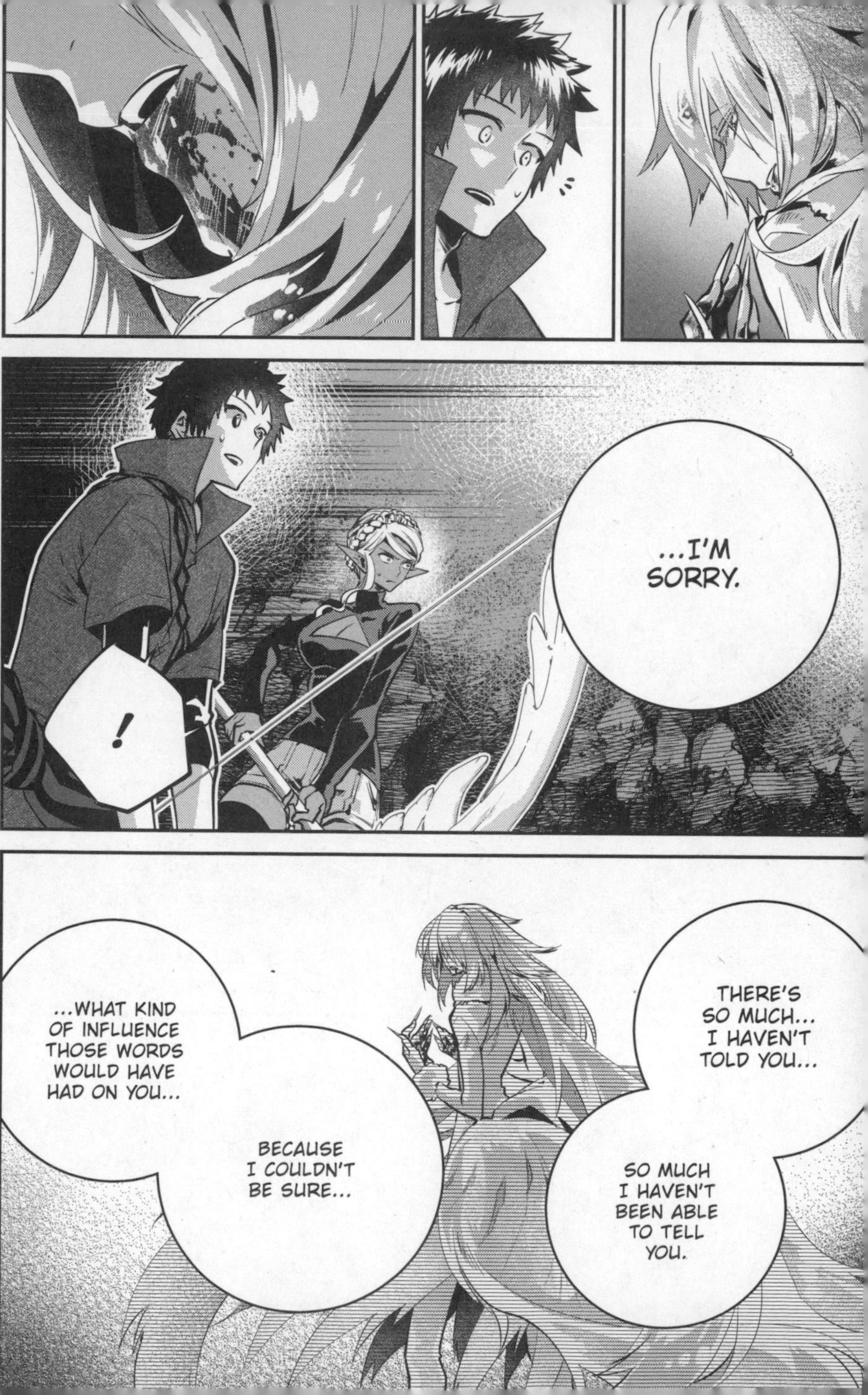
...I'M SORRY.
!
THERE'S SO MUCH... I HAVEN'T TOLD YOU...
SO MUCH I HAVEN'T BEEN ABLE TO TELL YOU.
BECAUSE I COULDN'T BE SURE...
...WHAT KIND OF INFLUENCE THOSE WORDS WOULD HAVE HAD ON YOU...

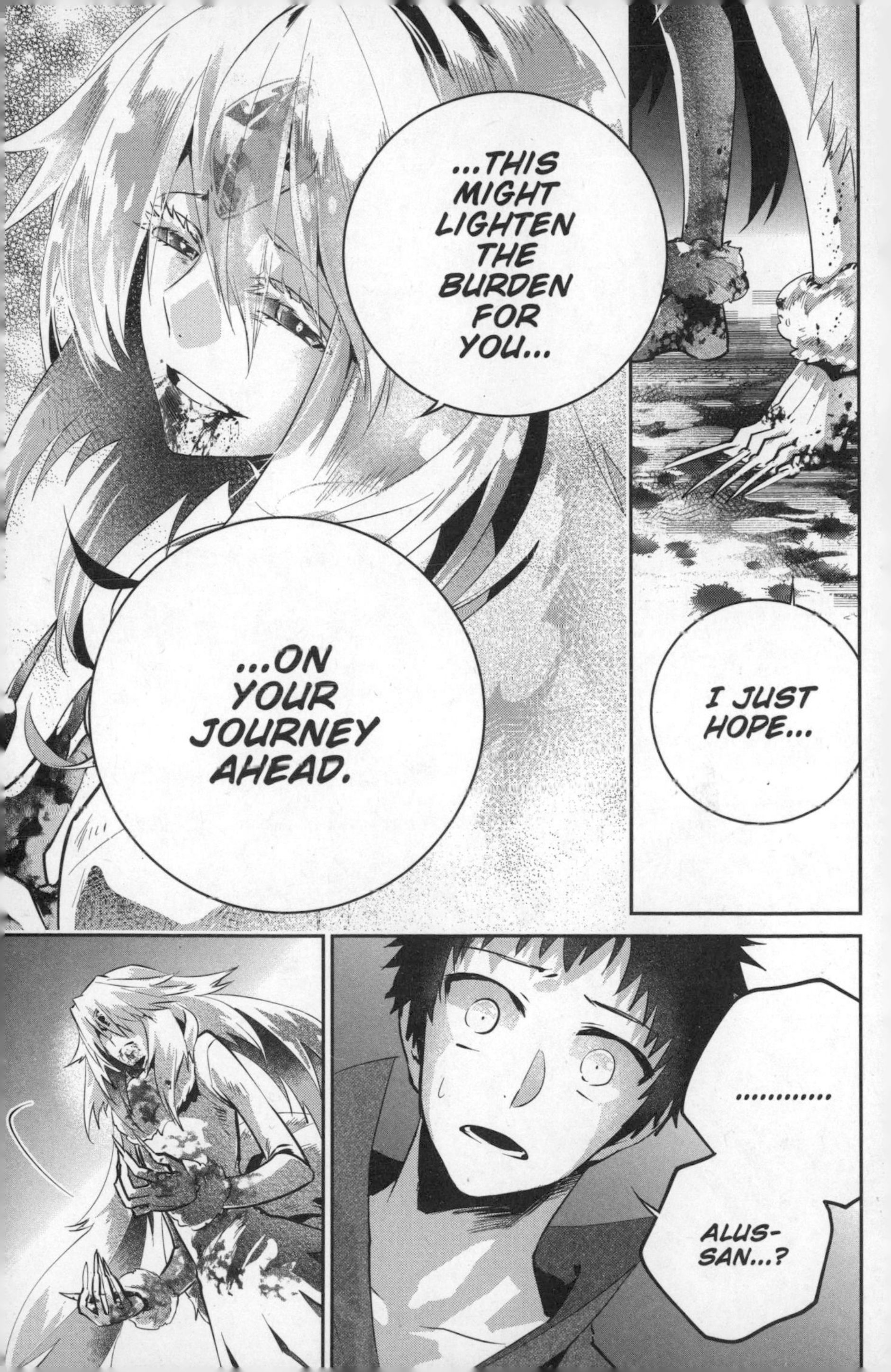
I JUST HOPE...
...THIS MIGHT LIGHTEN THE BURDEN FOR YOU...
...ON YOUR JOURNEY AHEAD.
............
ALUS-SAN...?

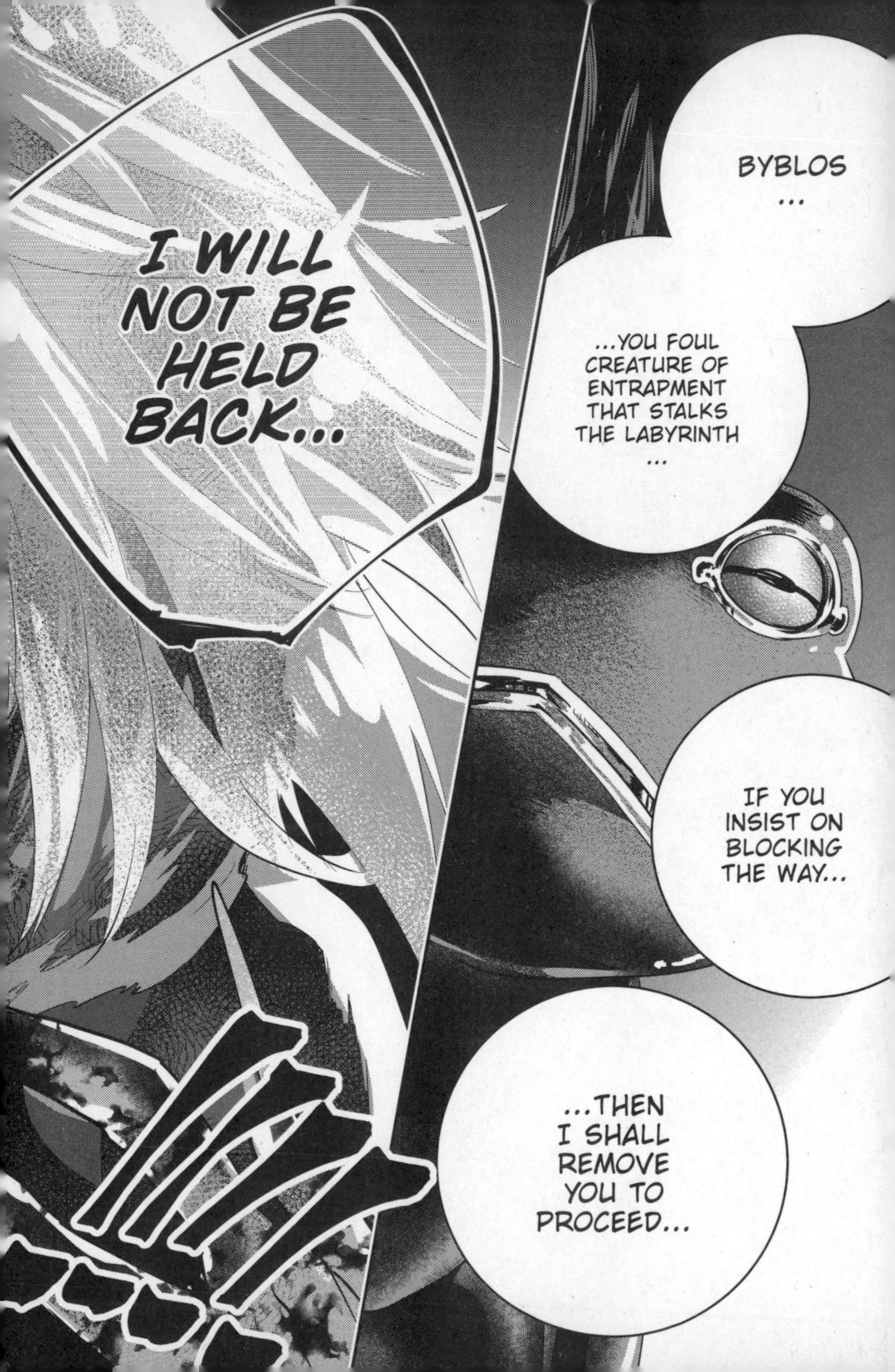
BYBLOS...
...YOU FOUL CREATURE OF ENTRAPMENT THAT STALKS THE LABYRINTH...
IF YOU INSIST ON BLOCKING THE WAY...
...THEN I SHALL REMOVE YOU TO PROCEED...
I WILL NOT BE HELD BACK...

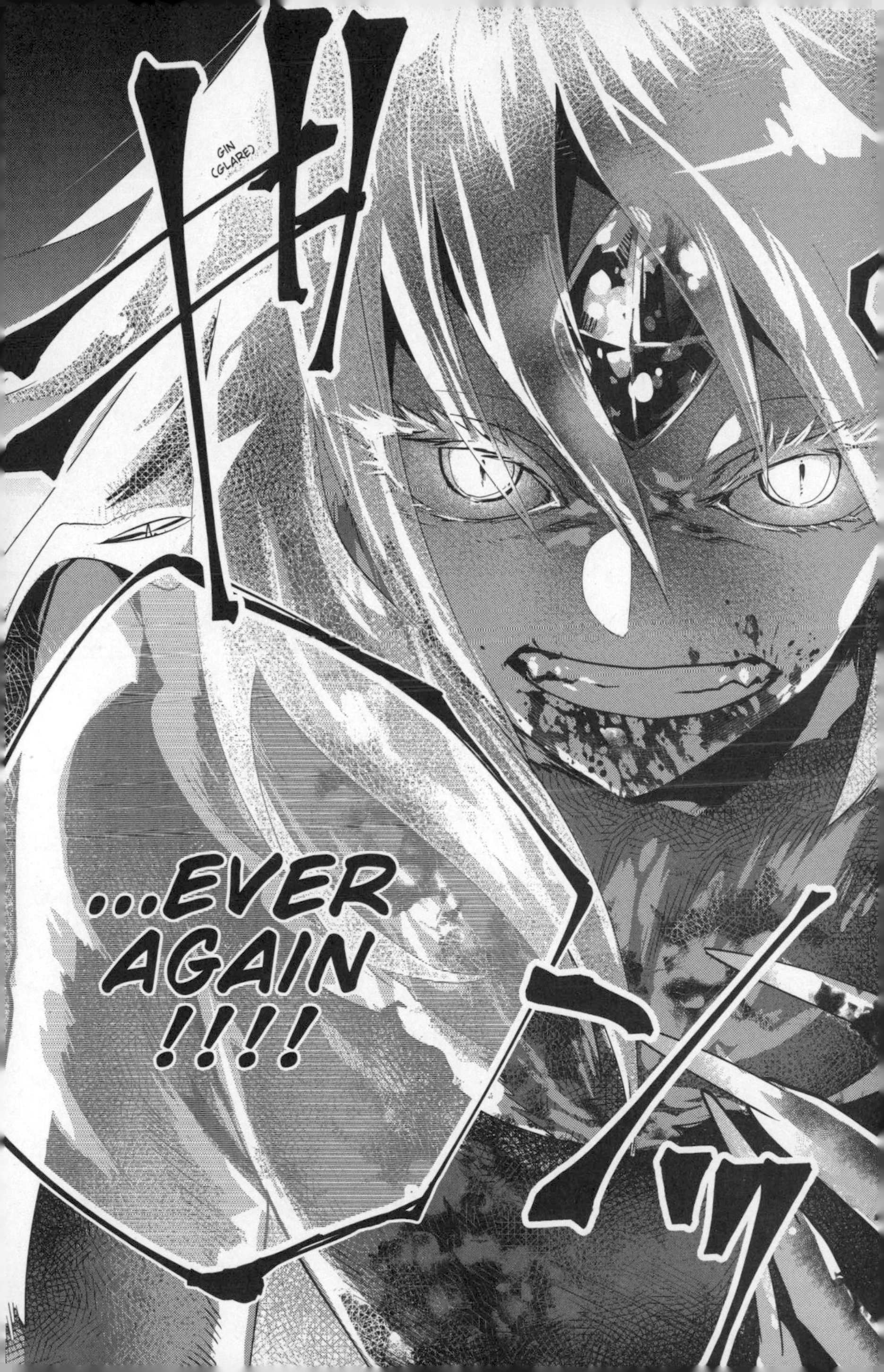
GIN (GLARE)
...EVER AGAIN !!!!

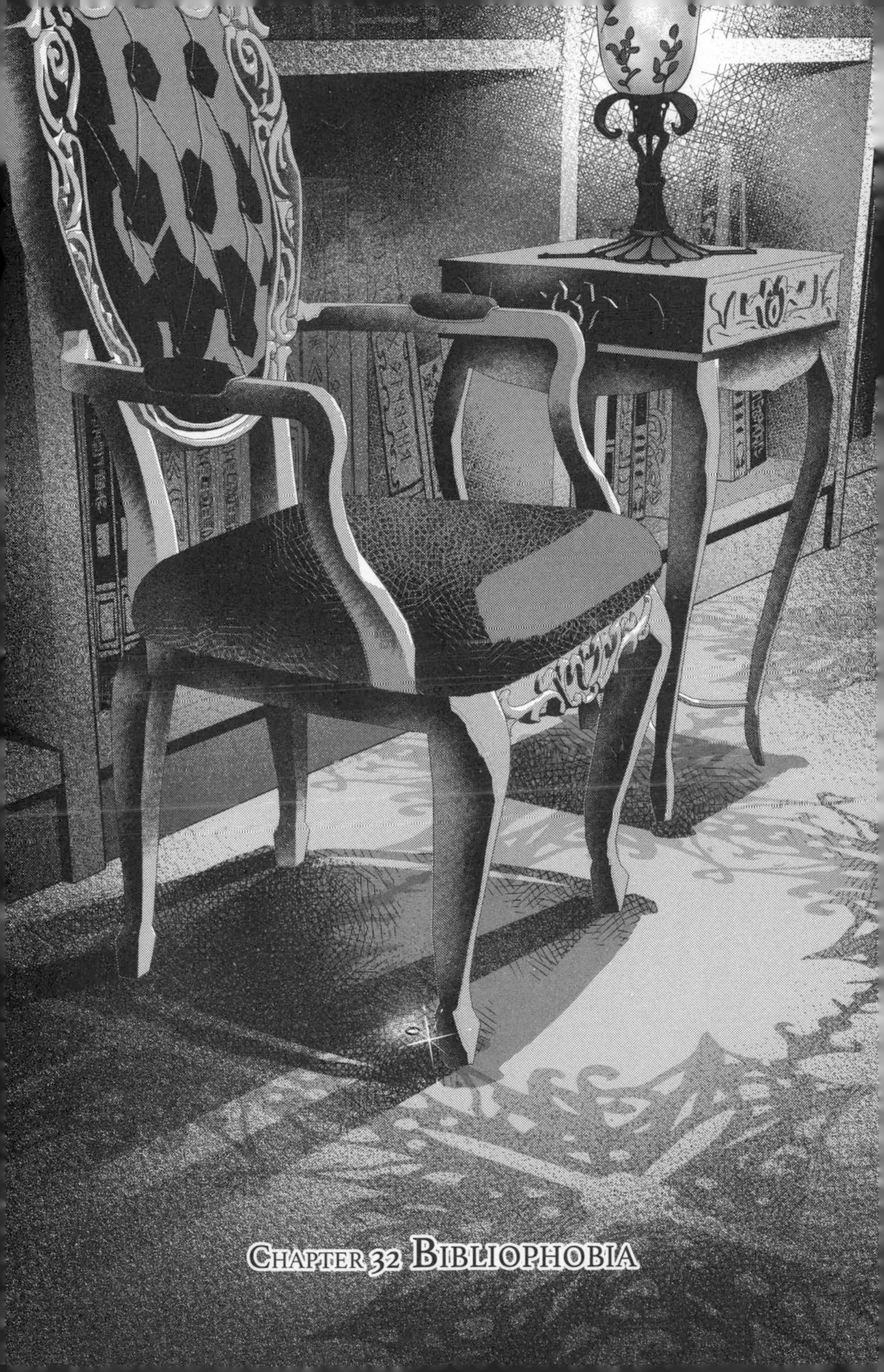

# Chapter 32 Bibliophobia

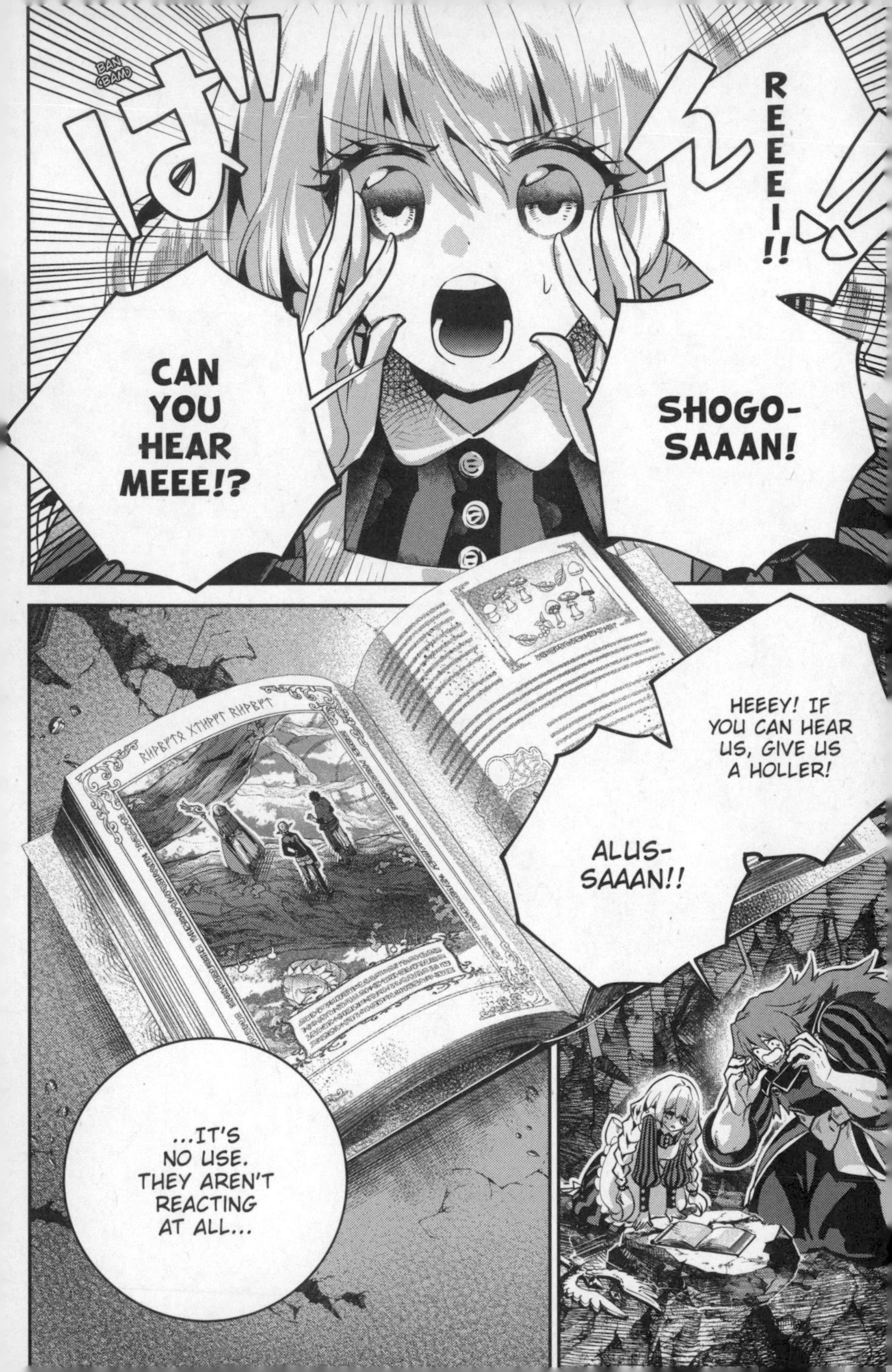
REEEI!!
SHOGO-SAAAN!
CAN YOU HEAR MEEE!?
BAN (BAM)
HEEEY! IF YOU CAN HEAR US, GIVE US A HOLLER!
ALUS-SAAAN!!
...IT'S NO USE. THEY AREN'T REACTING AT ALL...

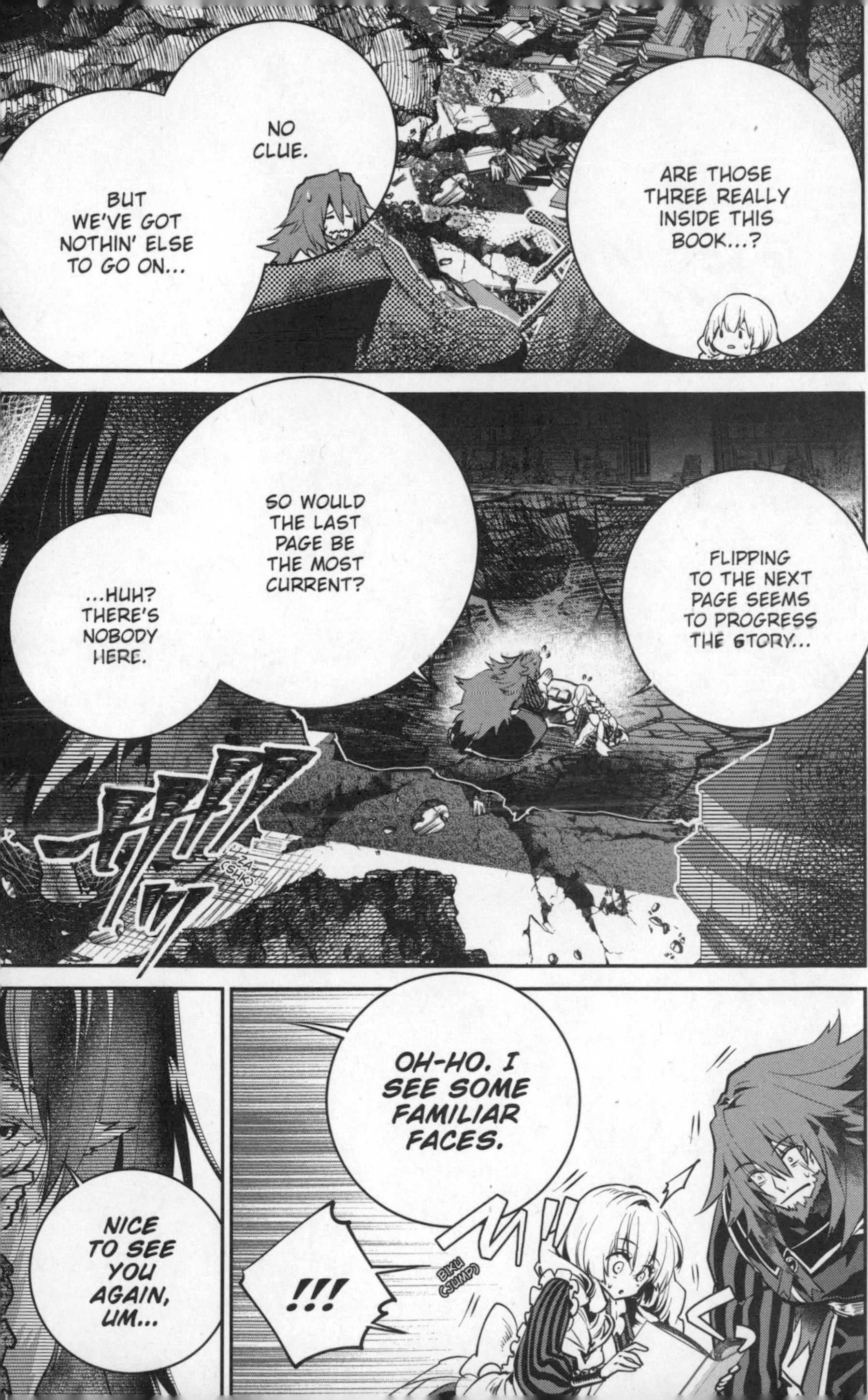
ARE THOSE THREE REALLY INSIDE THIS BOOK...?
NO CLUE.
BUT WE'VE GOT NOTHIN' ELSE TO GO ON...
FLIPPING TO THE NEXT PAGE SEEMS TO PROGRESS THE STORY...
SO WOULD THE LAST PAGE BE THE MOST CURRENT?
...HUH? THERE'S NOBODY HERE.
ZA (SHK)
OH-HO. I SEE SOME FAMILIAR FACES.
BIKU (JUMP)
!!!
NICE TO SEE YOU AGAIN, UM...

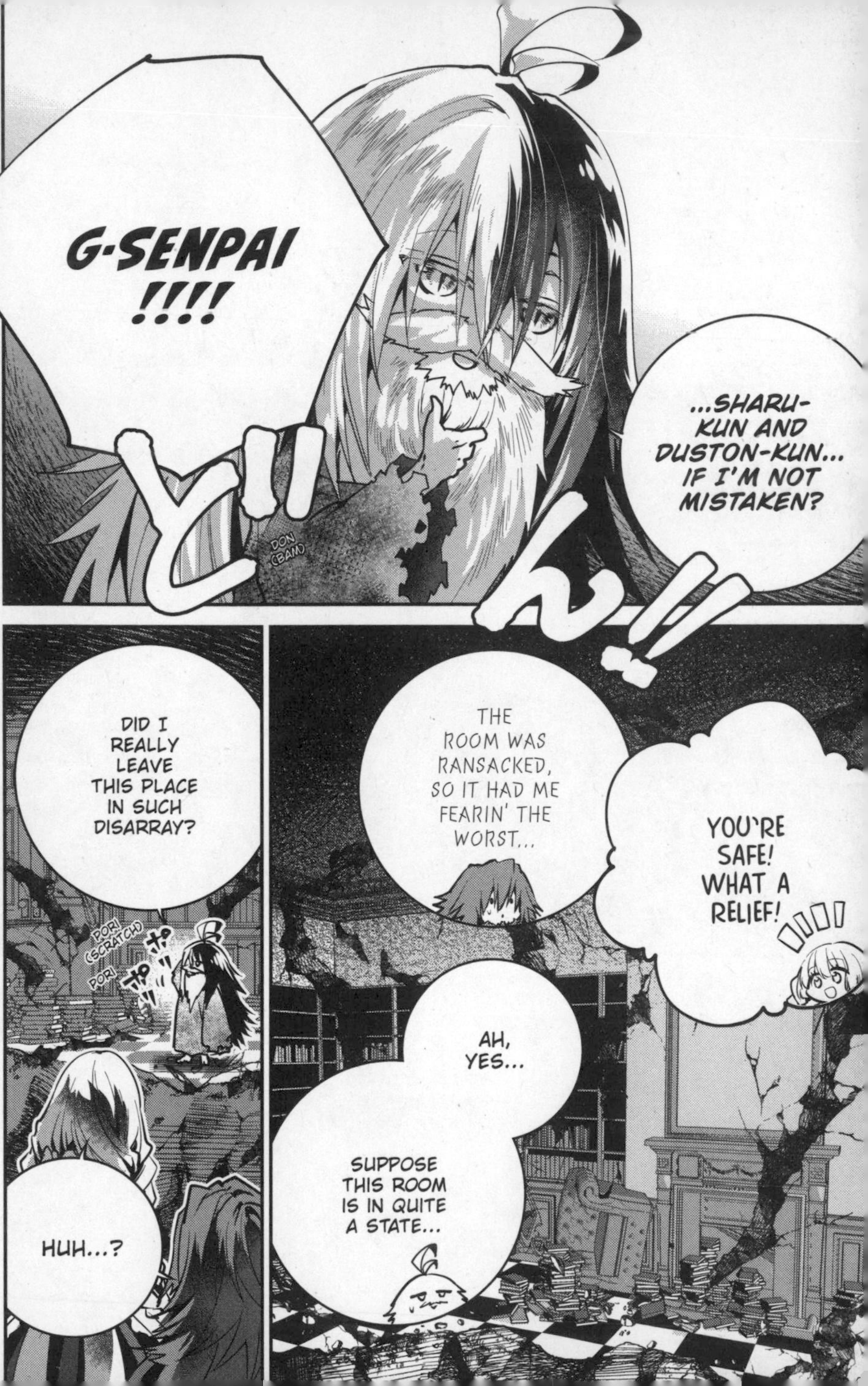
...SHARU-KUN AND DUSTON-KUN... IF I'M NOT MISTAKEN?
G-SENPAI !!!!
DON (BAM)
THE ROOM WAS RANSACKED, SO IT HAD ME FEARIN' THE WORST...
YOU'RE SAFE! WHAT A RELIEF!
AH, YES...
SUPPOSE THIS ROOM IS IN QUITE A STATE...
DID I REALLY LEAVE THIS PLACE IN SUCH DISARRAY?
PORI (SCRATCH) PORI
HUH...?

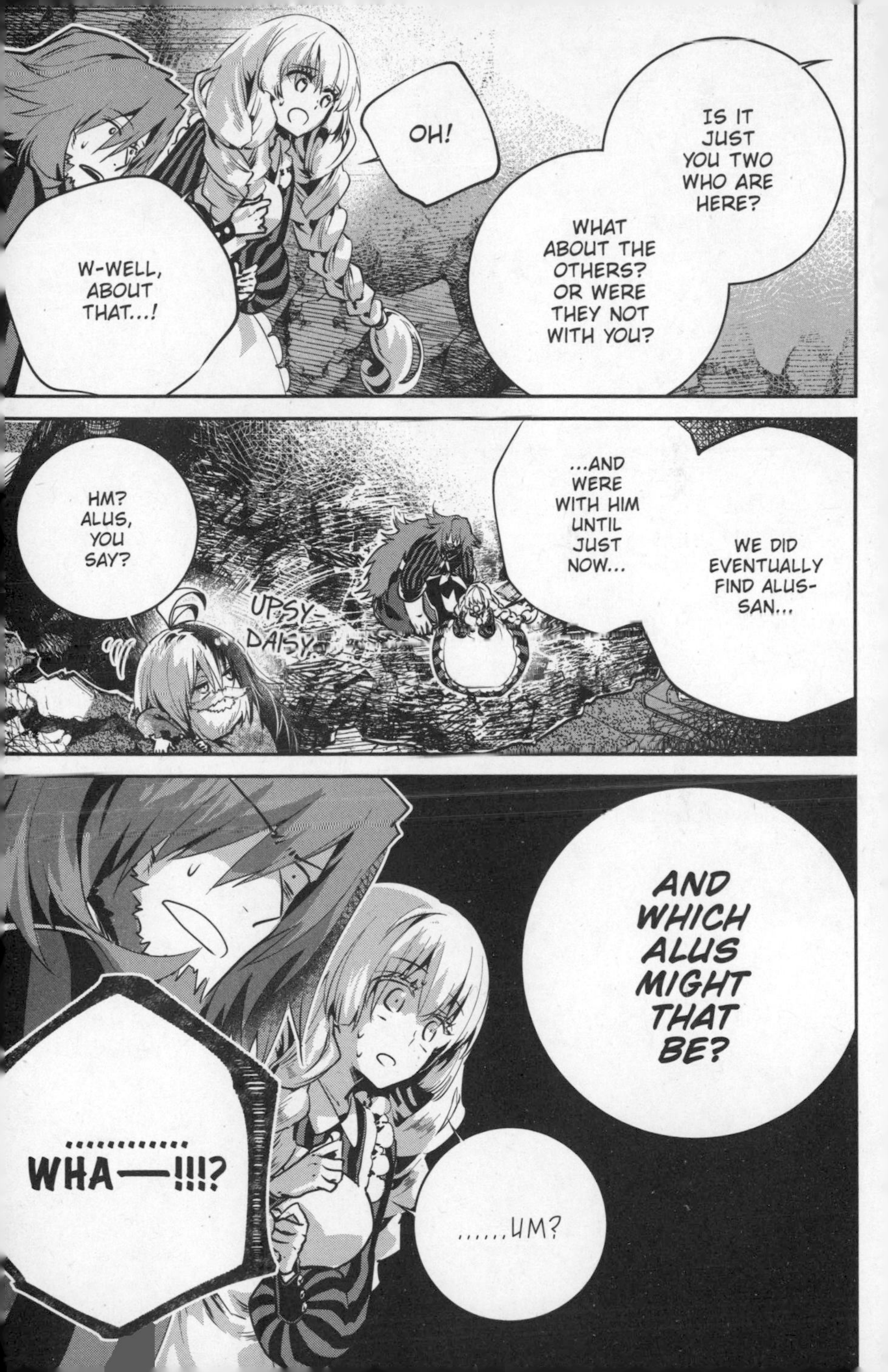
IS IT JUST YOU TWO WHO ARE HERE?
WHAT ABOUT THE OTHERS? OR WERE THEY NOT WITH YOU?
OH!
W-WELL, ABOUT THAT...!
WE DID EVENTUALLY FIND ALUS-SAN...
...AND WERE WITH HIM UNTIL JUST NOW...
UPSY-DAISY.
HM? ALUS, YOU SAY?
AND WHICH ALUS MIGHT THAT BE?
......UM?
............
WHA—!!!?

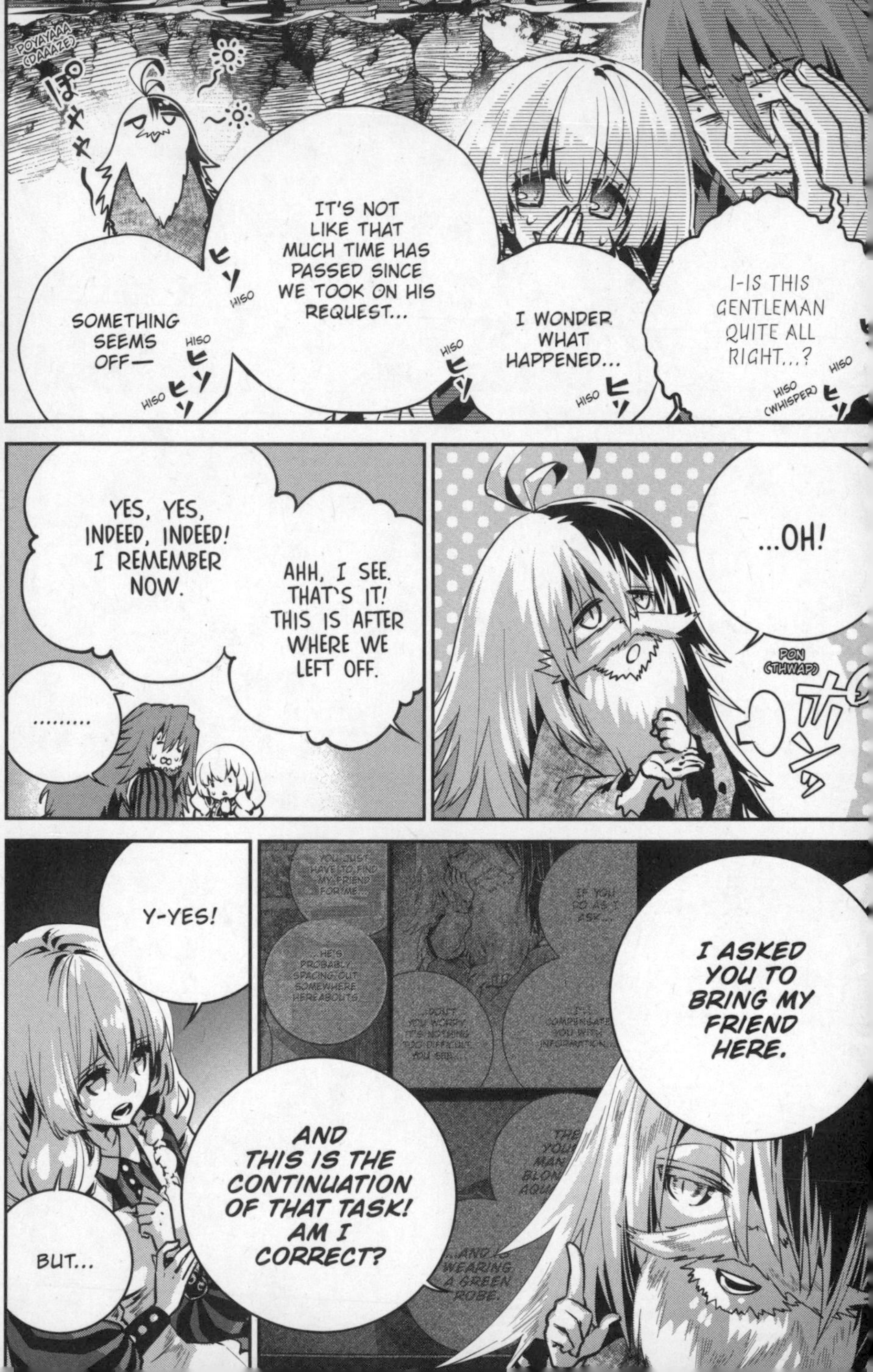

POYAYAAA (DAAAZE)
I-IS THIS GENTLEMAN QUITE ALL RIGHT...?
HISO (WHISPER)
I WONDER WHAT HAPPENED...
HISO
IT'S NOT LIKE THAT MUCH TIME HAS PASSED SINCE WE TOOK ON HIS REQUEST...
HISO
SOMETHING SEEMS OFF—
HISO
...OH!
PON (THWAP)
AHH, I SEE. THAT'S IT! THIS IS AFTER WHERE WE LEFT OFF.
YES, YES, INDEED, INDEED! I REMEMBER NOW.
.........
I ASKED YOU TO BRING MY FRIEND HERE.
IF YOU DO AS I ASK...
I'LL COMPENSATE YOU WITH INFORMATION...
YOU JUST HAVE TO FIND MY FRIEND FOR ME...
...HE'S PROBABLY SPACING OUT SOMEWHERE HEREABOUTS.
...DON'T YOU WORRY. IT'S NOTHING TOO DIFFICULT, YOU SEE...
...AND IS WEARING A GREEN ROBE.
AND THIS IS THE CONTINUATION OF THAT TASK! AM I CORRECT?
Y-YES!
BUT...

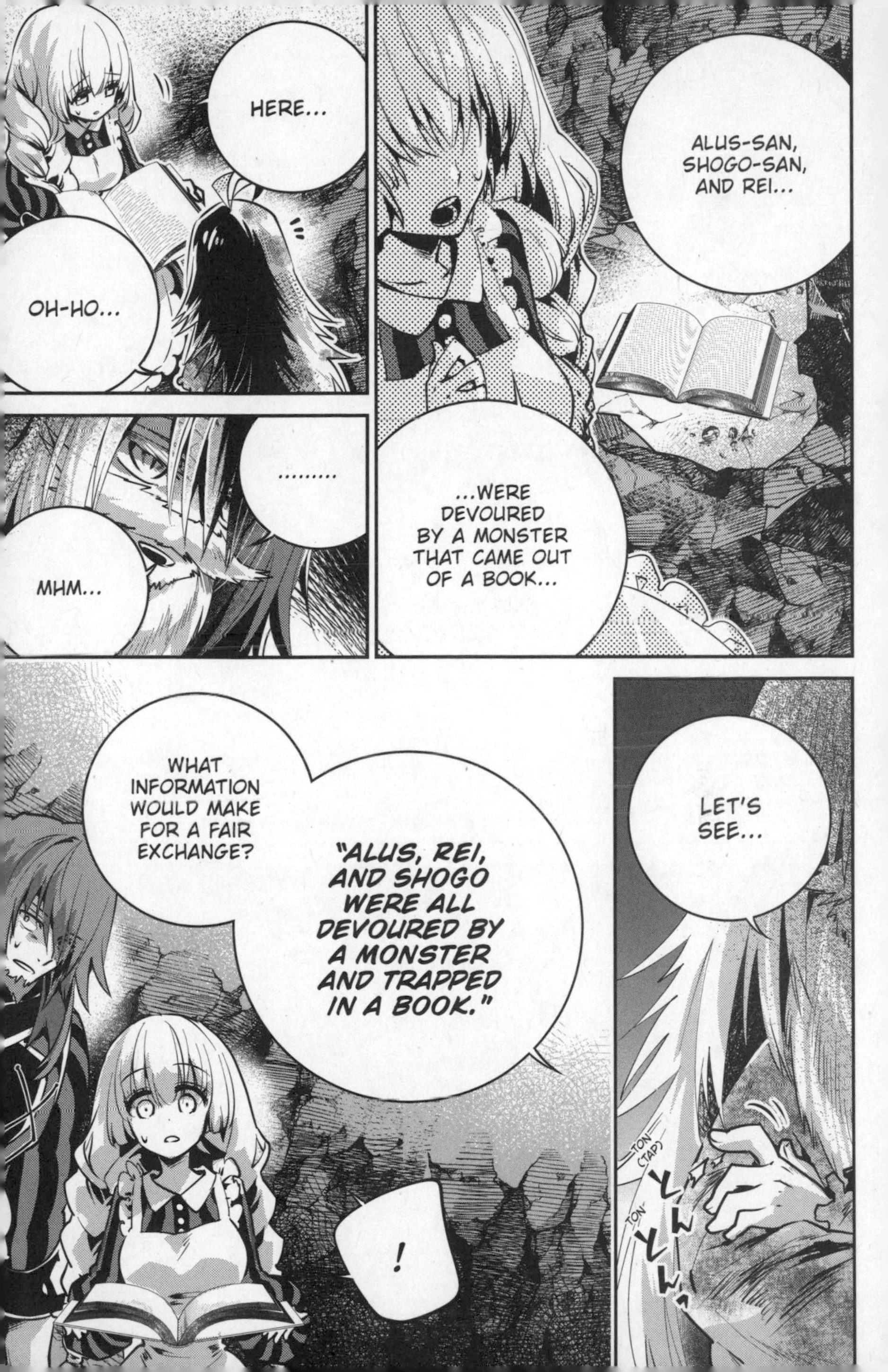
ALUS-SAN, SHOGO-SAN, AND REI...
...WERE DEVOURED BY A MONSTER THAT CAME OUT OF A BOOK...
HERE...
OH-HO...
.........
MHM...
LET'S SEE...
TON (TAP)
TON
WHAT INFORMATION WOULD MAKE FOR A FAIR EXCHANGE?
"ALUS, REI, AND SHOGO WERE ALL DEVOURED BY A MONSTER AND TRAPPED IN A BOOK."
!

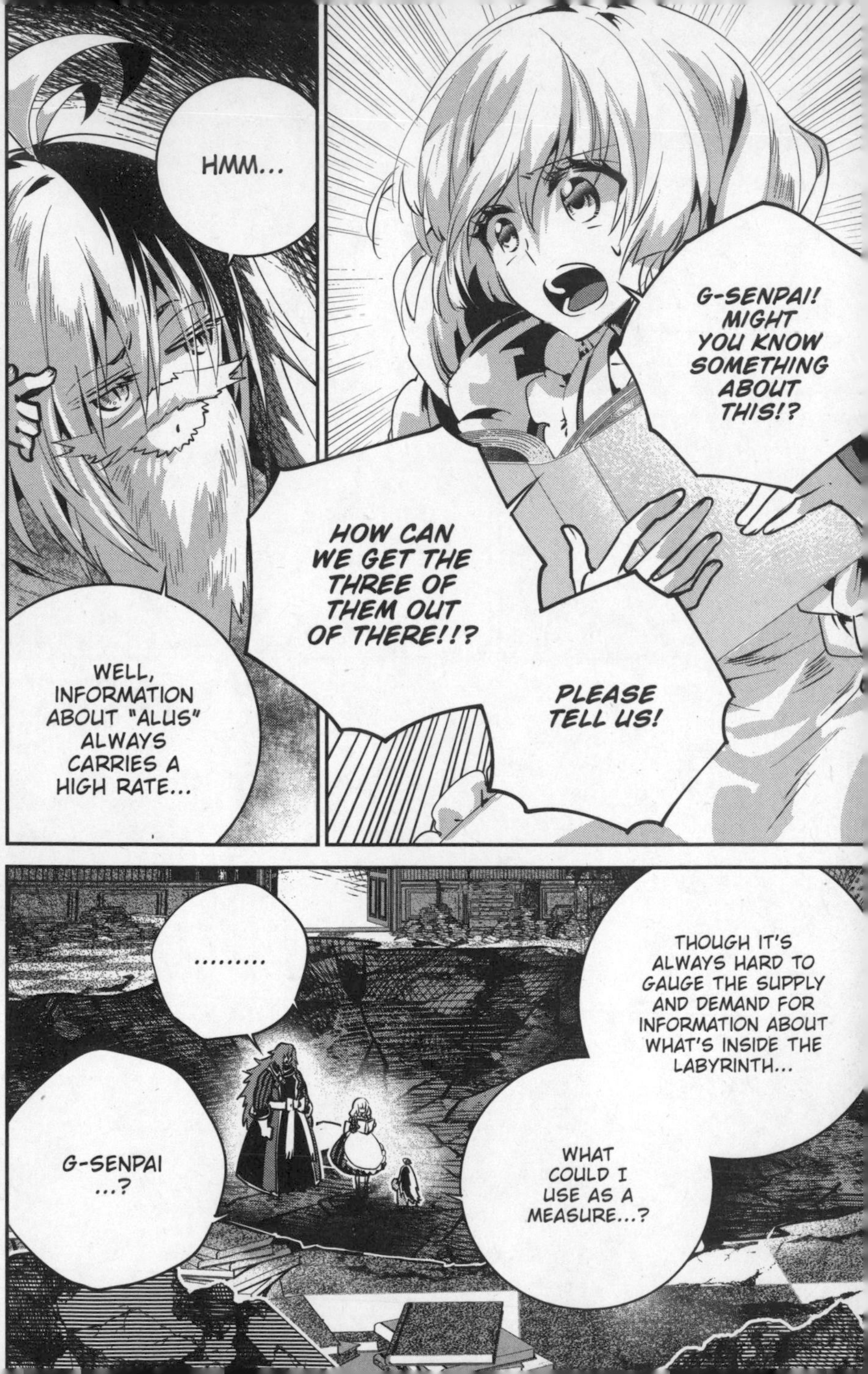
G-SENPAI! MIGHT YOU KNOW SOMETHING ABOUT THIS!?
HOW CAN WE GET THE THREE OF THEM OUT OF THERE!!?
PLEASE TELL US!
HMM...
WELL, INFORMATION ABOUT "ALUS" ALWAYS CARRIES A HIGH RATE...
THOUGH IT'S ALWAYS HARD TO GAUGE THE SUPPLY AND DEMAND FOR INFORMATION ABOUT WHAT'S INSIDE THE LABYRINTH...
WHAT COULD I USE AS A MEASURE...?
.........
G-SENPAI ...?

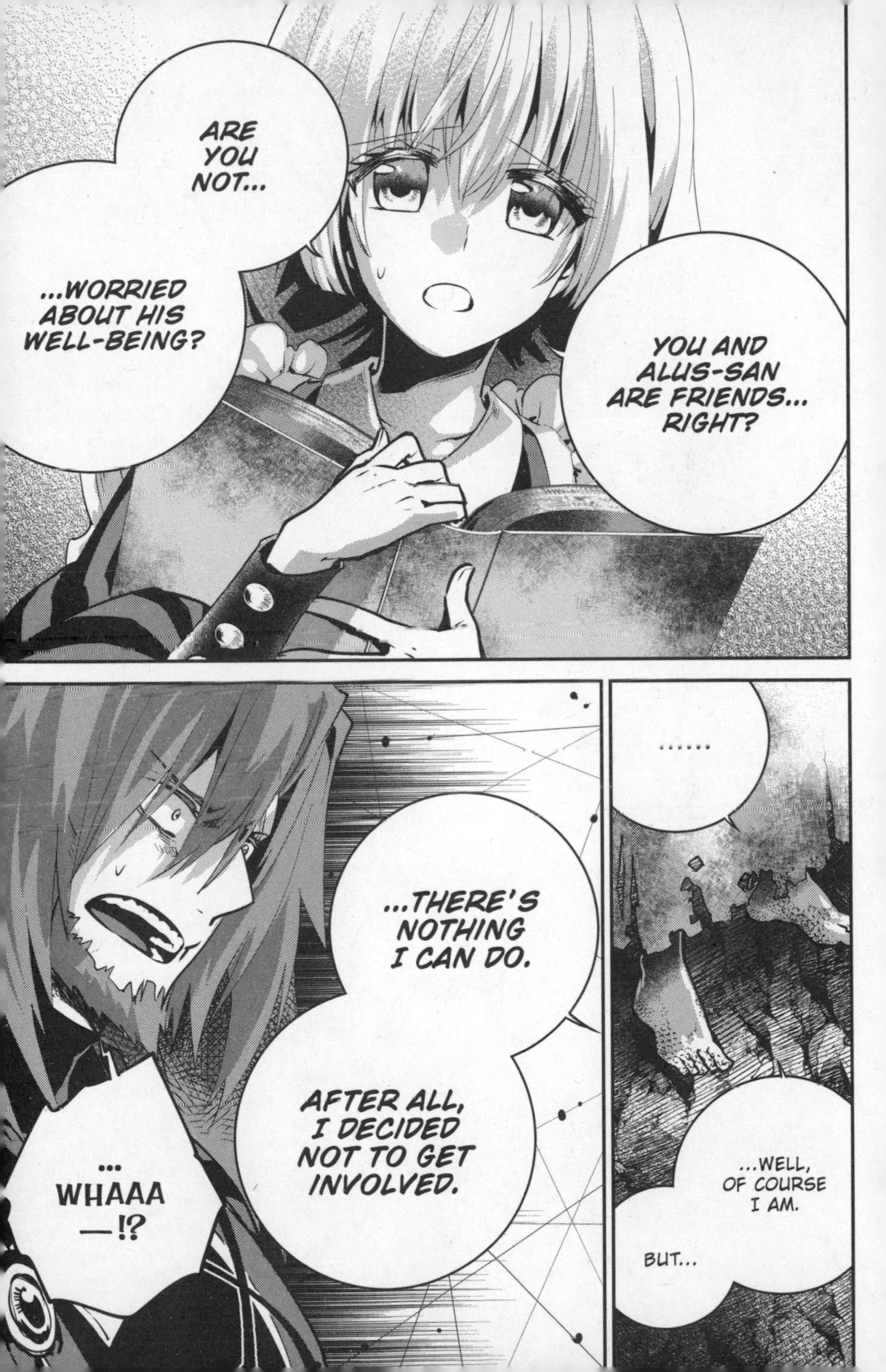
YOU AND ALUS-SAN ARE FRIENDS... RIGHT?
ARE YOU NOT...
...WORRIED ABOUT HIS WELL-BEING?
......
...WELL, OF COURSE I AM.
BUT...
...THERE'S NOTHING I CAN DO.
AFTER ALL, I DECIDED NOT TO GET INVOLVED.
...WHAAA—!?

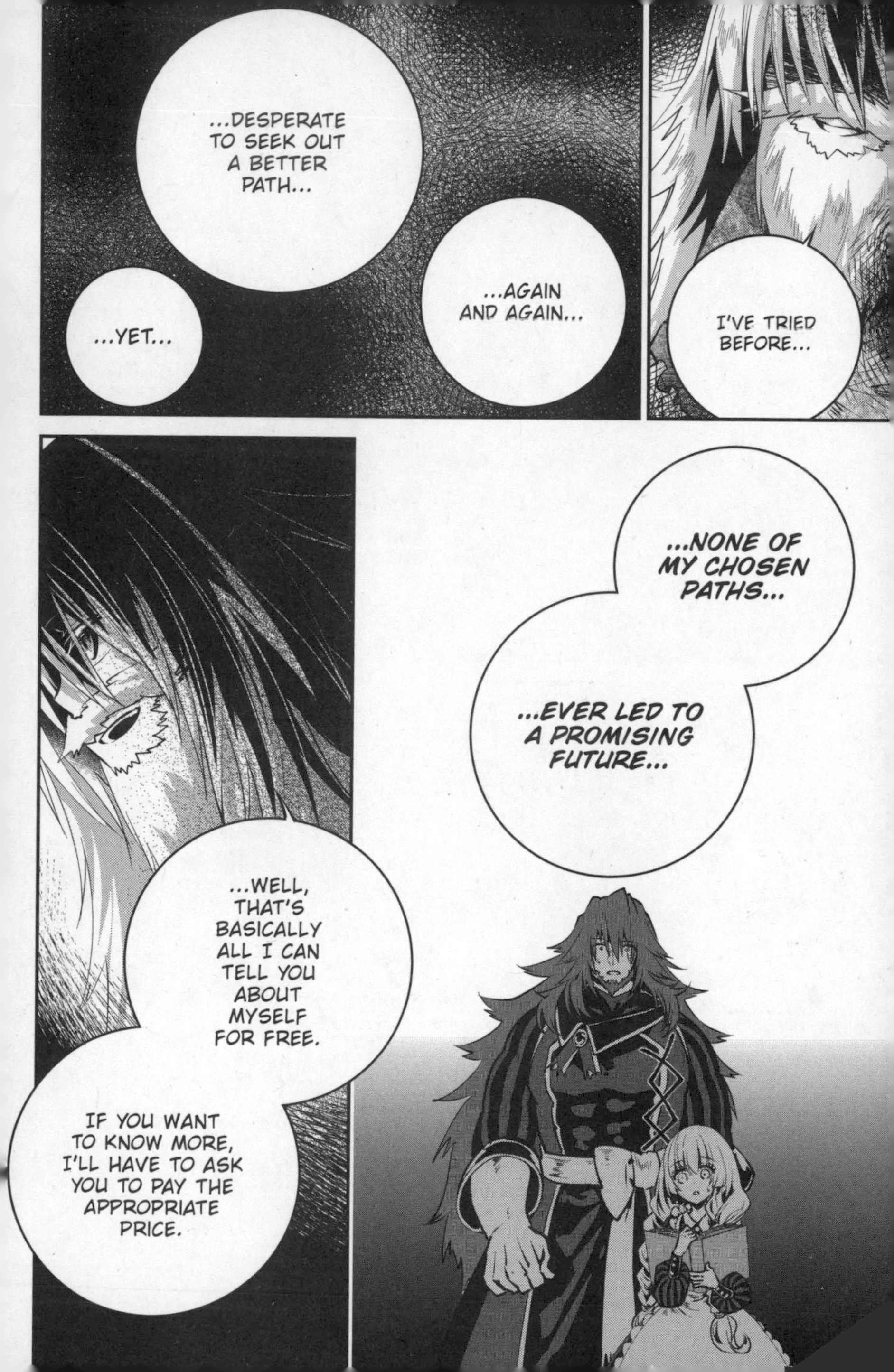
I'VE TRIED BEFORE...
...AGAIN AND AGAIN...
...DESPERATE TO SEEK OUT A BETTER PATH...
...YET...
...NONE OF MY CHOSEN PATHS...
...EVER LED TO A PROMISING FUTURE...
...WELL, THAT'S BASICALLY ALL I CAN TELL YOU ABOUT MYSELF FOR FREE.
IF YOU WANT TO KNOW MORE, I'LL HAVE TO ASK YOU TO PAY THE APPROPRIATE PRICE.

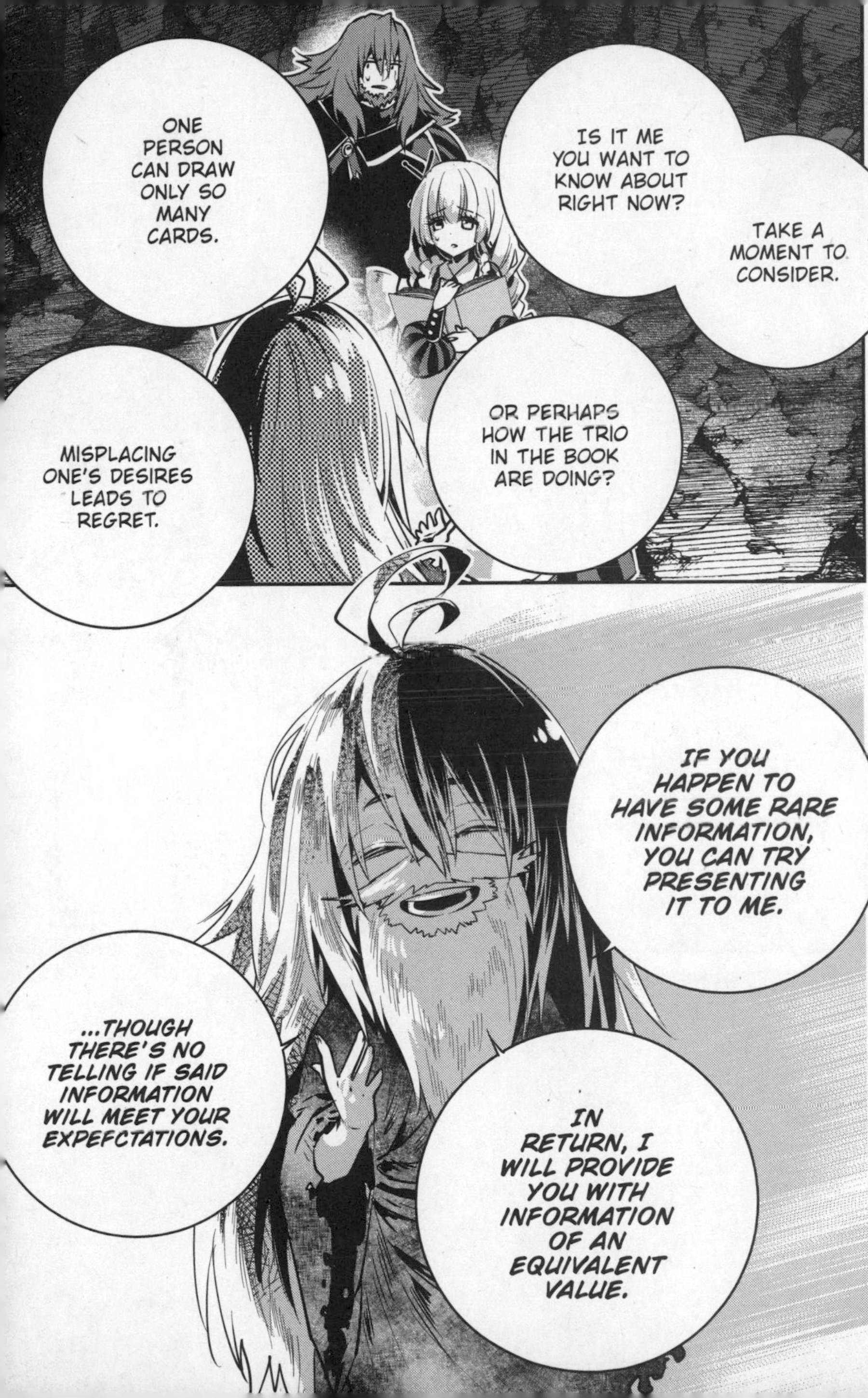
IS IT ME YOU WANT TO KNOW ABOUT RIGHT NOW?
TAKE A MOMENT TO CONSIDER.
OR PERHAPS HOW THE TRIO IN THE BOOK ARE DOING?
ONE PERSON CAN DRAW ONLY SO MANY CARDS.
MISPLACING ONE'S DESIRES LEADS TO REGRET.
IF YOU HAPPEN TO HAVE SOME RARE INFORMATION, YOU CAN TRY PRESENTING IT TO ME.
IN RETURN, I WILL PROVIDE YOU WITH INFORMATION OF AN EQUIVALENT VALUE.
...THOUGH THERE'S NO TELLING IF SAID INFORMATION WILL MEET YOUR EXPEFCTATIONS.

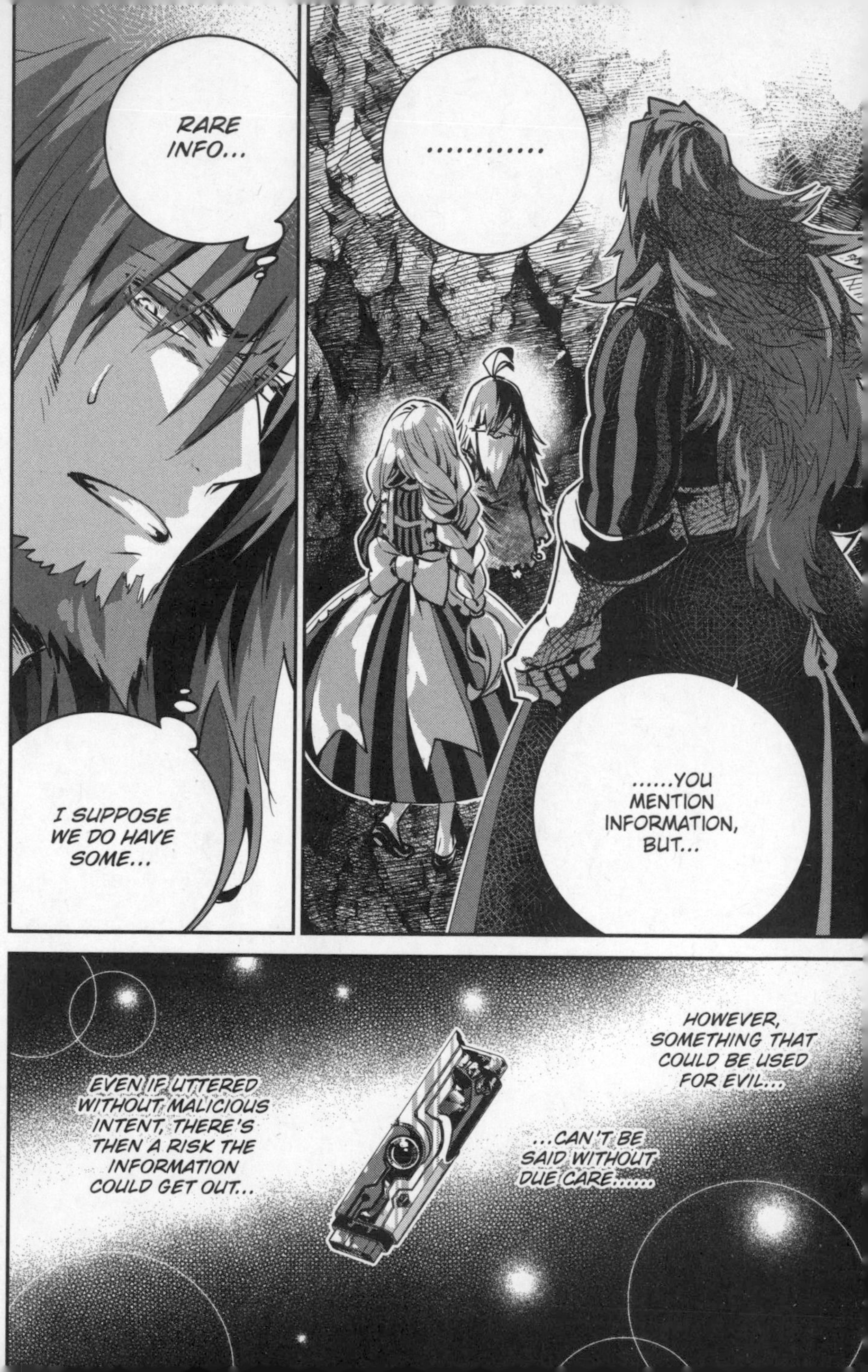
............
......YOU MENTION INFORMATION, BUT...
RARE INFO...
I SUPPOSE WE DO HAVE SOME...
HOWEVER, SOMETHING THAT COULD BE USED FOR EVIL...
...CAN'T BE SAID WITHOUT DUE CARE......
EVEN IF UTTERED WITHOUT MALICIOUS INTENT, THERE'S THEN A RISK THE INFORMATION COULD GET OUT...

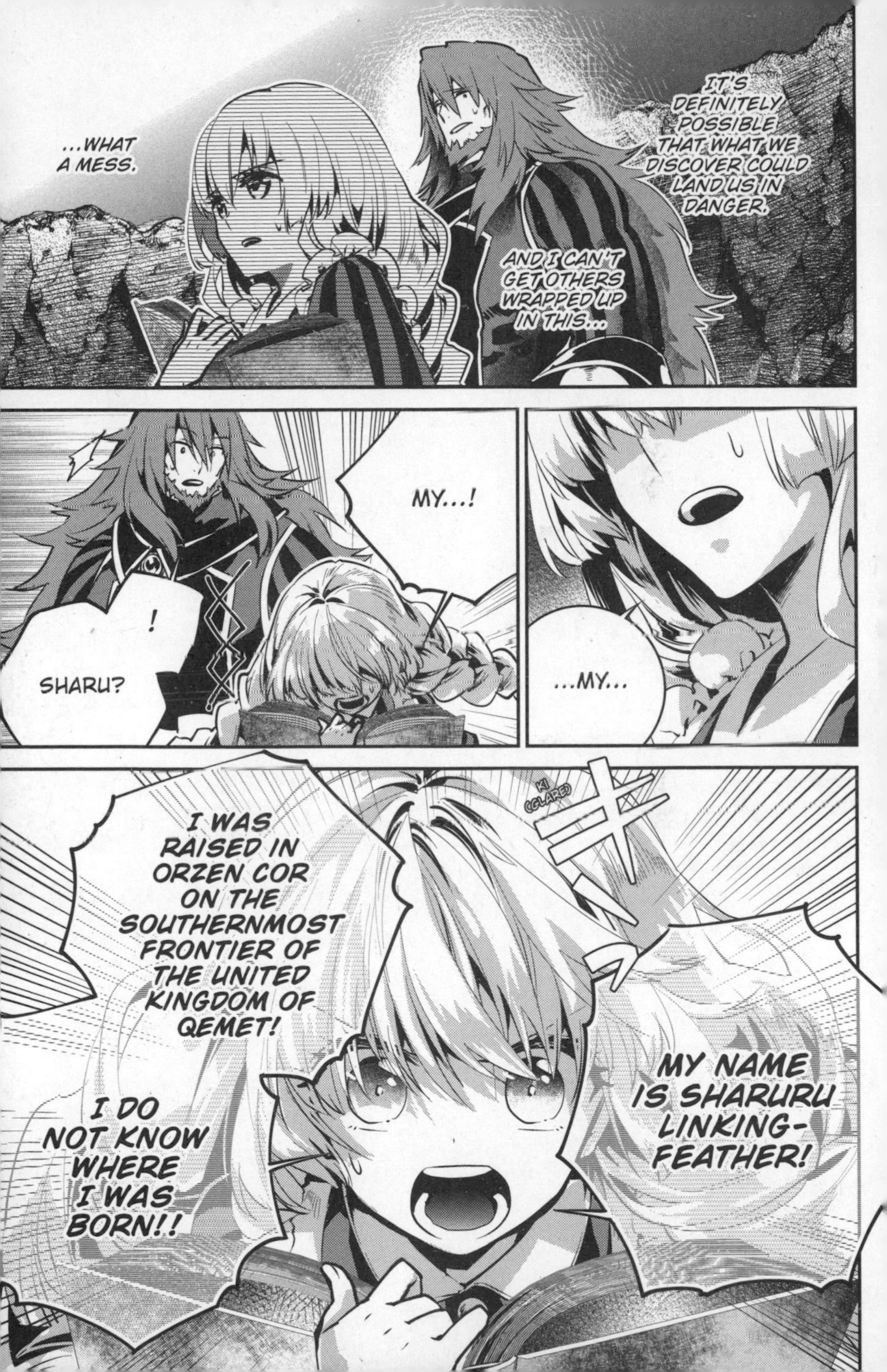
IT'S DEFINITELY POSSIBLE THAT WHAT WE DISCOVER COULD LAND US IN DANGER.
AND I CAN'T GET OTHERS WRAPPED UP IN THIS...
...WHAT A MESS.
...MY...
MY...!
!
SHARU?
KI (GLARE)
MY NAME IS SHARURU LINKING-FEATHER!
I WAS RAISED IN ORZEN COR ON THE SOUTHERNMOST FRONTIER OF THE UNITED KINGDOM OF QEMET!
I DO NOT KNOW WHERE I WAS BORN!!

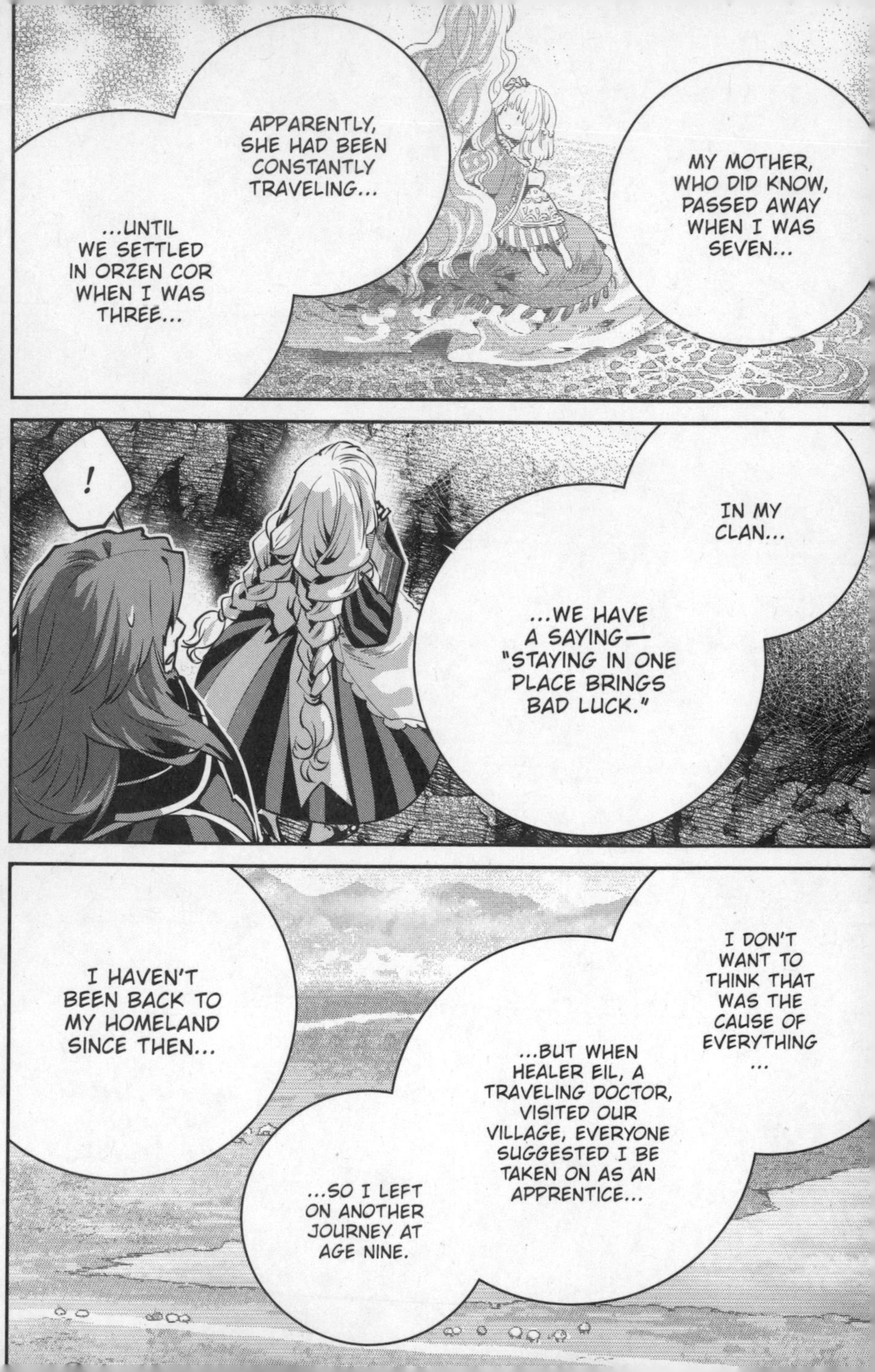
MY MOTHER, WHO DID KNOW, PASSED AWAY WHEN I WAS SEVEN...
APPARENTLY, SHE HAD BEEN CONSTANTLY TRAVELING...
...UNTIL WE SETTLED IN ORZEN COR WHEN I WAS THREE...
IN MY CLAN...
...WE HAVE A SAYING—"STAYING IN ONE PLACE BRINGS BAD LUCK."
!
I DON'T WANT TO THINK THAT WAS THE CAUSE OF EVERYTHING...
...BUT WHEN HEALER EIL, A TRAVELING DOCTOR, VISITED OUR VILLAGE, EVERYONE SUGGESTED I BE TAKEN ON AS AN APPRENTICE...
...SO I LEFT ON ANOTHER JOURNEY AT AGE NINE.
I HAVEN'T BEEN BACK TO MY HOMELAND SINCE THEN...

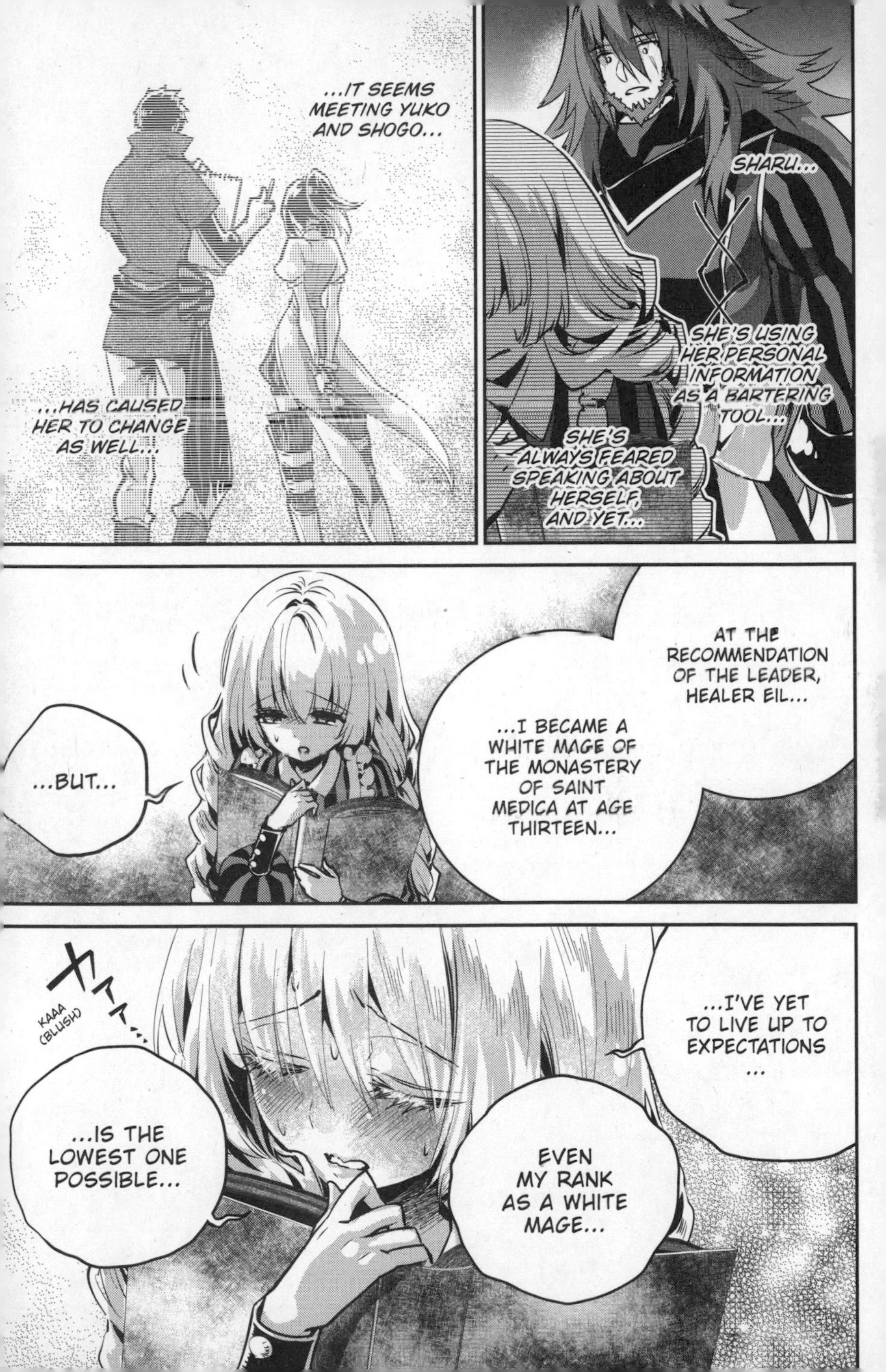
SHARU...
SHE'S USING HER PERSONAL INFORMATION AS A BARTERING TOOL...
SHE'S ALWAYS FEARED SPEAKING ABOUT HERSELF, AND YET...
...IT SEEMS MEETING YUKO AND SHOGO...
...HAS CAUSED HER TO CHANGE AS WELL...
AT THE RECOMMENDATION OF THE LEADER, HEALER EIL...
...I BECAME A WHITE MAGE OF THE MONASTERY OF SAINT MEDICA AT AGE THIRTEEN...
...BUT...
...I'VE YET TO LIVE UP TO EXPECTATIONS...
EVEN MY RANK AS A WHITE MAGE...
...IS THE LOWEST ONE POSSIBLE...
カァァ...
KAAA (BLUSH)

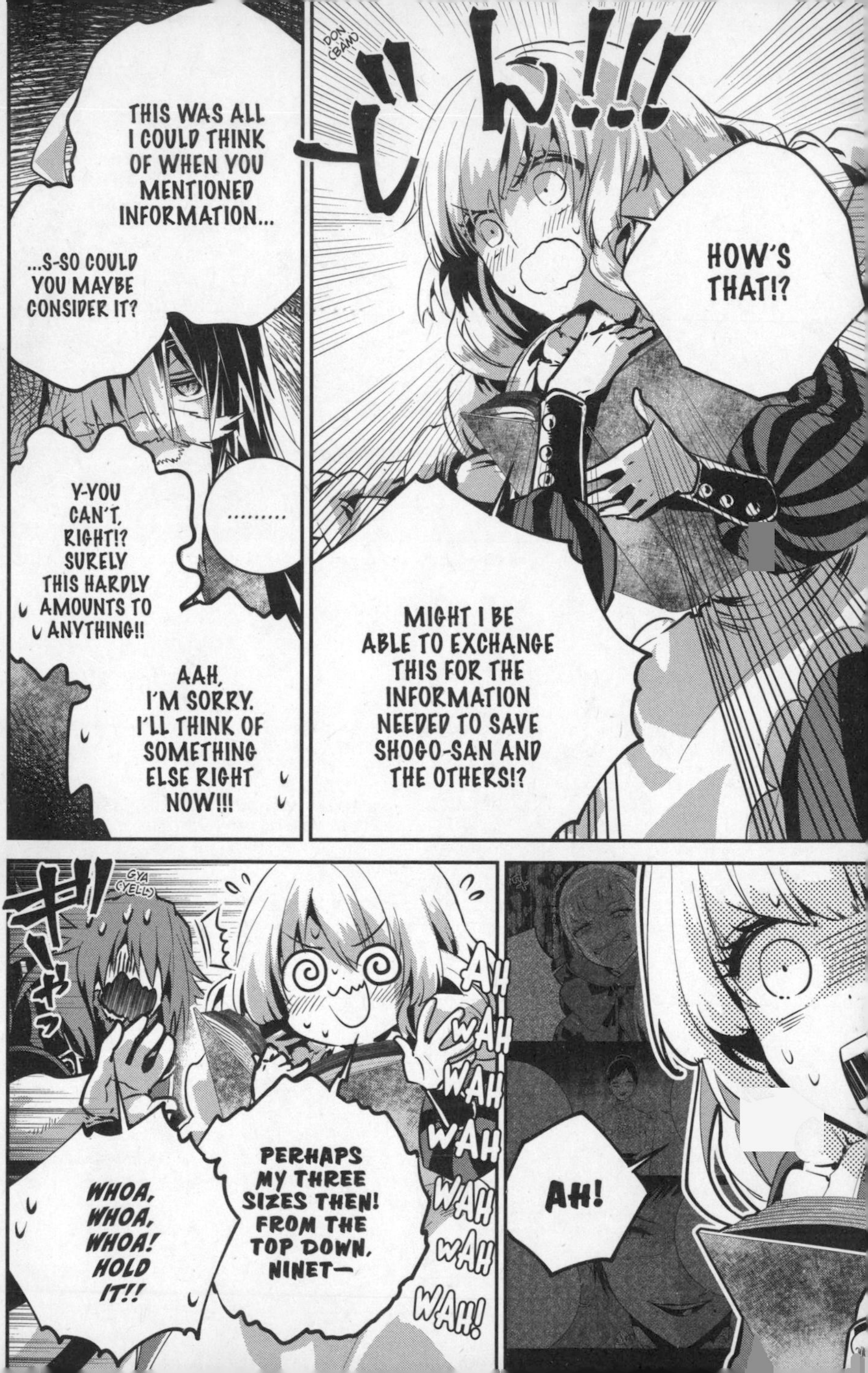
DON (BAM)
HOW'S THAT!?
MIGHT I BE ABLE TO EXCHANGE THIS FOR THE INFORMATION NEEDED TO SAVE SHOGO-SAN AND THE OTHERS!?
THIS WAS ALL I COULD THINK OF WHEN YOU MENTIONED INFORMATION...
...S-SO COULD YOU MAYBE CONSIDER IT?
..........
Y-YOU CAN'T, RIGHT!? SURELY THIS HARDLY AMOUNTS TO ANYTHING!!
AAH, I'M SORRY. I'LL THINK OF SOMETHING ELSE RIGHT NOW!!!
AH!
AH WAH WAH WAH WAH WAH WAH!
GYA (YELL)
PERHAPS MY THREE SIZES THEN! FROM THE TOP DOWN, NINET—
WHOA, WHOA, WHOA! HOLD IT!!

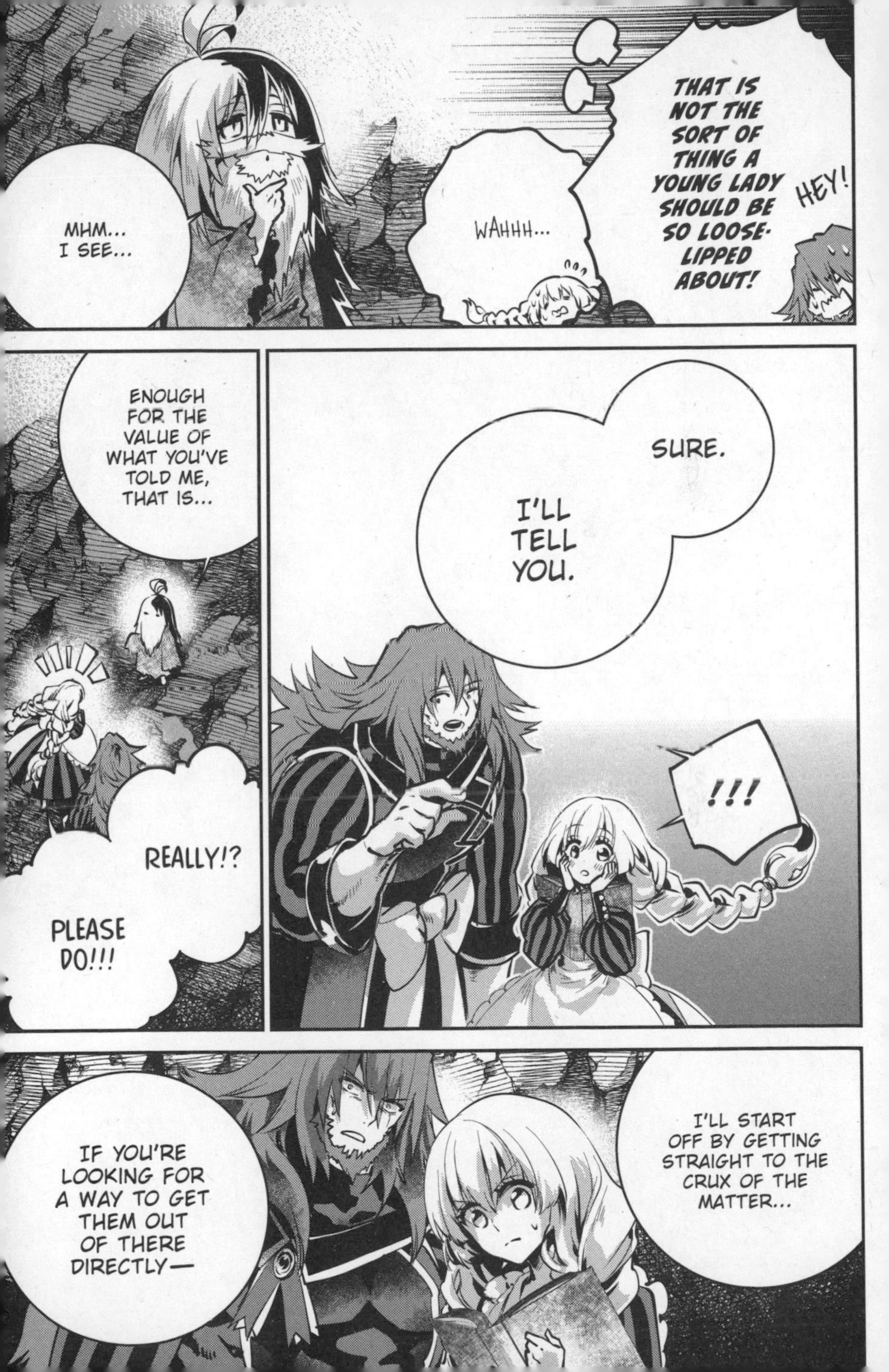
HEY!
THAT IS NOT THE SORT OF THING A YOUNG LADY SHOULD BE SO LOOSE-LIPPED ABOUT!
WAHHH...
MHM... I SEE...
SURE.
I'LL TELL YOU.
!!!
ENOUGH FOR THE VALUE OF WHAT YOU'VE TOLD ME, THAT IS...
REALLY!?
PLEASE DO!!!
I'LL START OFF BY GETTING STRAIGHT TO THE CRUX OF THE MATTER...
IF YOU'RE LOOKING FOR A WAY TO GET THEM OUT OF THERE DIRECTLY—

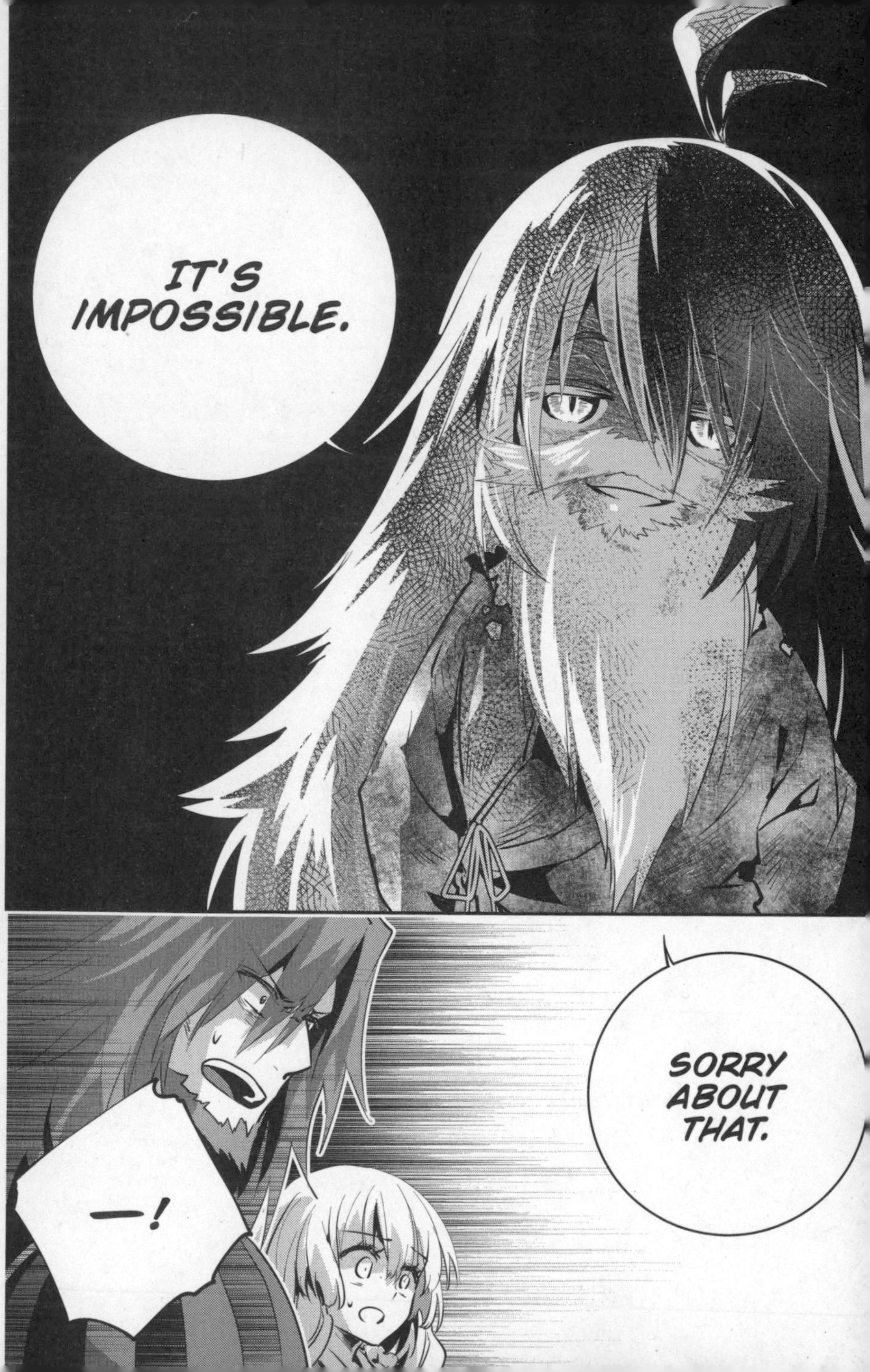
IT'S IMPOSSIBLE.
SORRY ABOUT THAT.
—!

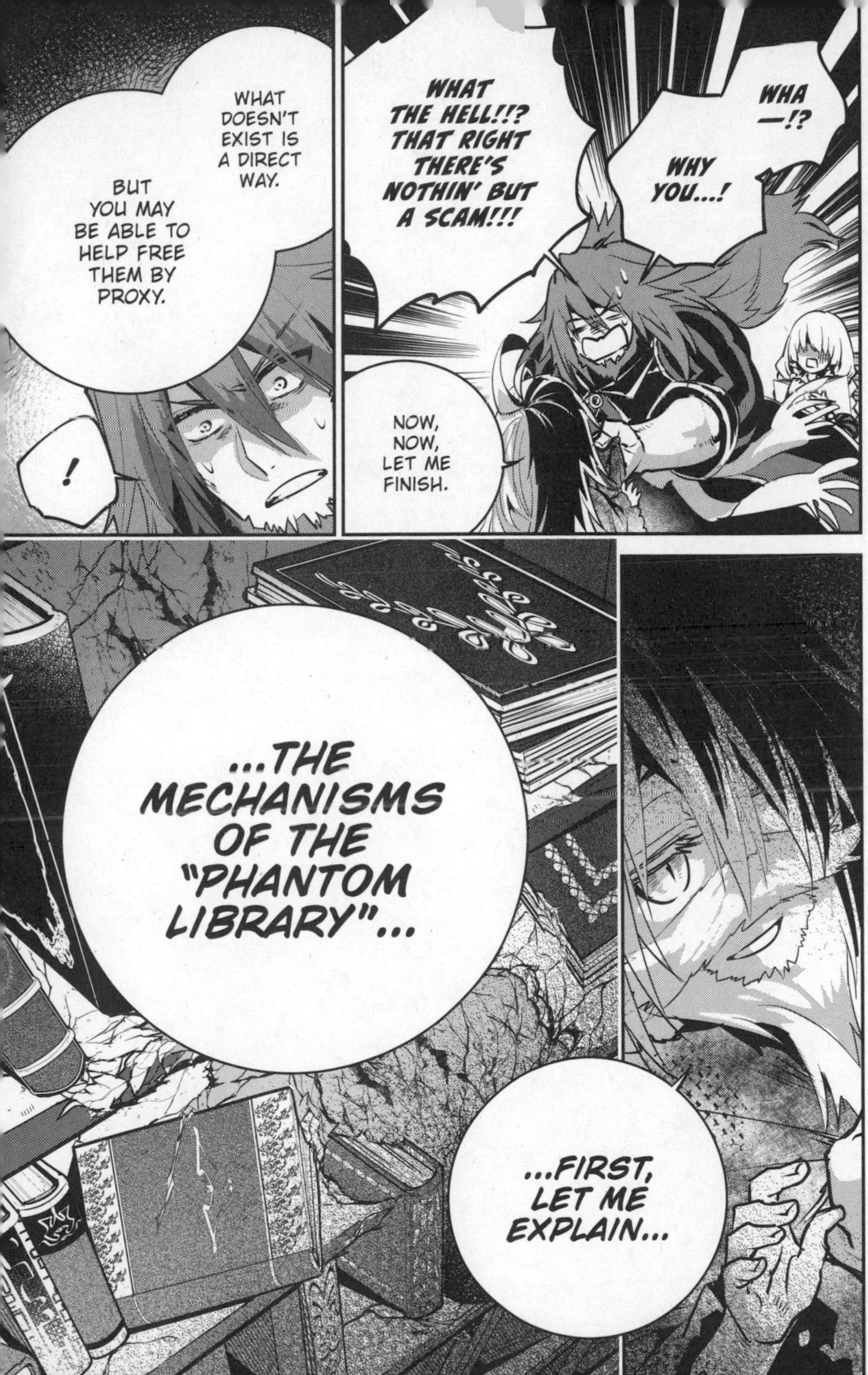
WHA—!?
WHY YOU...!
WHAT THE HELL!!? THAT RIGHT THERE'S NOTHIN' BUT A SCAM!!!
NOW, NOW, LET ME FINISH.
WHAT DOESN'T EXIST IS A DIRECT WAY.
BUT YOU MAY BE ABLE TO HELP FREE THEM BY PROXY.
!
...FIRST, LET ME EXPLAIN...
...THE MECHANISMS OF THE "PHANTOM LIBRARY"...

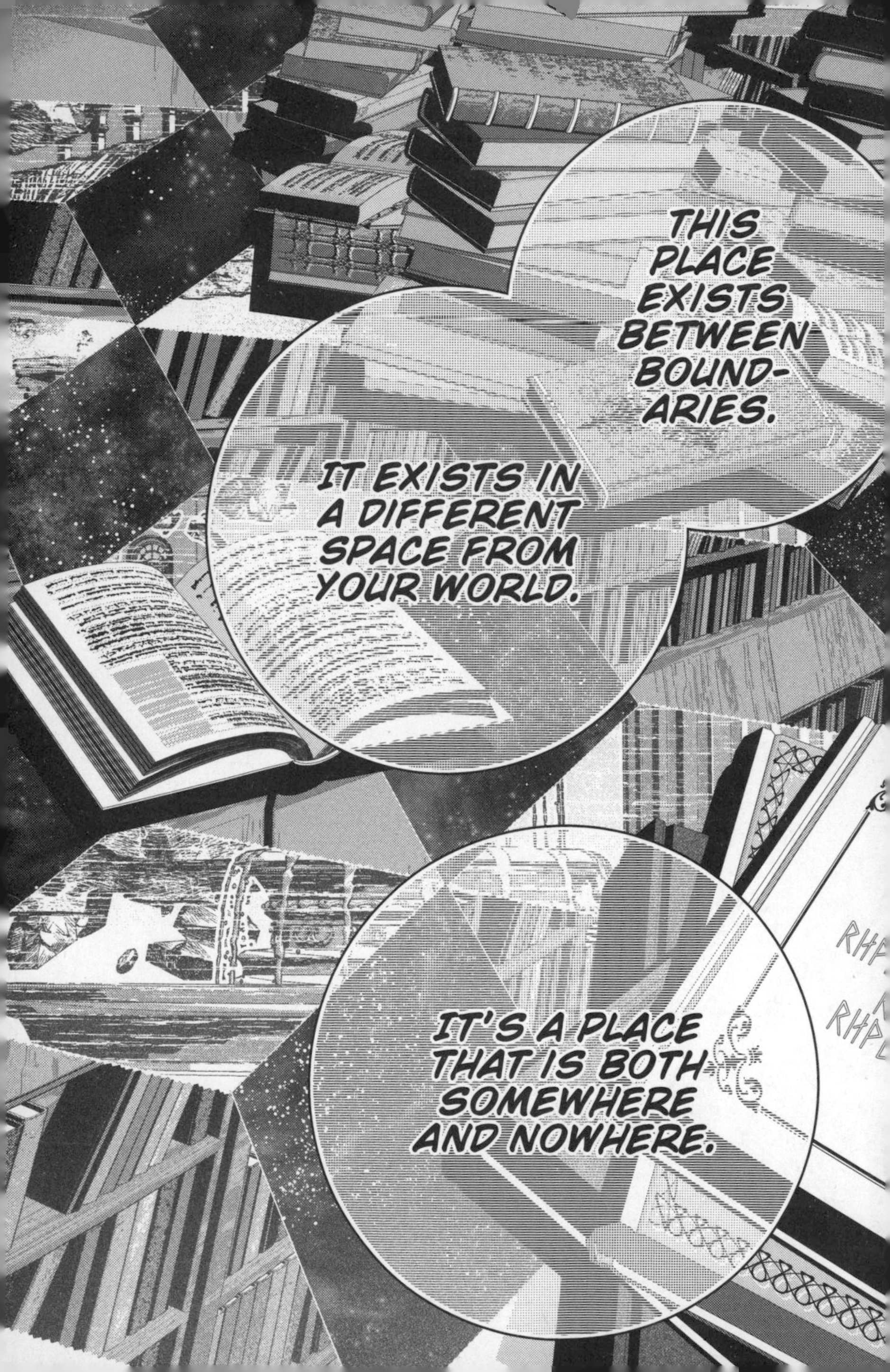
THIS PLACE EXISTS BETWEEN BOUND-ARIES.
IT EXISTS IN A DIFFERENT SPACE FROM YOUR WORLD.
IT'S A PLACE THAT IS BOTH SOMEWHERE AND NOWHERE.

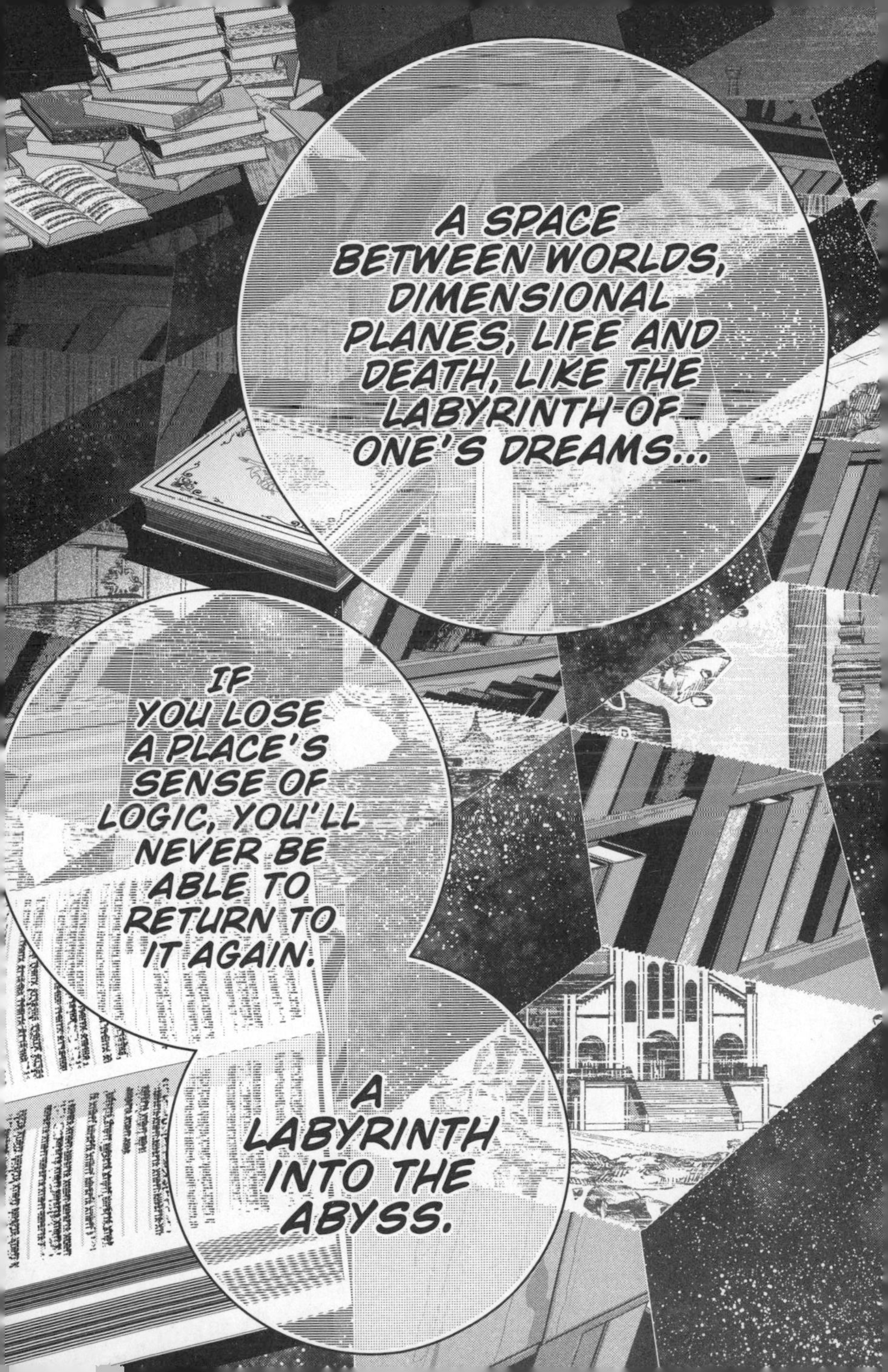
A SPACE BETWEEN WORLDS, DIMENSIONAL PLANES, LIFE AND DEATH, LIKE THE LABYRINTH OF ONE'S DREAMS...
IF YOU LOSE A PLACE'S SENSE OF LOGIC, YOU'LL NEVER BE ABLE TO RETURN TO IT AGAIN.
A LABYRINTH INTO THE ABYSS.

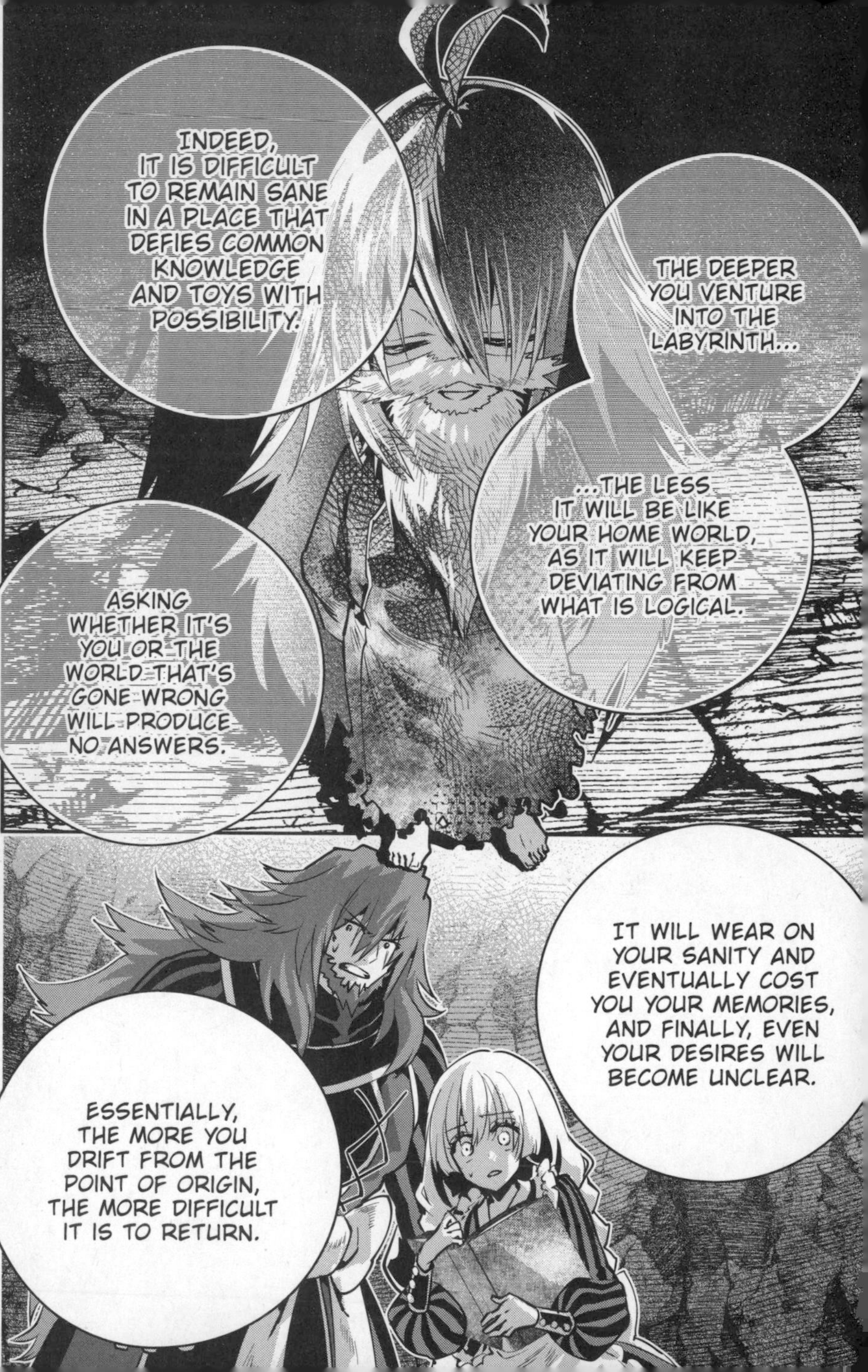
INDEED, IT IS DIFFICULT TO REMAIN SANE IN A PLACE THAT DEFIES COMMON KNOWLEDGE AND TOYS WITH POSSIBILITY.
THE DEEPER YOU VENTURE INTO THE LABYRINTH...
...THE LESS IT WILL BE LIKE YOUR HOME WORLD, AS IT WILL KEEP DEVIATING FROM WHAT IS LOGICAL.
ASKING WHETHER IT'S YOU OR THE WORLD THAT'S GONE WRONG WILL PRODUCE NO ANSWERS.
IT WILL WEAR ON YOUR SANITY AND EVENTUALLY COST YOU YOUR MEMORIES, AND FINALLY, EVEN YOUR DESIRES WILL BECOME UNCLEAR.
ESSENTIALLY, THE MORE YOU DRIFT FROM THE POINT OF ORIGIN, THE MORE DIFFICULT IT IS TO RETURN.

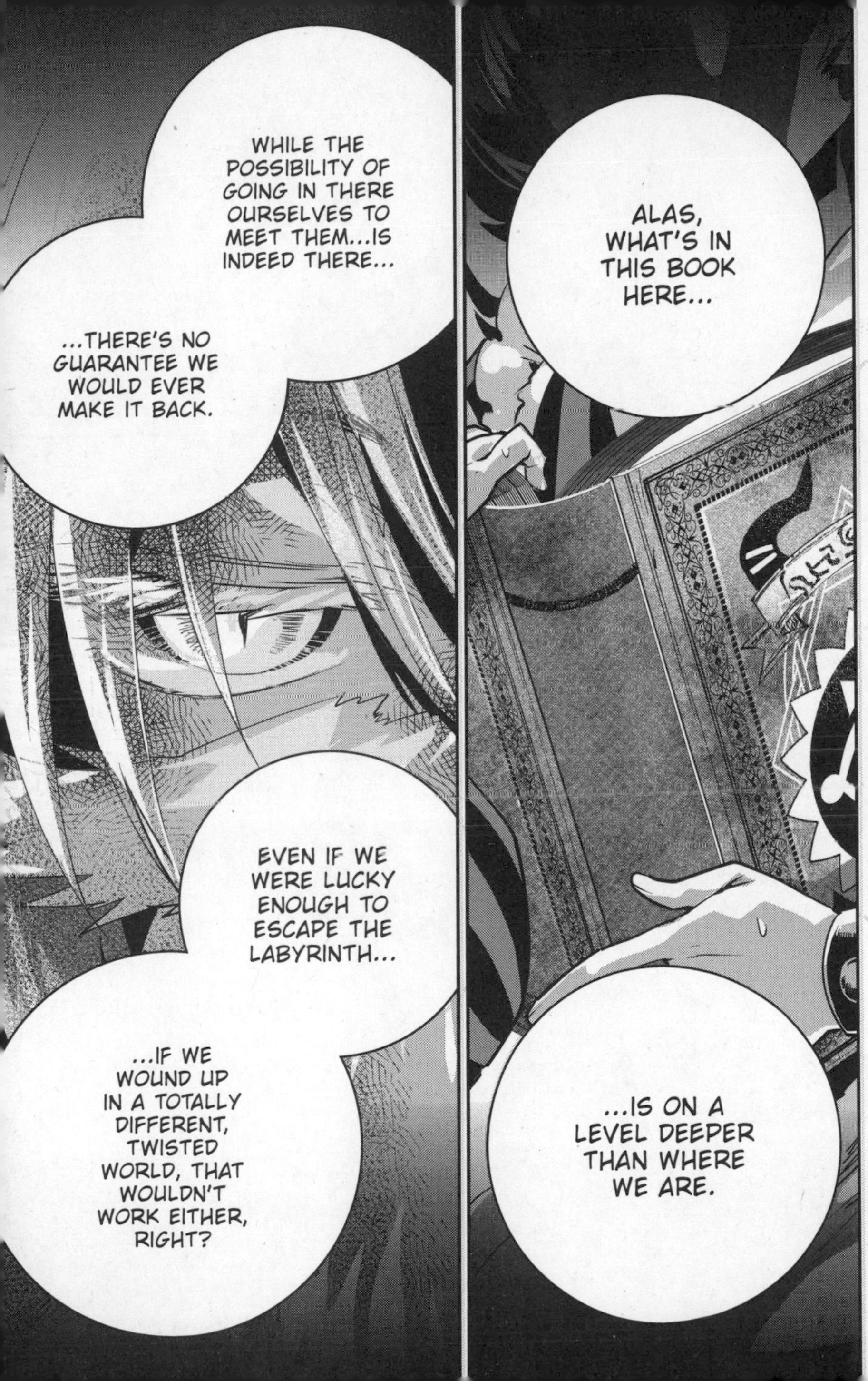
ALAS, WHAT'S IN THIS BOOK HERE...
...IS ON A LEVEL DEEPER THAN WHERE WE ARE.
WHILE THE POSSIBILITY OF GOING IN THERE OURSELVES TO MEET THEM...IS INDEED THERE...
...THERE'S NO GUARANTEE WE WOULD EVER MAKE IT BACK.
EVEN IF WE WERE LUCKY ENOUGH TO ESCAPE THE LABYRINTH...
...IF WE WOUND UP IN A TOTALLY DIFFERENT, TWISTED WORLD, THAT WOULDN'T WORK EITHER, RIGHT?

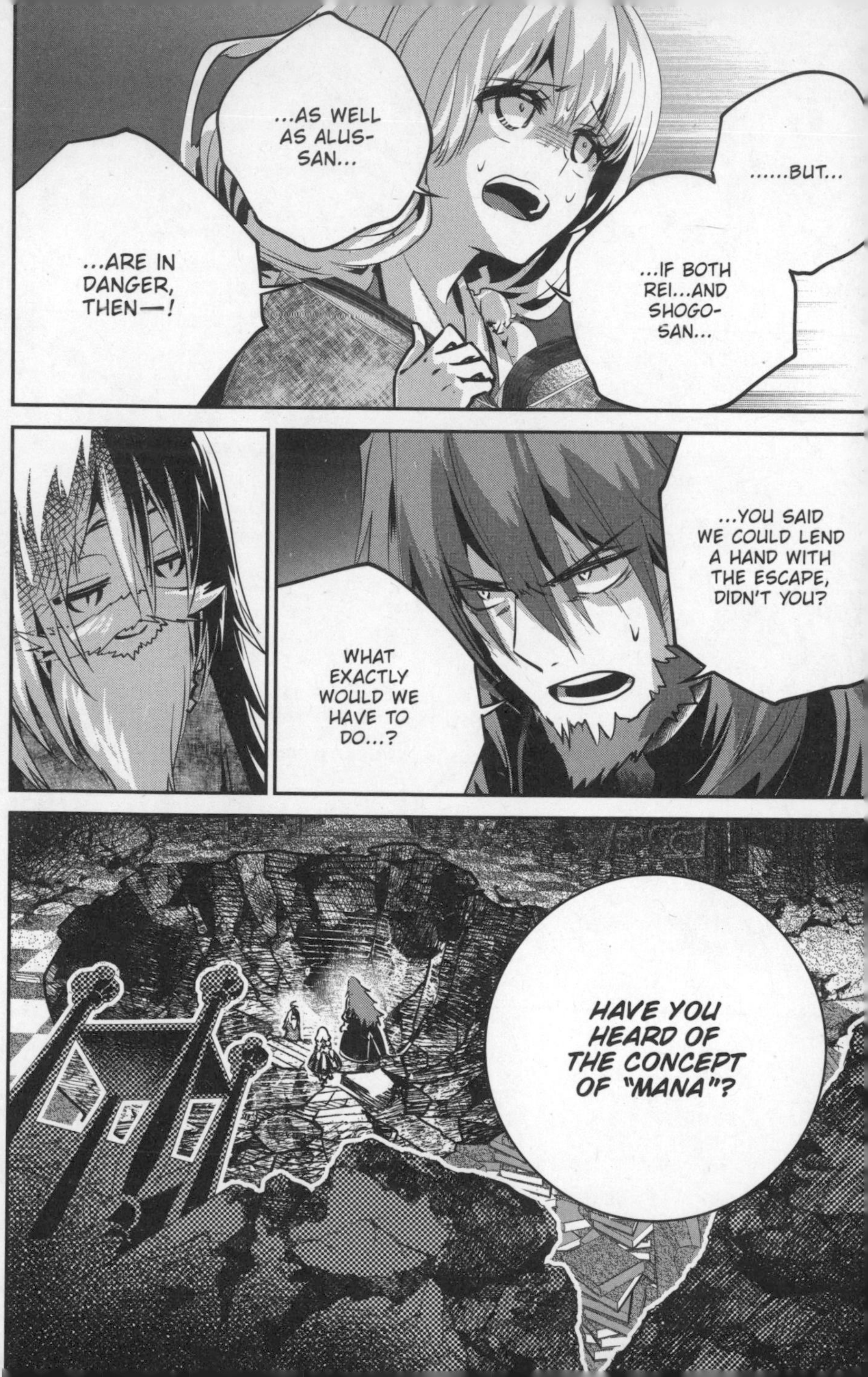

......BUT...
...IF BOTH REI...AND SHOGO-SAN...
...AS WELL AS ALUS-SAN...
...ARE IN DANGER, THEN—!
...YOU SAID WE COULD LEND A HAND WITH THE ESCAPE, DIDN'T YOU?
WHAT EXACTLY WOULD WE HAVE TO DO...?
HAVE YOU HEARD OF THE CONCEPT OF "MANA"?

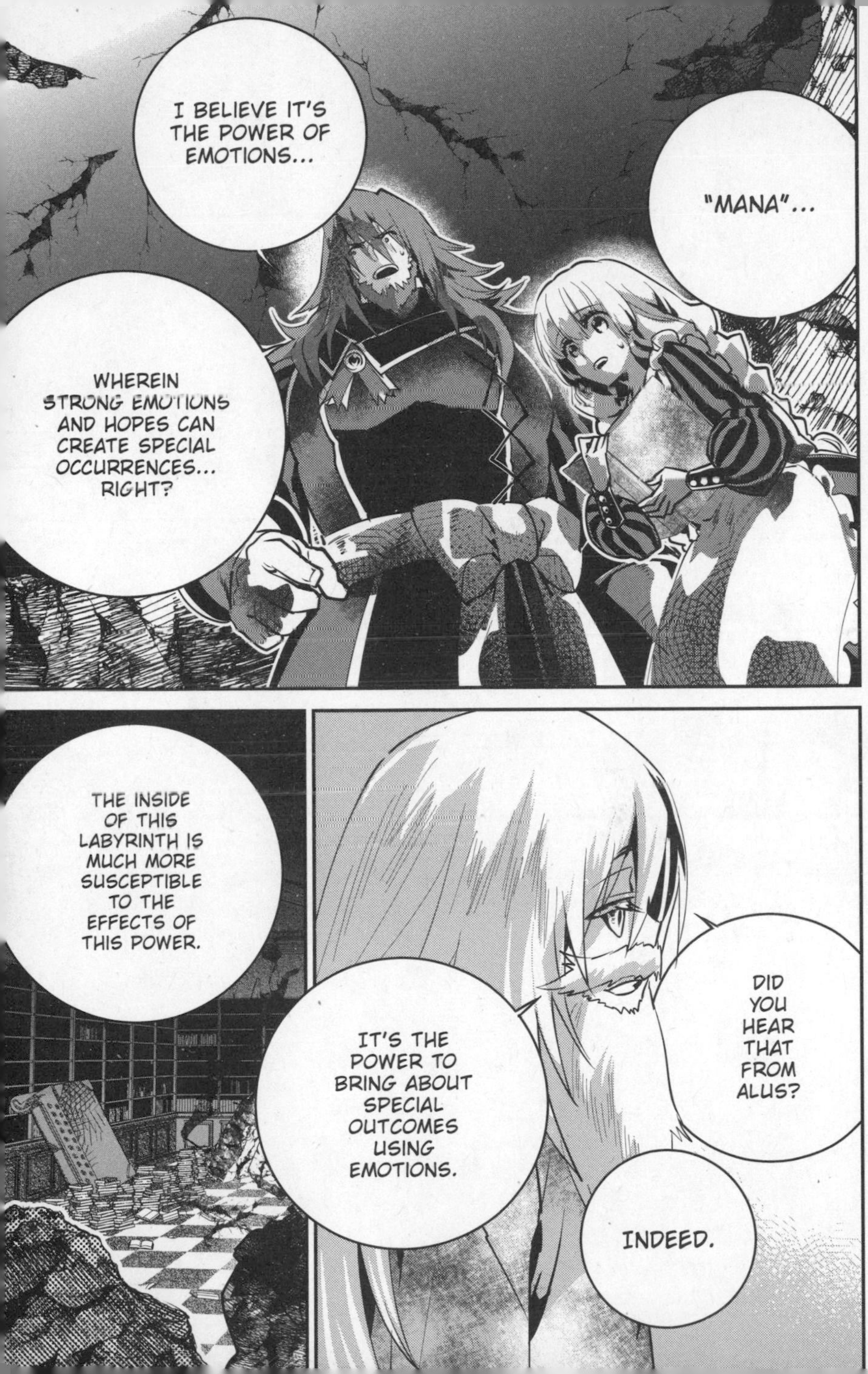
"MANA"...
I BELIEVE IT'S THE POWER OF EMOTIONS...
WHEREIN STRONG EMOTIONS AND HOPES CAN CREATE SPECIAL OCCURRENCES... RIGHT?
DID YOU HEAR THAT FROM ALUS?
INDEED.
IT'S THE POWER TO BRING ABOUT SPECIAL OUTCOMES USING EMOTIONS.
THE INSIDE OF THIS LABYRINTH IS MUCH MORE SUSCEPTIBLE TO THE EFFECTS OF THIS POWER.

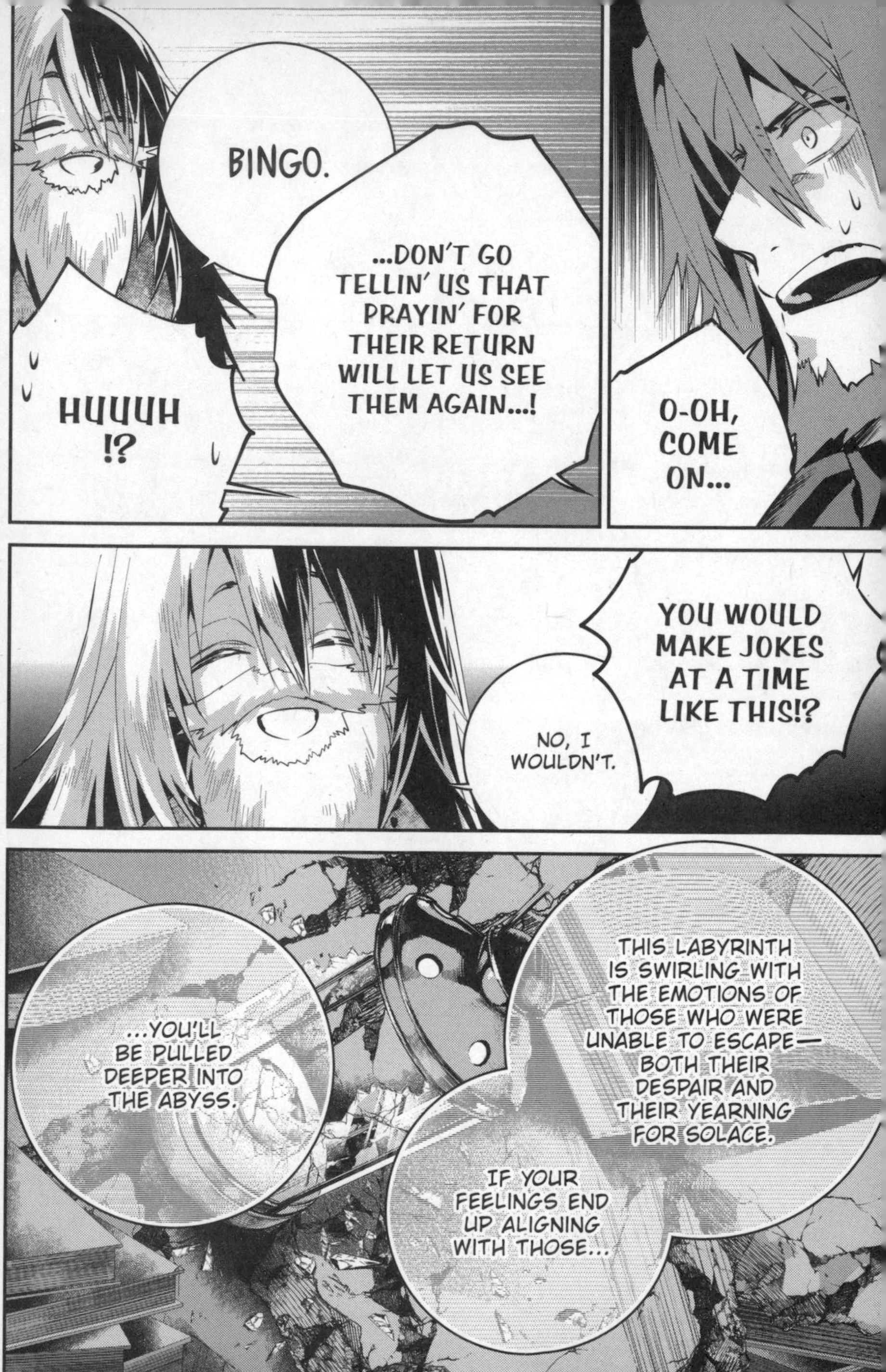
O-OH, COME ON...
BINGO.
...DON'T GO TELLIN' US THAT PRAYIN' FOR THEIR RETURN WILL LET US SEE THEM AGAIN...!
HUUUH !?
YOU WOULD MAKE JOKES AT A TIME LIKE THIS!?
NO, I WOULDN'T.
THIS LABYRINTH IS SWIRLING WITH THE EMOTIONS OF THOSE WHO WERE UNABLE TO ESCAPE—BOTH THEIR DESPAIR AND THEIR YEARNING FOR SOLACE.
IF YOUR FEELINGS END UP ALIGNING WITH THOSE...
...YOU'LL BE PULLED DEEPER INTO THE ABYSS.

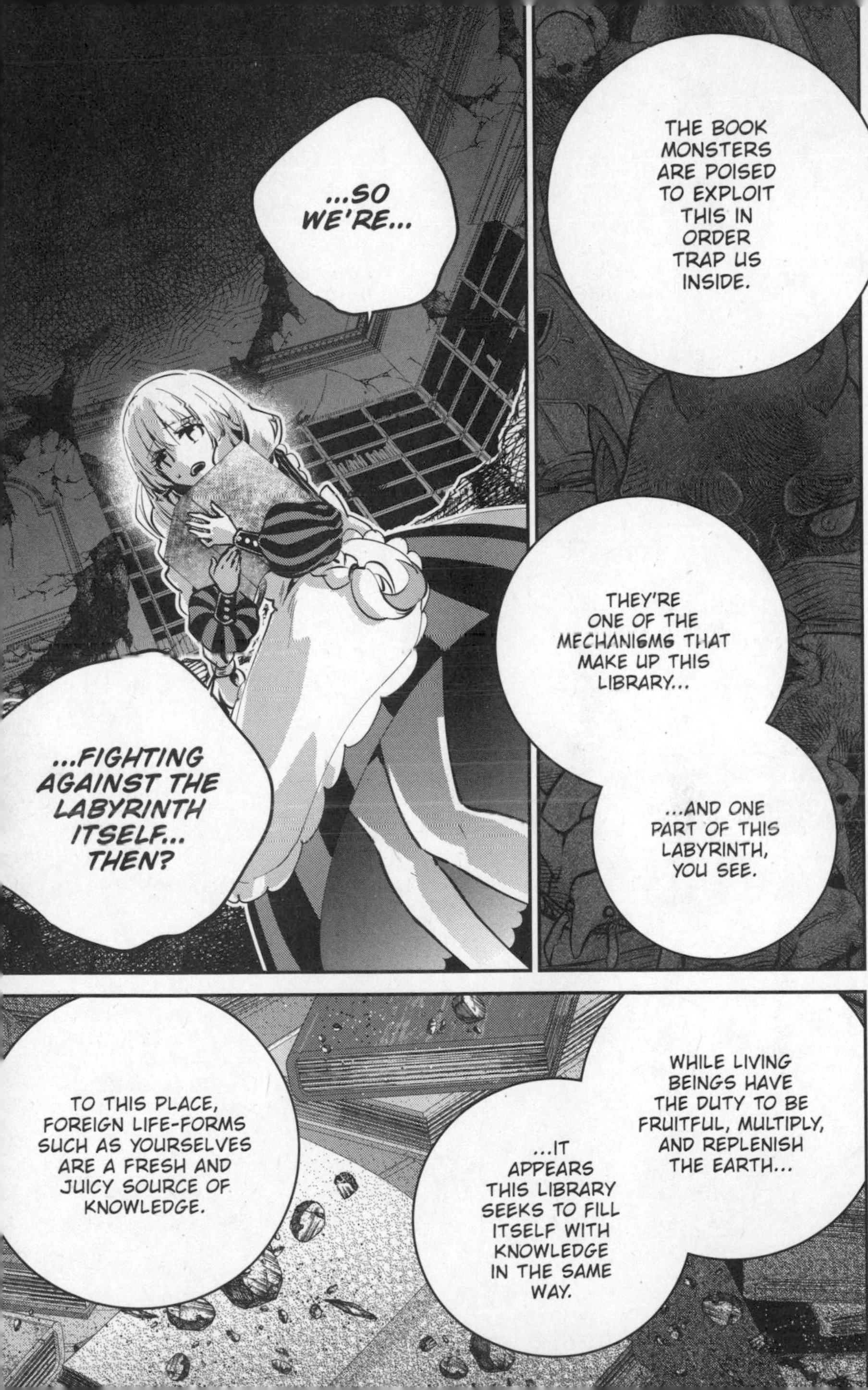
THE BOOK MONSTERS ARE POISED TO EXPLOIT THIS IN ORDER TRAP US INSIDE.
THEY'RE ONE OF THE MECHANISMS THAT MAKE UP THIS LIBRARY...
...AND ONE PART OF THIS LABYRINTH, YOU SEE.
...SO WE'RE...
...FIGHTING AGAINST THE LABYRINTH ITSELF... THEN?
WHILE LIVING BEINGS HAVE THE DUTY TO BE FRUITFUL, MULTIPLY, AND REPLENISH THE EARTH...
...IT APPEARS THIS LIBRARY SEEKS TO FILL ITSELF WITH KNOWLEDGE IN THE SAME WAY.
TO THIS PLACE, FOREIGN LIFE-FORMS SUCH AS YOURSELVES ARE A FRESH AND JUICY SOURCE OF KNOWLEDGE.

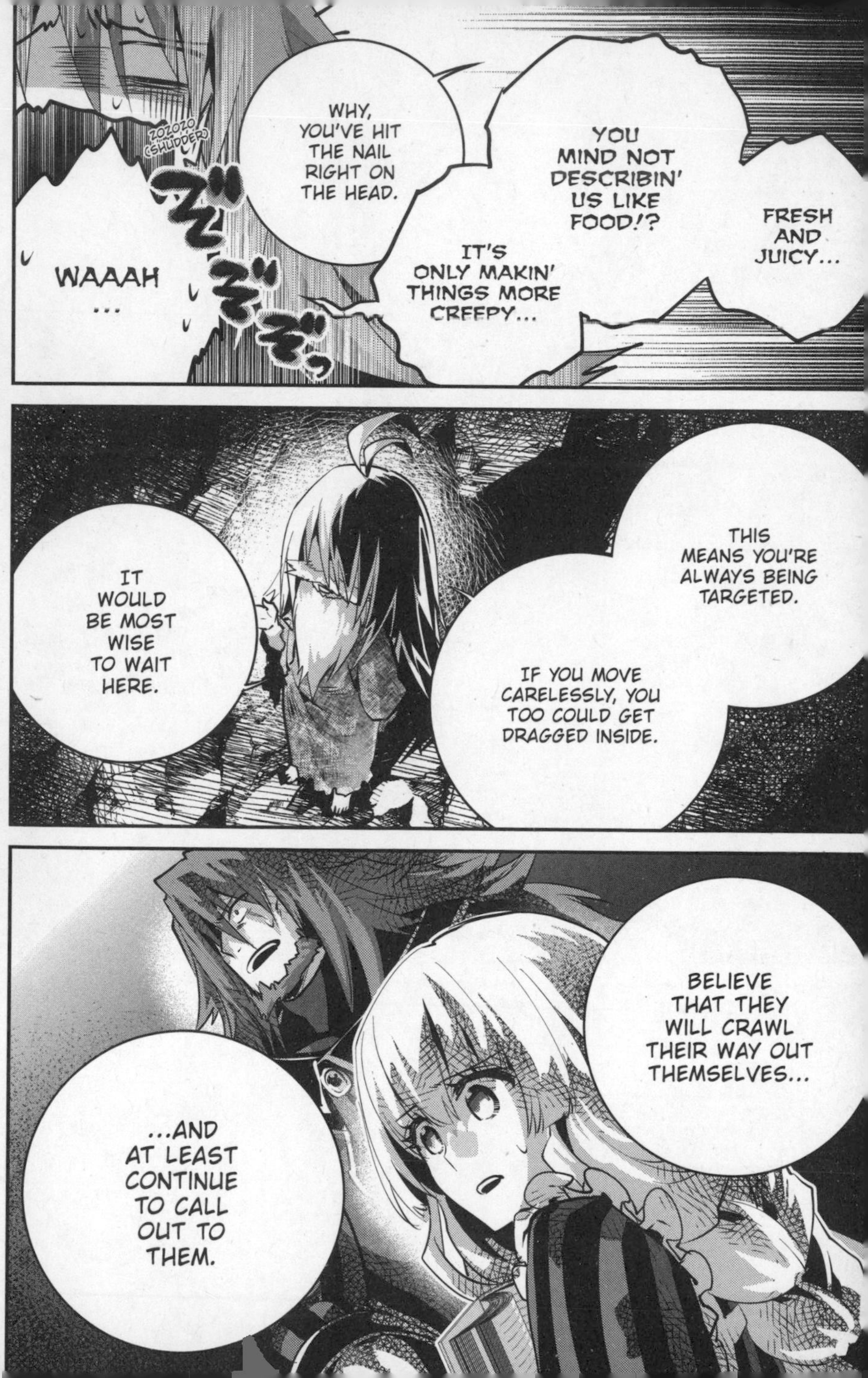
FRESH AND JUICY...
YOU MIND NOT DESCRIBIN' US LIKE FOOD!?
IT'S ONLY MAKIN' THINGS MORE CREEPY...
WHY, YOU'VE HIT THE NAIL RIGHT ON THE HEAD.
ZOZOZO (SHUDDER)
WAAAH ...
THIS MEANS YOU'RE ALWAYS BEING TARGETED.
IF YOU MOVE CARELESSLY, YOU TOO COULD GET DRAGGED INSIDE.
IT WOULD BE MOST WISE TO WAIT HERE.
BELIEVE THAT THEY WILL CRAWL THEIR WAY OUT THEMSELVES...
...AND AT LEAST CONTINUE TO CALL OUT TO THEM.

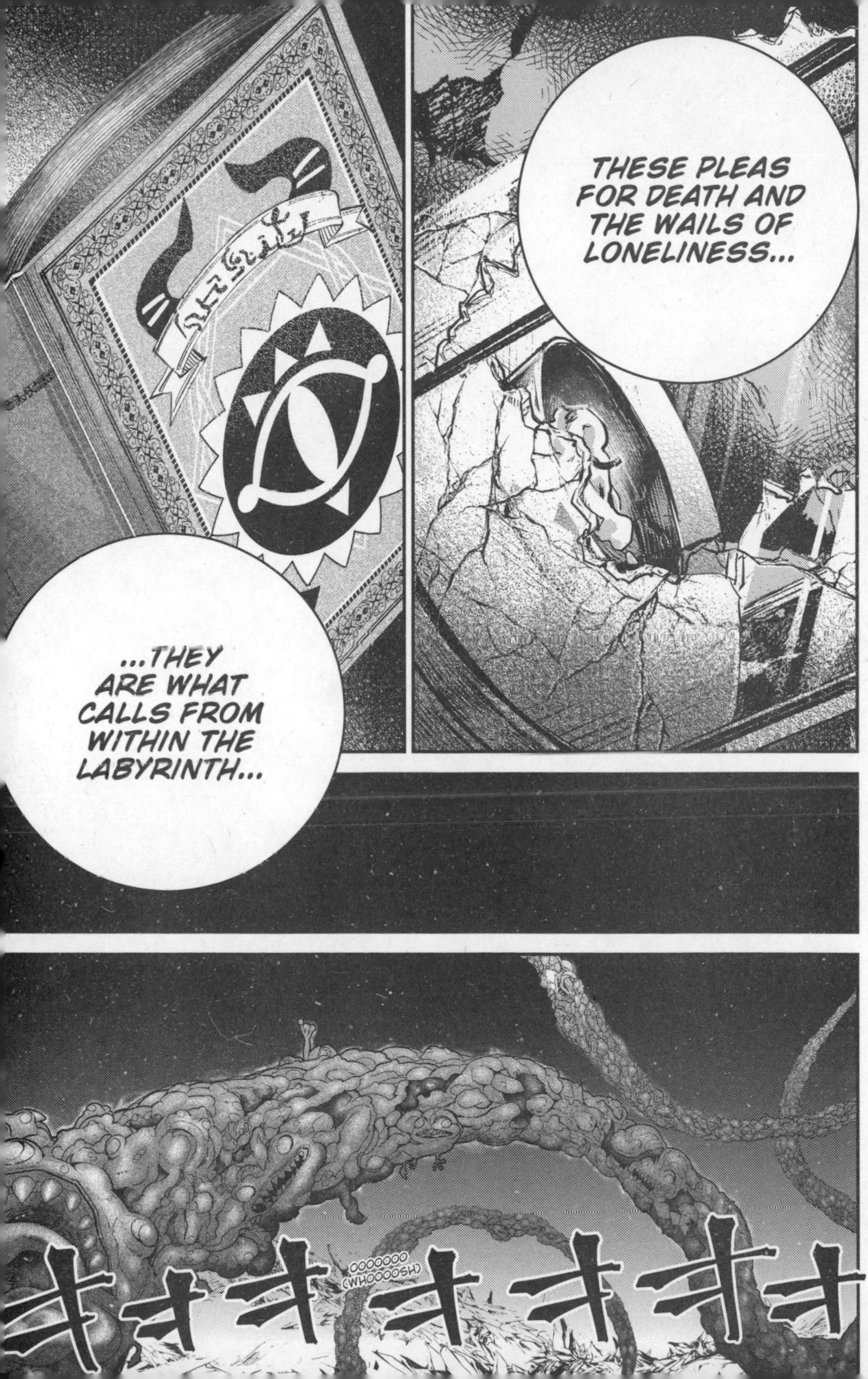
THESE PLEAS FOR DEATH AND THE WAILS OF LONELINESS...
...THEY ARE WHAT CALLS FROM WITHIN THE LABYRINTH...
OOOOOOO
(WHOOOOSH)

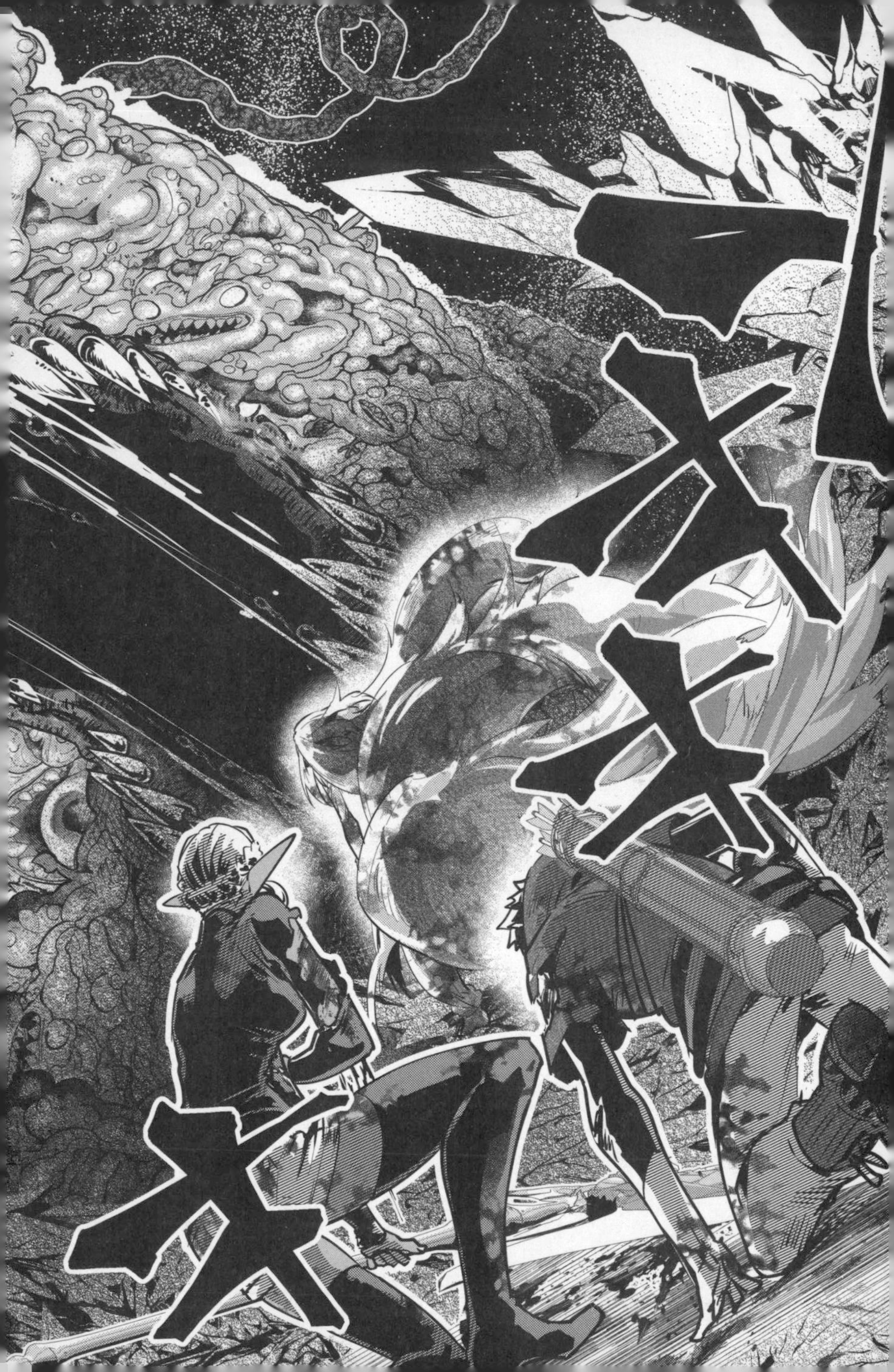

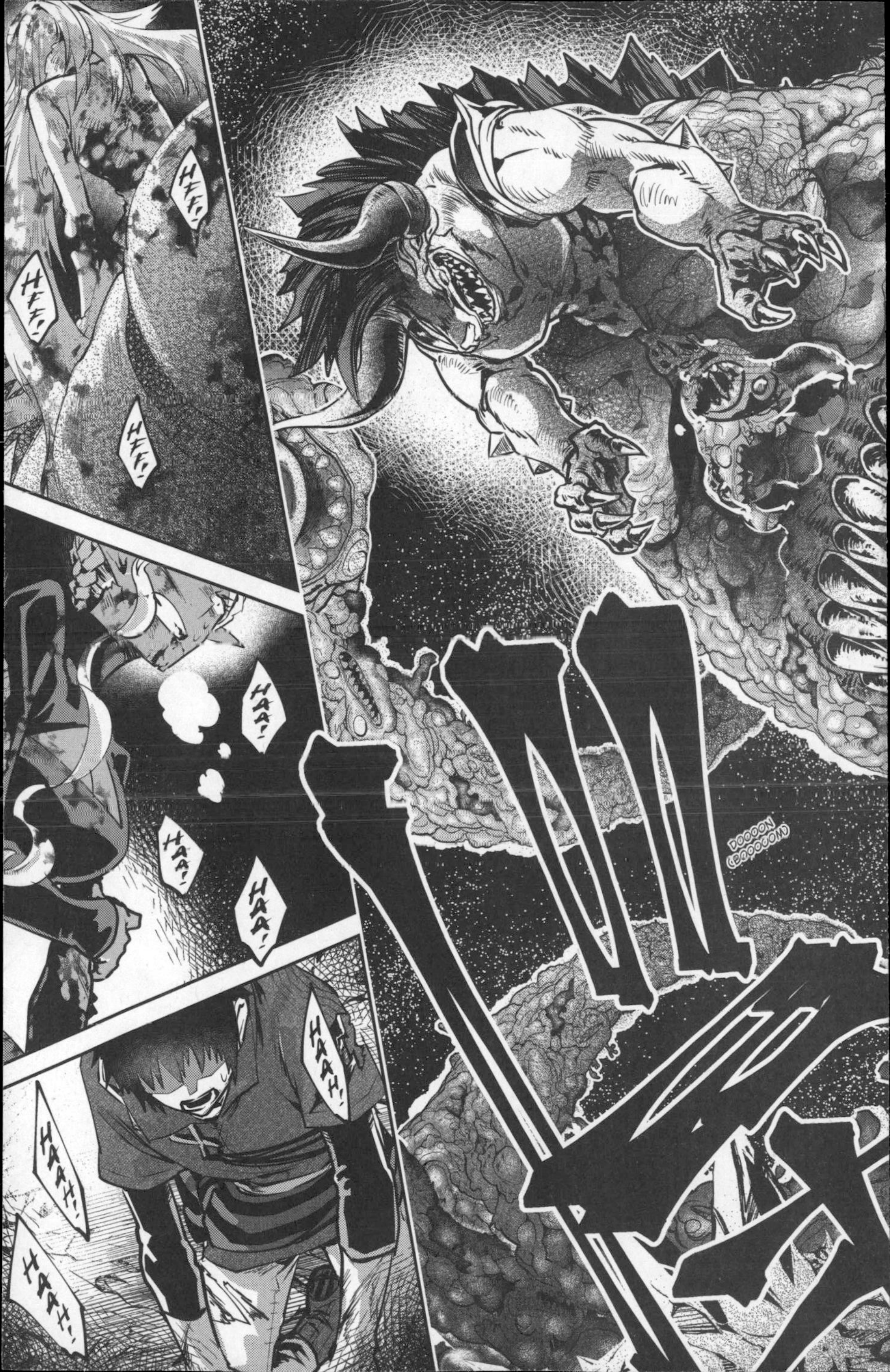
DOOOON (BOOOOOM)
HEF!
HEF!
HEF!
HAA!
HAA!
HAA!
HAAAH!
HAAAH!
HAAAH!

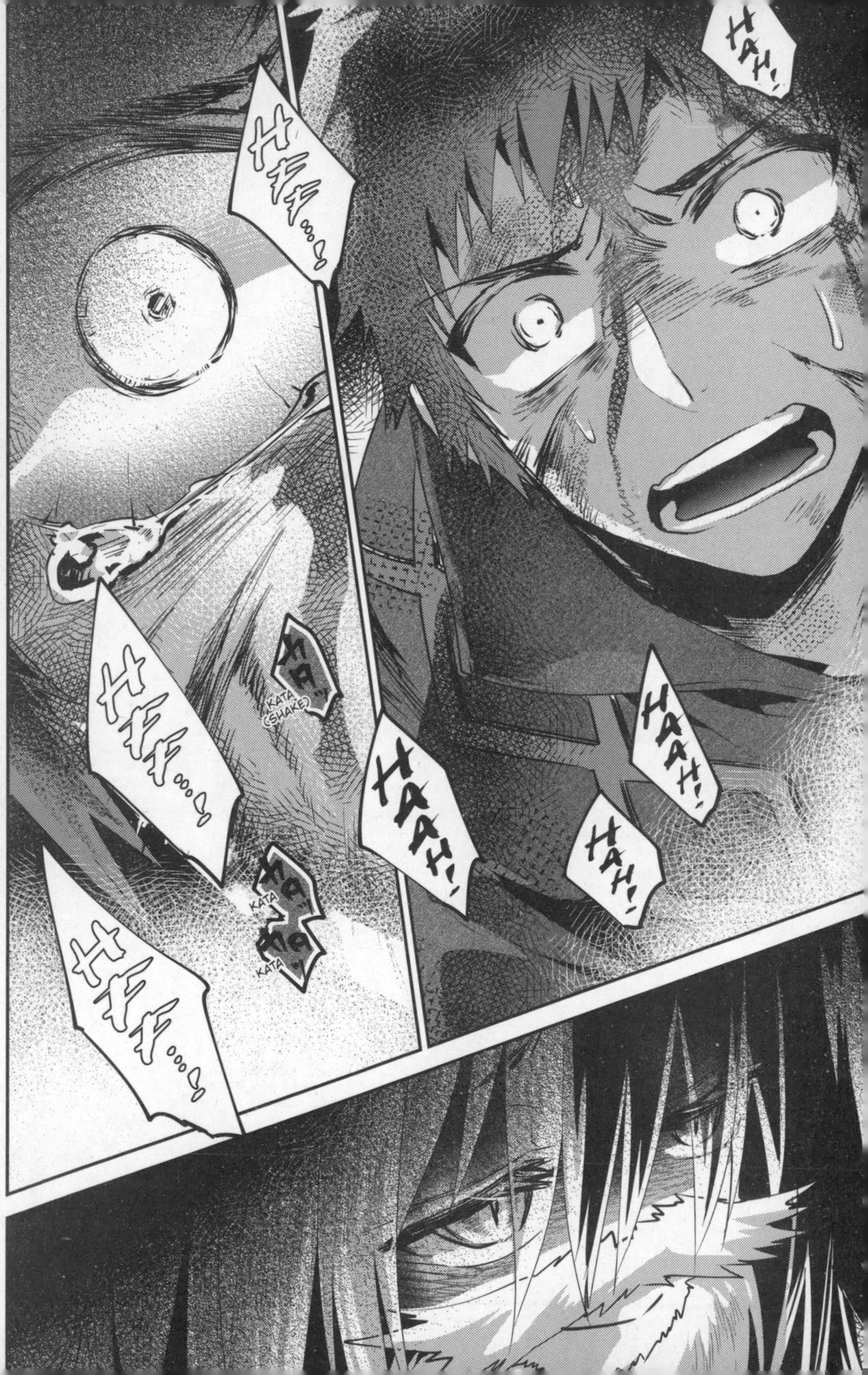

HAH!
HAAH!
HAH!
HAAH!
KATA (SHAKE)
KATA
KATA

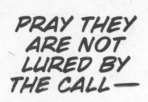
PRAY THEY
ARE NOT
LURED BY
THE CALL—

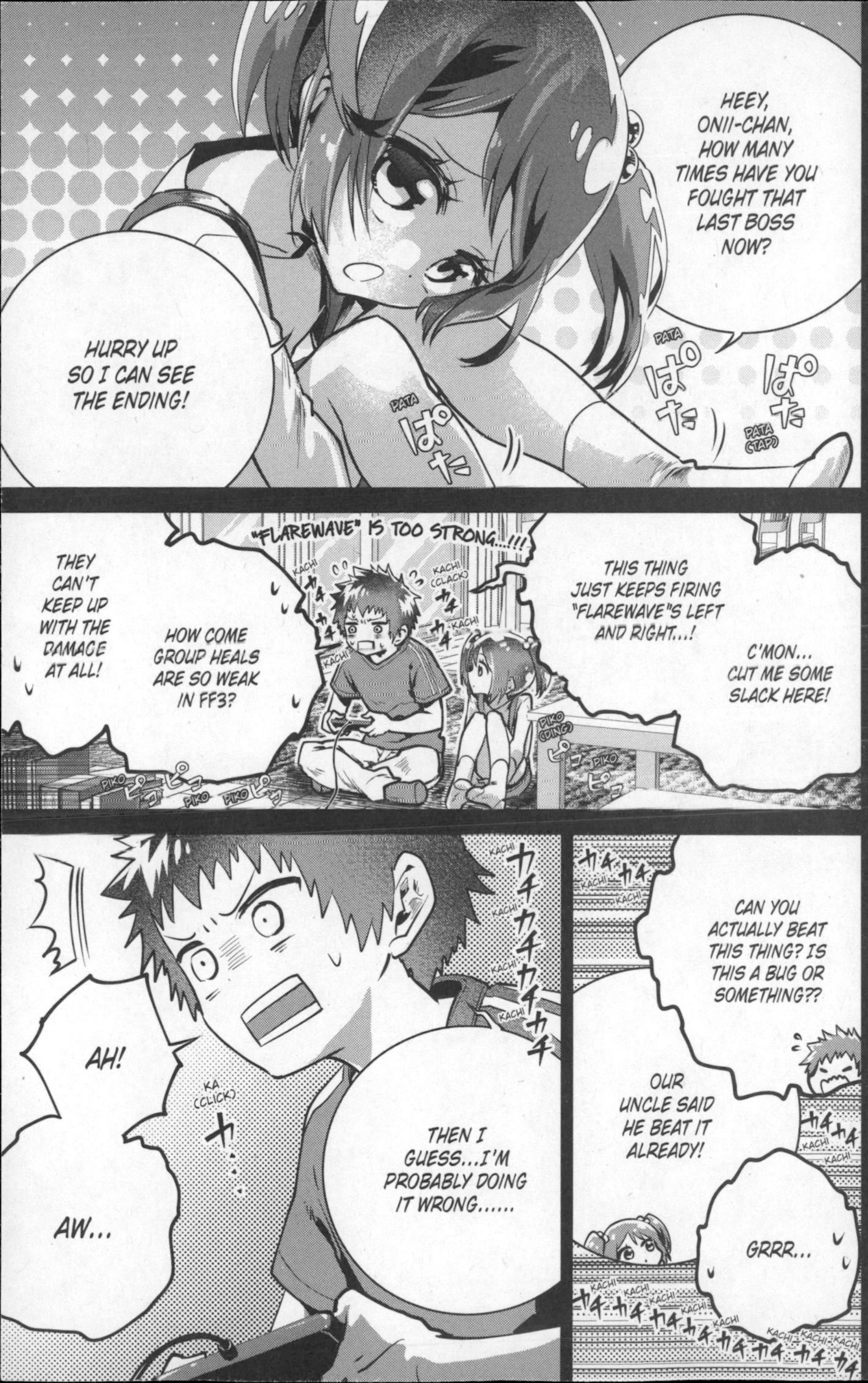
HEEY, ONII-CHAN, HOW MANY TIMES HAVE YOU FOUGHT THAT LAST BOSS NOW?
PATA
PATA (TAP)
HURRY UP SO I CAN SEE THE ENDING!
PATA
C'MON... CUT ME SOME SLACK HERE!
THIS THING JUST KEEPS FIRING "FLAREWAVE"S LEFT AND RIGHT...!
"FLAREWAVE" IS TOO STRONG...!!!
KACHI (CLACK)
KACHI
HOW COME GROUP HEALS ARE SO WEAK IN FF3?
THEY CAN'T KEEP UP WITH THE DAMAGE AT ALL!
PIKO (DING)
PIKO
CAN YOU ACTUALLY BEAT THIS THING? IS THIS A BUG OR SOMETHING??
OUR UNCLE SAID HE BEAT IT ALREADY!
GRRR...
KACHI
THEN I GUESS...I'M PROBABLY DOING IT WRONG......
KA (CLICK)
AH!
AW...

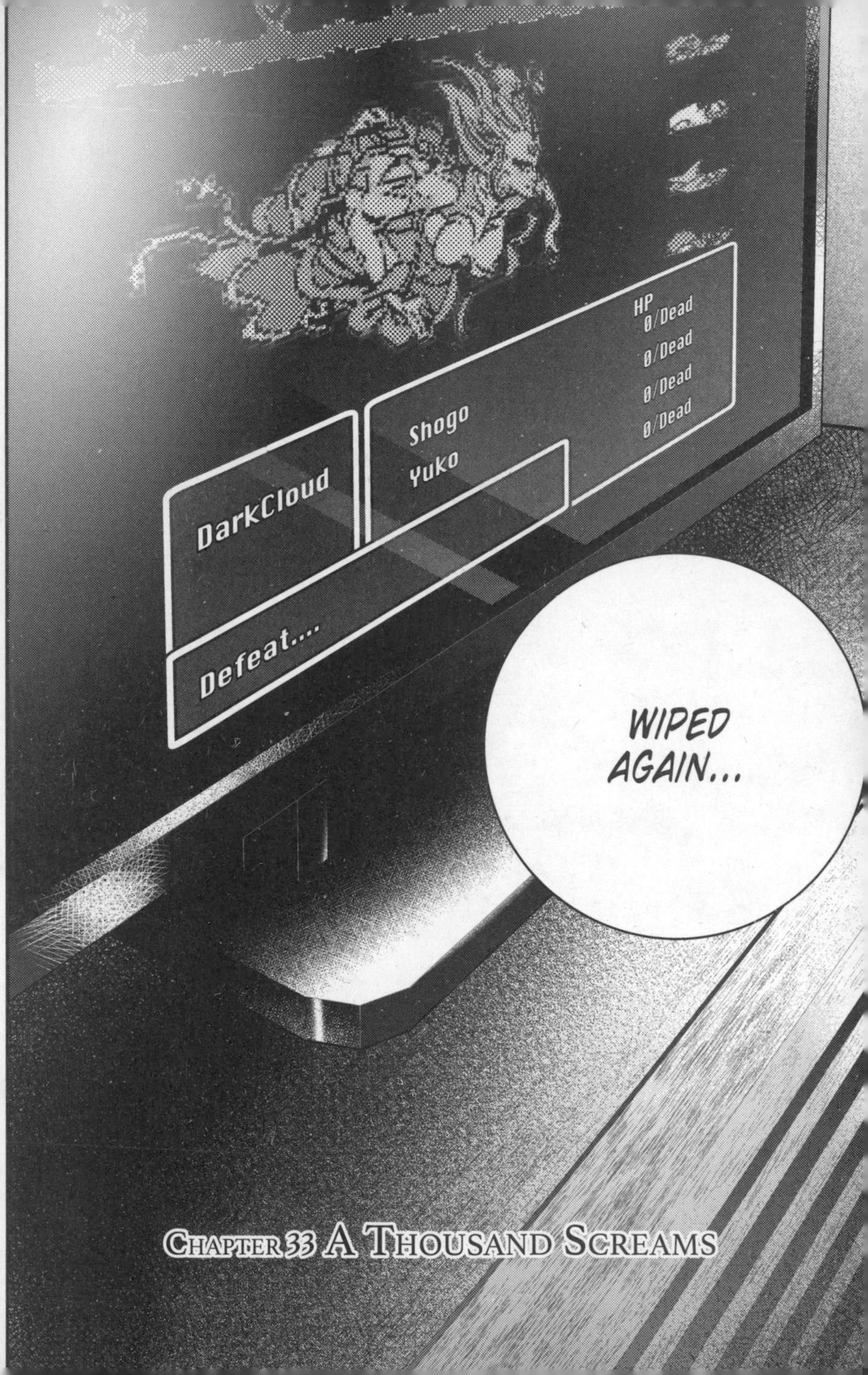
HP
0/Dead
0/Dead
0/Dead
0/Dead
Shogo
Yuko
DarkCloud
Defeat....
WIPED AGAIN...

# Chapter 33 A Thousand Screams

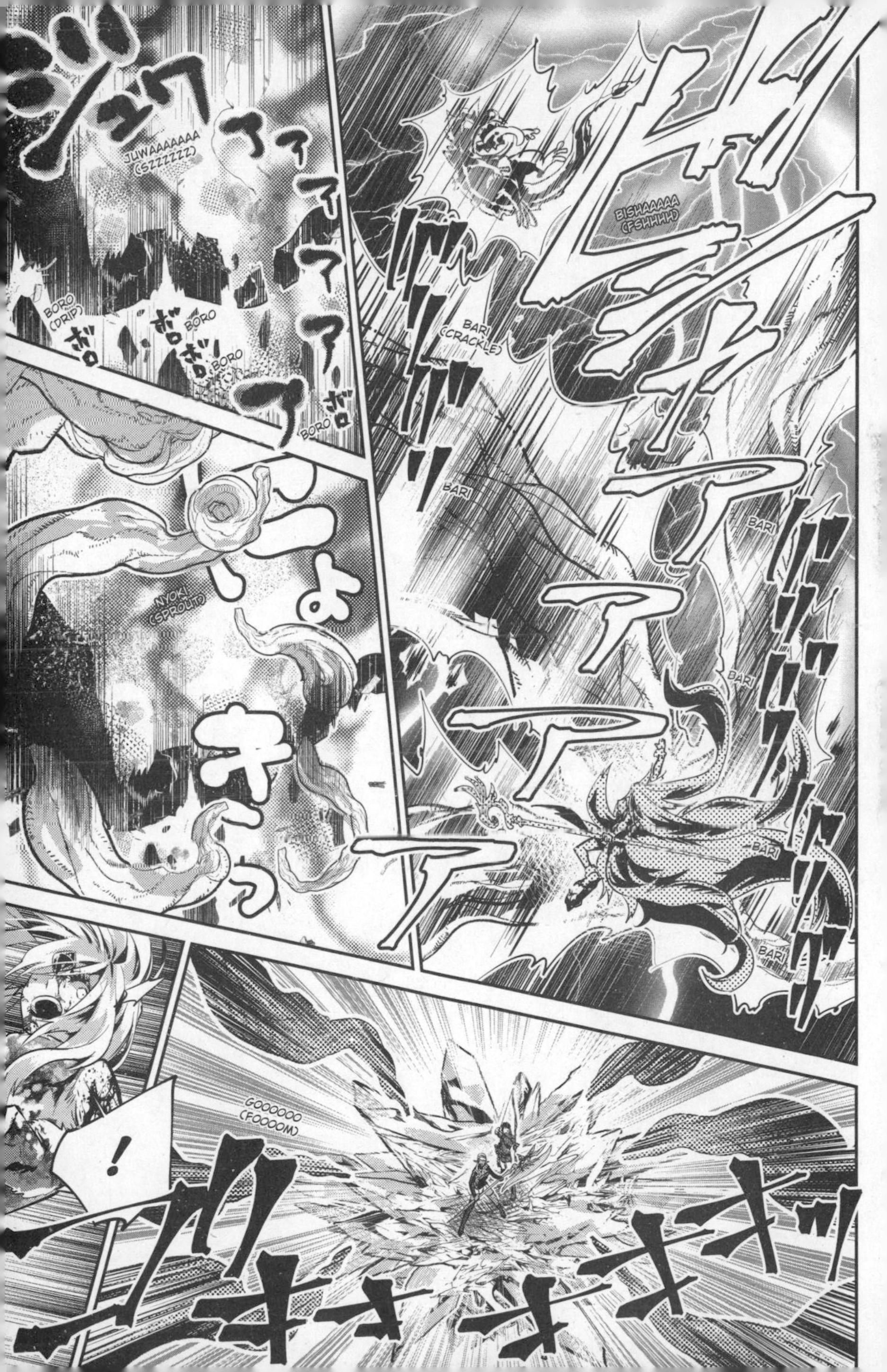
BISHAAAAA (FSHHHH)
BARI (CRACKLE)
BARI
BARI
BARI
BARI
BARI
JUWAAAAAAAA (SZZZZZZ)
BORO (DRIP)
BORO
BORO
BORO
NYOKI (SPROUT)
GOOOOOO (FOOOOM)
!

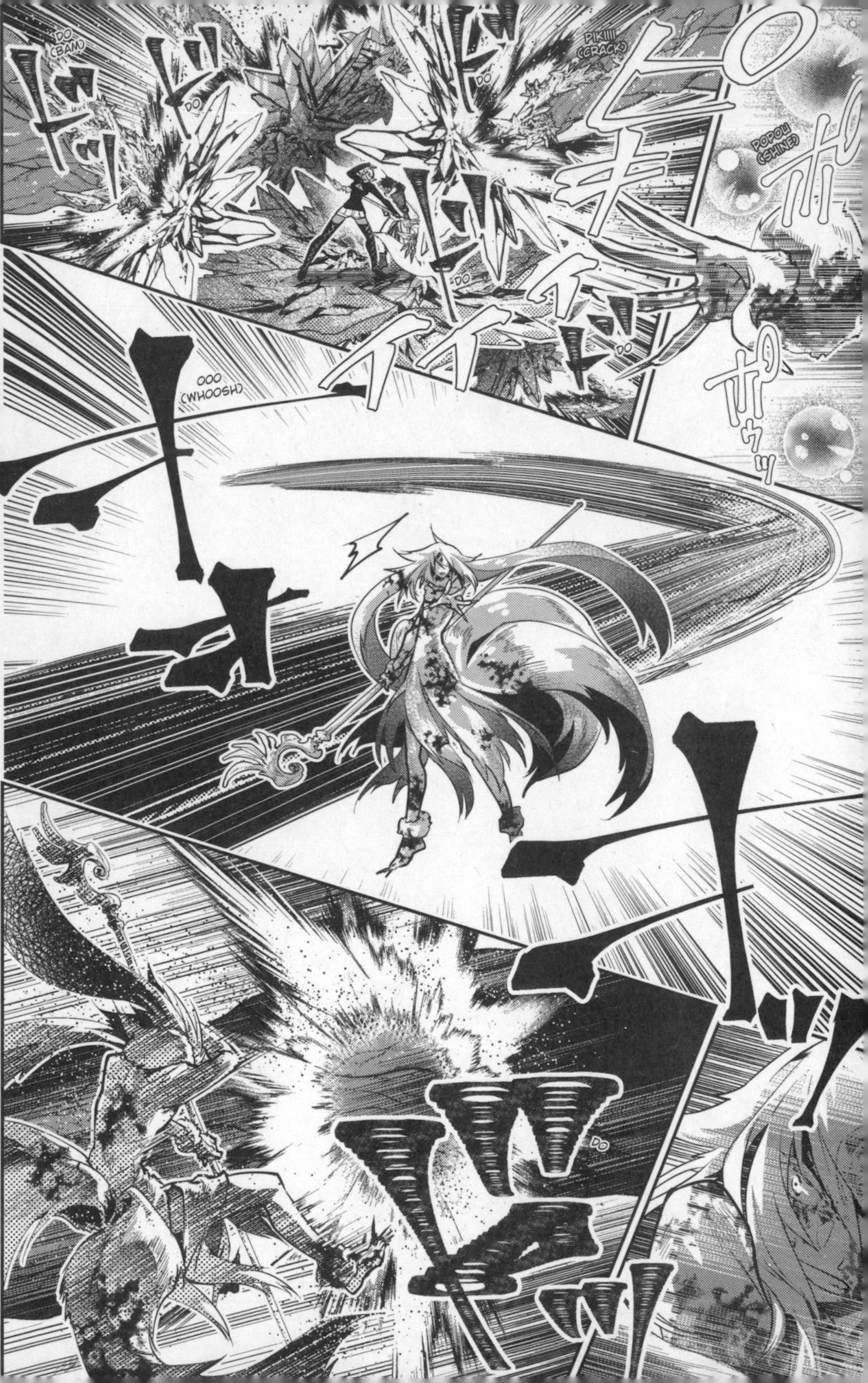
POPOU (SHINE)
PIKIIII (CRACK)
DO
DO
DO (BAM)
DO
DO
OOO (WHOOSH)
DO

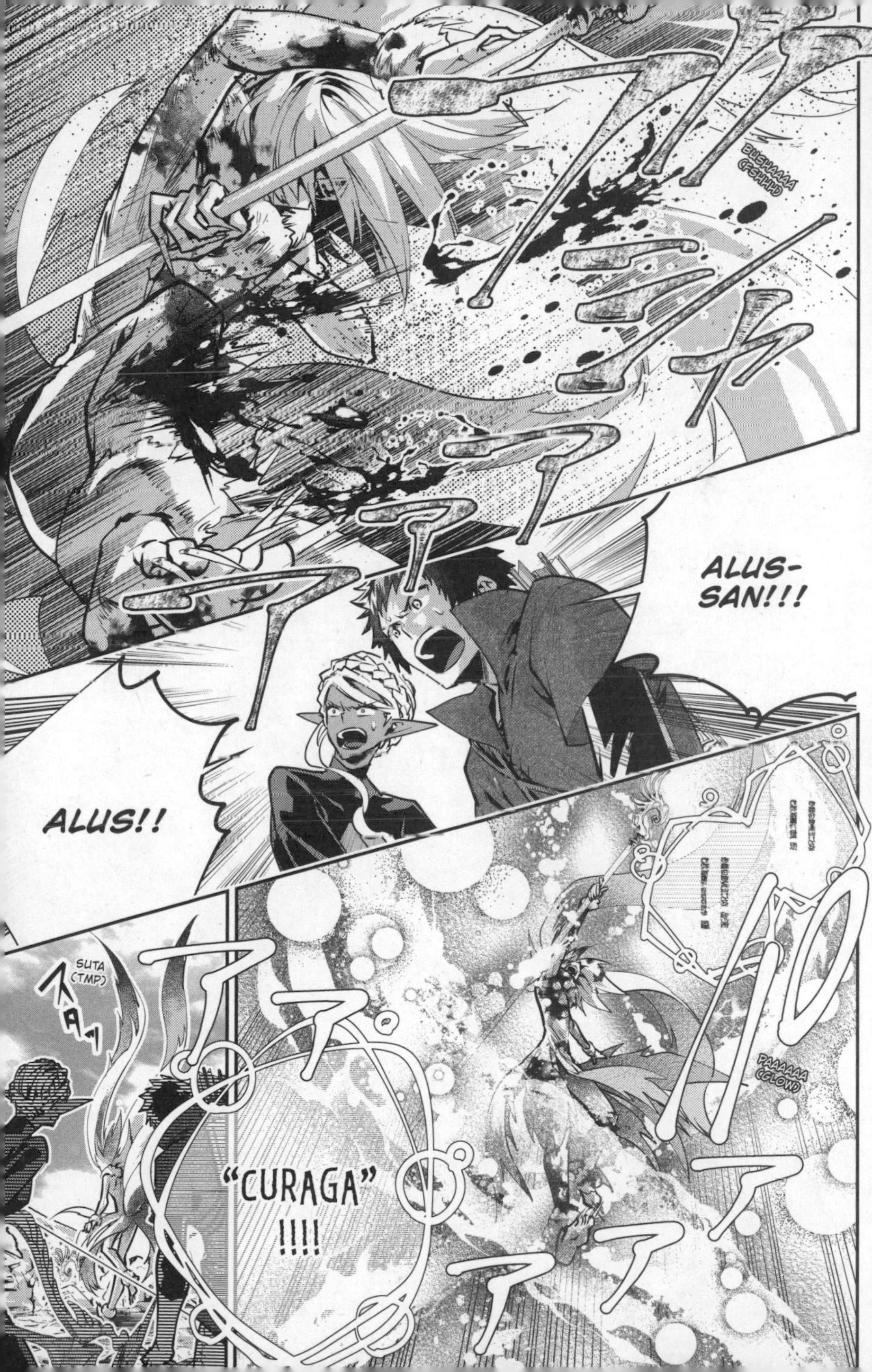
BUSHAAAA (FSHHH)
ALUS-SAN!!!
ALUS!!
PAAAAAA (GLOW)
"CURAGA"!!!!
SUTA (TMP)

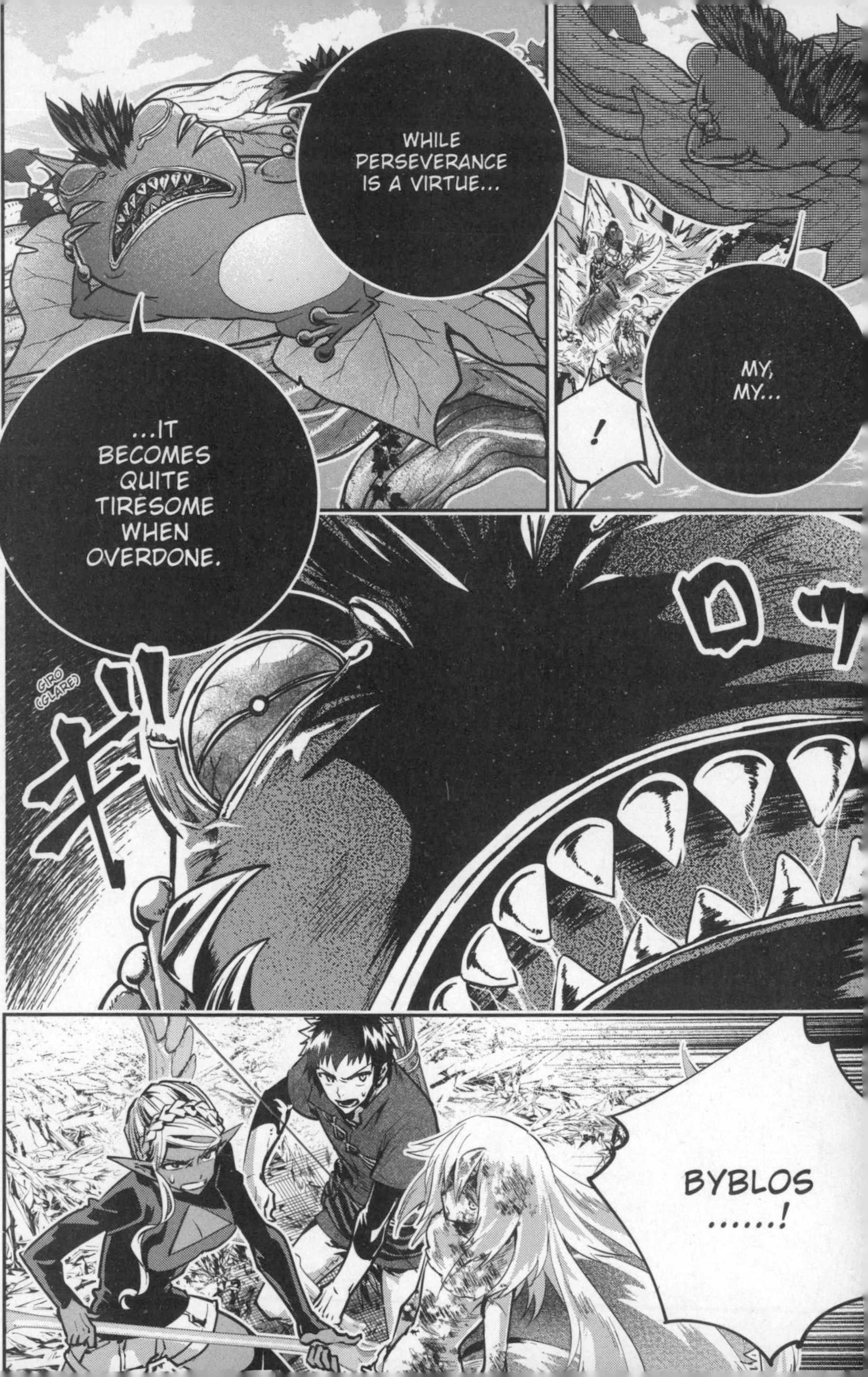
MY, MY...
!
WHILE PERSEVERANCE IS A VIRTUE...
...IT BECOMES QUITE TIRESOME WHEN OVERDONE.
GIRO (GLARE)
BYBLOS ......!

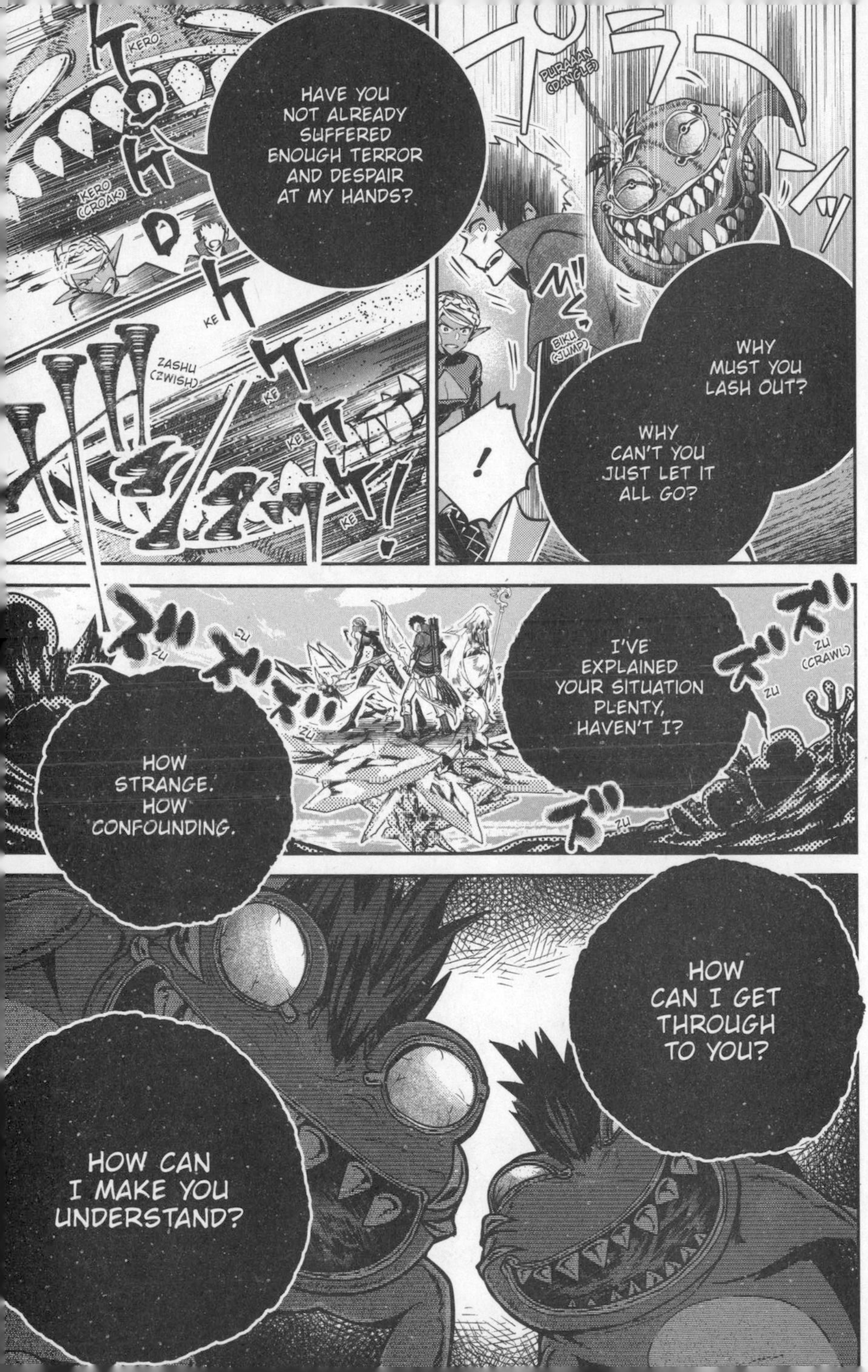
PURAAAN (DANGLE)
BIKU (JUMP)
WHY MUST YOU LASH OUT?
WHY CAN'T YOU JUST LET IT ALL GO?
!
KERO
KERO (CROAK)
HAVE YOU NOT ALREADY SUFFERED ENOUGH TERROR AND DESPAIR AT MY HANDS?
KE
ZASHU (ZWISH)
KE
KE
KE
ZU (CRAWL)
ZU
I'VE EXPLAINED YOUR SITUATION PLENTY, HAVEN'T I?
ZU
ZU
ZU
ZU
HOW STRANGE. HOW CONFOUNDING.
HOW CAN I GET THROUGH TO YOU?
HOW CAN I MAKE YOU UNDERSTAND?

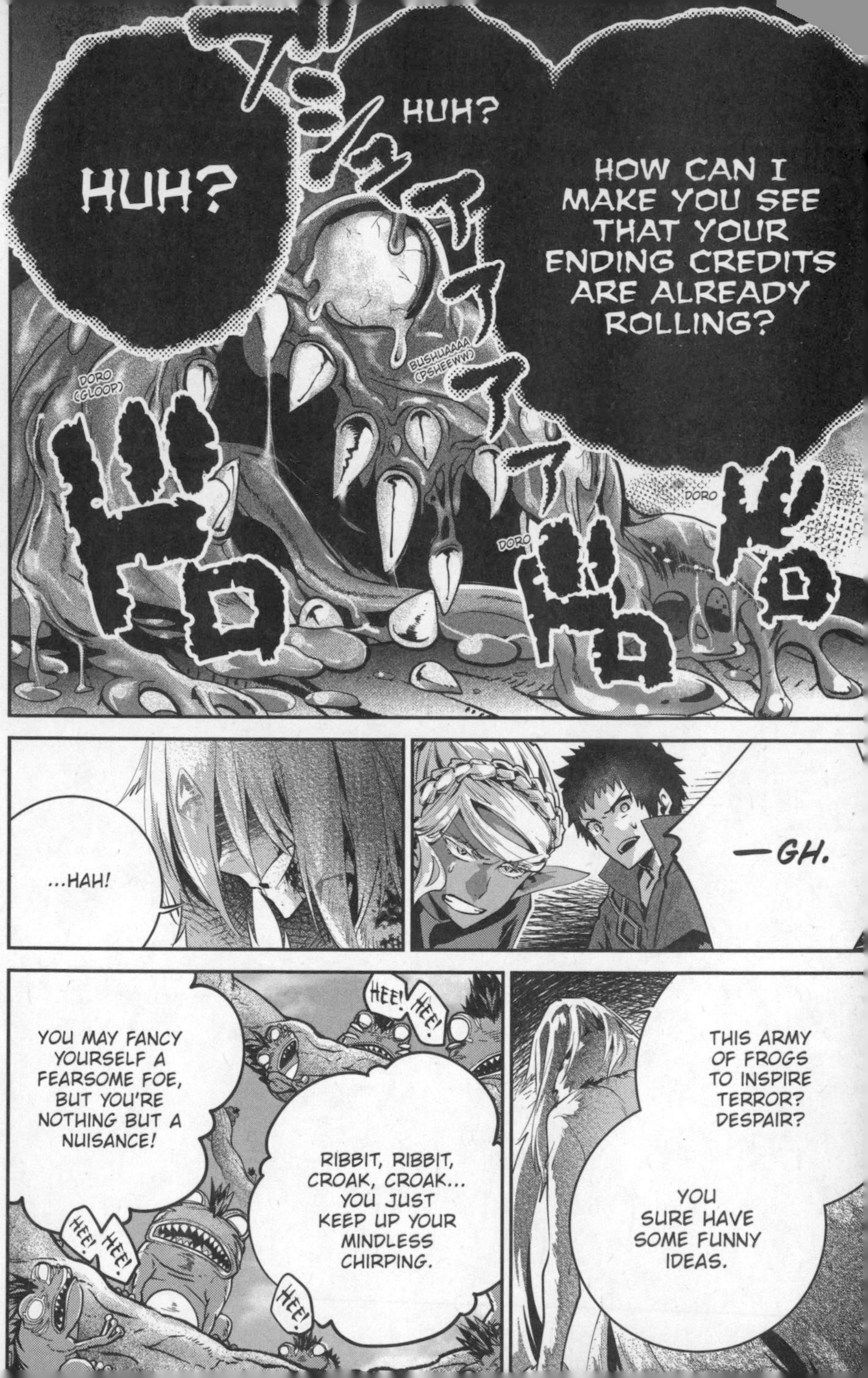
HOW CAN I MAKE YOU SEE THAT YOUR ENDING CREDITS ARE ALREADY ROLLING?
HUH?
HUH?
BUSHUAAAA (PSHEEWW)
DORO (GLOOP)
DORO
DORO
—GH.
...HAH!
THIS ARMY OF FROGS TO INSPIRE TERROR? DESPAIR?
YOU SURE HAVE SOME FUNNY IDEAS.
HEE! HEE!
YOU MAY FANCY YOURSELF A FEARSOME FOE, BUT YOU'RE NOTHING BUT A NUISANCE!
RIBBIT, RIBBIT, CROAK, CROAK... YOU JUST KEEP UP YOUR MINDLESS CHIRPING.
HEE! HEE!
HEE!

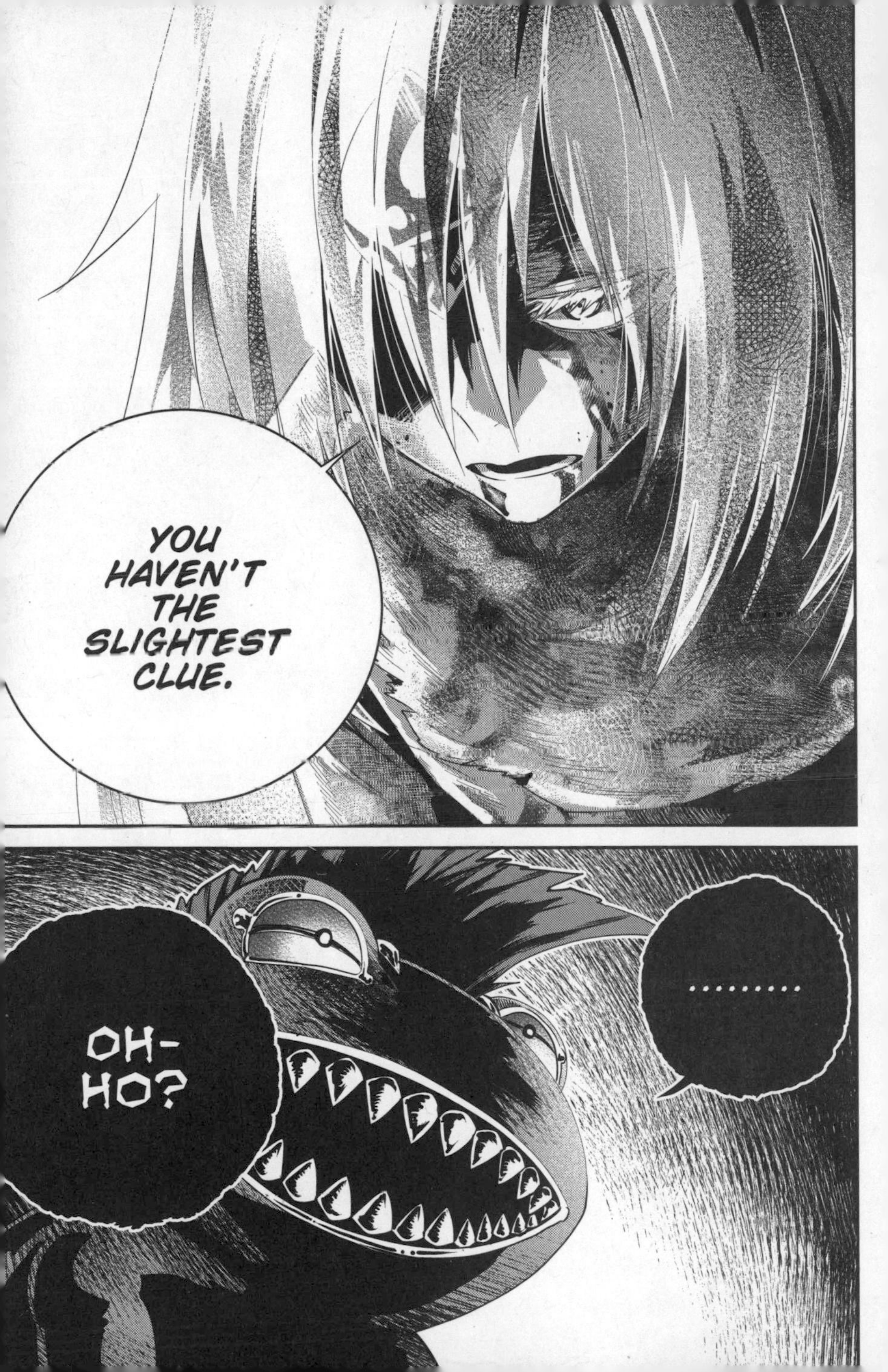
YOU HAVEN'T THE SLIGHTEST CLUE.
........
OH-HO?

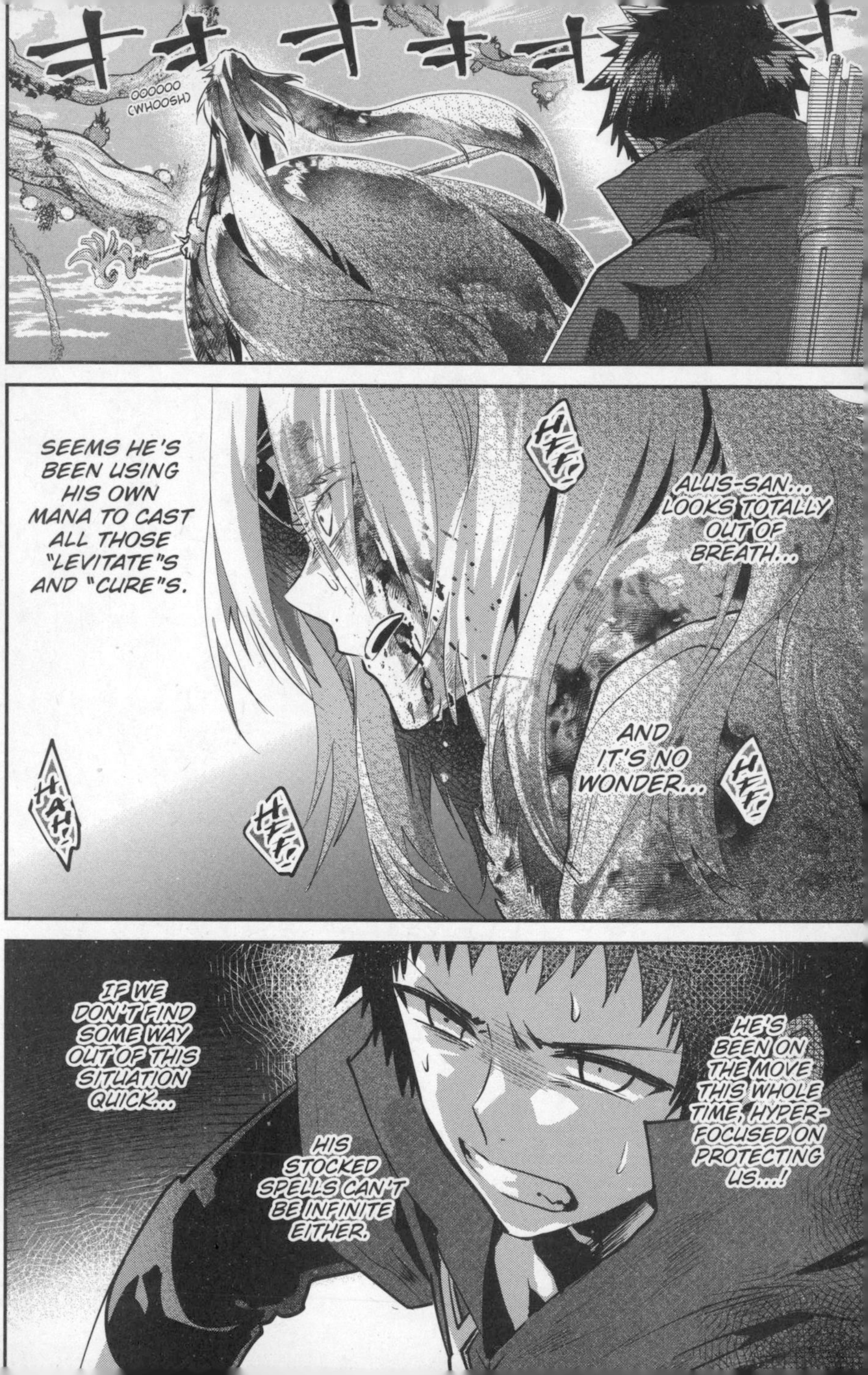
オオオオオオ
OOOOOO (WHOOSH)
ALUS-SAN... LOOKS TOTALLY OUT OF BREATH...
HFF
AND IT'S NO WONDER...
HFF
SEEMS HE'S BEEN USING HIS OWN MANA TO CAST ALL THOSE "LEVITATE"S AND "CURE"S.
HFF
HAH
HE'S BEEN ON THE MOVE THIS WHOLE TIME, HYPER-FOCUSED ON PROTECTING US...!
HIS STOCKED SPELLS CAN'T BE INFINITE EITHER.
IF WE DON'T FIND SOME WAY OUT OF THIS SITUATION QUICK...

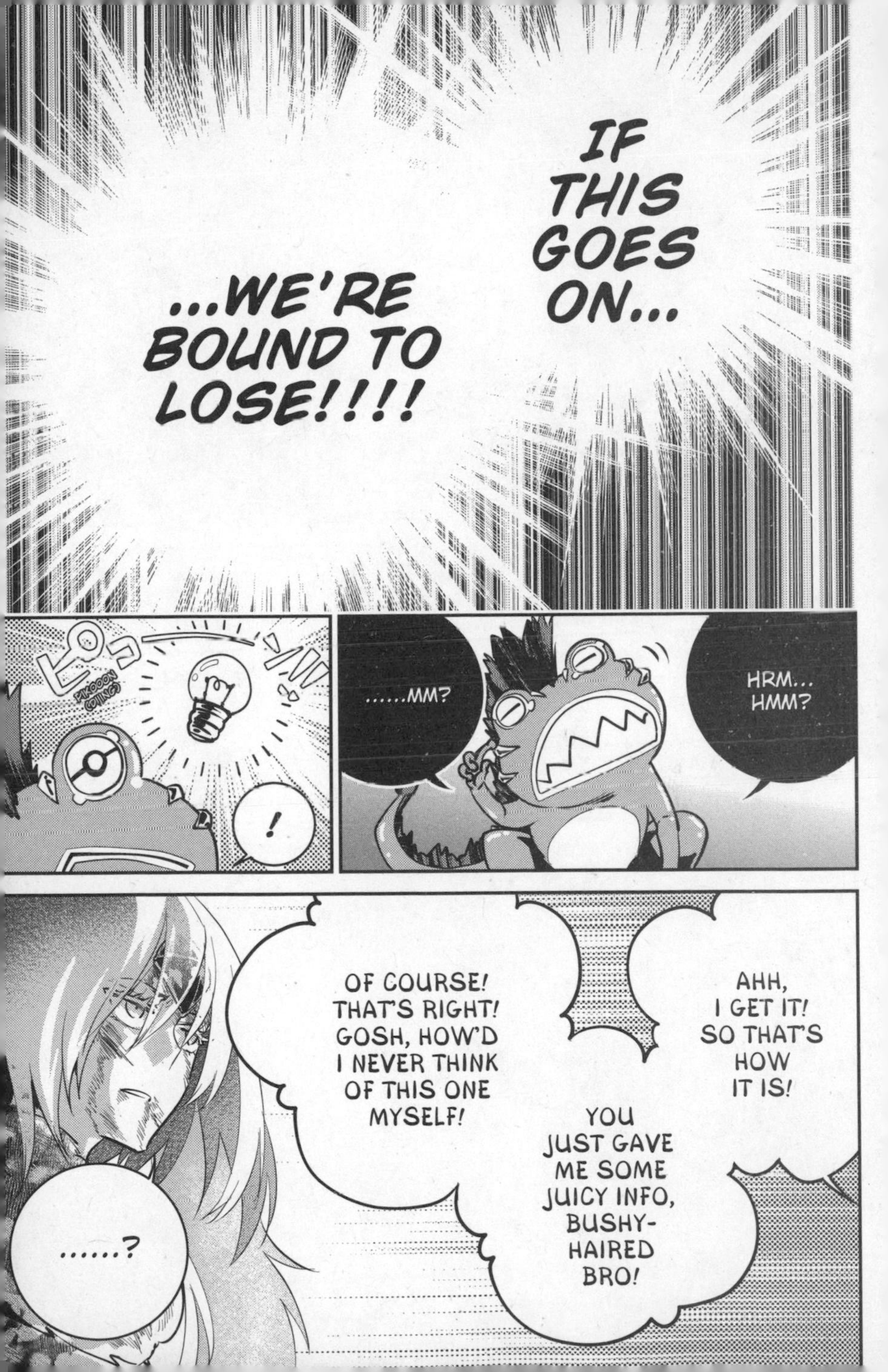
IF THIS GOES ON...
...WE'RE BOUND TO LOSE!!!!
HRM... HMM?
......MM?
PIKOOON (DING)
!
AHH, I GET IT! SO THAT'S HOW IT IS!
OF COURSE! THAT'S RIGHT! GOSH, HOW'D I NEVER THINK OF THIS ONE MYSELF!
YOU JUST GAVE ME SOME JUICY INFO, BUSHY-HAIRED BRO!
......?

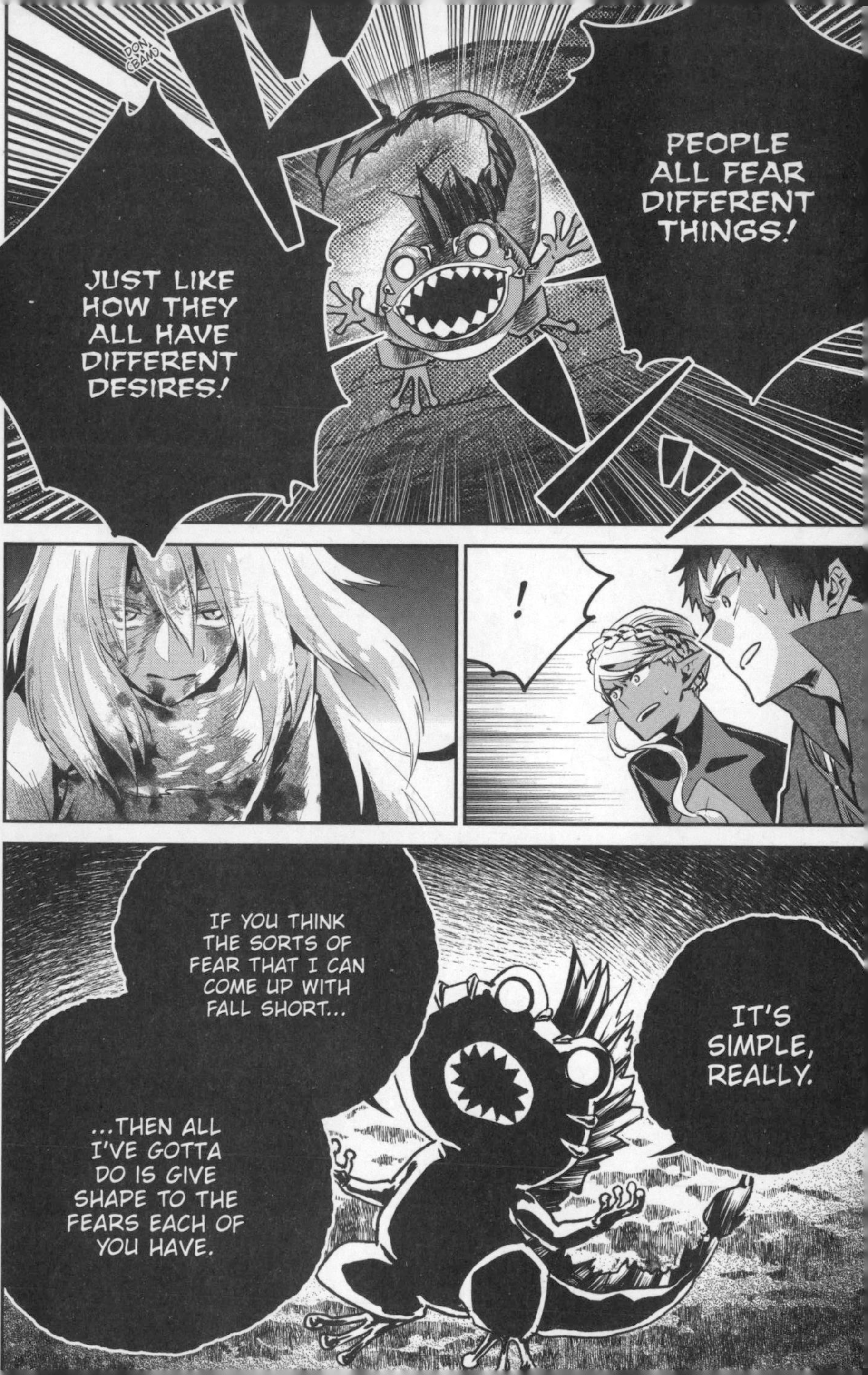
DON (BAN)
PEOPLE ALL FEAR DIFFERENT THINGS!
JUST LIKE HOW THEY ALL HAVE DIFFERENT DESIRES!
!
IT'S SIMPLE, REALLY.
IF YOU THINK THE SORTS OF FEAR THAT I CAN COME UP WITH FALL SHORT...
...THEN ALL I'VE GOTTA DO IS GIVE SHAPE TO THE FEARS EACH OF YOU HAVE.

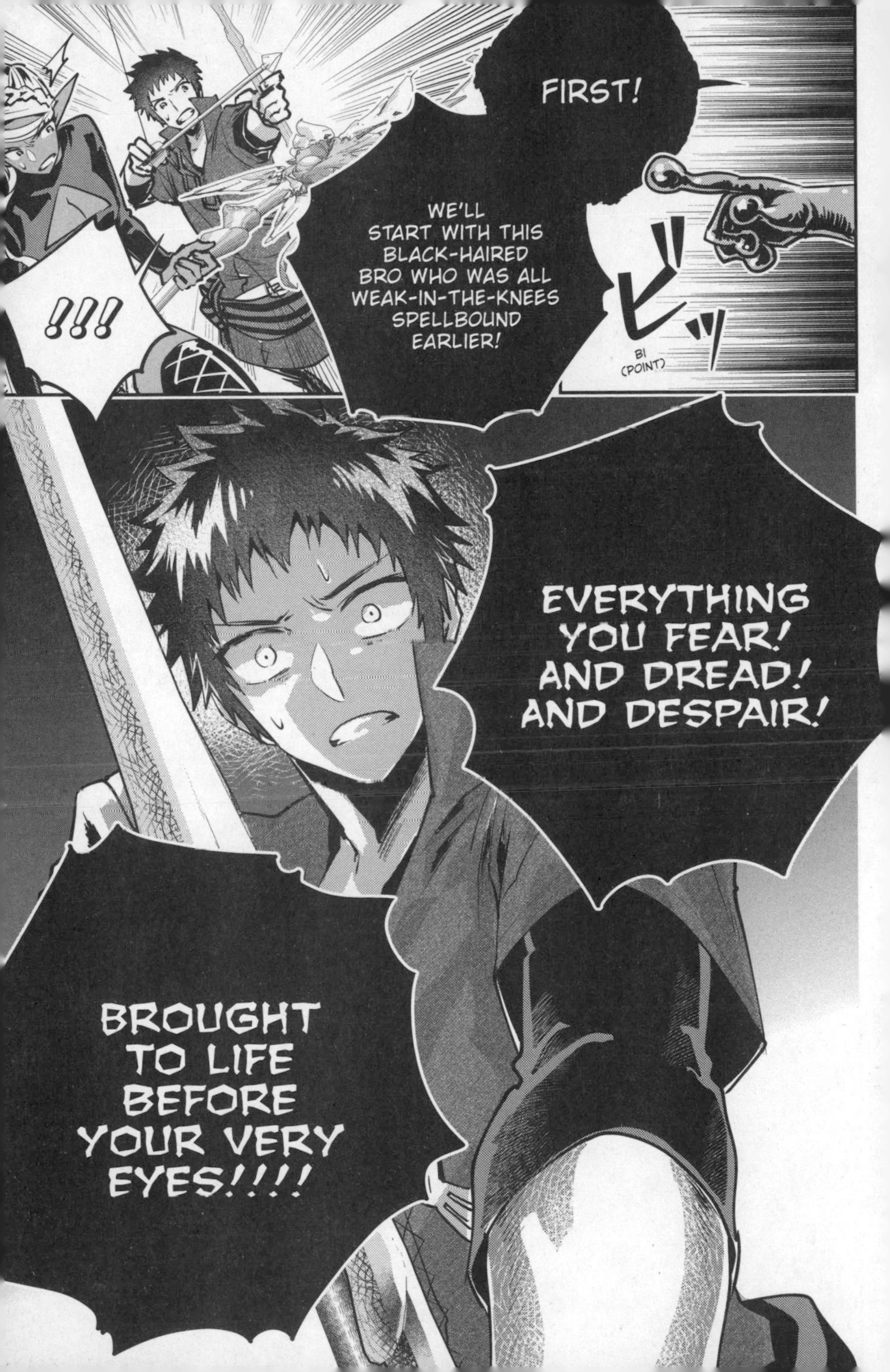

FIRST!
WE'LL START WITH THIS BLACK-HAIRED BRO WHO WAS ALL WEAK-IN-THE-KNEES SPELLBOUND EARLIER!
ビッ
BI (POINT)
!!!
EVERYTHING YOU FEAR! AND DREAD! AND DESPAIR!
BROUGHT TO LIFE BEFORE YOUR VERY EYES!!!!

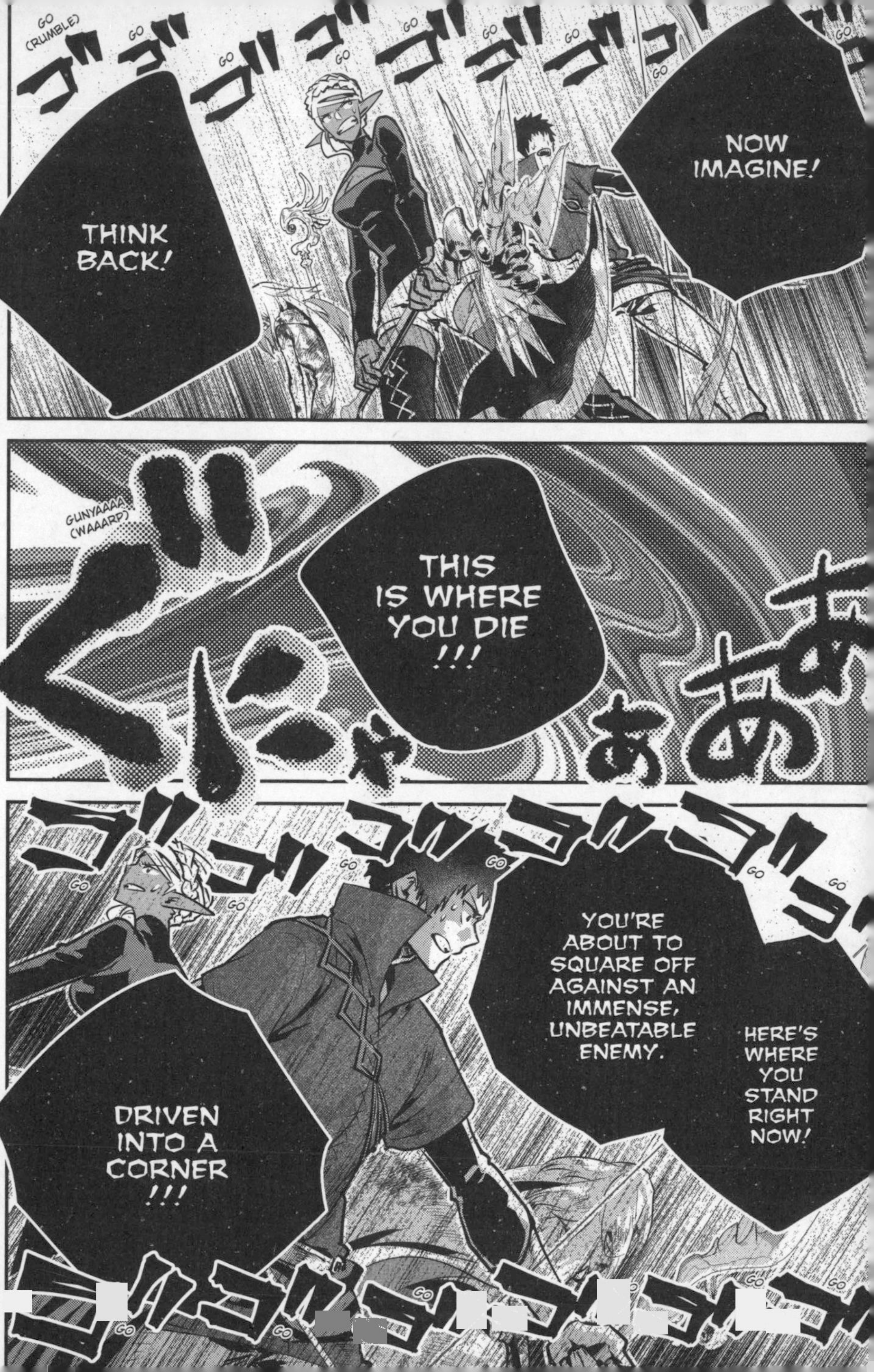
GO (RUMBLE)
GO GO GO GO GO GO GO GO
NOW IMAGINE!
THINK BACK!
GUNYAAAA (WAAARP)
THIS IS WHERE YOU DIE!!!
GO GO GO GO GO GO
YOU'RE ABOUT TO SQUARE OFF AGAINST AN IMMENSE, UNBEATABLE ENEMY.
HERE'S WHERE YOU STAND RIGHT NOW!
DRIVEN INTO A CORNER!!!
GO GO GO GO

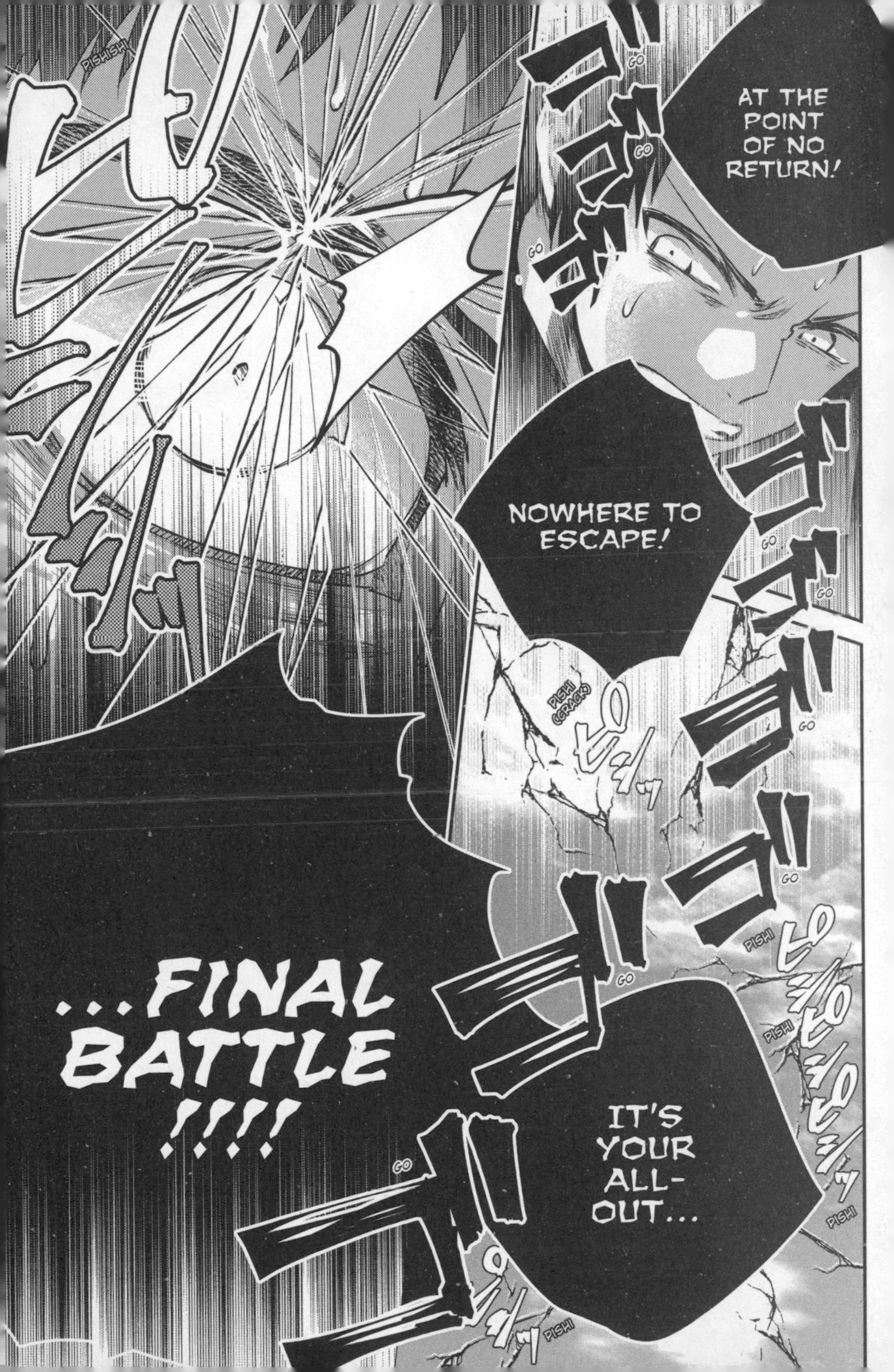

GO GO GO
AT THE POINT OF NO RETURN!
PISHISHI
NOWHERE TO ESCAPE!
GO GO GO GO
PISHI (CRACK)
PISHI PISHI PISHI
IT'S YOUR ALL-OUT...
GO GO
...FINAL BATTLE!!!!
PISHI

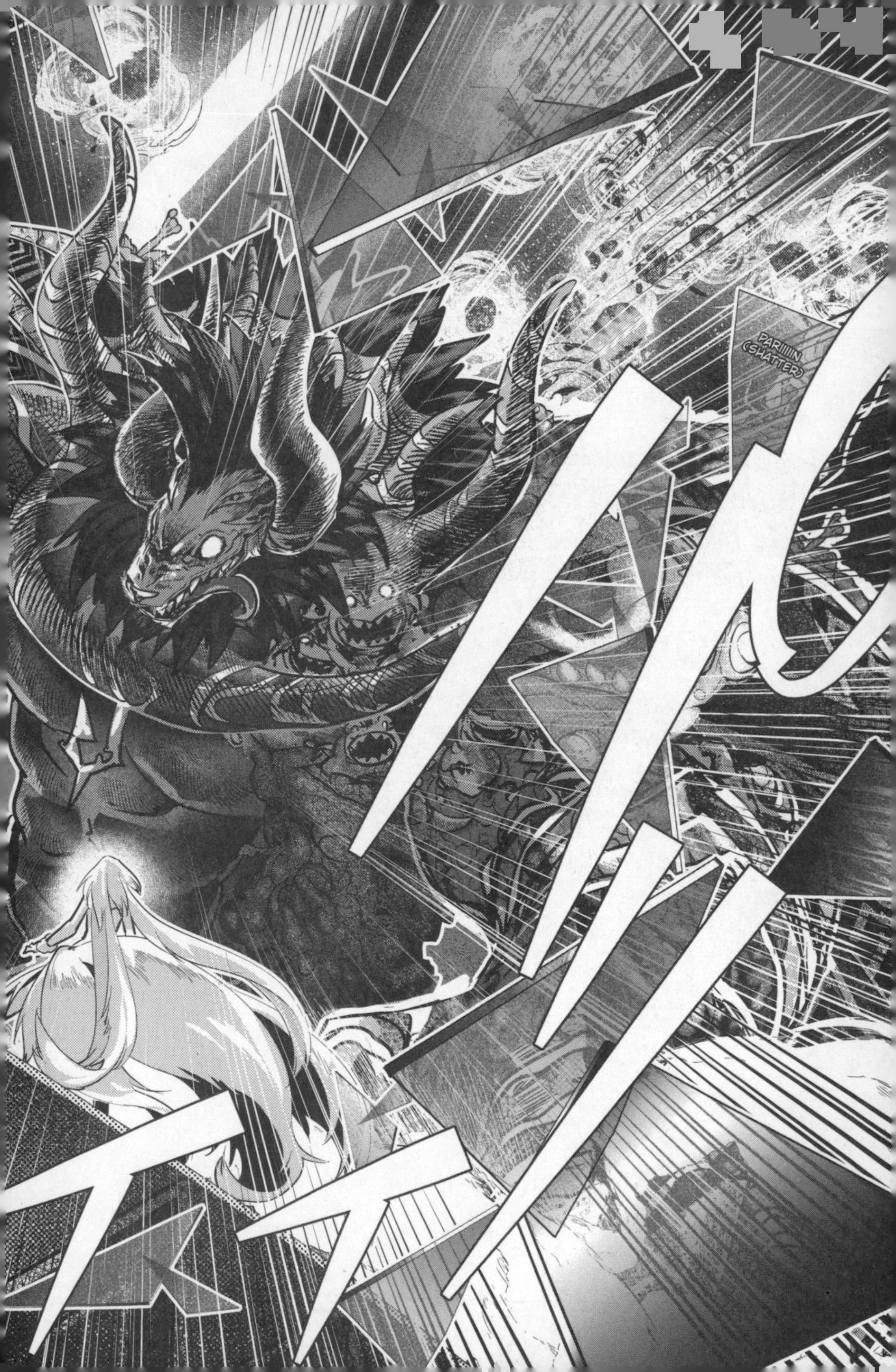
PARIIIIIN
(SHATTER)

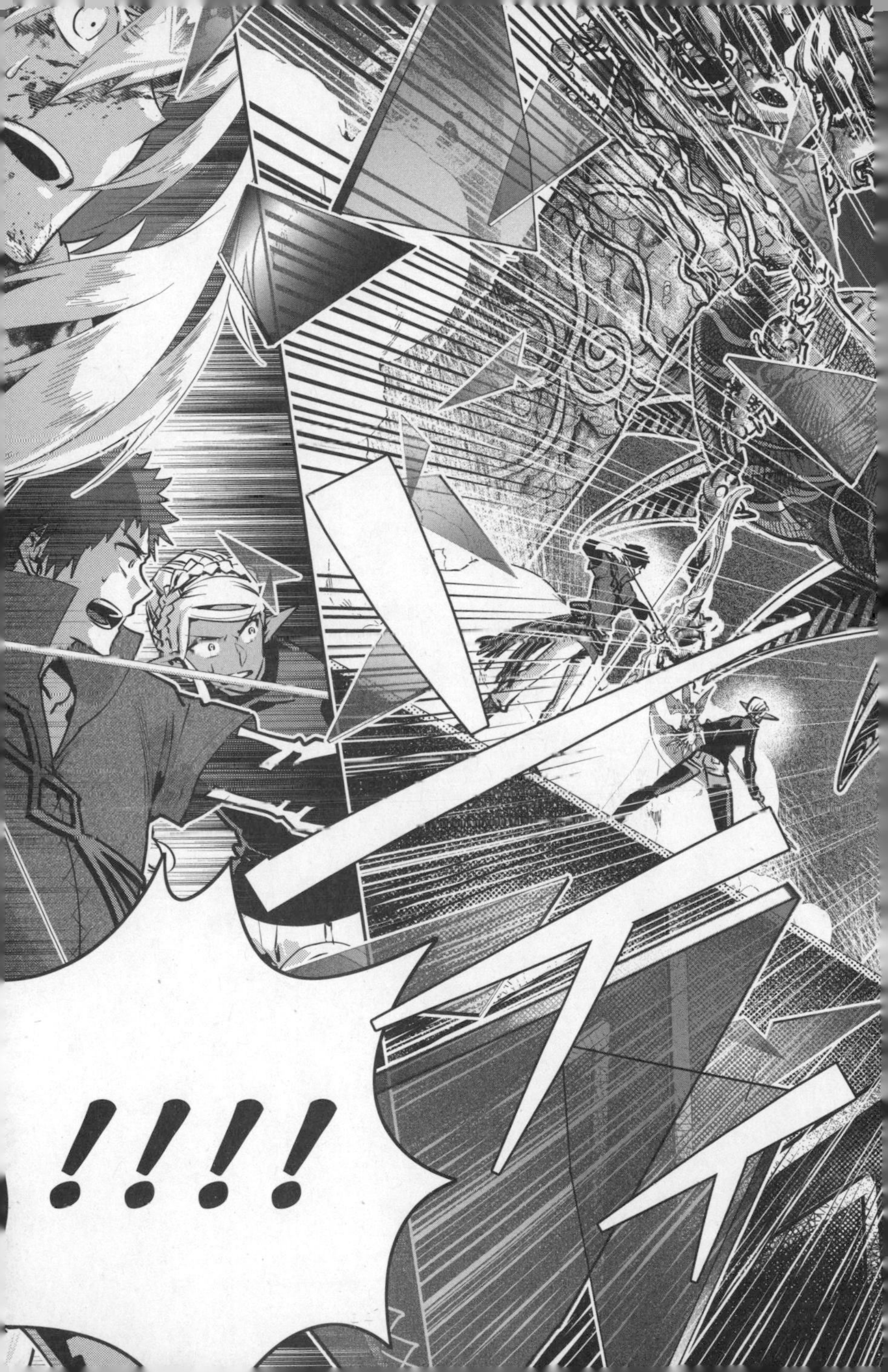
!!!!

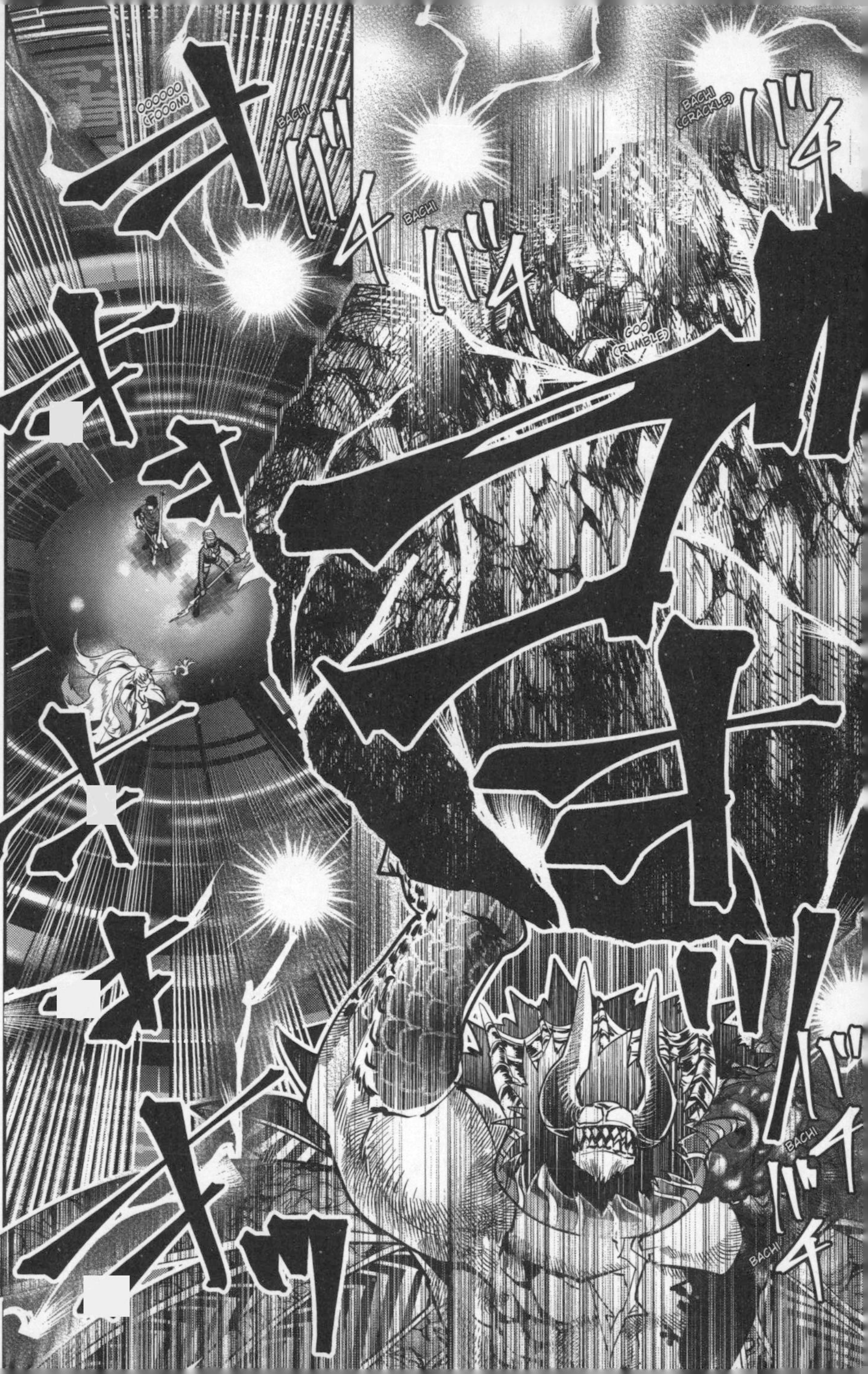
BACHI (CRACKLE)
GOO (RUMBLE)
BACHI
BACHI
OOOOOO (FOOOM)
BACHI
BACHI

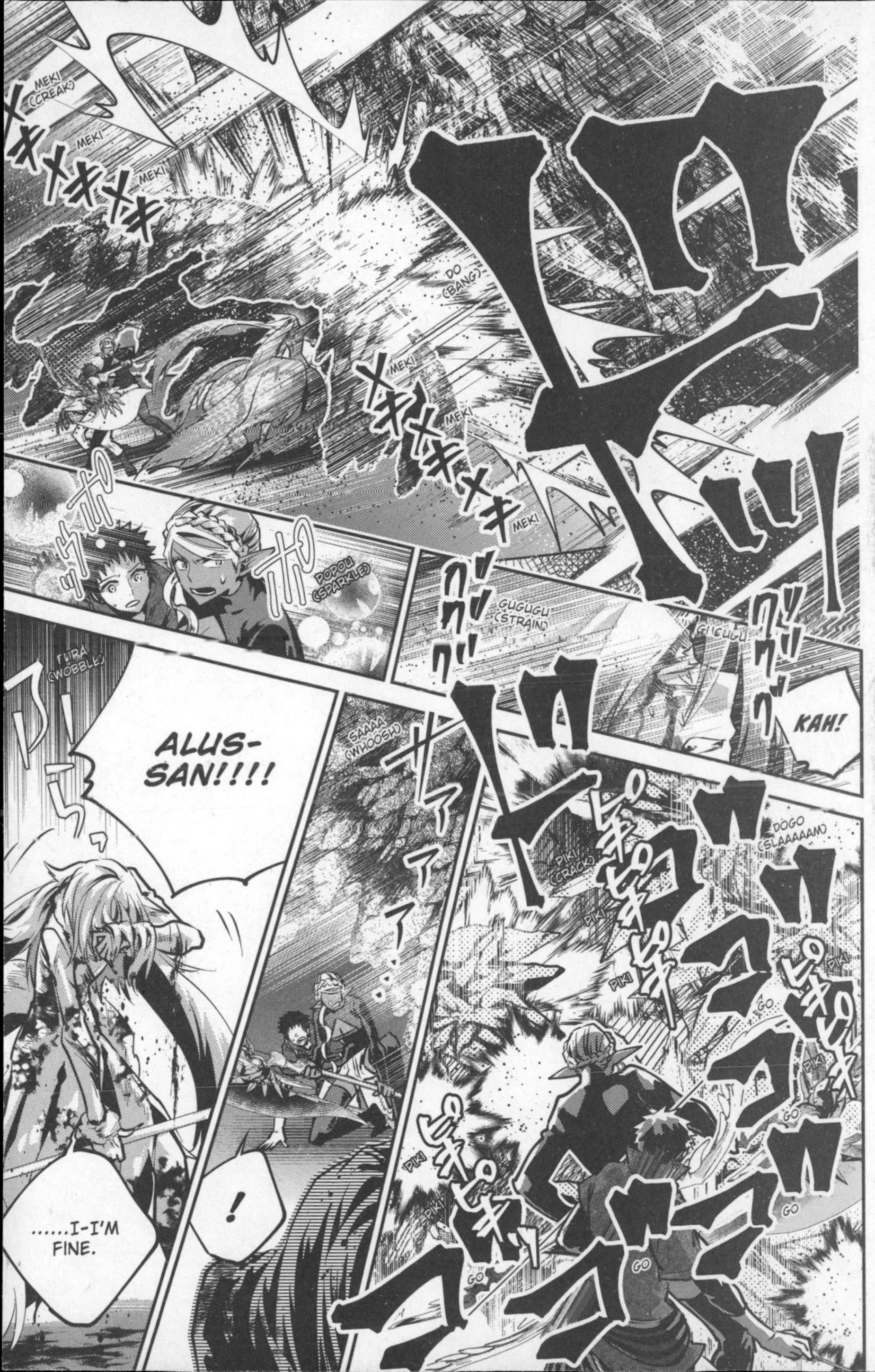
DO (BANG)
MEKI (CREAK)
MEKI
MEKI
MEKI
MEKI
MEKI
GUGUGU (STRAIN)
GUGUGU
KAH!
POPOU (SPARKLE)
DOGO (SLAAAAAM)
PIKI (CRACK)
PIKI
PIKI
PIKI
GO
GO
GO
PIKI
PIKI
GO
GO
SAAAA (WHOOSH)
ALUS-SAN!!!!
FURA (WOBBLE)
!
......I-I'M FINE.

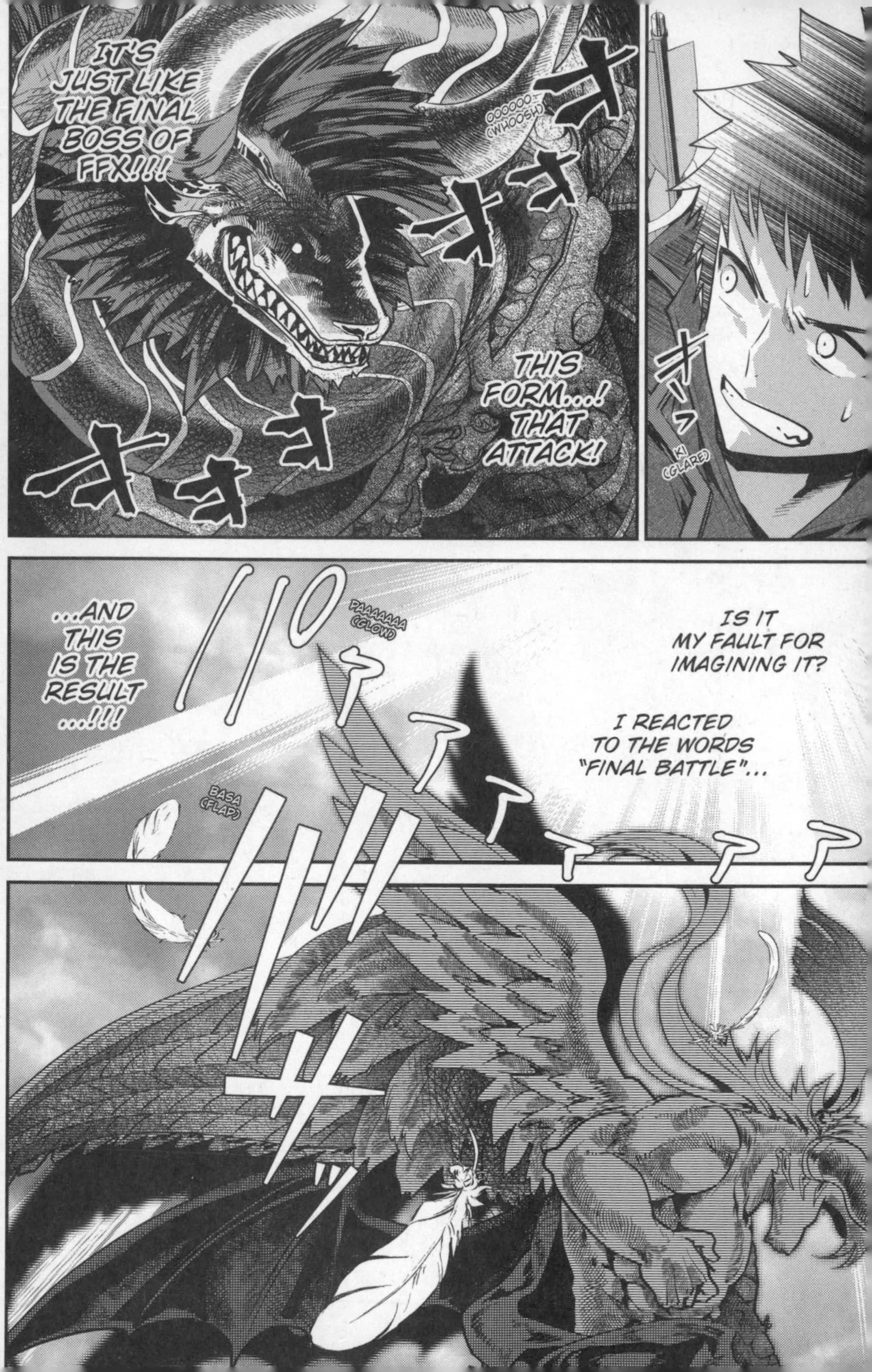
KI (GLARE)
OOOOOO (WHOOSH)
THIS FORM...! THAT ATTACK!
IT'S JUST LIKE THE FINAL BOSS OF FFX!!!
IS IT MY FAULT FOR IMAGINING IT?
I REACTED TO THE WORDS "FINAL BATTLE"...
PAAAAAAA (GLOW)
...AND THIS IS THE RESULT ...!!!
BASA (FLAP)

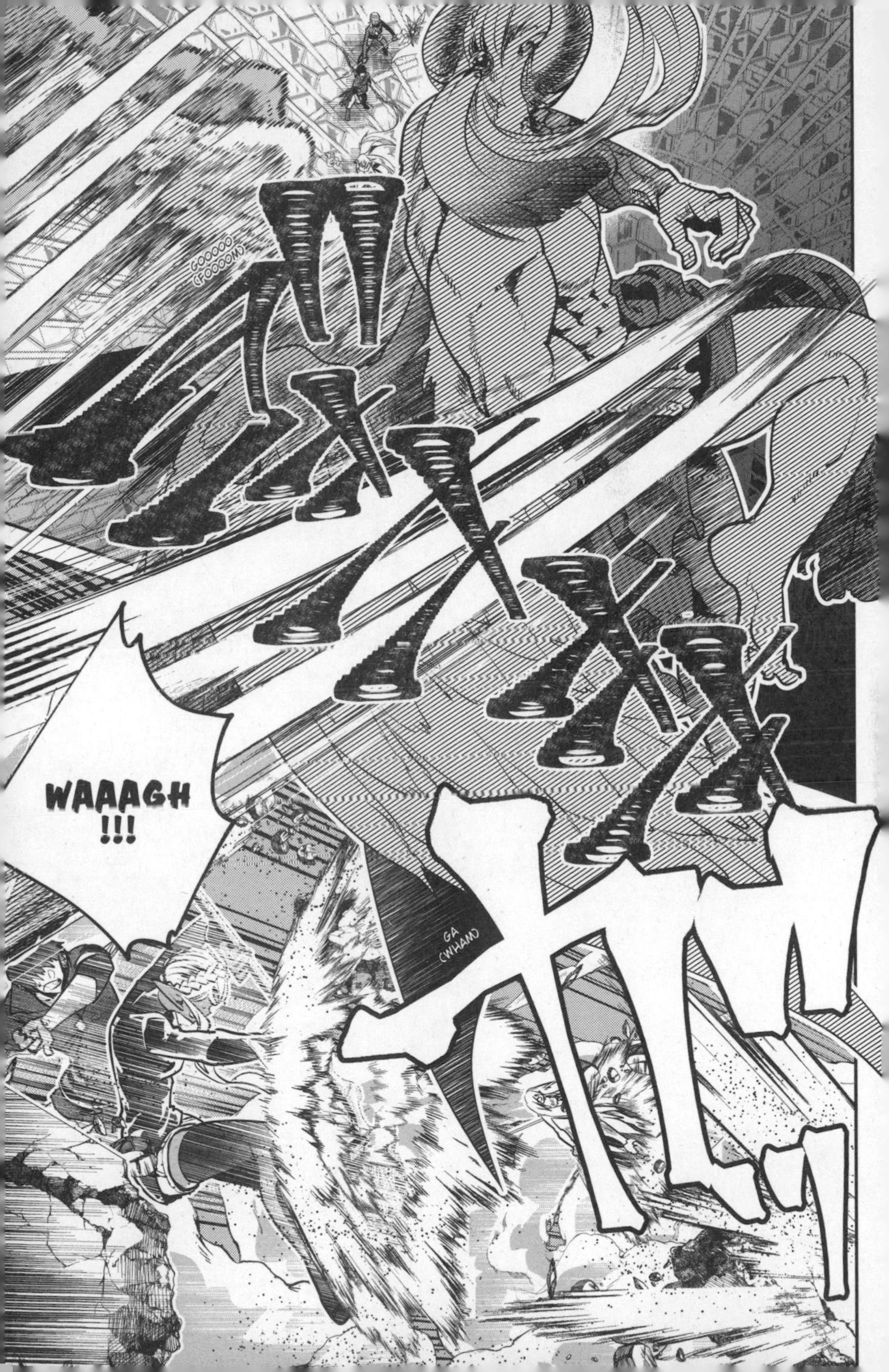
GOOOOO
(FOOOOM)
WAAAGH !!!
GA
(WHAM)

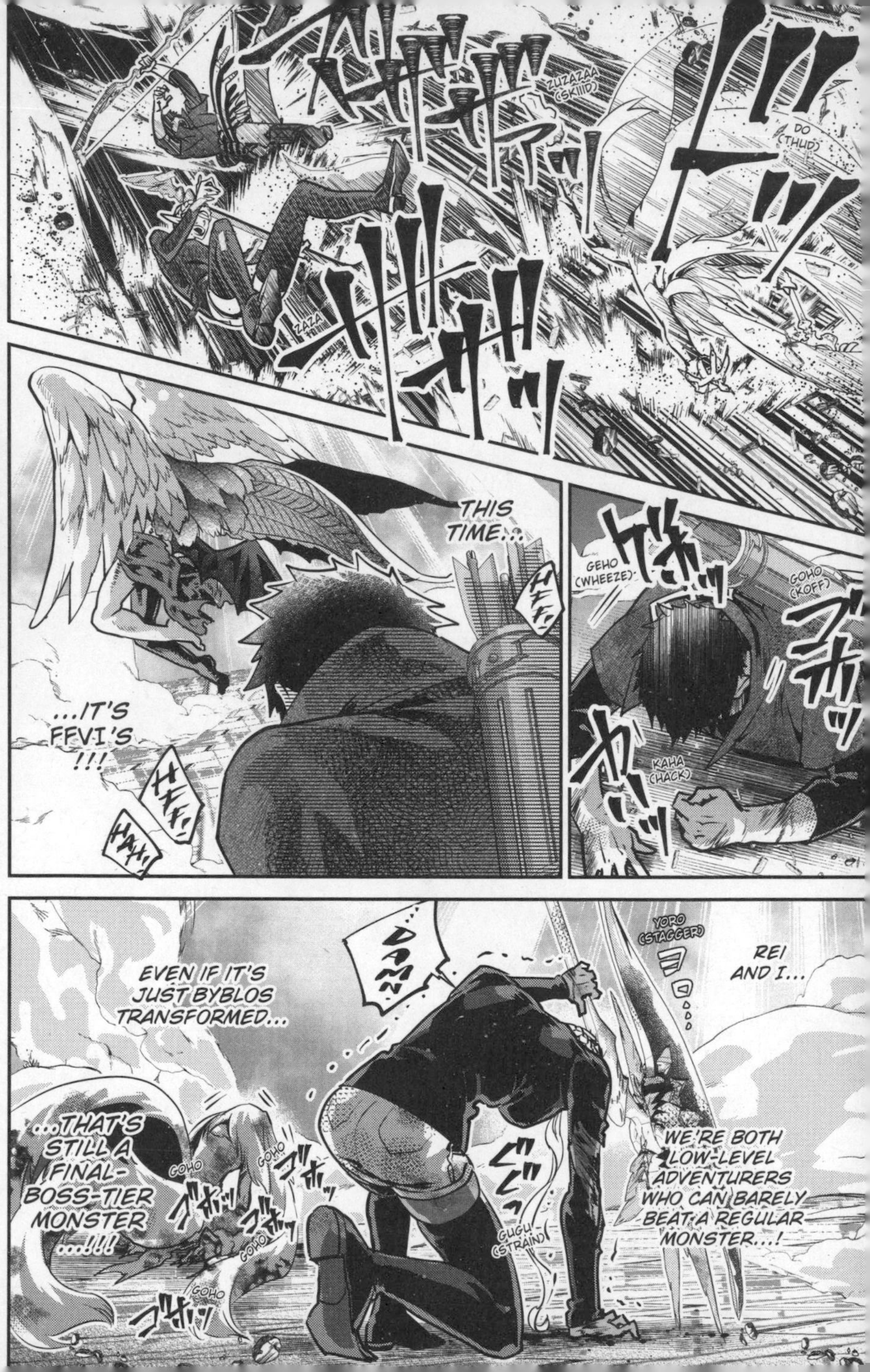
DO (THUD)
ZUZAZAA (SKIIID)
ZAZA
GOHO (KOFF)
GEHO (WHEEZE)
KAHA (HACK)
THIS TIME...
HEFF
...IT'S FFVI'S !!!
HEFF
HAH
YORO (STAGGER)
REI AND I...
WE'RE BOTH LOW-LEVEL ADVENTURERS WHO CAN BARELY BEAT A REGULAR MONSTER...!
GUGU (STRAIN)
DAMN
EVEN IF IT'S JUST BYBLOS TRANSFORMED...
...THAT'S STILL A FINAL-BOSS-TIER MONSTER ...!!!
GOHO
GOHO
GOHO
GOHO

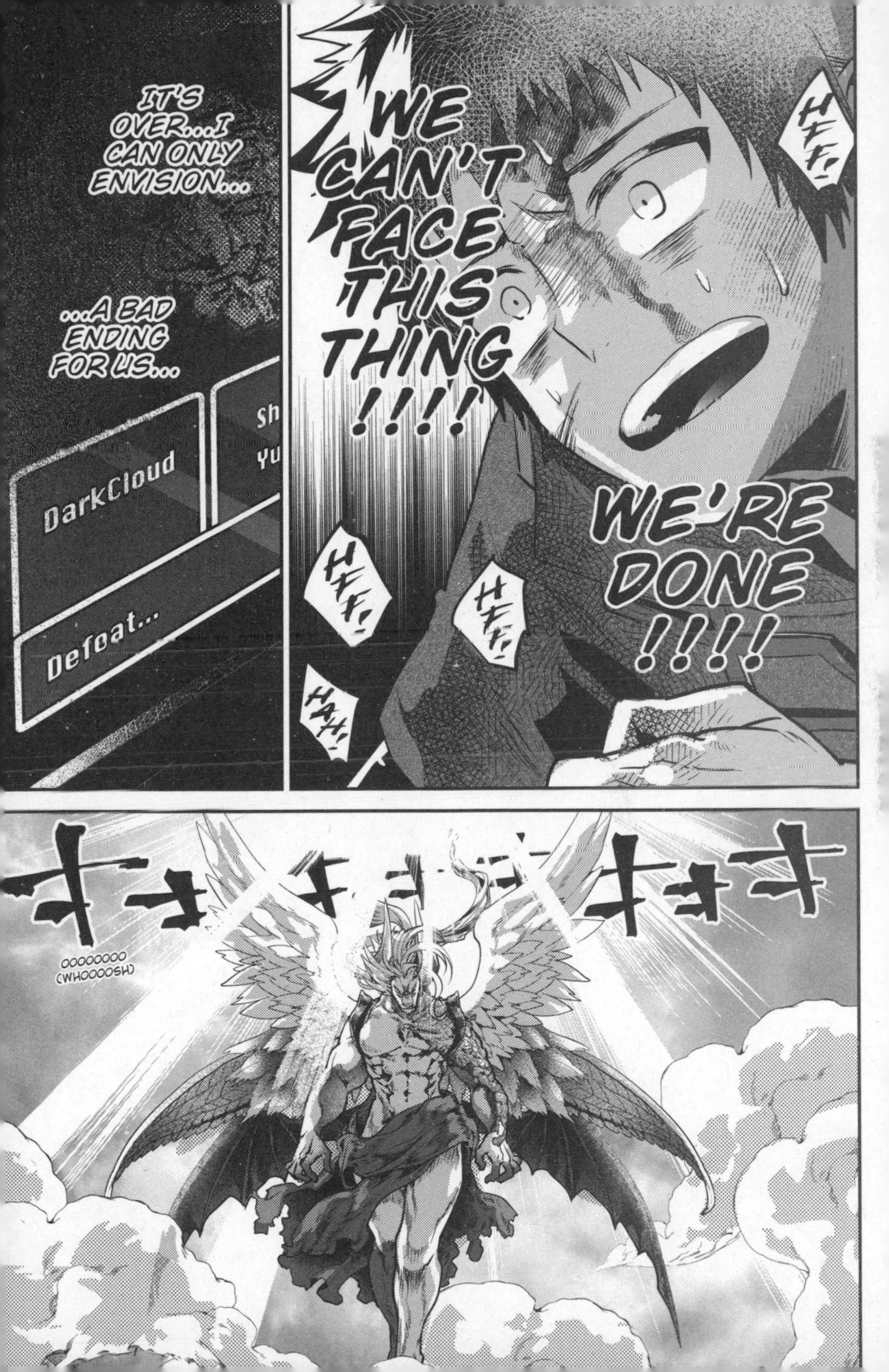
HFF!
WE CAN'T FACE THIS THING!!!!
WE'RE DONE!!!!
HFF!
HFF!
HAH!
IT'S OVER...I CAN ONLY ENVISION...
...A BAD ENDING FOR US...
DarkCloud
Defeat...
OOOOOOOO (WHOOOOSH)

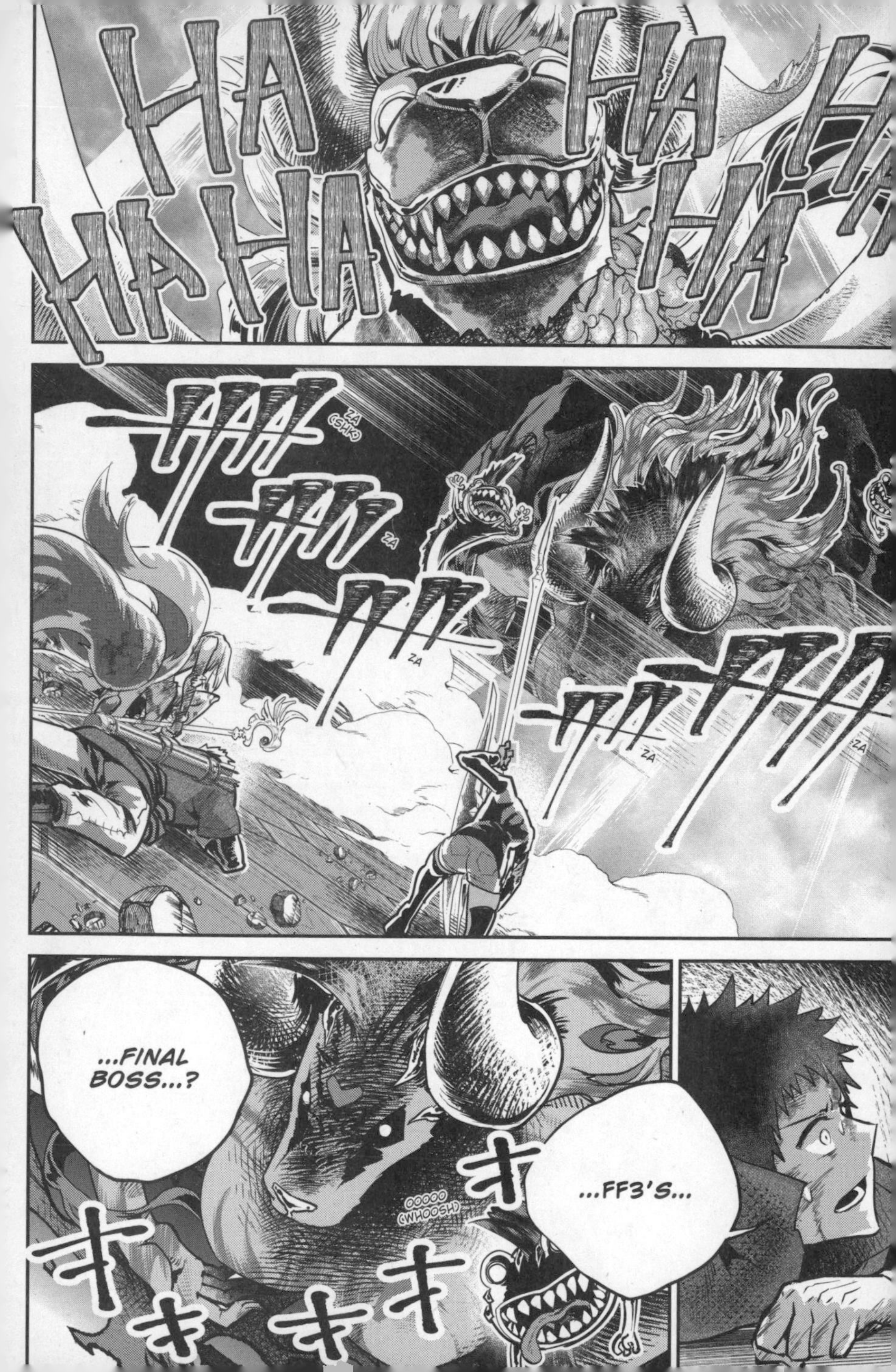

HA HA HA HA HA HA HA HA
ZA (SHK)
ZA
ZA
ZA
ZA
OOOOO (WHOOSH)
...FF3'S...
...FINAL BOSS...?

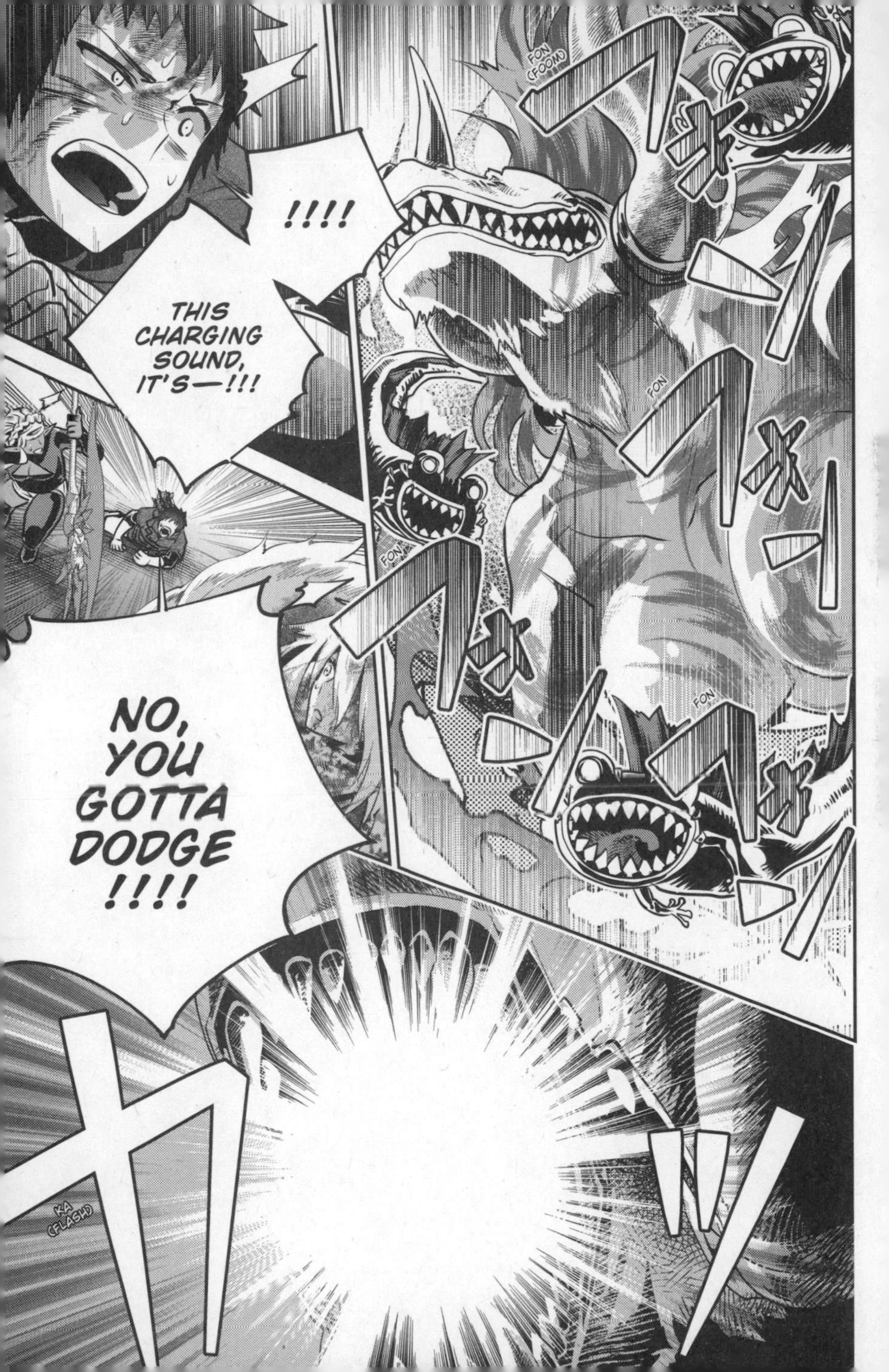
FON (FOOM)
FON
FON
FON
!!!!
THIS CHARGING SOUND, IT'S—!!!
NO, YOU GOTTA DODGE!!!!
KA (FLASH)

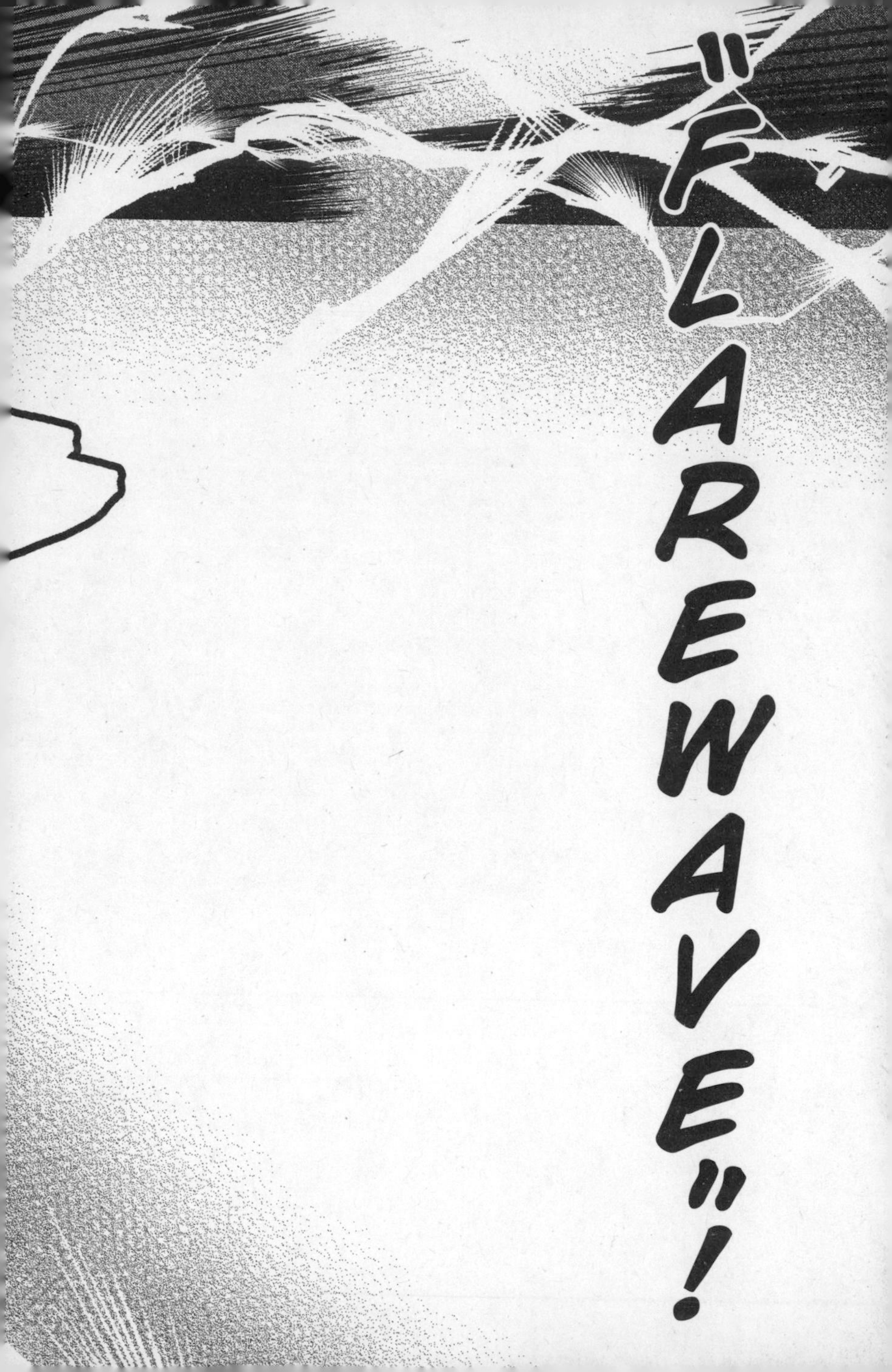
"FLAREWAVE"!

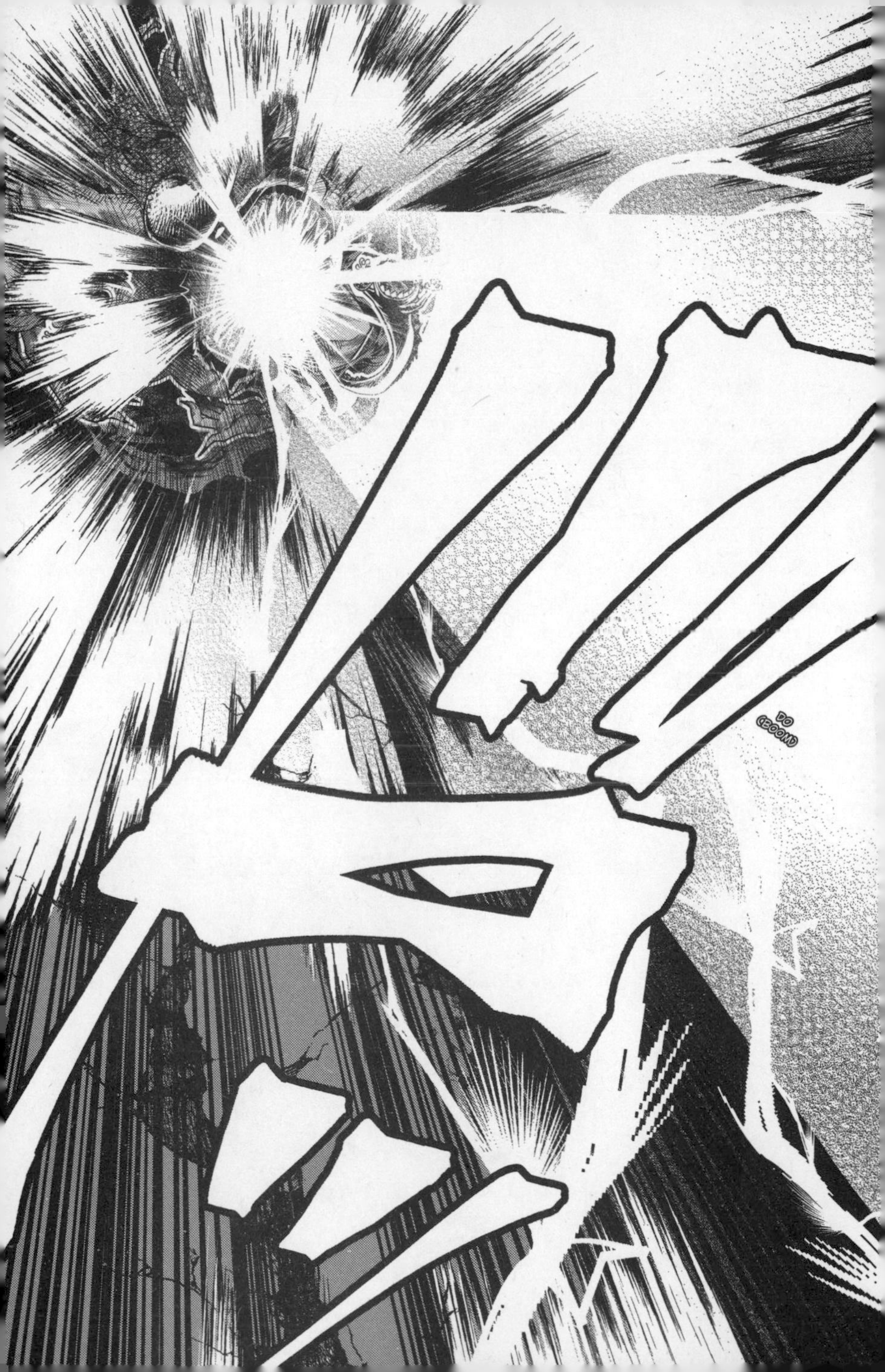
DO
(BOOM)

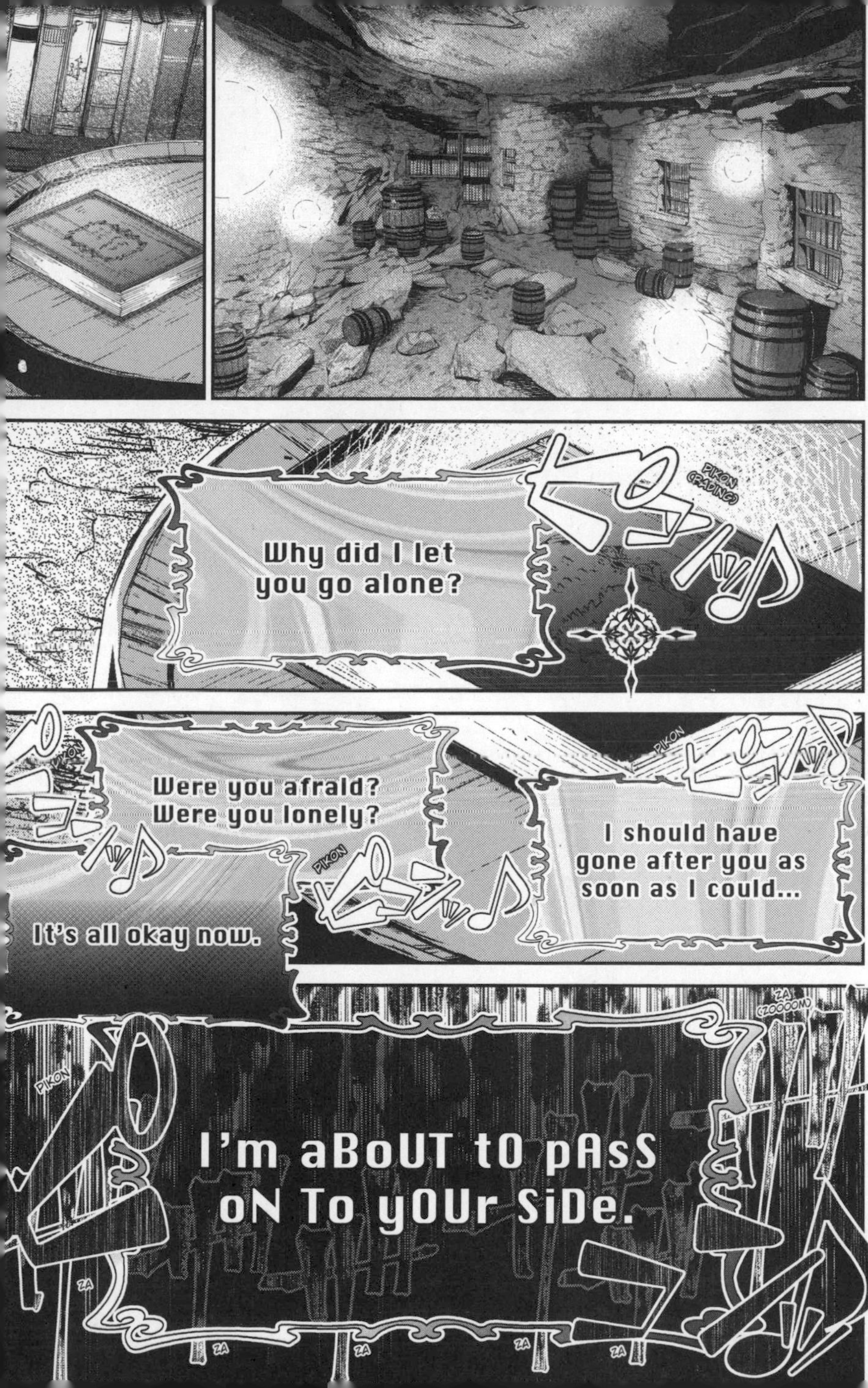
PIKON (FADING)
Why did I let you go alone?
PIKON
I should have gone after you as soon as I could...
PIKON
Were you afraid? Were you lonely?
PIKON
It's all okay now.
ZA (ZOOOOM)
PIKON
I'm aBoUT tO pAsS oN To yOUr SiDe.
ZA
ZA
ZA
ZA
ZA

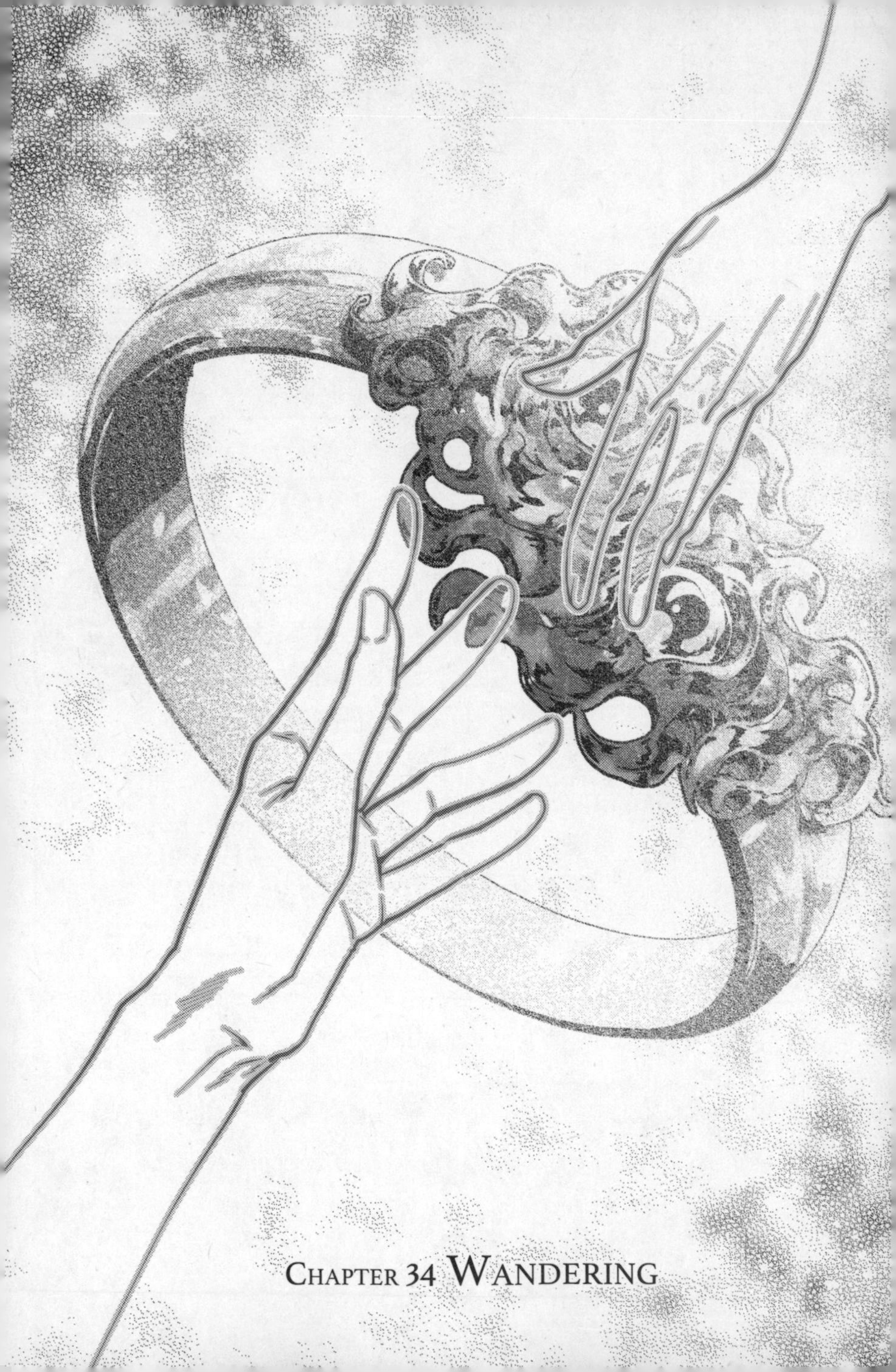

# Chapter 34 Wandering

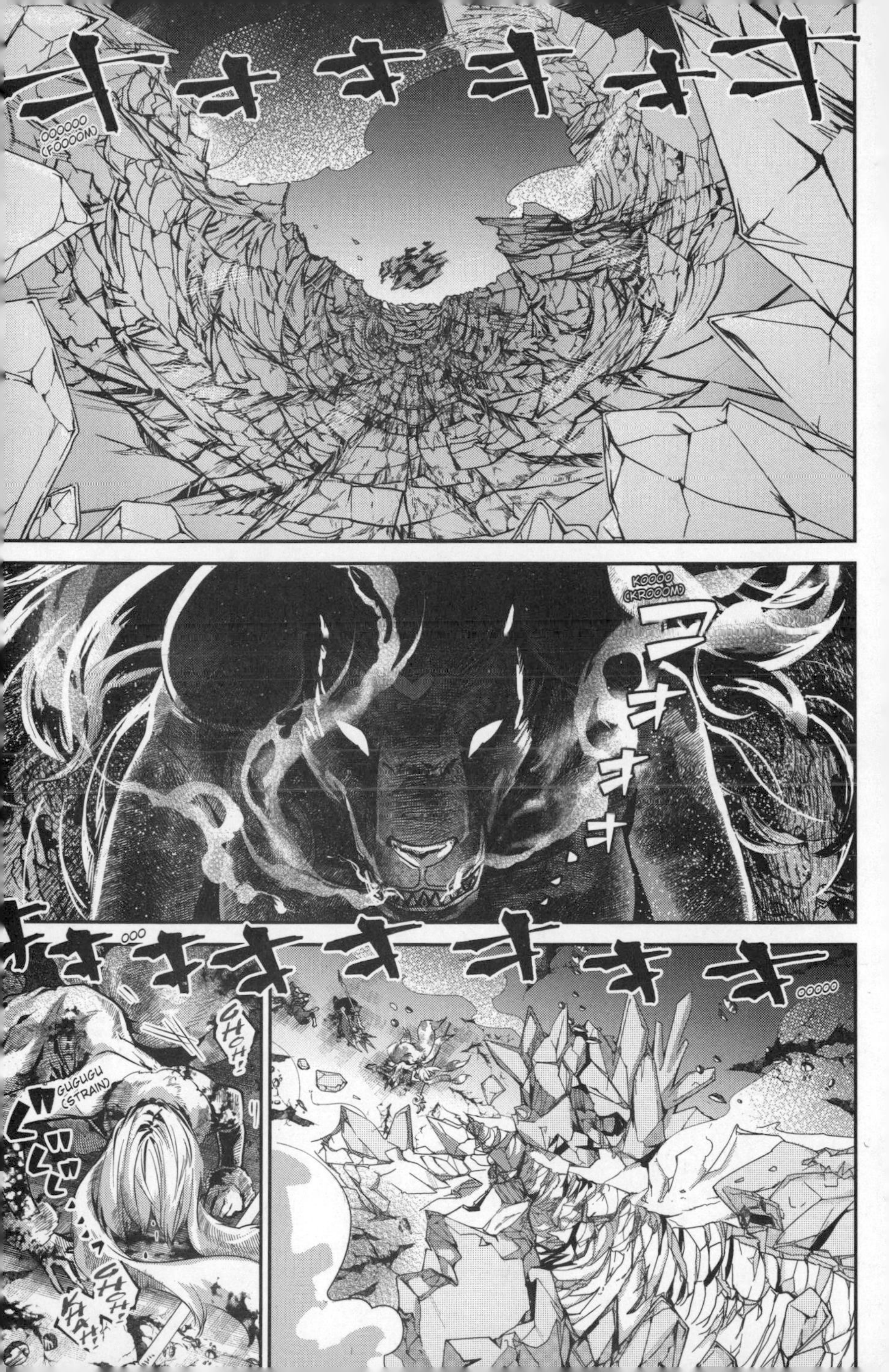
OOOOOO (FOOOOM)
KOOOO (KROOOM)
OOOOO
OOO
GUGUGU (STRAIN)
GHGH!
GHGH! KAH!

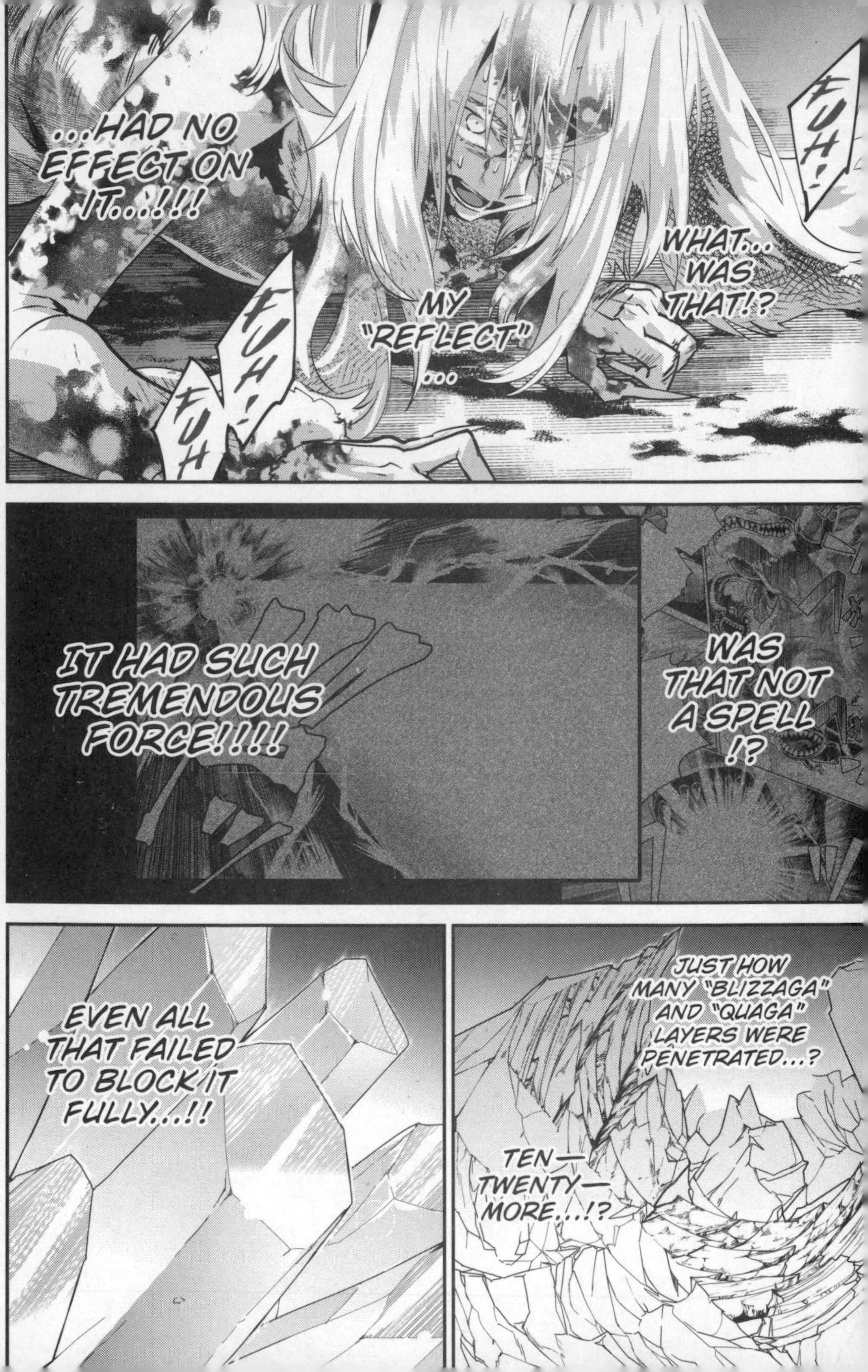
FUH!
WHAT... WAS THAT!?
MY "REFLECT"...
FUH!
FUH
...HAD NO EFFECT ON IT...!!!
WAS THAT NOT A SPELL!?
IT HAD SUCH TREMENDOUS FORCE!!!!
JUST HOW MANY "BLIZZAGA" AND "QUAGA" LAYERS WERE PENETRATED...?
TEN— TWENTY— MORE...!?
EVEN ALL THAT FAILED TO BLOCK IT FULLY...!!

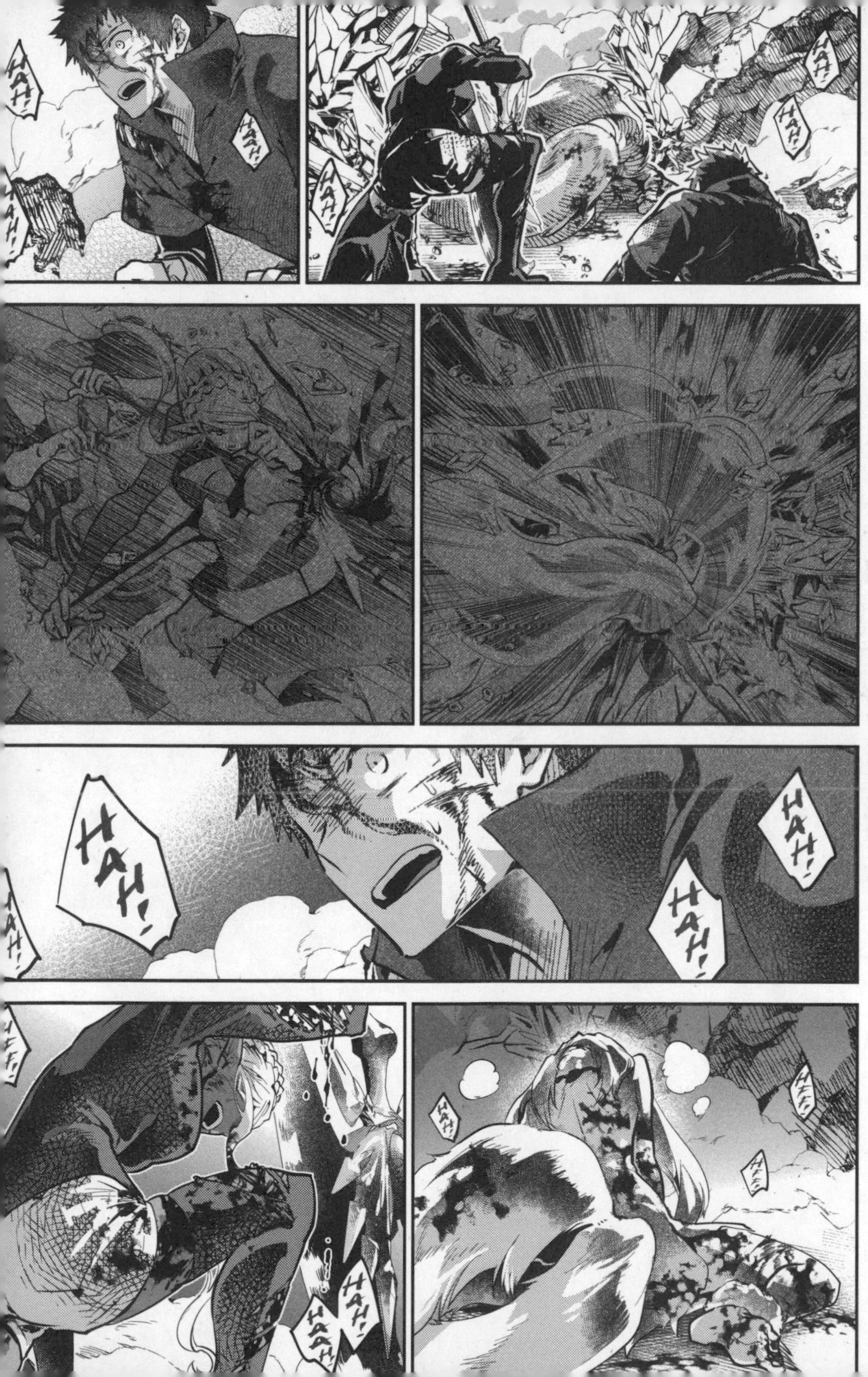

HAH!
HAH!
HAH!
HAAH!
HAH!
HAH!
HAH!
HAH!
HAH!
HAH!
HAH!
HAAH!

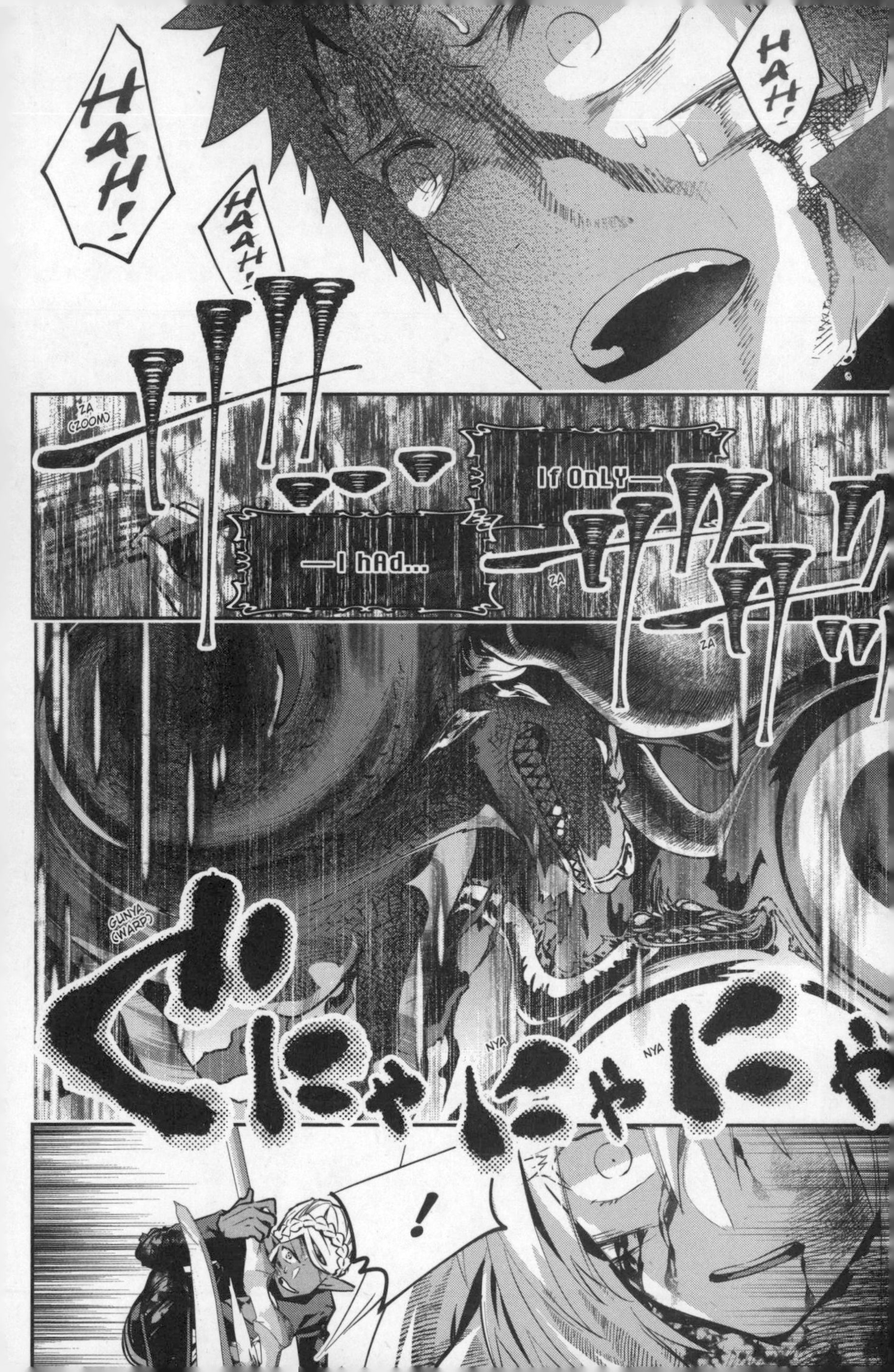
HAH!
HAH!
HAAH!
If ONLY—
—I hAd...
ZA
ZA
ZA (ZOOM)
NYA
NYA
GUNYA (WARP)
!

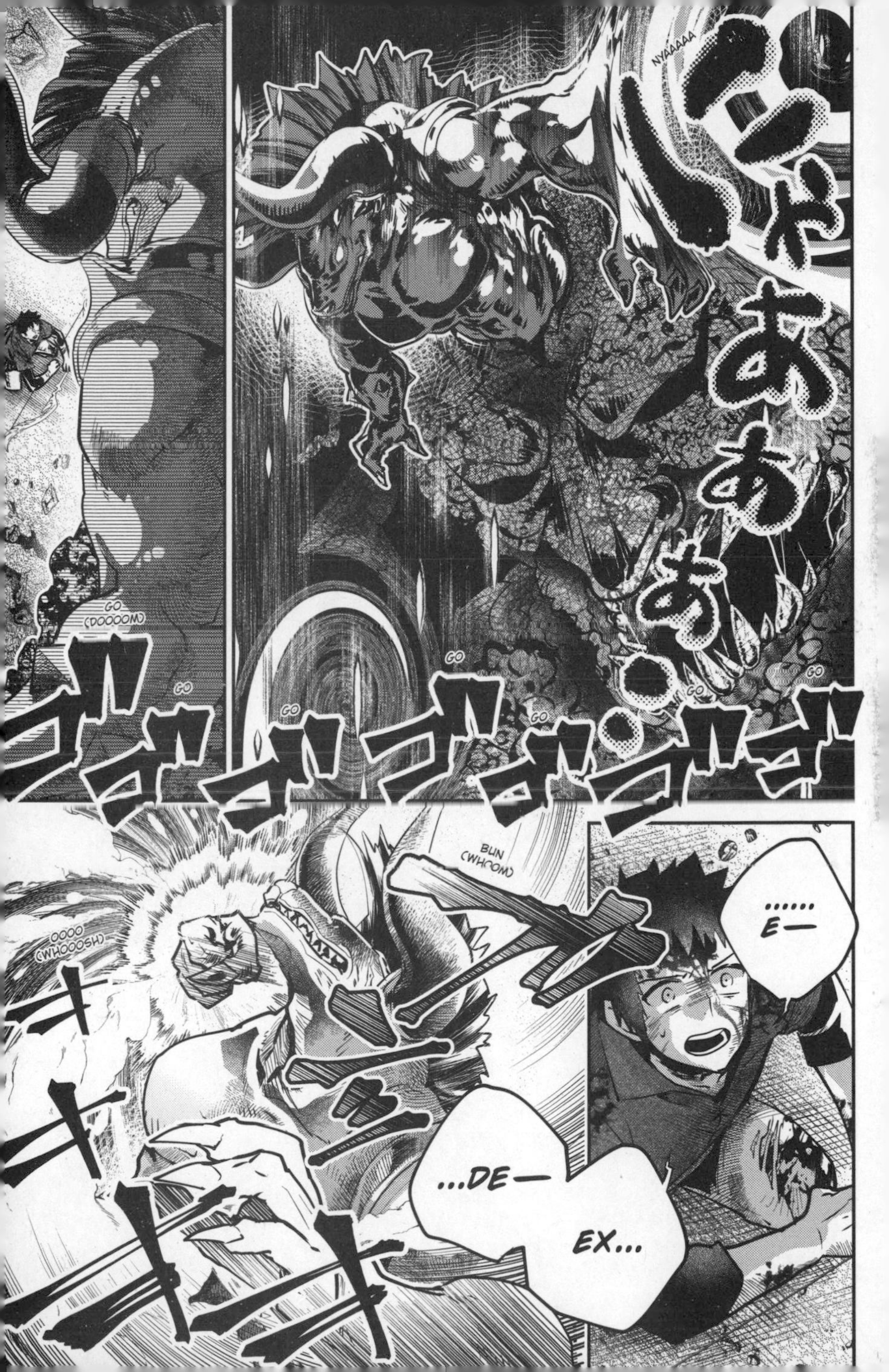
NYAAAAA
GO
GO
GO
GO
GO (DOOOOM)
GO
......E—
BUN (WHOOM)
OOOO (WHOOOSH)
...DE—
EX...

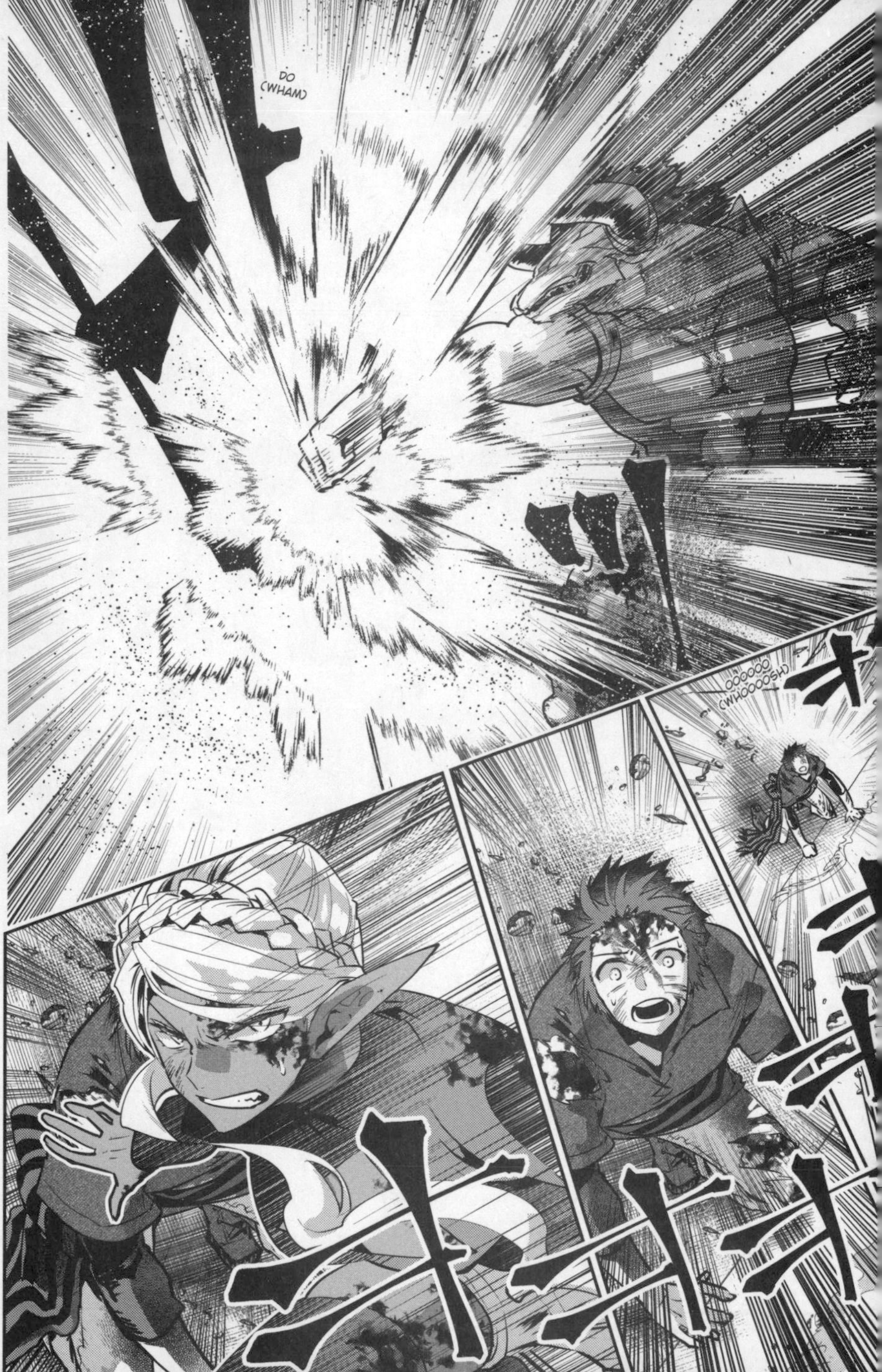
DO (WHAM)
OOOOOO (WHOOOOSH)

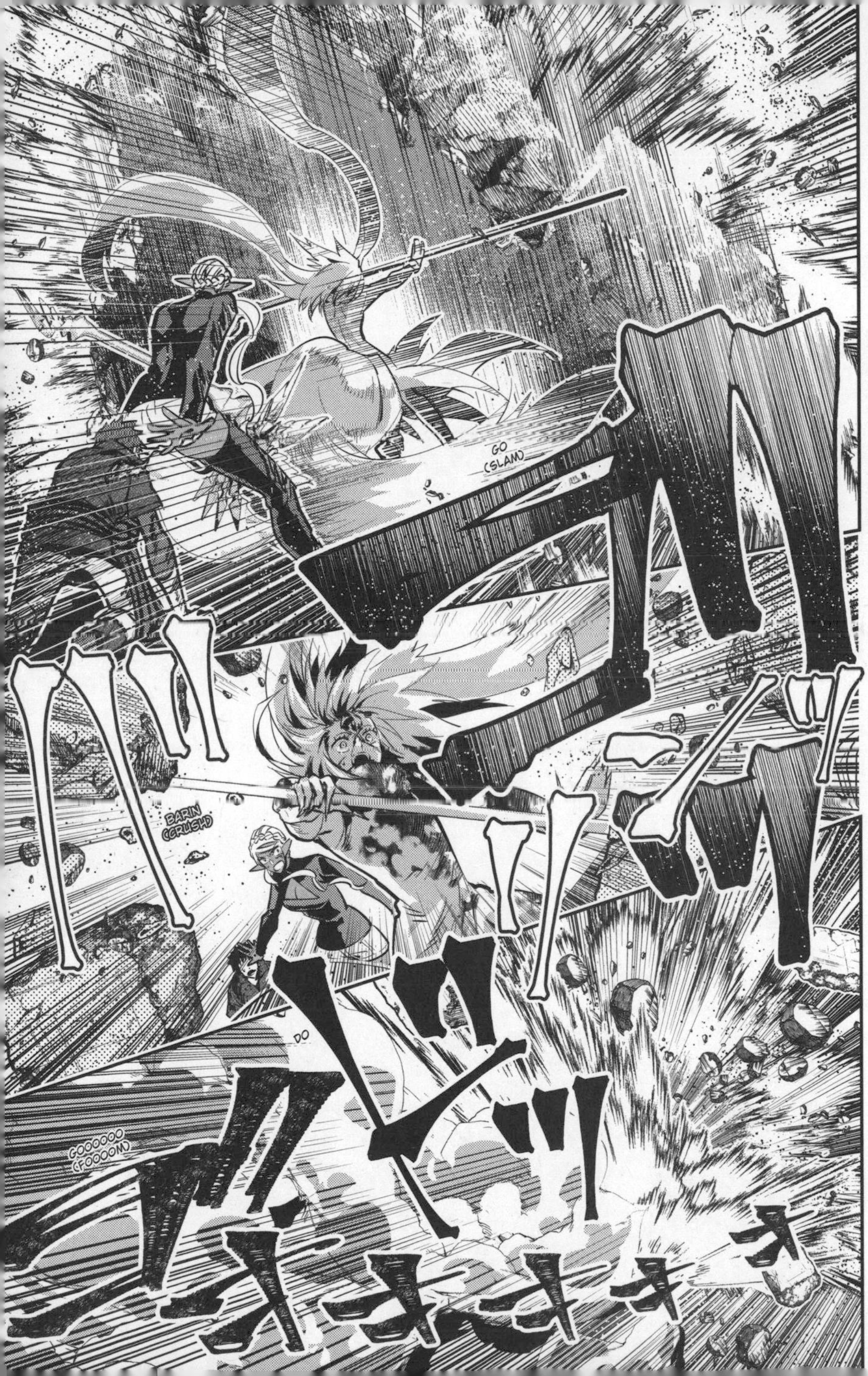
GO (SLAM)
BARIN (CRUSH)
DO
GOOOOOO (FOOOOM)

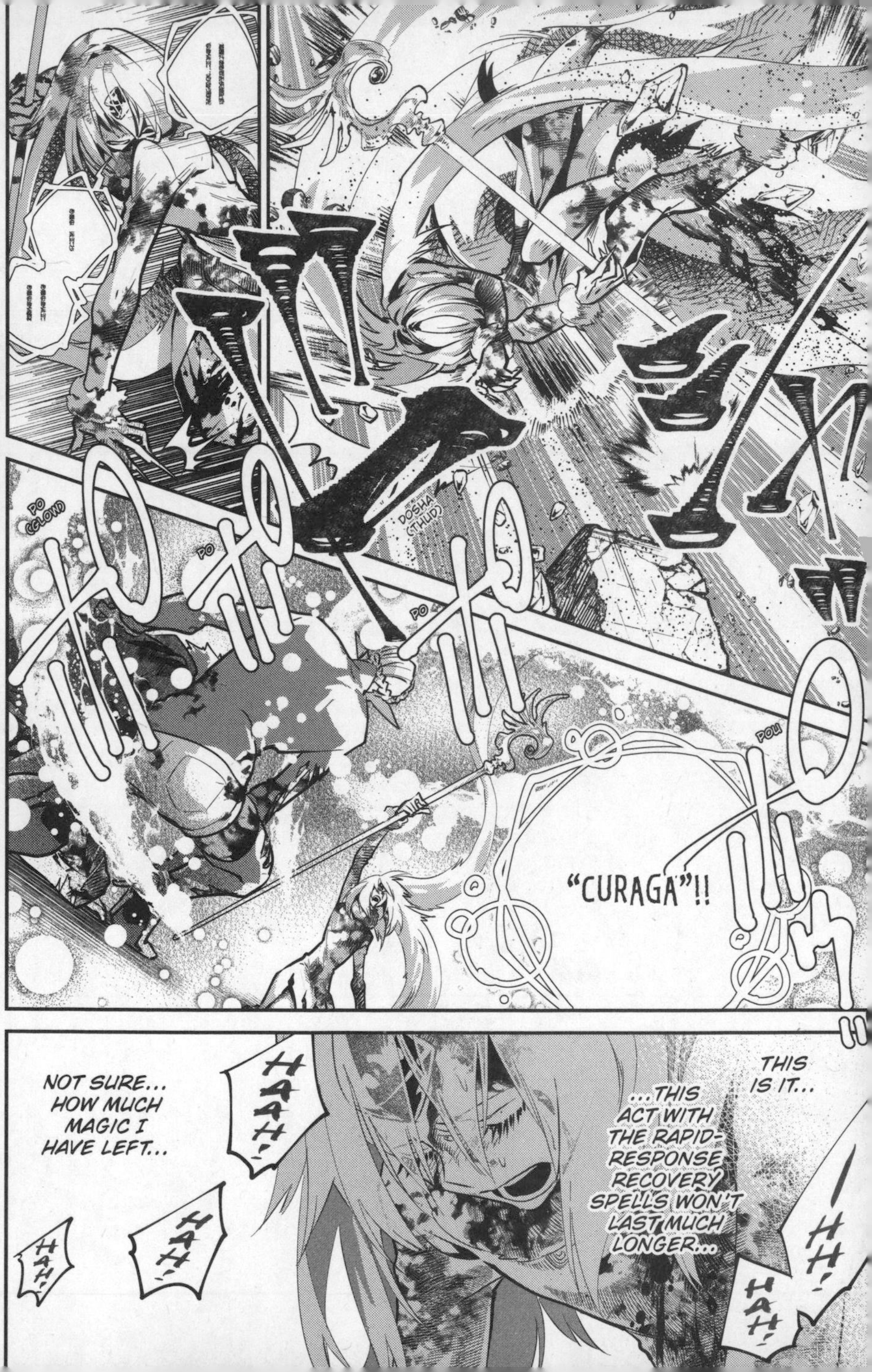
PO (GLOW)
PO
DOSHA (THUD)
PO
POU
"CURAGA"!!
THIS IS IT...
...THIS ACT WITH THE RAPID-RESPONSE RECOVERY SPELLS WON'T LAST MUCH LONGER...
HH!
HAH!
HAAH!
NOT SURE... HOW MUCH MAGIC I HAVE LEFT...
HAH!
HAH!

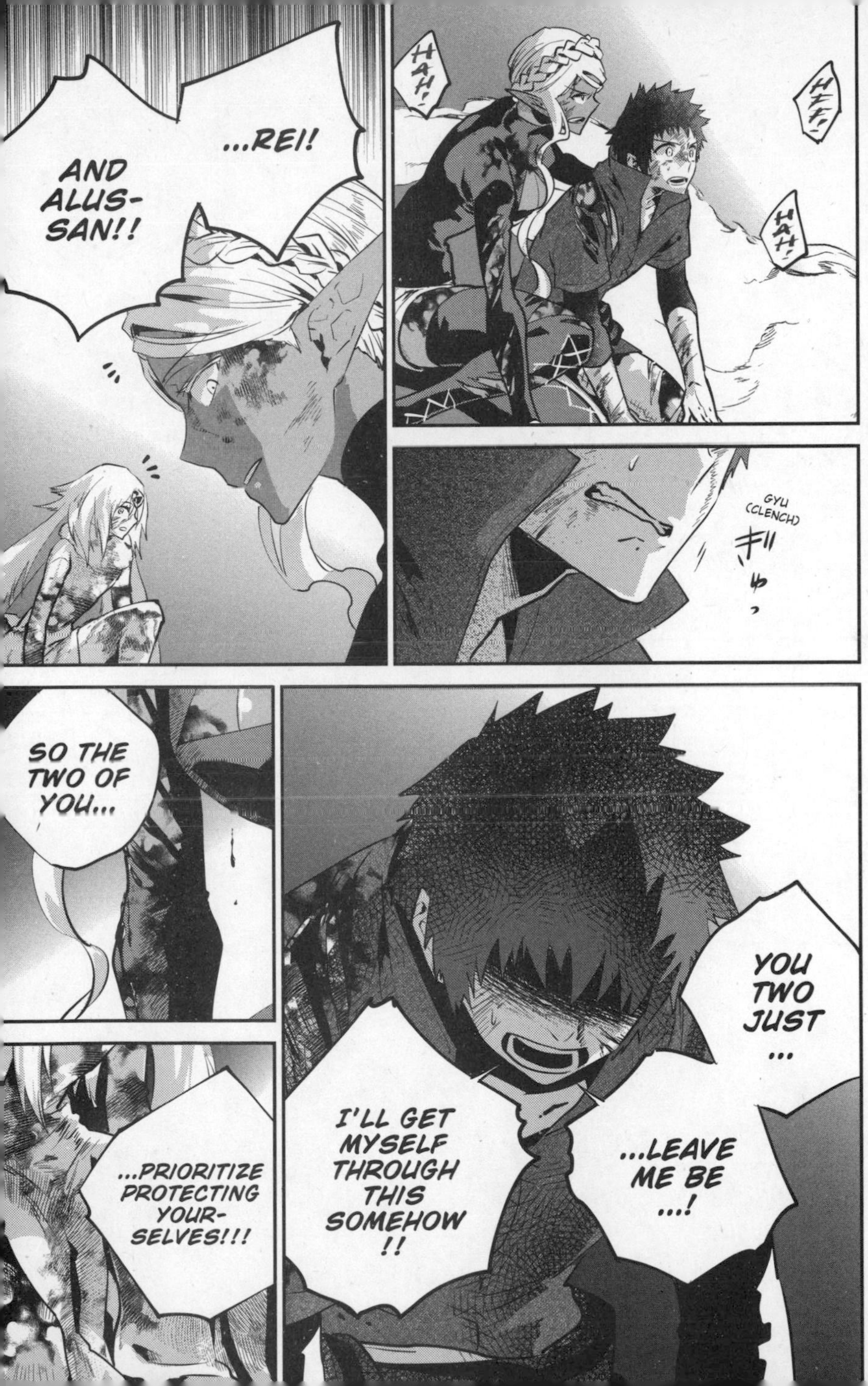
HFF!
HAH!
HAH!
GYU (CLENCH)
...REI!
AND ALUS-SAN!!
YOU TWO JUST...
...LEAVE ME BE...!
I'LL GET MYSELF THROUGH THIS SOMEHOW!!
SO THE TWO OF YOU...
...PRIORITIZE PROTECTING YOUR-SELVES!!!

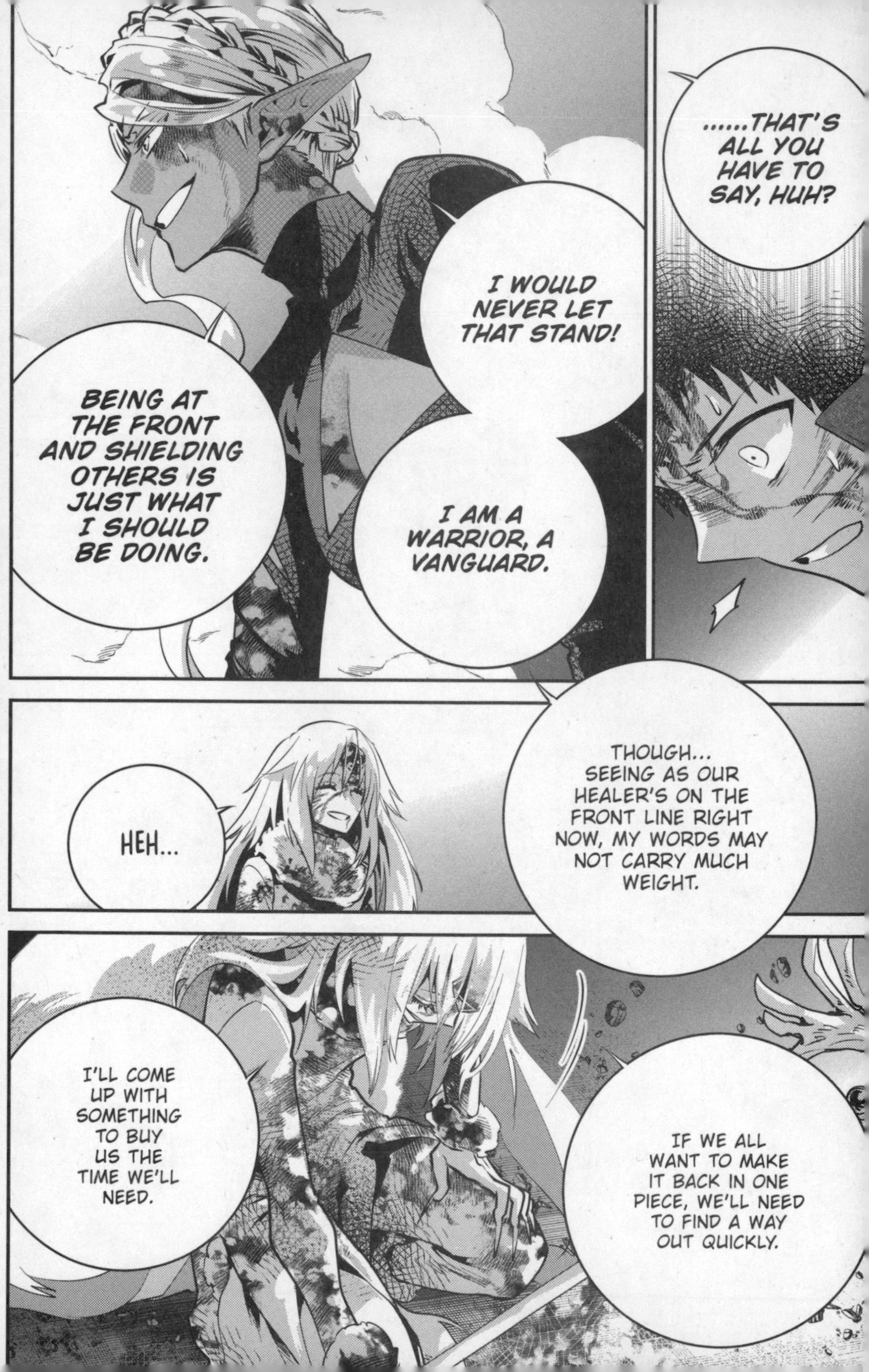
......THAT'S ALL YOU HAVE TO SAY, HUH?
I WOULD NEVER LET THAT STAND!
I AM A WARRIOR, A VANGUARD.
BEING AT THE FRONT AND SHIELDING OTHERS IS JUST WHAT I SHOULD BE DOING.
THOUGH... SEEING AS OUR HEALER'S ON THE FRONT LINE RIGHT NOW, MY WORDS MAY NOT CARRY MUCH WEIGHT.
HEH...
IF WE ALL WANT TO MAKE IT BACK IN ONE PIECE, WE'LL NEED TO FIND A WAY OUT QUICKLY.
I'LL COME UP WITH SOMETHING TO BUY US THE TIME WE'LL NEED.

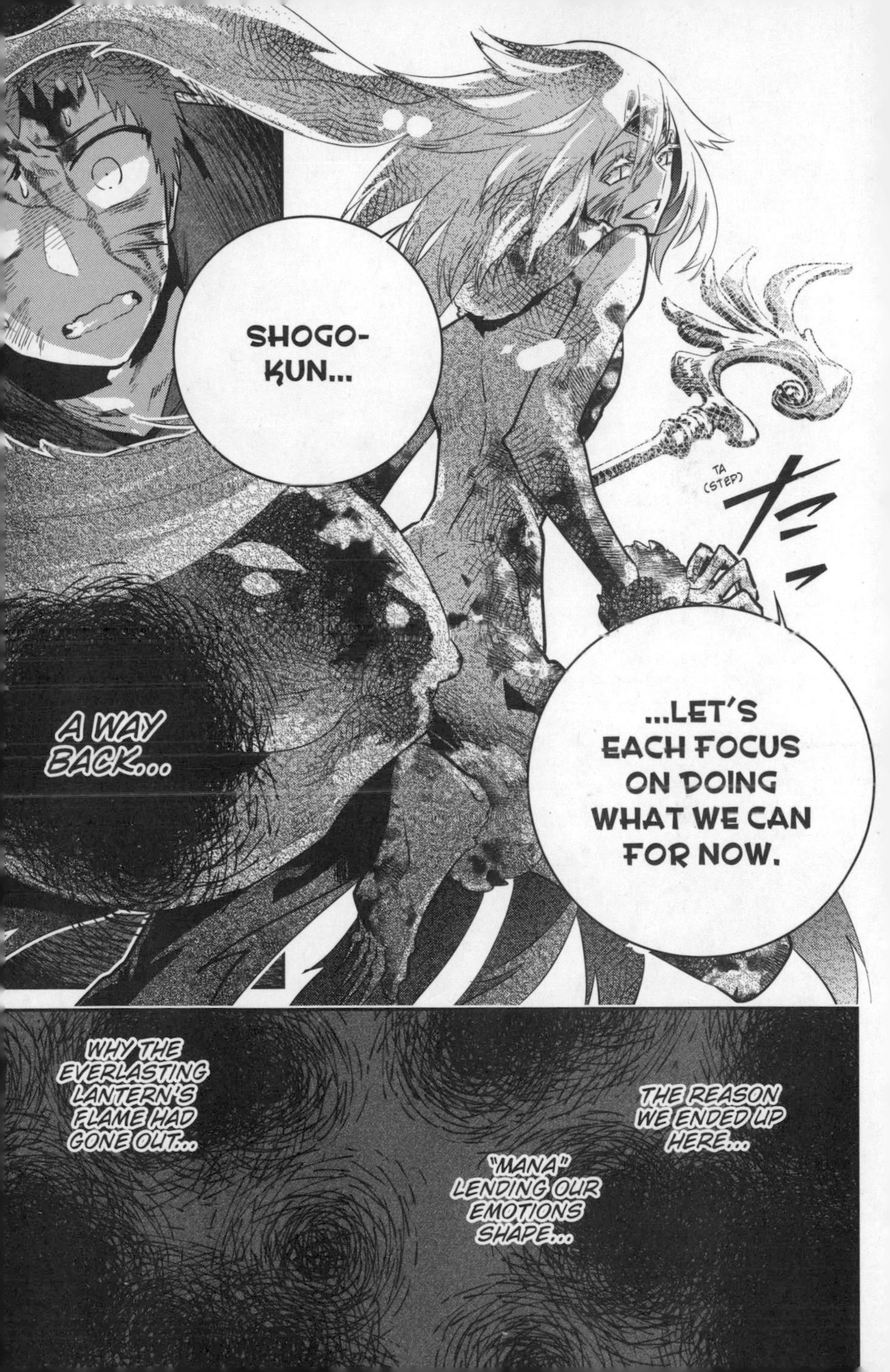
SHOGO-KUN...
TA (STEP)
...LET'S EACH FOCUS ON DOING WHAT WE CAN FOR NOW.
A WAY BACK...
THE REASON WE ENDED UP HERE...
WHY THE EVERLASTING LANTERN'S FLAME HAD GONE OUT...
"MANA" LENDING OUR EMOTIONS SHAPE...

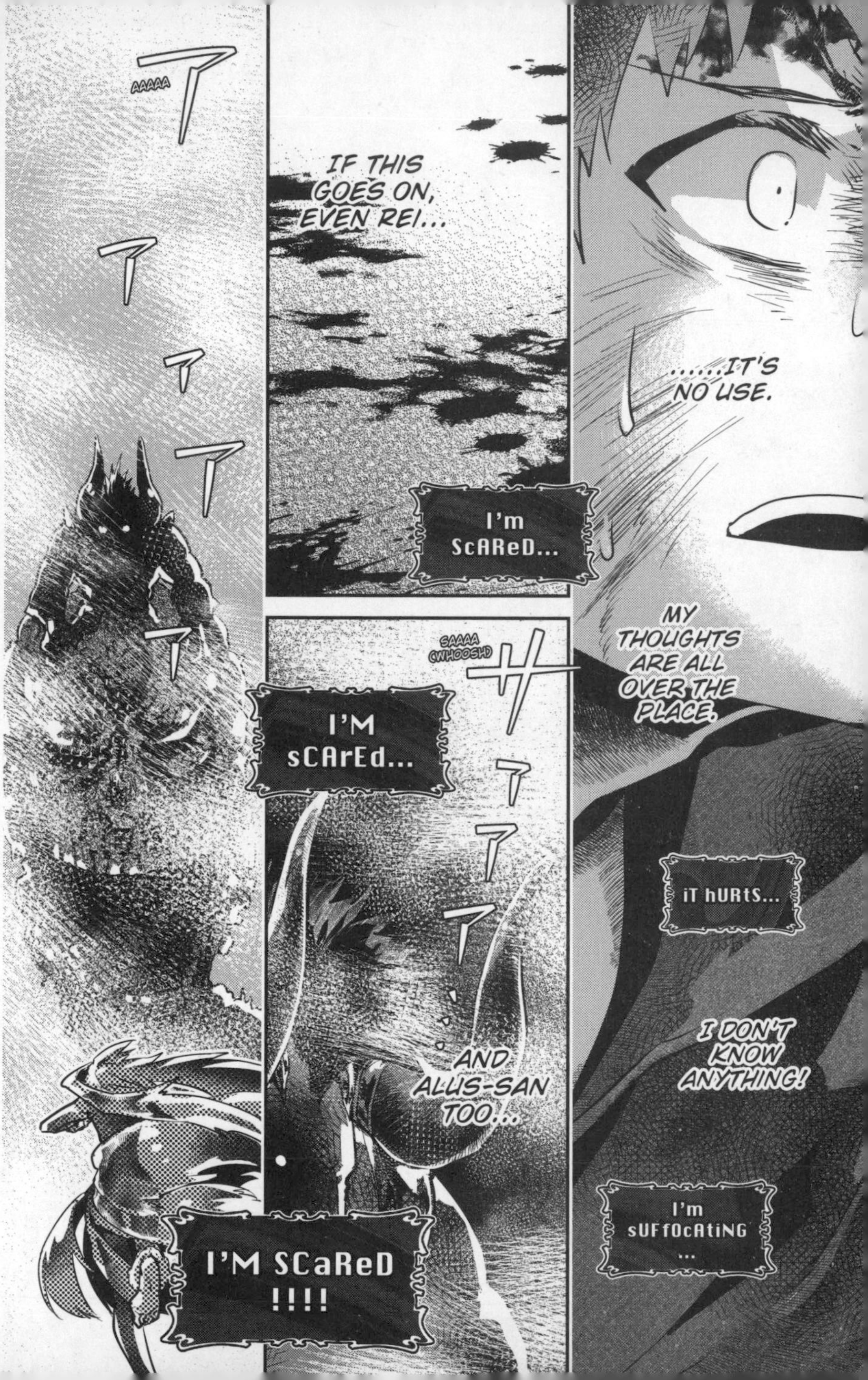
......IT'S NO USE.
MY THOUGHTS ARE ALL OVER THE PLACE.
iT hURtS...
I DON'T KNOW ANYTHING!
I'm sUFfOcAtiNG ...
IF THIS GOES ON, EVEN REI...
I'm ScAReD...
SAAAA (WHOOSH)
I'M sCArEd...
AND ALUS-SAN TOO...
AAAAA
I'M SCaReD !!!!

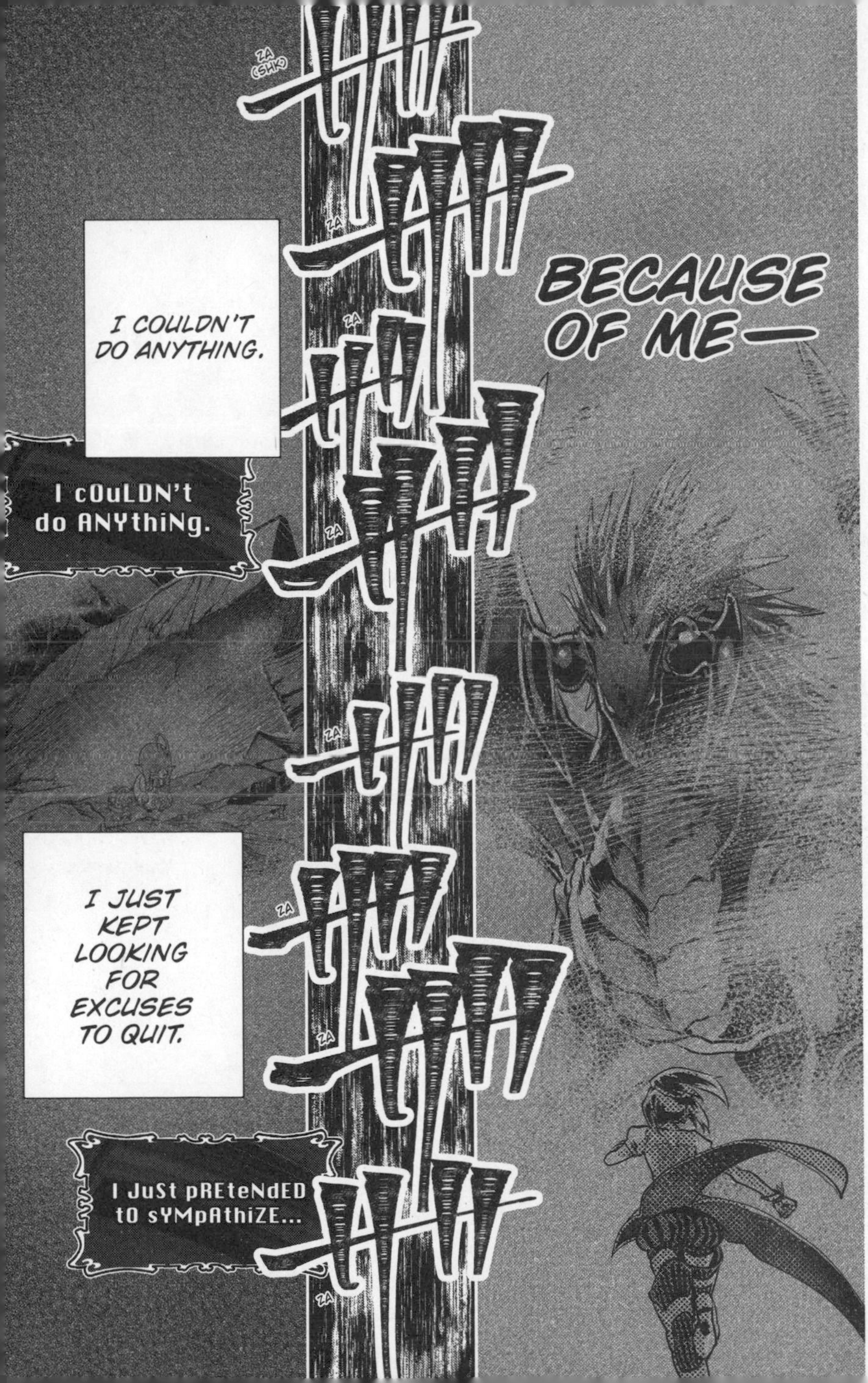
BECAUSE OF ME—
ZA (SHK)
I COULDN'T DO ANYTHING.
I cOuLDN't do ANYthiNg.
I JUST KEPT LOOKING FOR EXCUSES TO QUIT.
I JuSt pREteNdED tO sYMpAthiZE...

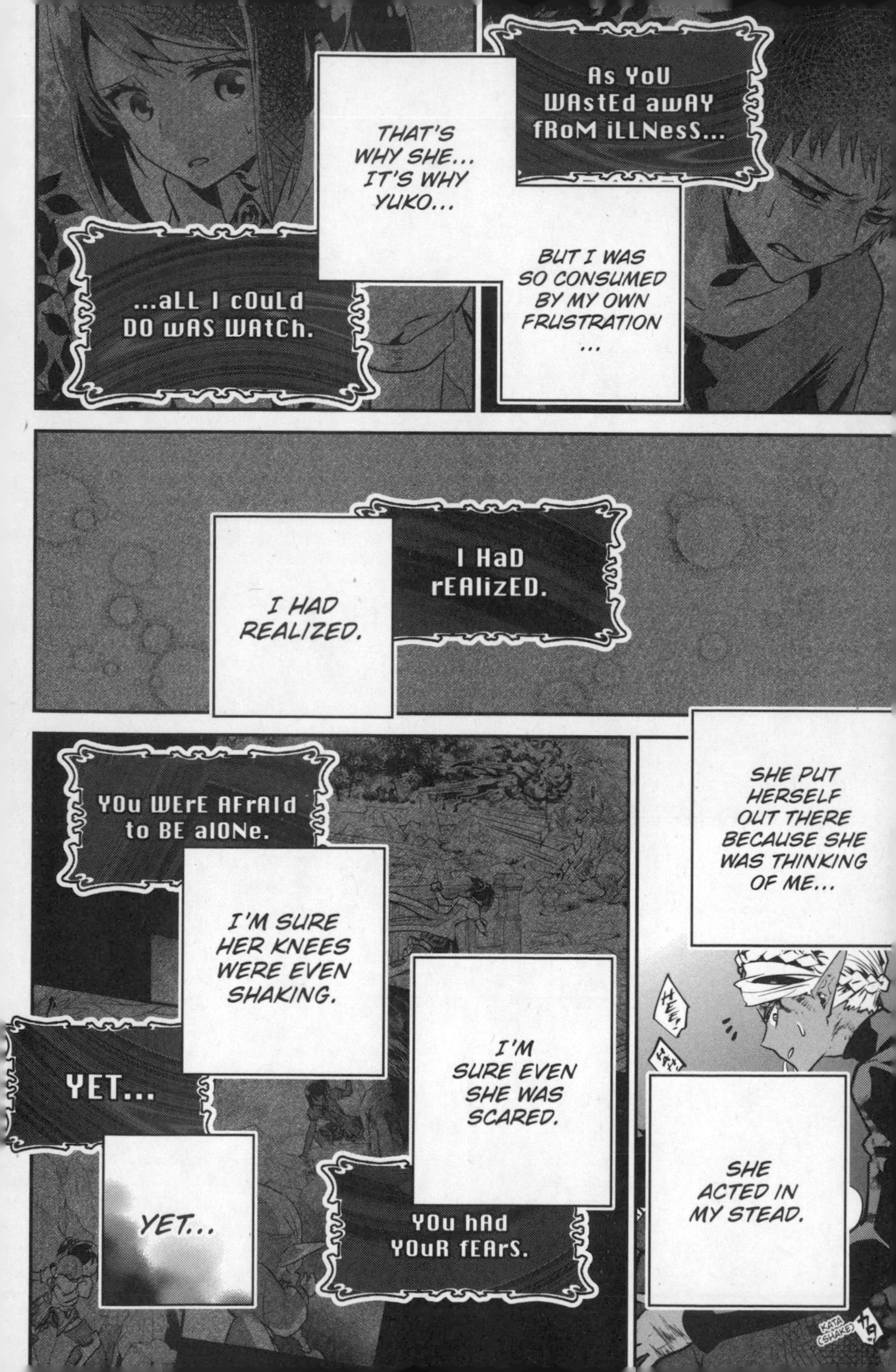
As YoU WAstEd awAY fRoM iLLNesS...
THAT'S WHY SHE... IT'S WHY YUKO...
BUT I WAS SO CONSUMED BY MY OWN FRUSTRATION ...
...aLL I cOuLd DO wAS WAtCh.
I HaD rEAlizED.
I HAD REALIZED.
SHE PUT HERSELF OUT THERE BECAUSE SHE WAS THINKING OF ME...
SHE ACTED IN MY STEAD.
KATA (SHAKE)
YOu WErE AFrAId to BE alONe.
I'M SURE HER KNEES WERE EVEN SHAKING.
I'M SURE EVEN SHE WAS SCARED.
YET...
YOu hAd YOuR fEArS.
YET...

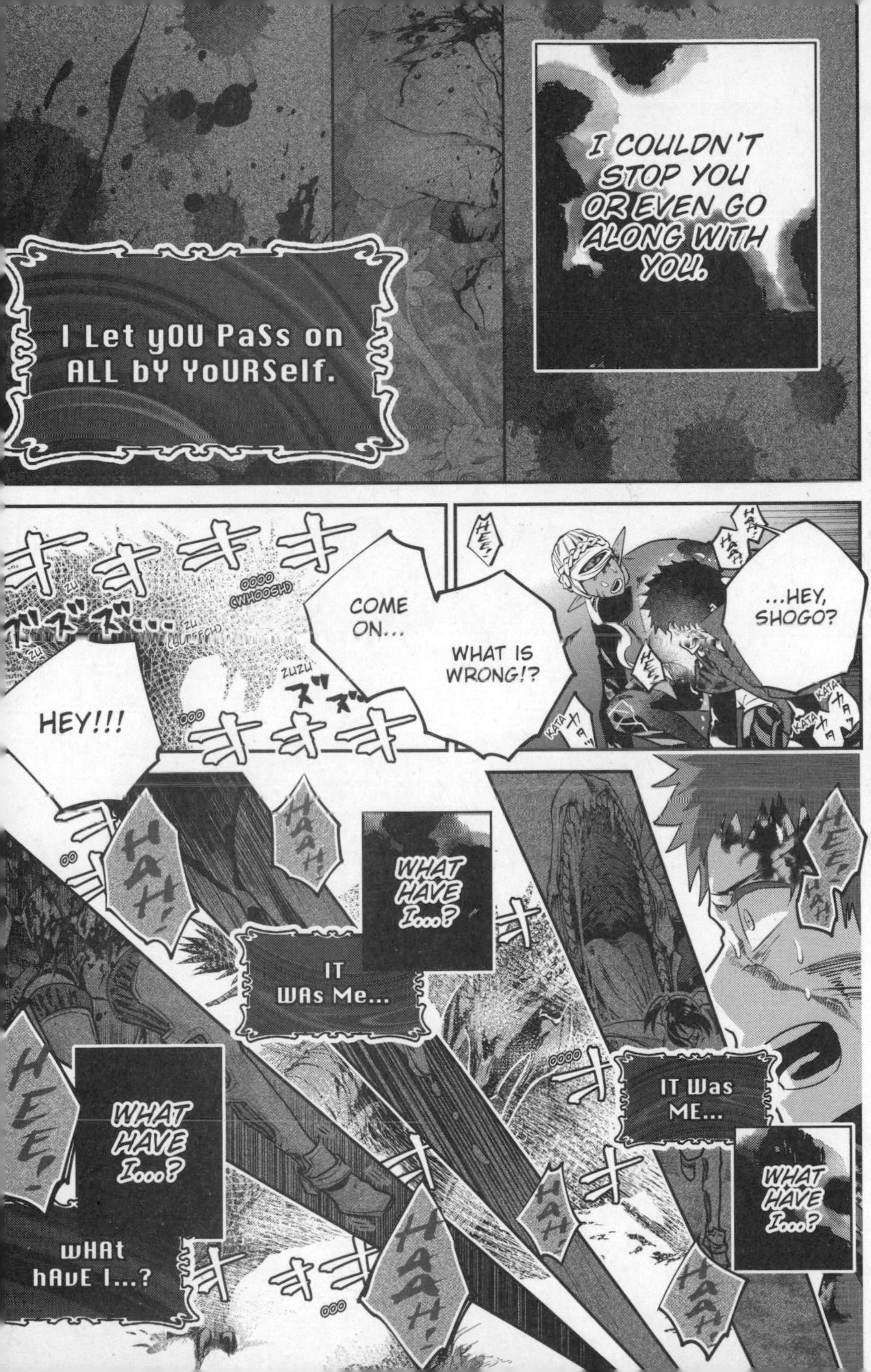
I COULDN'T STOP YOU OR EVEN GO ALONG WITH YOU.
I Let yOU PaSs on ALL bY YoURSelf.
HAH HAH
HEE!
...HEY, SHOGO?
WHAT IS WRONG!?
COME ON...
KATA KATA
OOOO (WHOOSH)
ZU ZU
ZUZU
OOO
HEY!!!
HEE HAH
IT Was ME...
WHAT HAVE I...?
OOOO
WHAT HAVE I...?
IT WAs Me...
HAAH!
HAH!
WHAT HAVE I...?
wHAt hAvE I...?
OOO

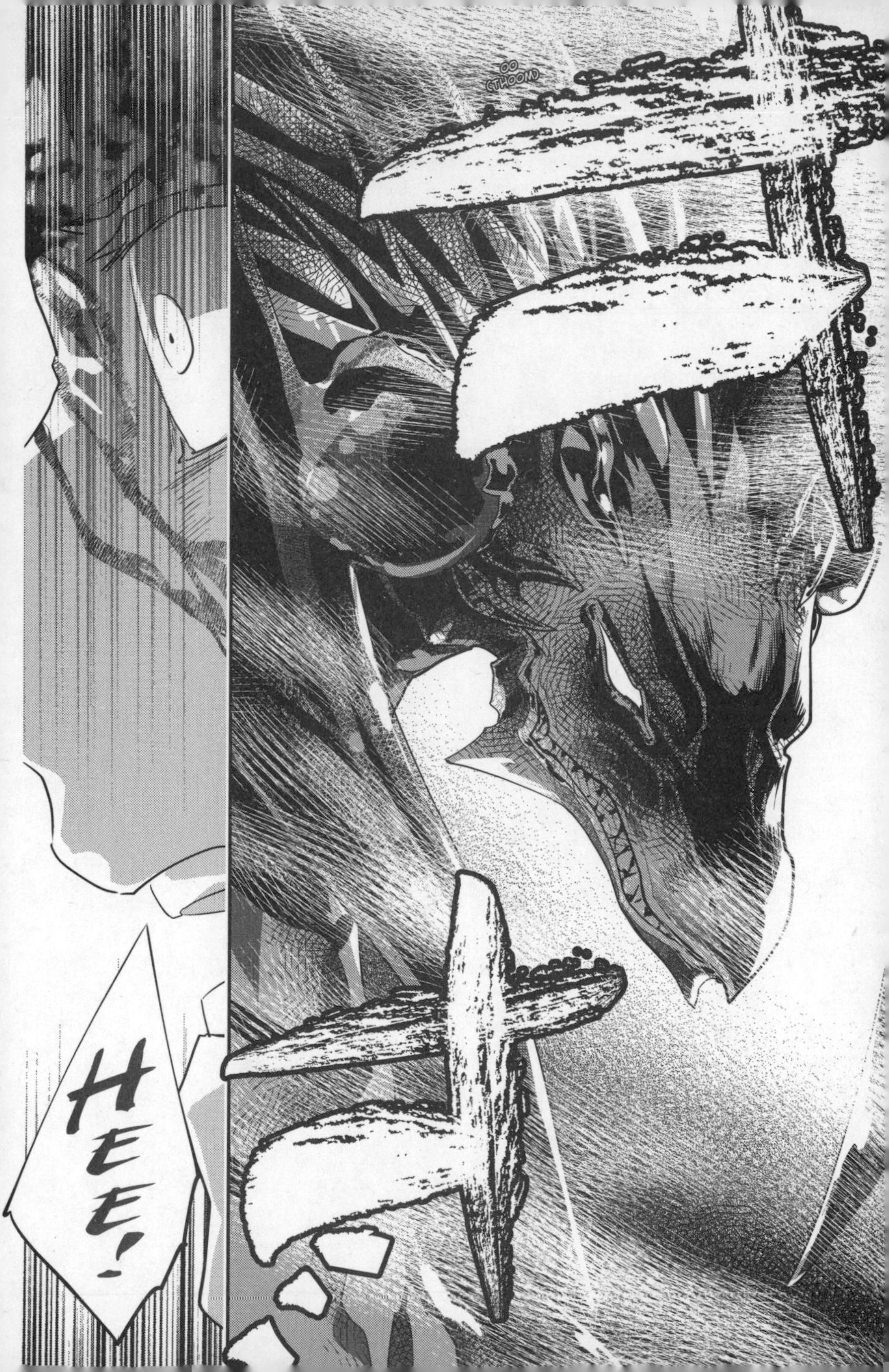
OO (THOOM)
HEE!

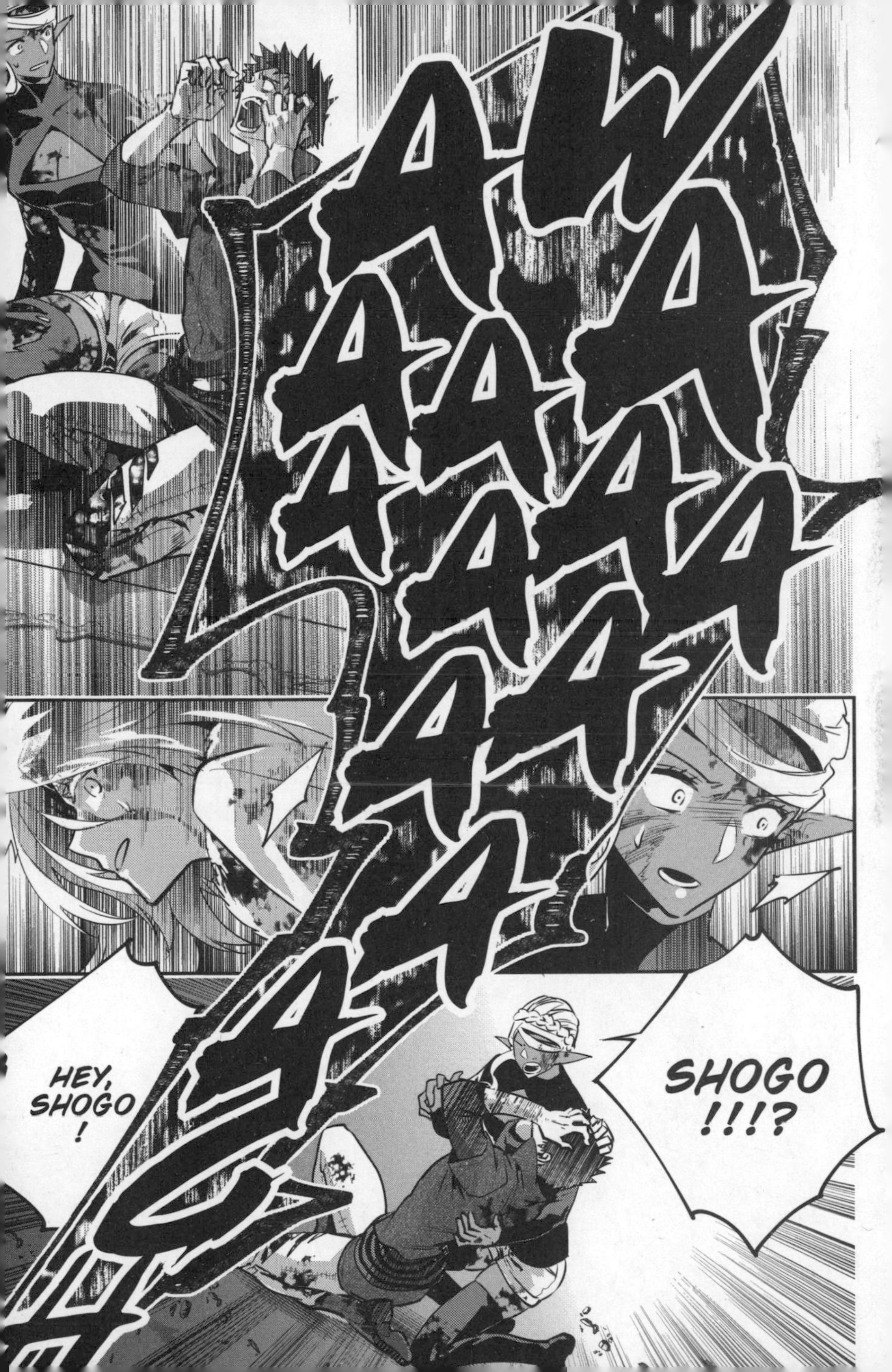
SHOGO!!!?
HEY, SHOGO!

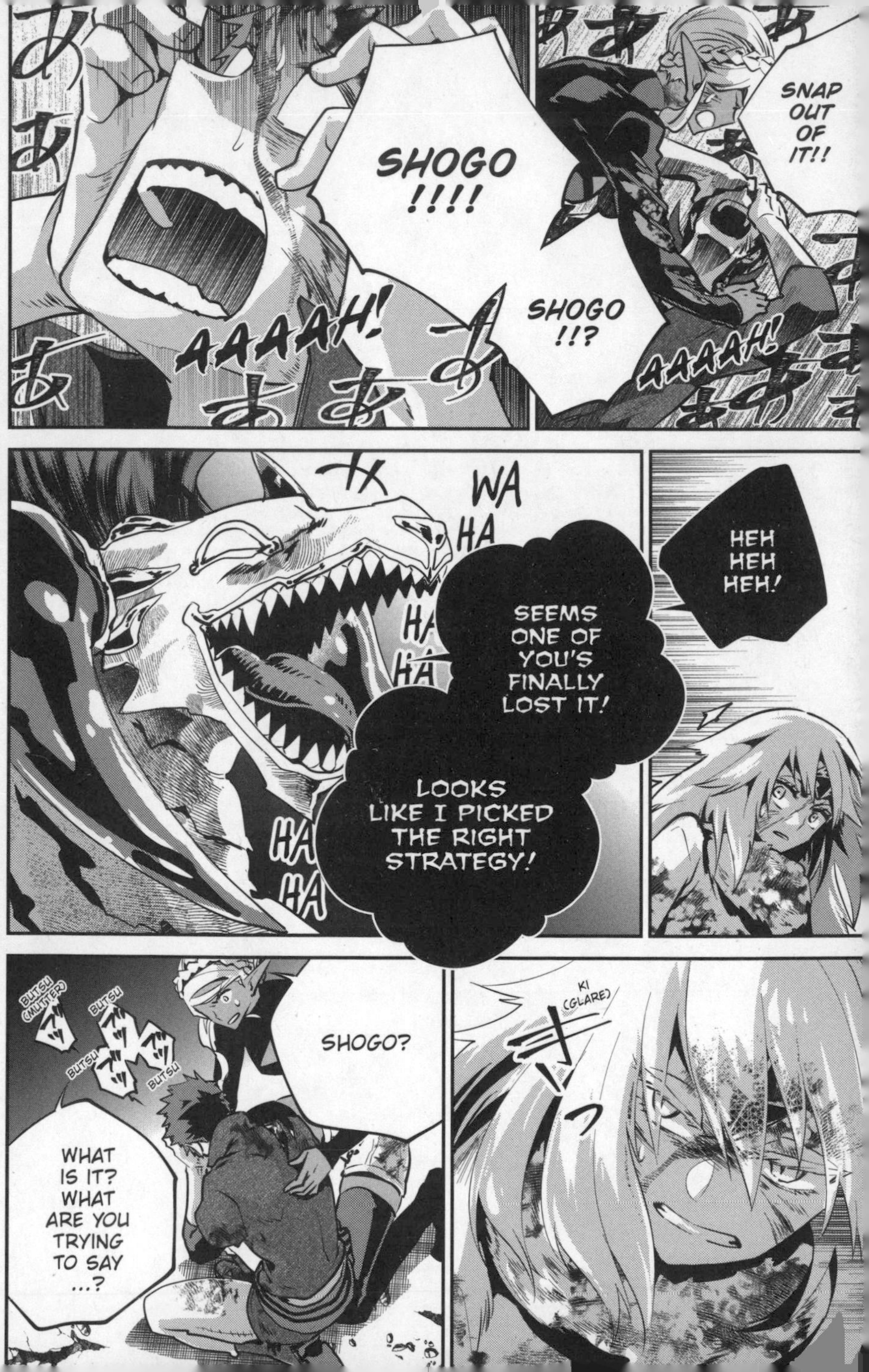
SNAP OUT OF IT!!
SHOGO !!?
AAAAAH!
SHOGO !!!!
AAAAAH!
HEH HEH HEH!
WA HA HA HA HA HA
SEEMS ONE OF YOU'S FINALLY LOST IT!
LOOKS LIKE I PICKED THE RIGHT STRATEGY!
KI (GLARE)
SHOGO?
BUTSU (MUTTER) BUTSU BUTSU BUTSU
WHAT IS IT? WHAT ARE YOU TRYING TO SAY ...?

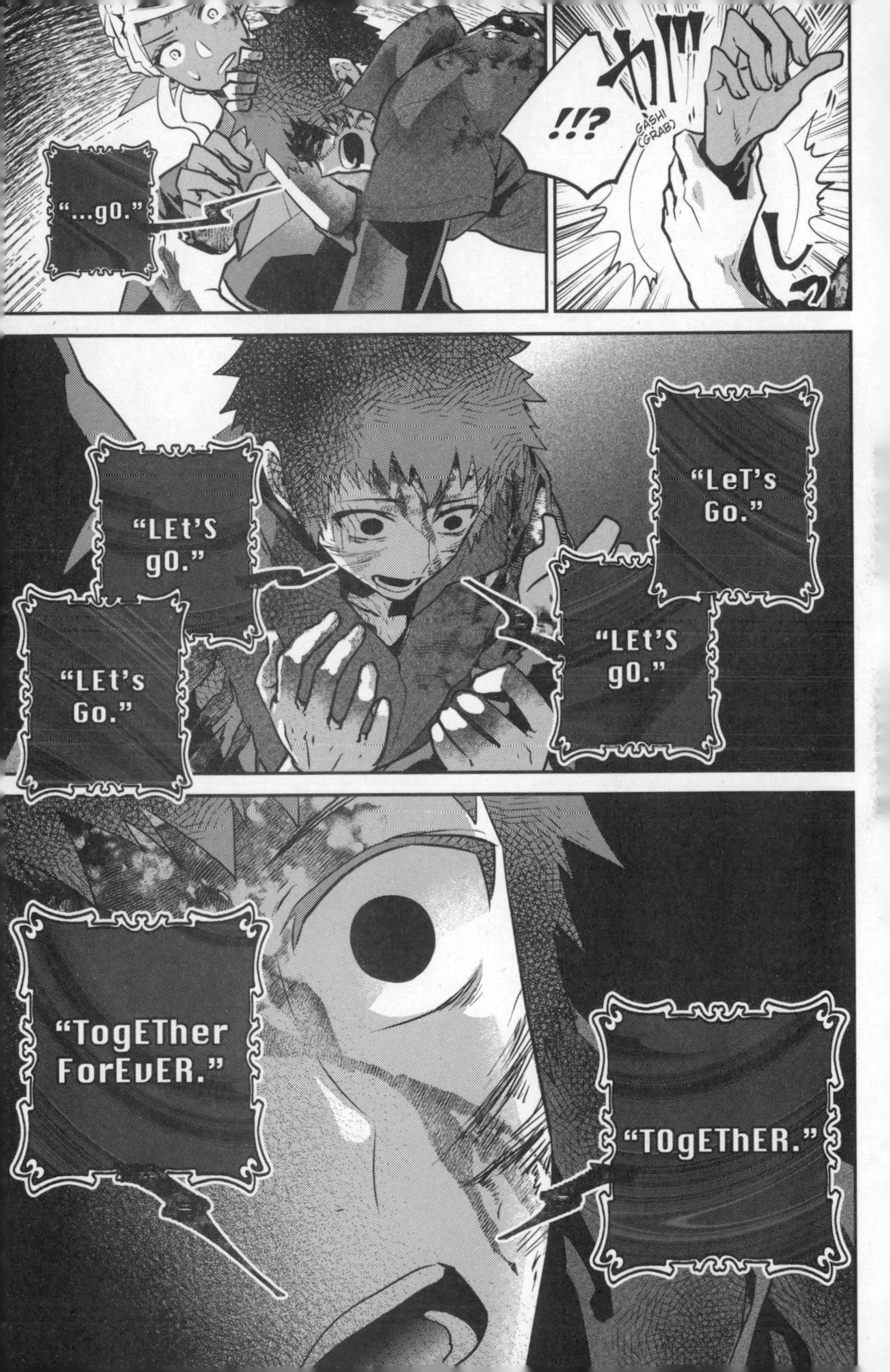

!!?
GASHI (GRAB)
"...gO."
"LeT's Go."
"LEt'S gO."
"LEt'S gO."
"LEt's Go."
"TOgEThER."
"TogETher ForEvER."

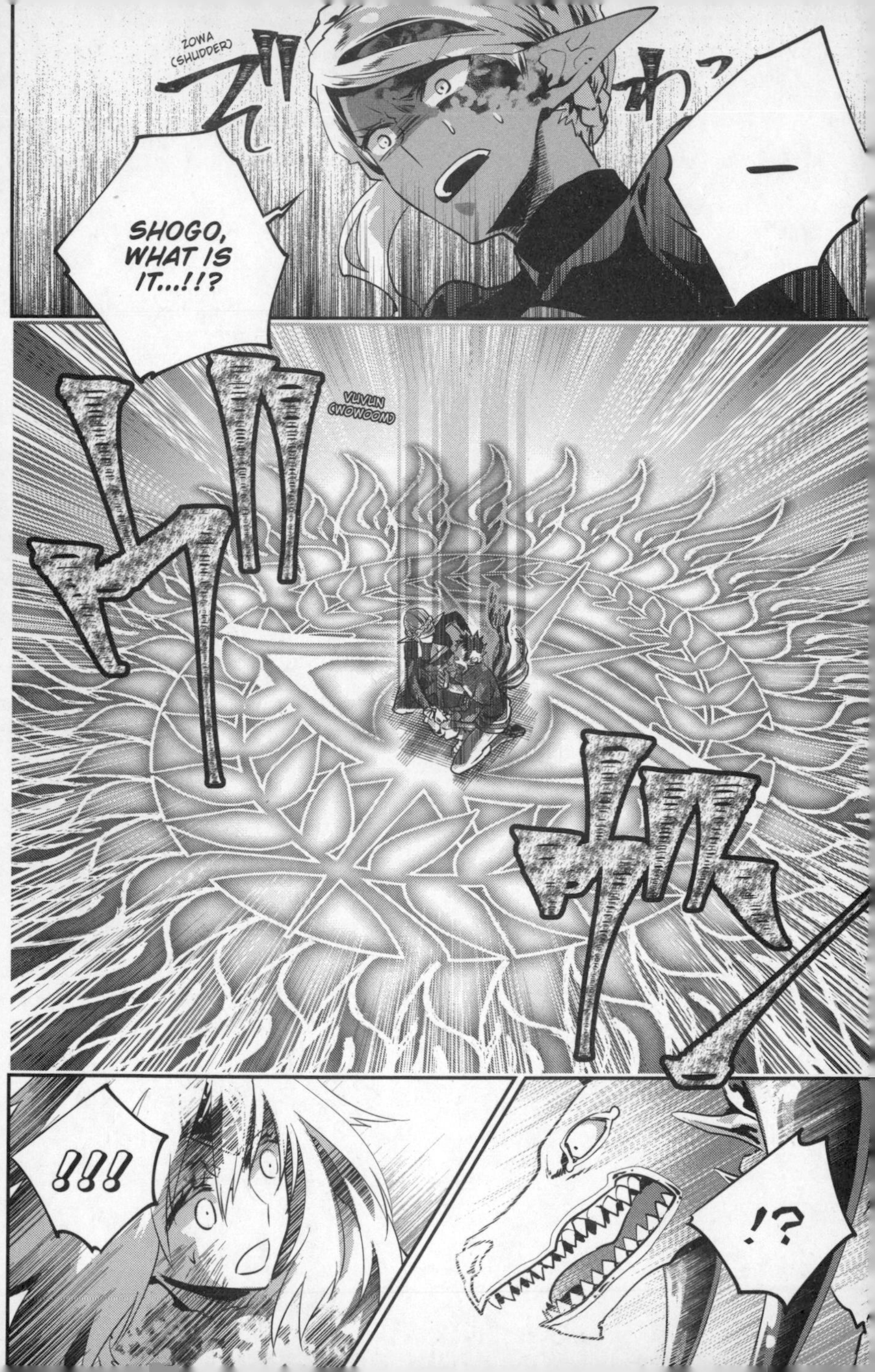
ZOWA (SHUDDER)
—
SHOGO, WHAT IS IT...!!?
VUVUN (WOWOOM)
!?
!!!

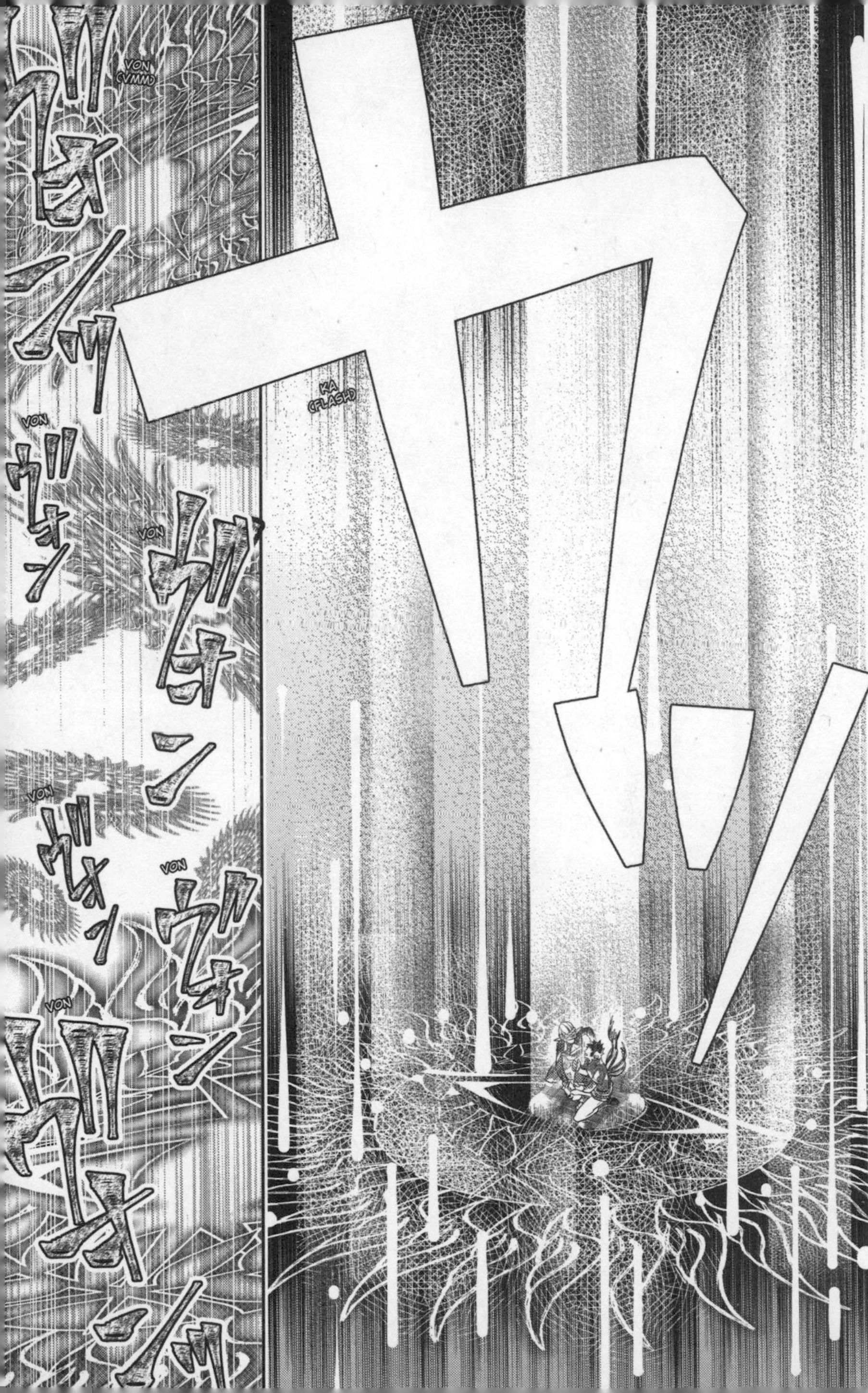
KA (FLASH)
VON (VMMM)
VON
VON
VON
VON
VON

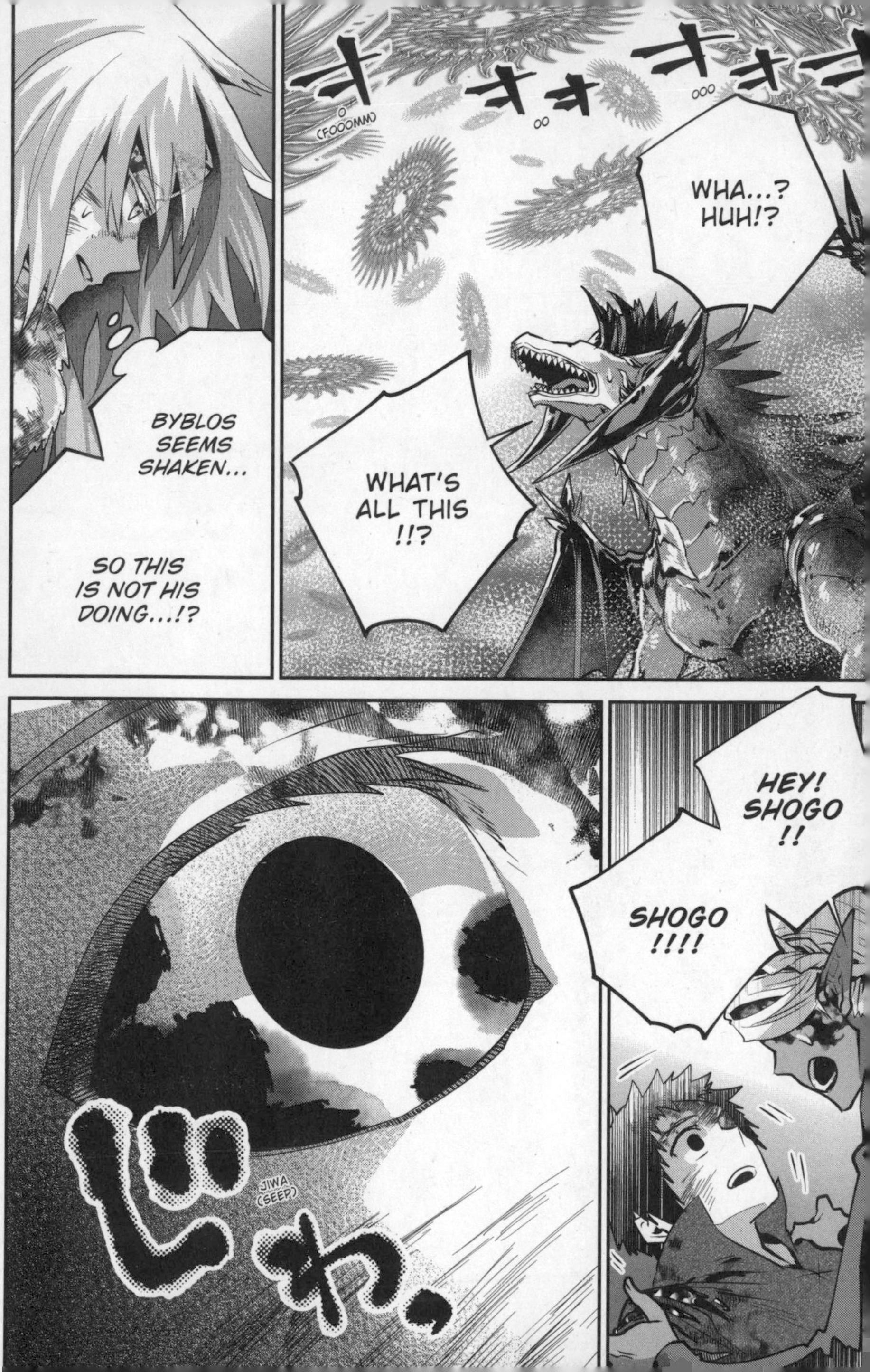
(FOOOMM)
WHA...? HUH!?
WHAT'S ALL THIS!!?
BYBLOS SEEMS SHAKEN...
SO THIS IS NOT HIS DOING...!?
HEY! SHOGO!!
SHOGO!!!!
JIWA (SEEP)

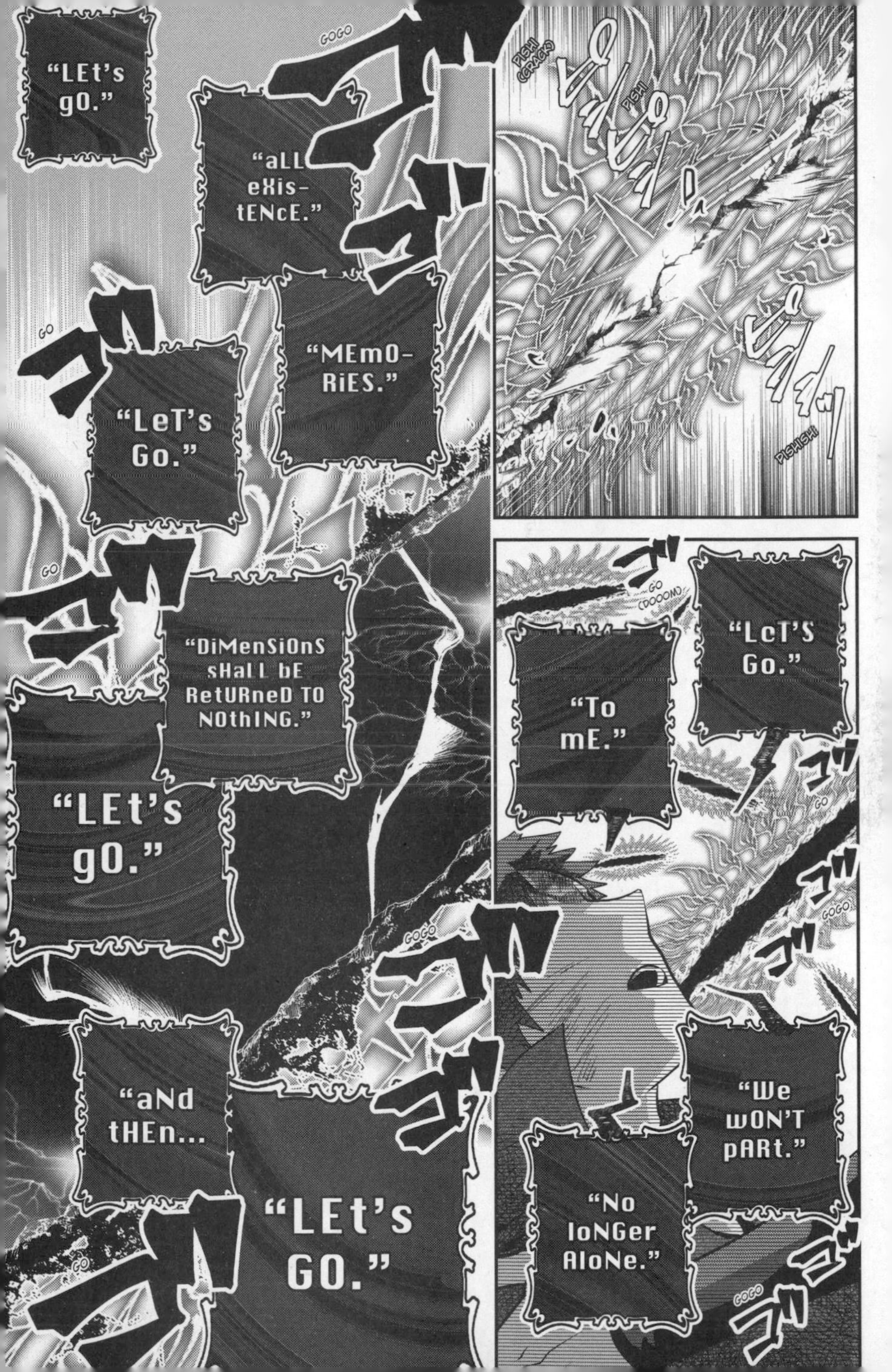
PISHI (CRACK)
PISHI
PISHI!
GO (DOOOM)
"LeT'S Go."
"To mE."
GO
GOGO
"We wON'T pARt."
"No loNGer AloNe."
GOGO
GOGO
"aLL eXis-tENcE."
"LEt's gO."
"MEmORiES."
GO
"LeT's Go."
GO
"DiMenSiOnS sHalL bE RetURneD TO NOthING."
"LEt's gO."
GOGO
"aNd tHEn...
"LEt's GO."
GO

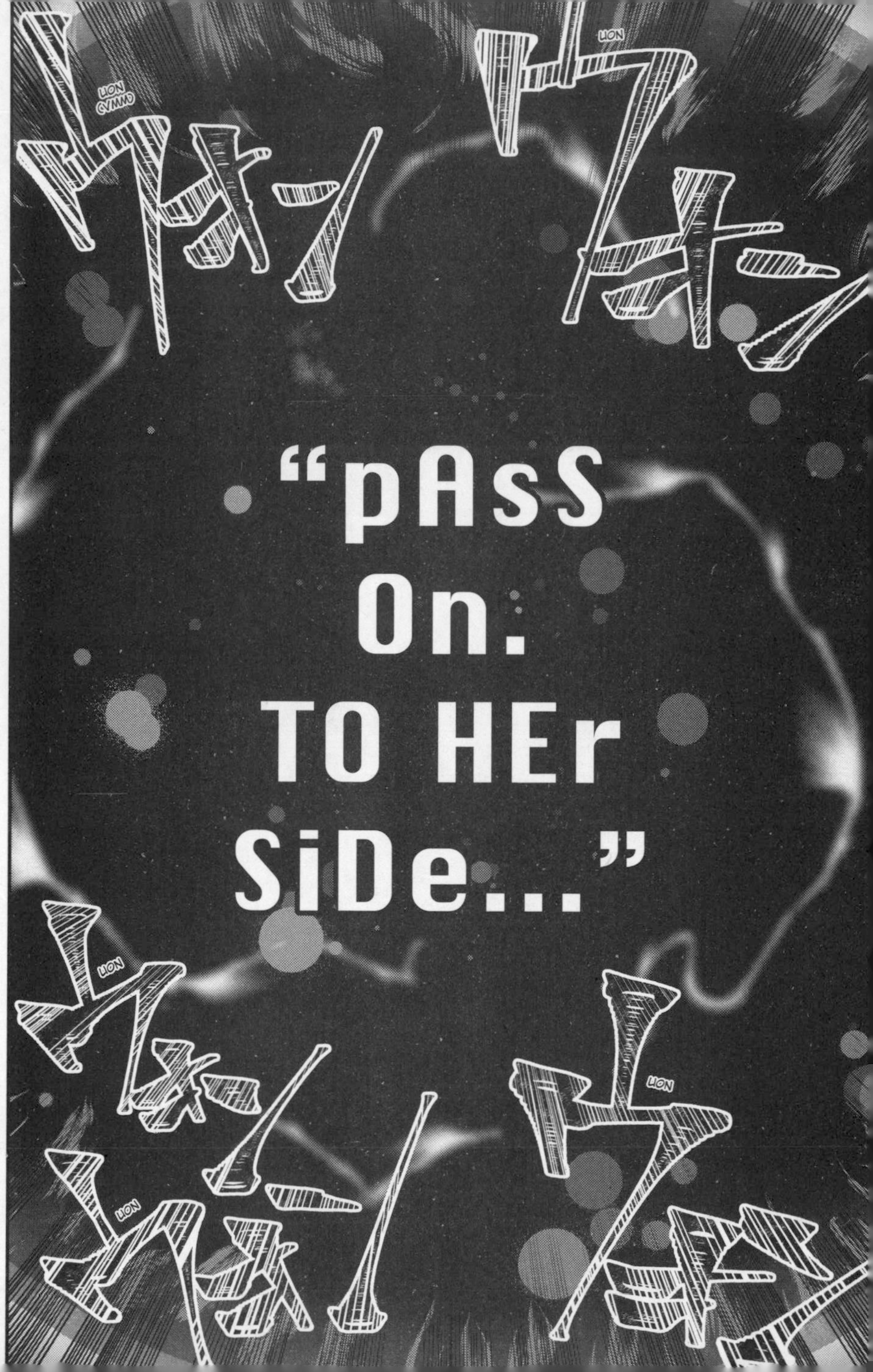
“pAsS On. TO HEr SiDe...”

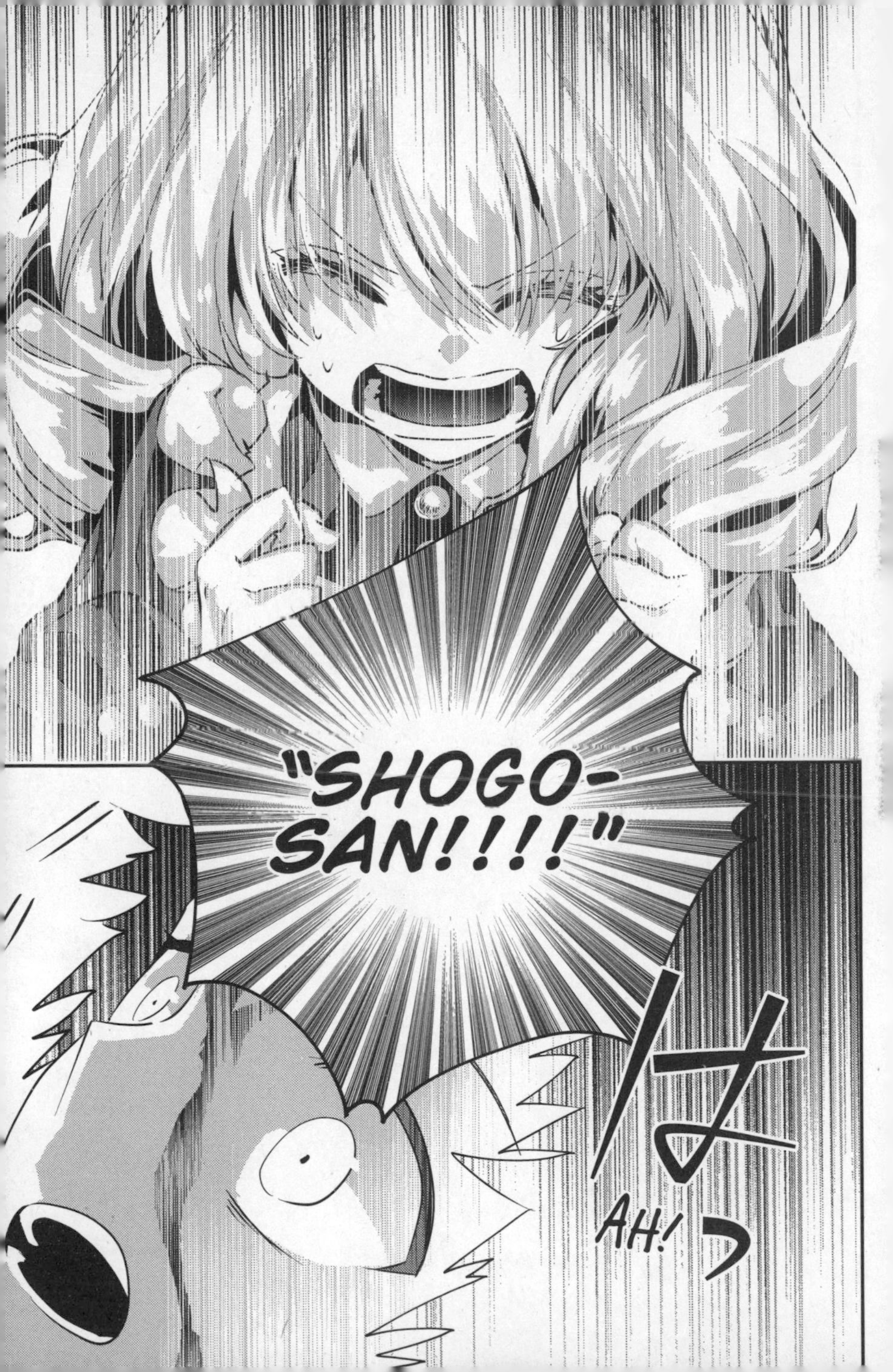
"SHOGO-SAN!!!!"
はっ
AH!

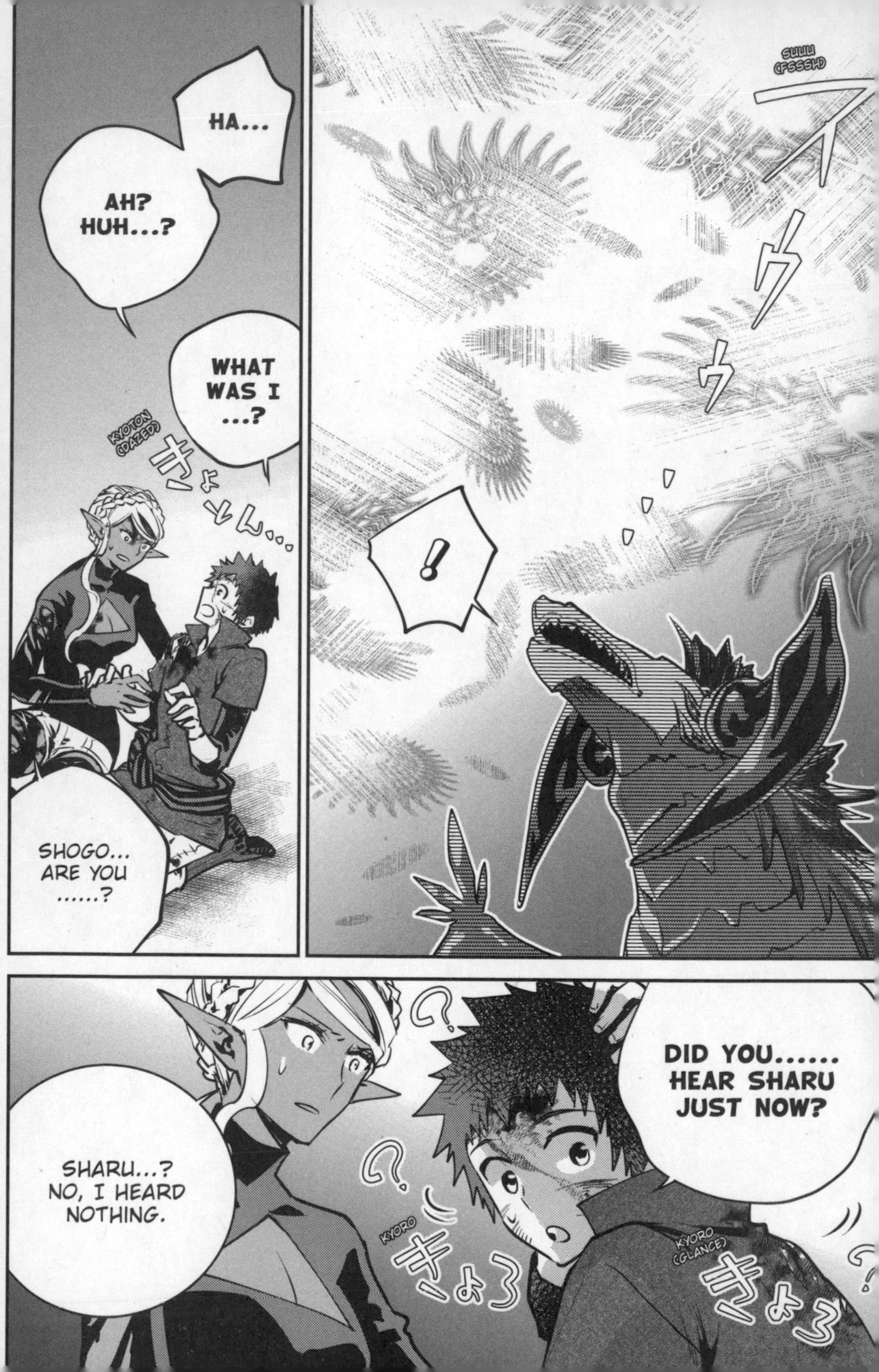
SUUU (FSSSH)
スウゥゥ
!
HA...
AH? HUH...?
WHAT WAS I ...?
KYOTON (DAZED)
きょとん...
SHOGO... ARE YOU ......?
DID YOU...... HEAR SHARU JUST NOW?
KYORO (GLANCE)
きょろ
KYORO
きょろ
SHARU...? NO, I HEARD NOTHING.

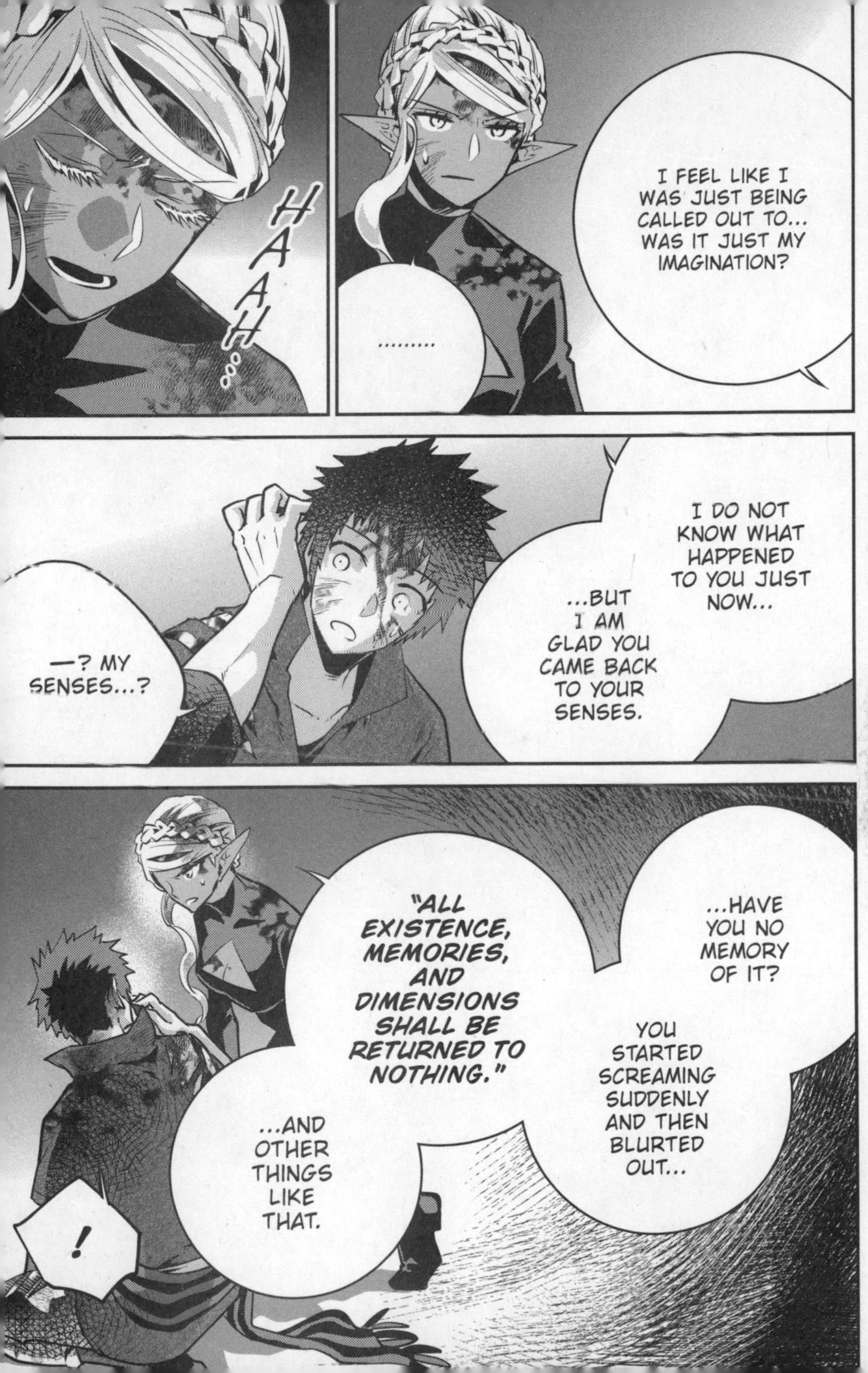
I FEEL LIKE I WAS JUST BEING CALLED OUT TO... WAS IT JUST MY IMAGINATION?
.........
HAAH
I DO NOT KNOW WHAT HAPPENED TO YOU JUST NOW...
...BUT I AM GLAD YOU CAME BACK TO YOUR SENSES.
—? MY SENSES...?
...HAVE YOU NO MEMORY OF IT?
YOU STARTED SCREAMING SUDDENLY AND THEN BLURTED OUT...
"ALL EXISTENCE, MEMORIES, AND DIMENSIONS SHALL BE RETURNED TO NOTHING."
...AND OTHER THINGS LIKE THAT.
!

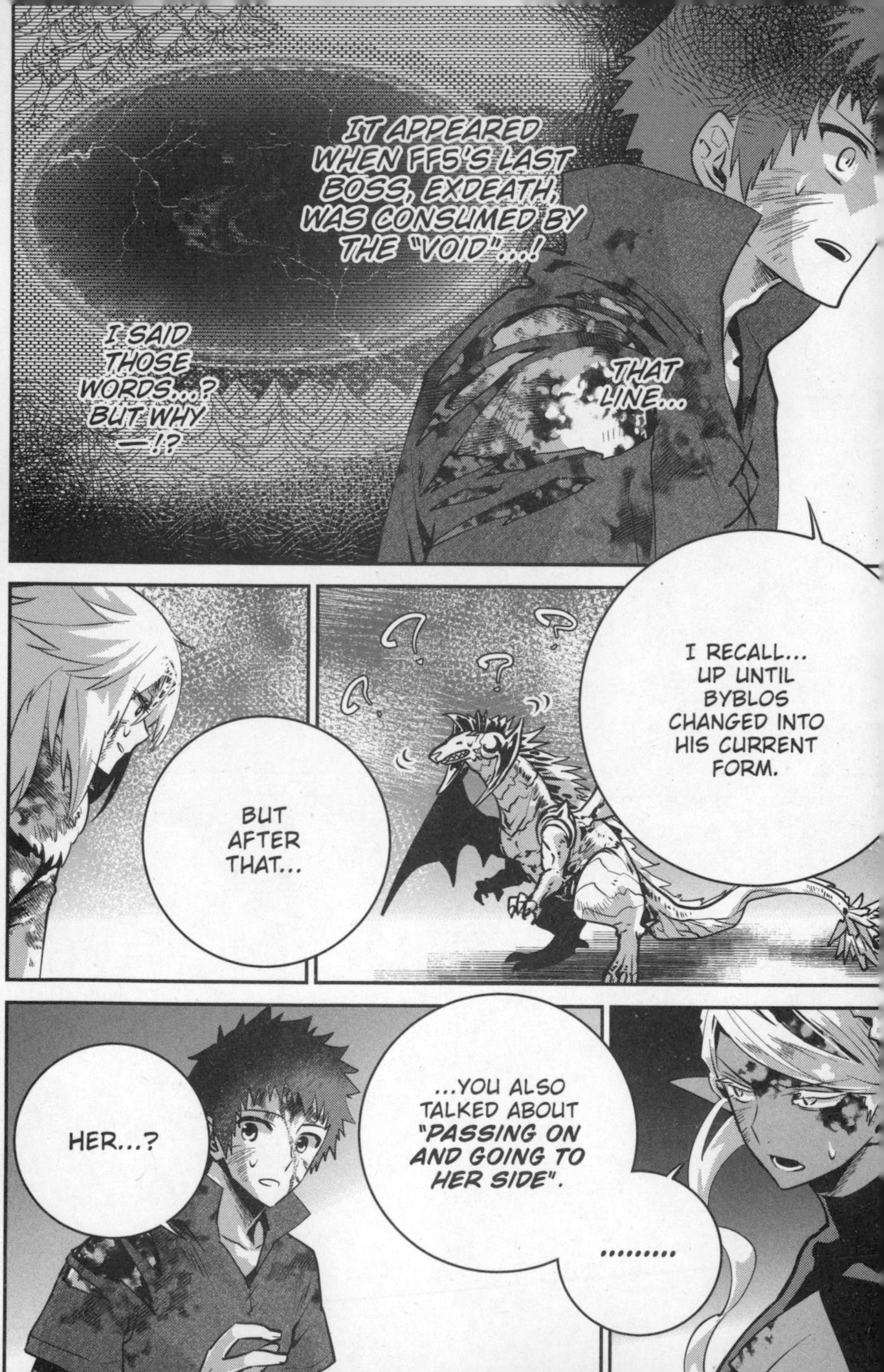
IT APPEARED WHEN FF5'S LAST BOSS, EXDEATH, WAS CONSUMED BY THE "VOID"...!
THAT LINE...
I SAID THOSE WORDS...? BUT WHY —!?
I RECALL... UP UNTIL BYBLOS CHANGED INTO HIS CURRENT FORM.
BUT AFTER THAT...
...YOU ALSO TALKED ABOUT "PASSING ON AND GOING TO HER SIDE".
.........
HER...?

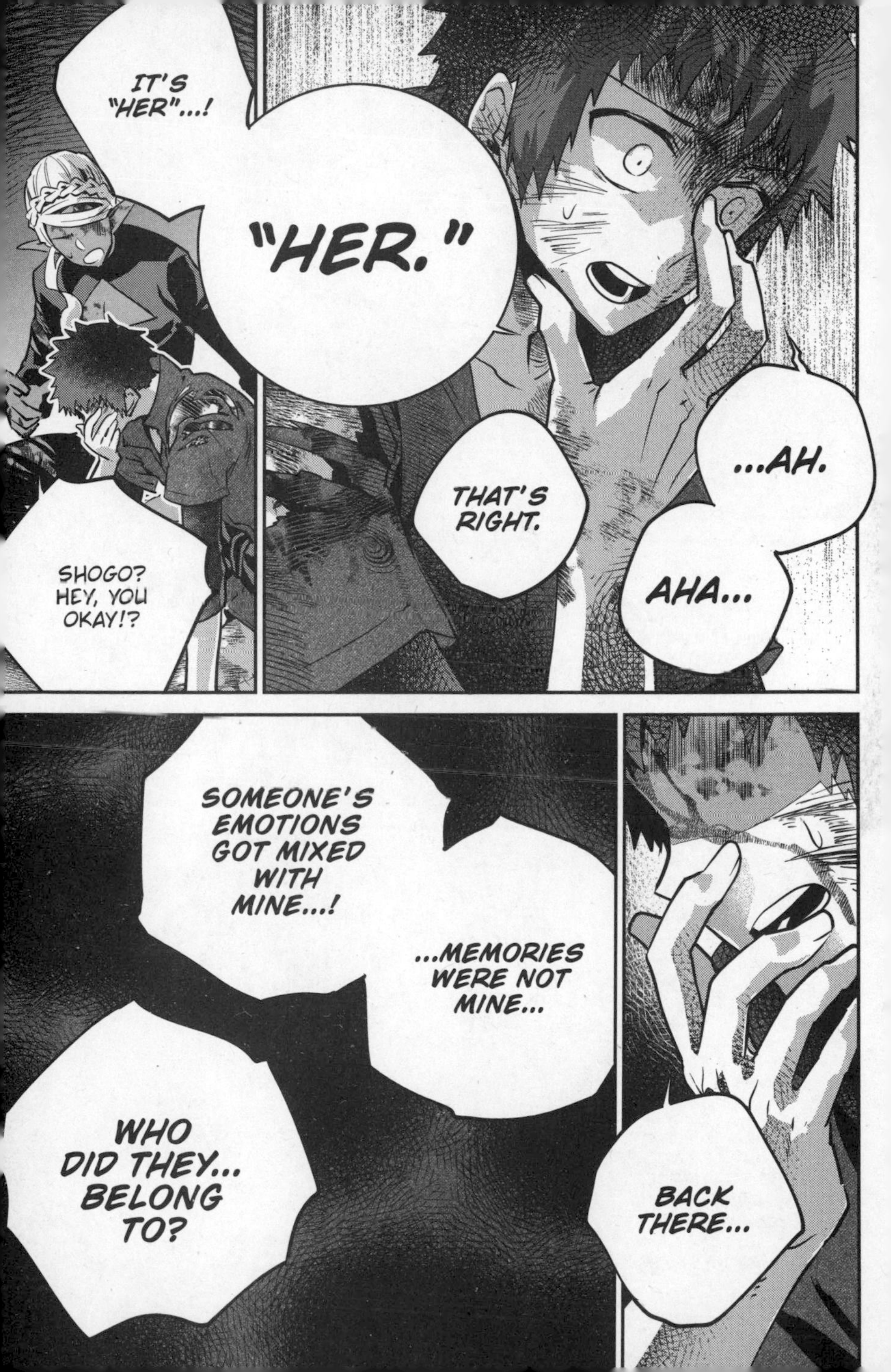
"HER."
...AH.
AHA...
THAT'S RIGHT.
IT'S "HER"...!
SHOGO? HEY, YOU OKAY!?
BACK THERE...
SOMEONE'S EMOTIONS GOT MIXED WITH MINE...!
...MEMORIES WERE NOT MINE...
WHO DID THEY... BELONG TO?

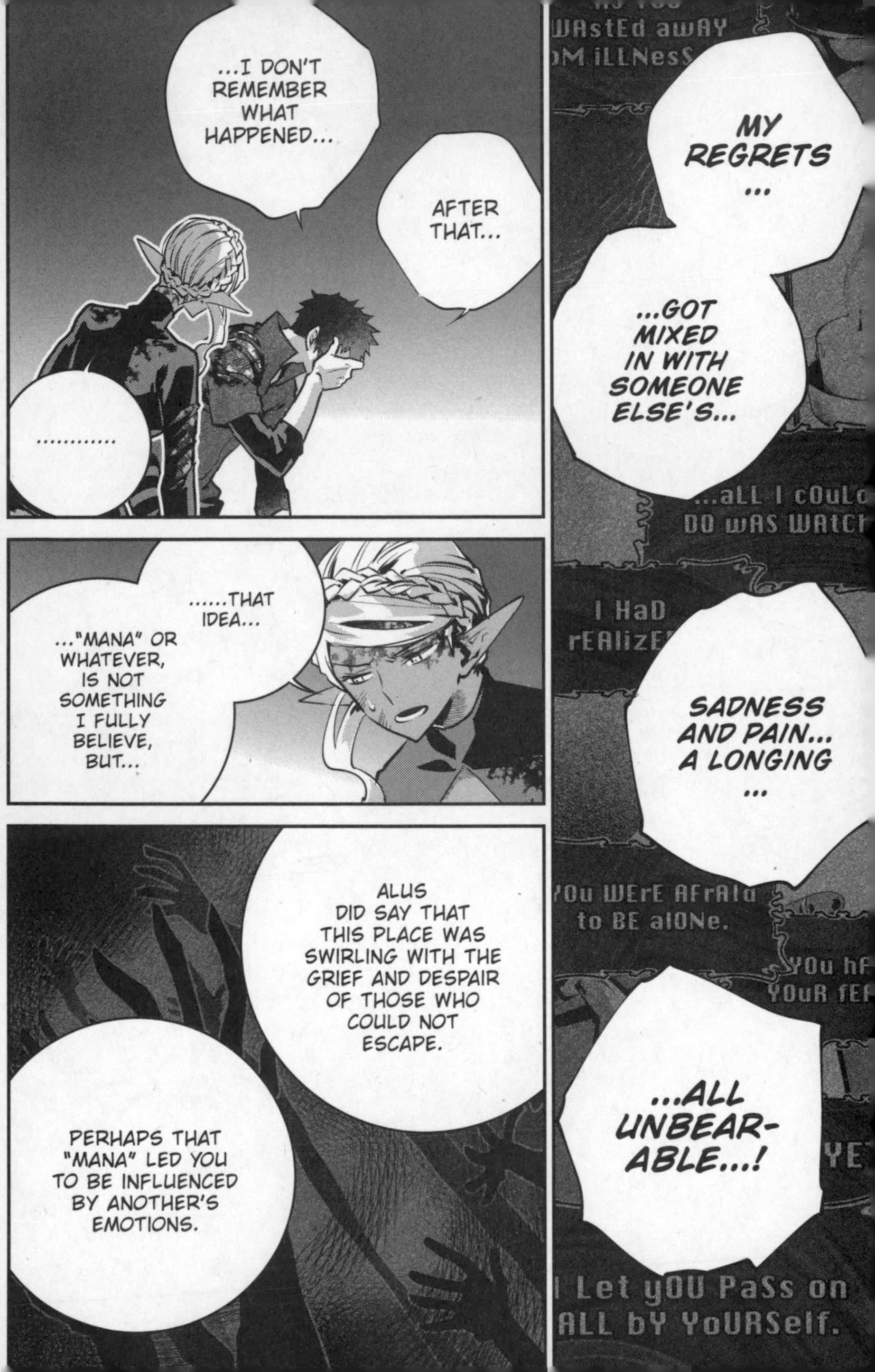
WAstEd awAY
M iLLNesS
MY REGRETS...
...GOT MIXED IN WITH SOMEONE ELSE'S...
...aLL I cOuLd
DO wAS WAtc
I HaD
rEAlizE
SADNESS AND PAIN... A LONGING...
YOu WErE AFrAId to BE alONe.
YOu h
YOuR fE
...ALL UNBEARABLE...!
YE
I Let yOU PaSs on ALL bY YoURSelf.
...I DON'T REMEMBER WHAT HAPPENED...
AFTER THAT...
............
......THAT IDEA...
..."MANA" OR WHATEVER, IS NOT SOMETHING I FULLY BELIEVE, BUT...
ALUS DID SAY THAT THIS PLACE WAS SWIRLING WITH THE GRIEF AND DESPAIR OF THOSE WHO COULD NOT ESCAPE.
PERHAPS THAT "MANA" LED YOU TO BE INFLUENCED BY ANOTHER'S EMOTIONS.

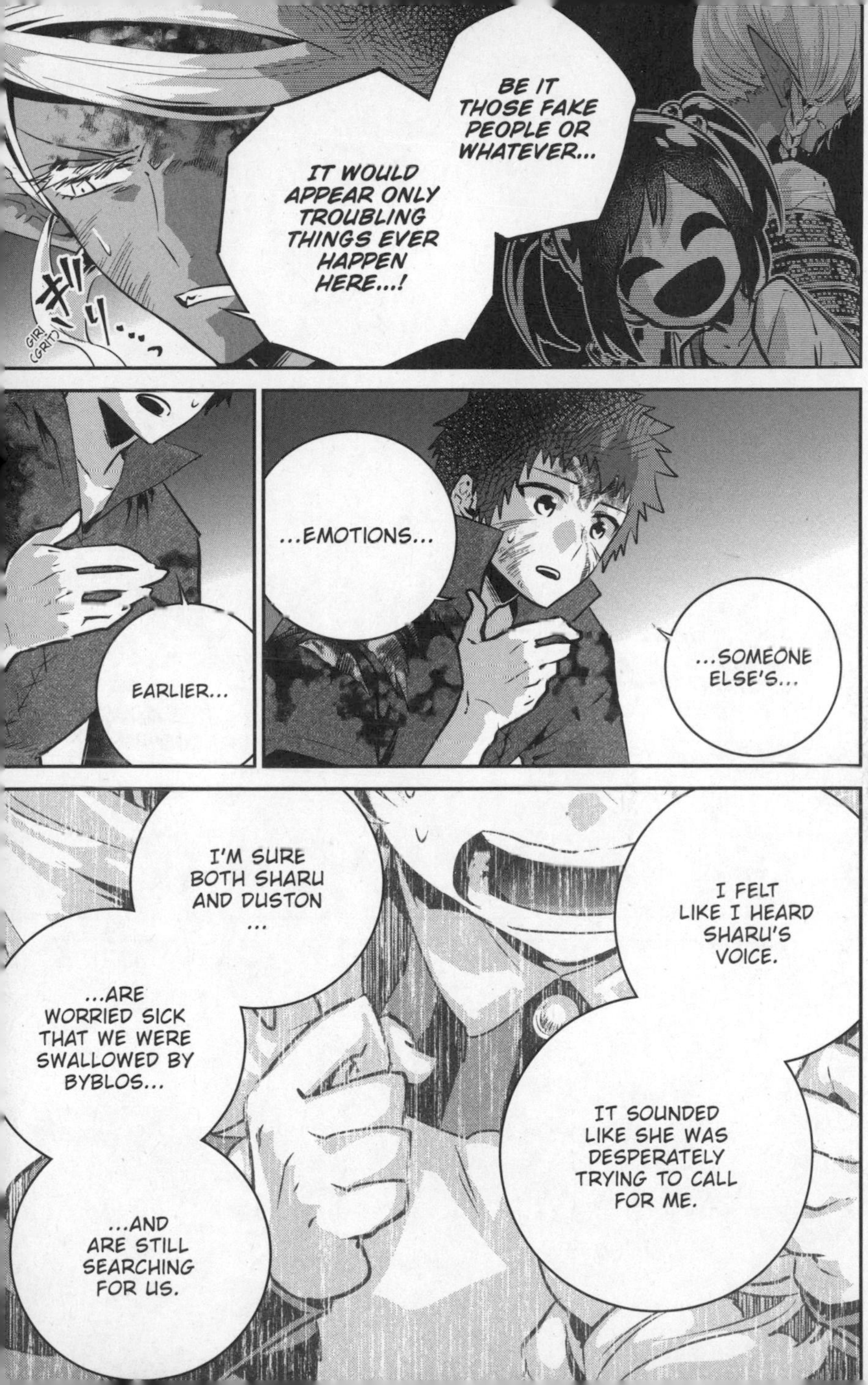
BE IT THOSE FAKE PEOPLE OR WHATEVER...
IT WOULD APPEAR ONLY TROUBLING THINGS EVER HAPPEN HERE...!
GIRI (GRIT)
...SOMEONE ELSE'S...
...EMOTIONS...
EARLIER...
I FELT LIKE I HEARD SHARU'S VOICE.
IT SOUNDED LIKE SHE WAS DESPERATELY TRYING TO CALL FOR ME.
I'M SURE BOTH SHARU AND DUSTON ...
...ARE WORRIED SICK THAT WE WERE SWALLOWED BY BYBLOS...
...AND ARE STILL SEARCHING FOR US.

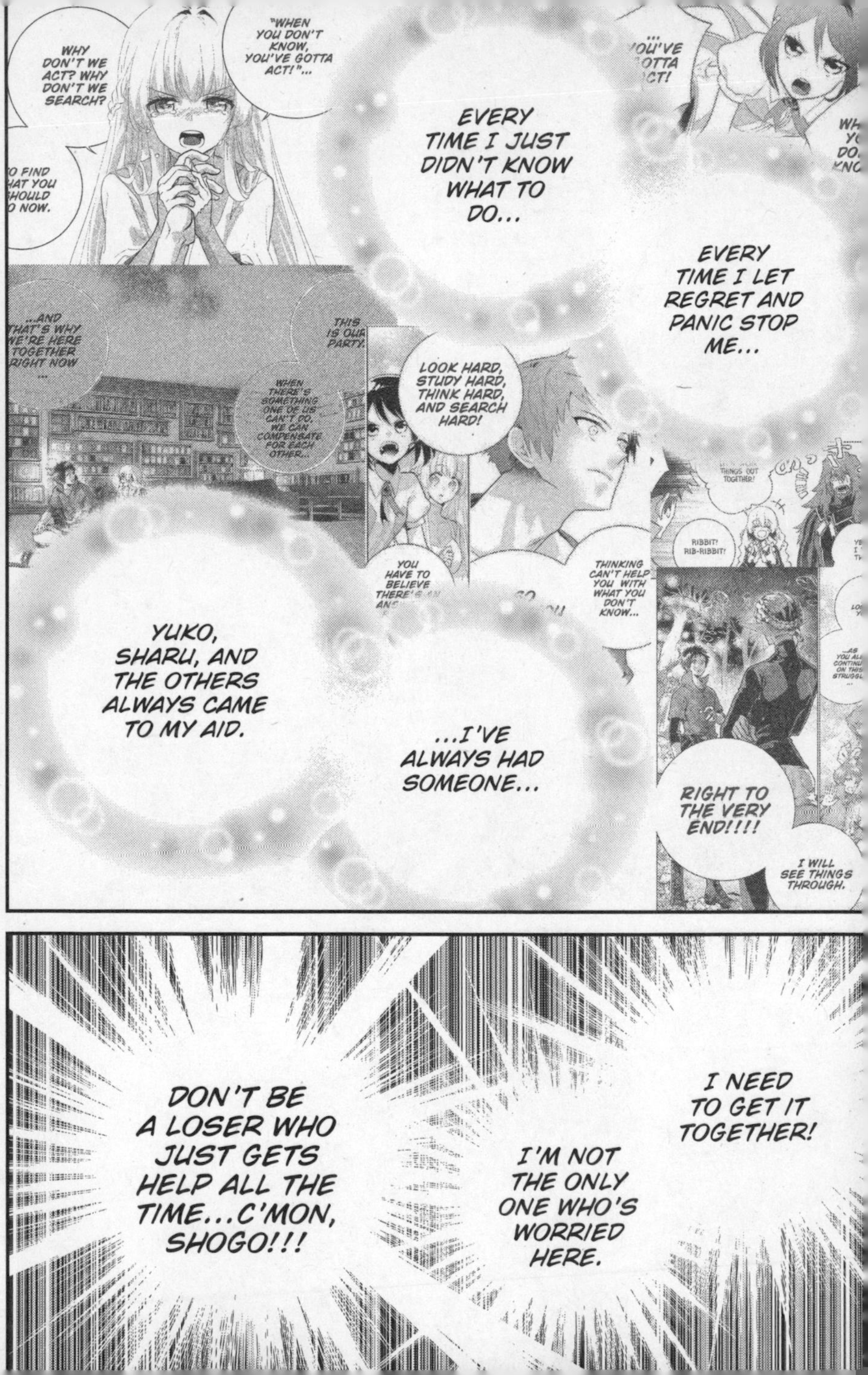
EVERY TIME I JUST DIDN'T KNOW WHAT TO DO...
"WHEN YOU DON'T KNOW, YOU'VE GOTTA ACT!"...
WHY DON'T WE ACT? WHY DON'T WE SEARCH?
EVERY TIME I LET REGRET AND PANIC STOP ME...
THINGS OUT TOGETHER!
RIBBIT! RIB-RIBBIT!
RIGHT TO THE VERY END!!!!
I WILL SEE THINGS THROUGH.
LOOK HARD, STUDY HARD, THINK HARD, AND SEARCH HARD!
THINKING CAN'T HELP YOU WITH WHAT YOU DON'T KNOW...
WHEN THERE'S SOMETHING ONE OF US CAN'T DO, WE CAN COMPENSATE FOR EACH OTHER...
...I'VE ALWAYS HAD SOMEONE...
YUKO, SHARU, AND THE OTHERS ALWAYS CAME TO MY AID.
I NEED TO GET IT TOGETHER!
I'M NOT THE ONLY ONE WHO'S WORRIED HERE.
DON'T BE A LOSER WHO JUST GETS HELP ALL THE TIME...C'MON, SHOGO!!!

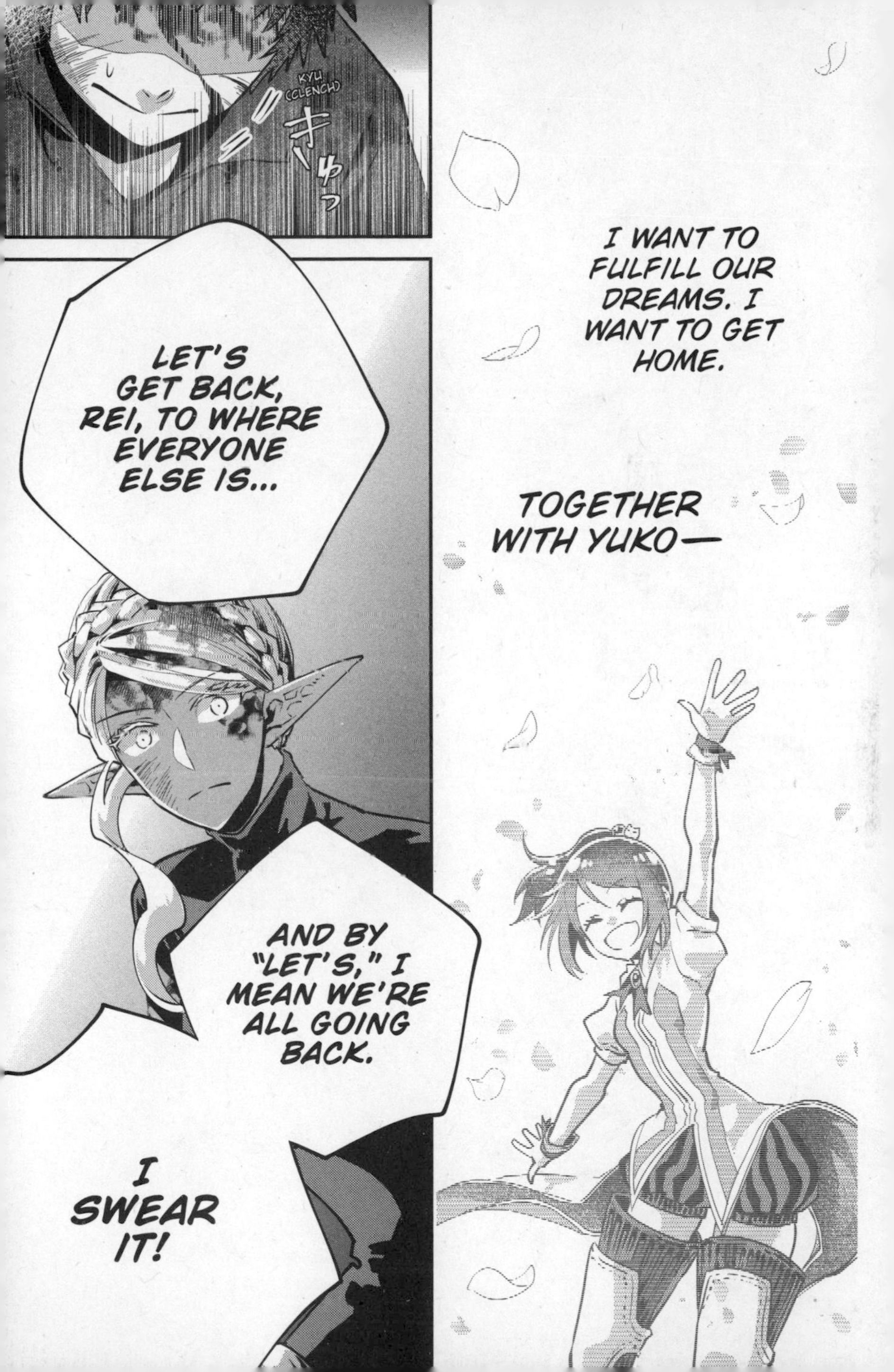
I WANT TO FULFILL OUR DREAMS. I WANT TO GET HOME.
TOGETHER WITH YUKO—
KYU (CLENCH)
きゅっ
LET'S GET BACK, REI, TO WHERE EVERYONE ELSE IS...
AND BY "LET'S," I MEAN WE'RE ALL GOING BACK.
I SWEAR IT!

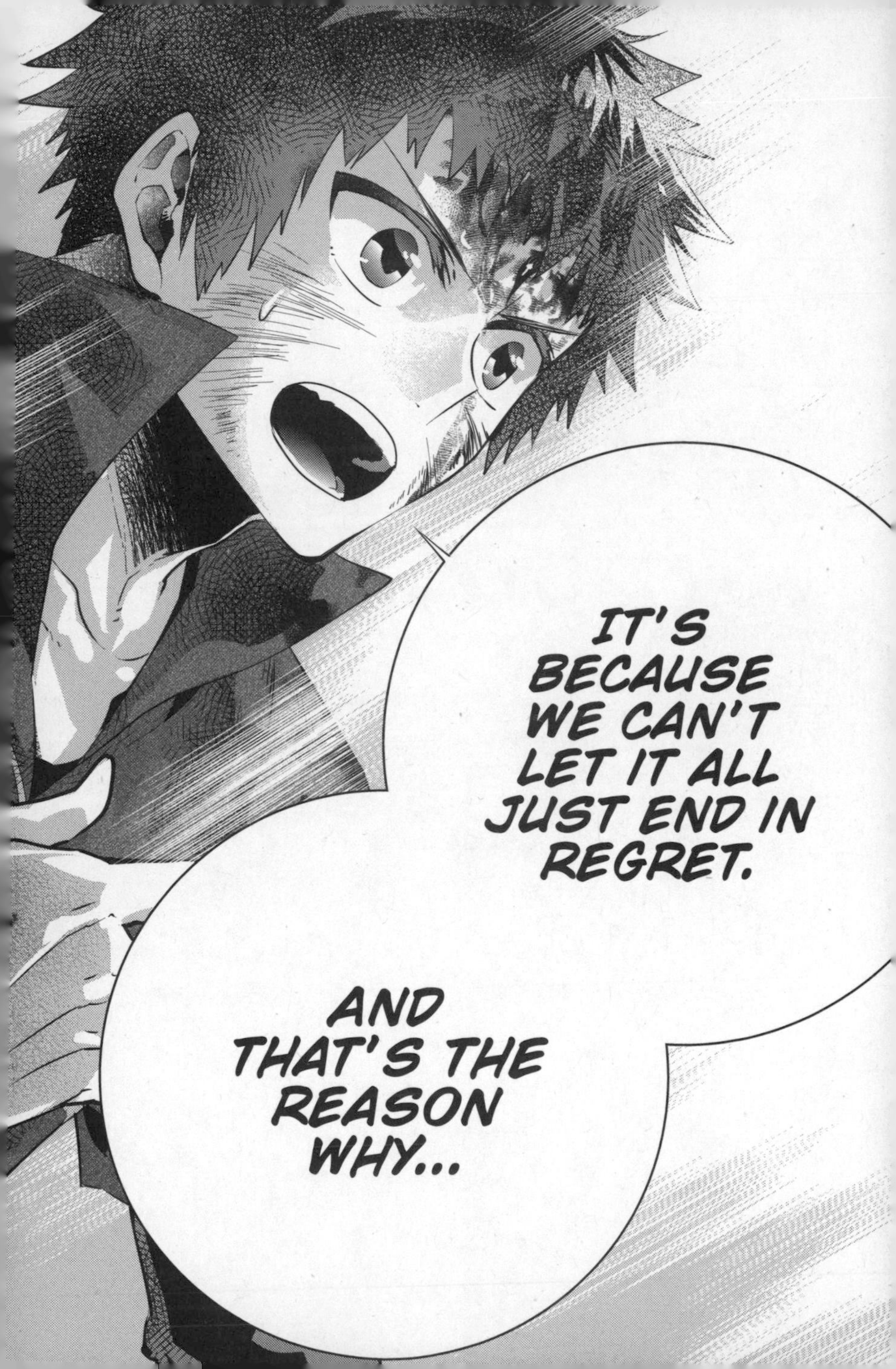
IT'S BECAUSE WE CAN'T LET IT ALL JUST END IN REGRET.
AND THAT'S THE REASON WHY...

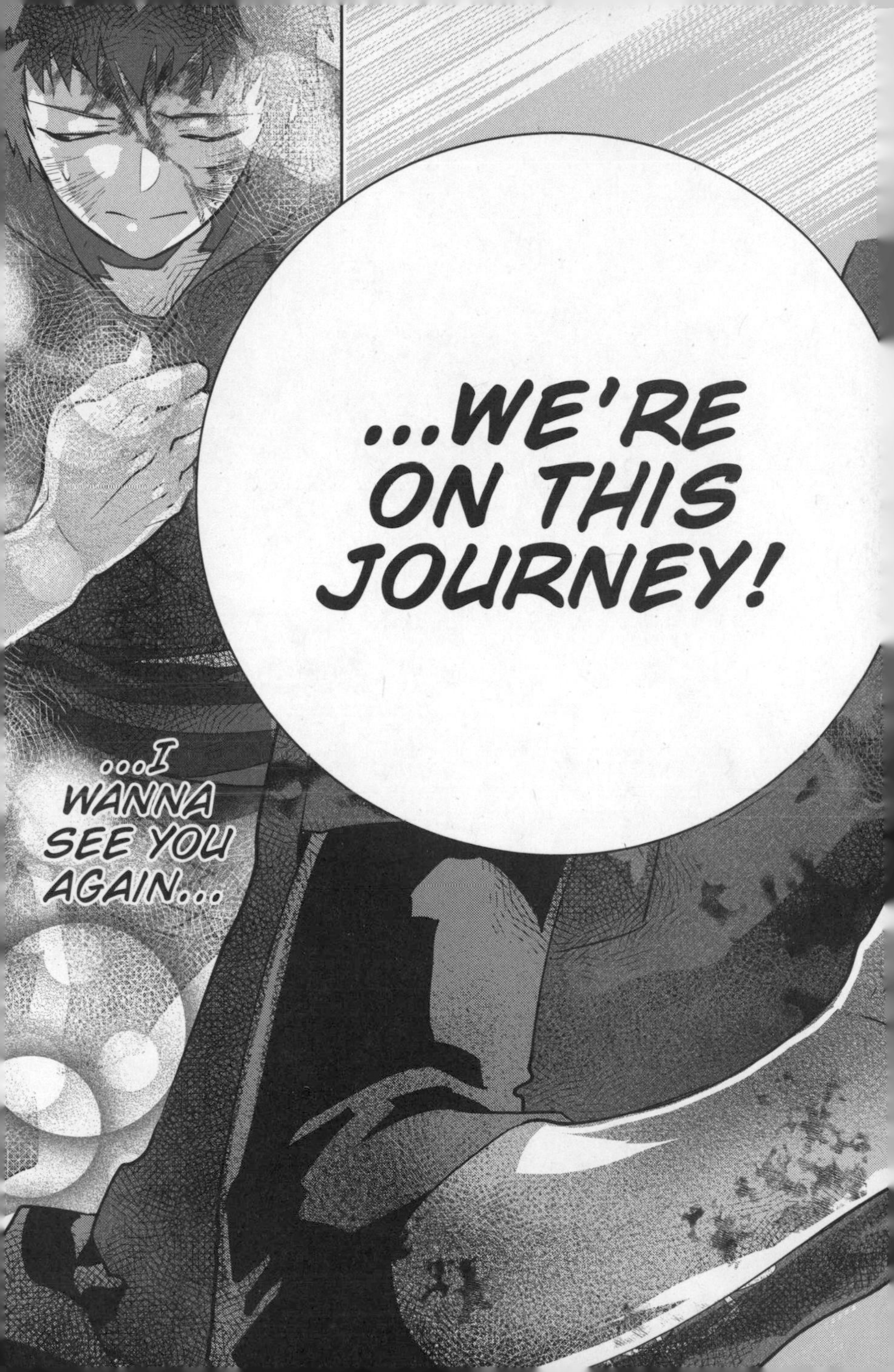
...WE'RE ON THIS JOURNEY!
...I WANNA SEE YOU AGAIN...

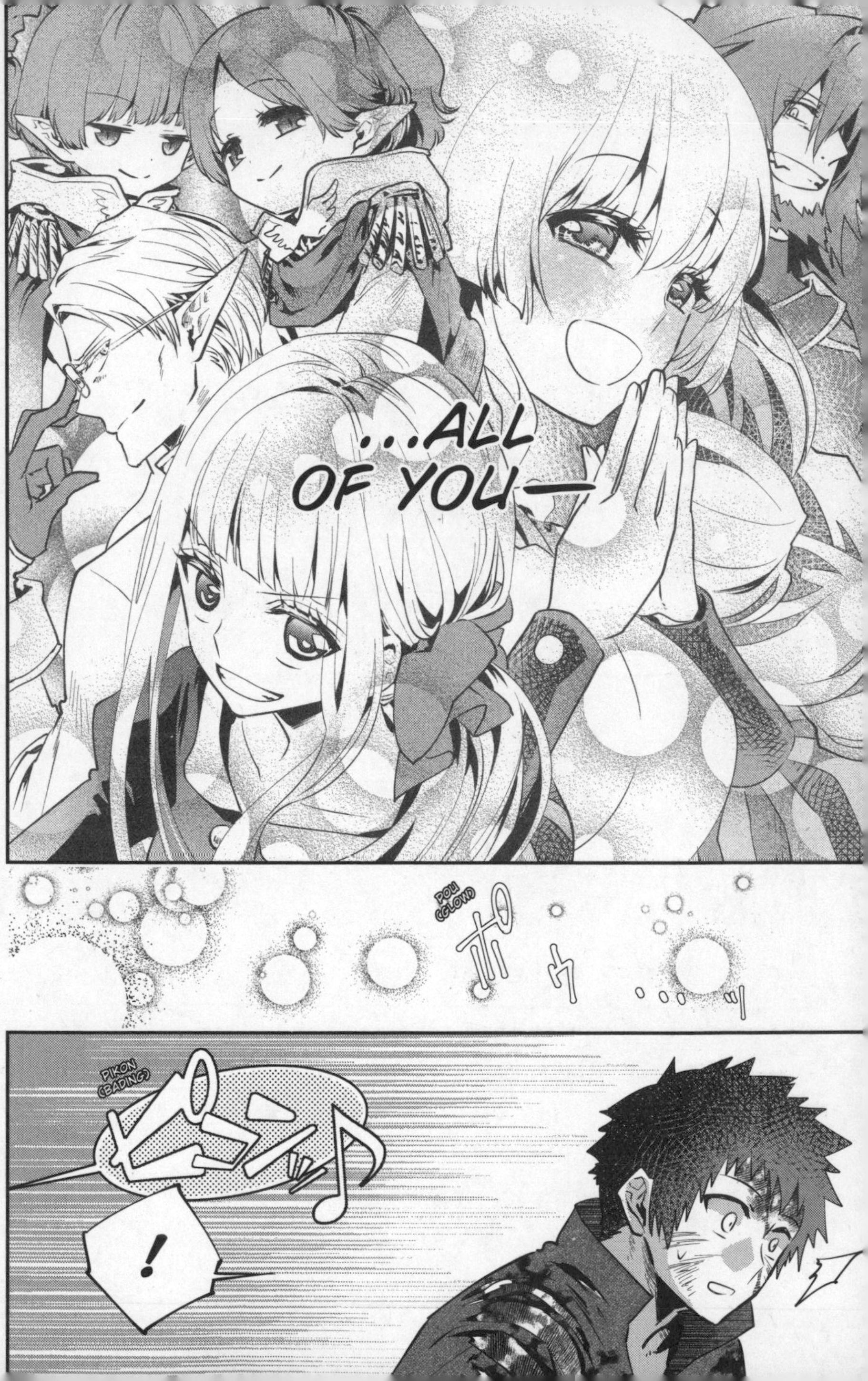
...ALL OF YOU—
POU (GLOW)
PIKON (BADING)
!

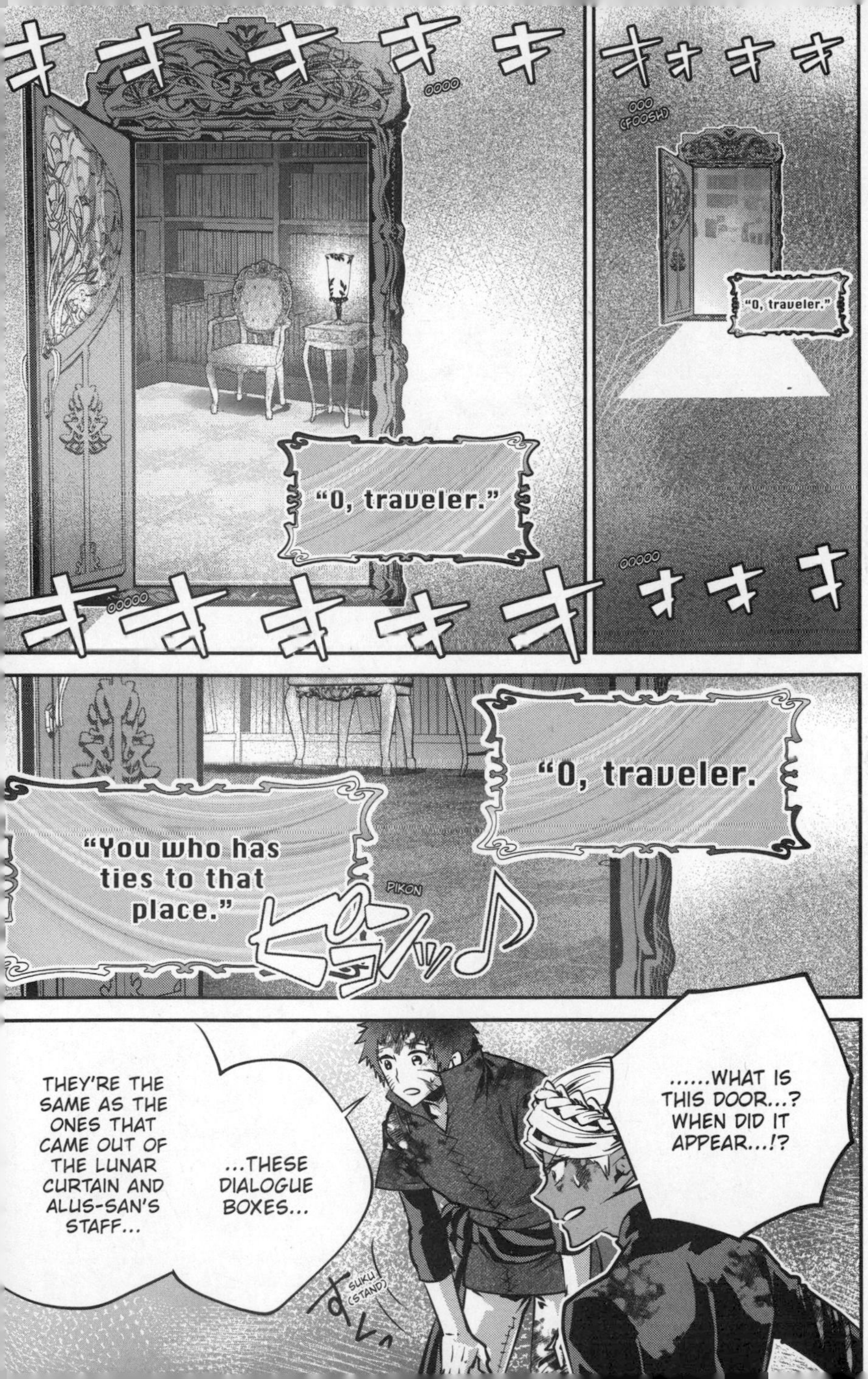
OOO (FOOSH)
"O, traveler."
OOOOO
OOOO
"O, traveler."
OOOOO
"O, traveler.
"You who has ties to that place."
PIKON
......WHAT IS THIS DOOR...? WHEN DID IT APPEAR...!?
...THESE DIALOGUE BOXES...
THEY'RE THE SAME AS THE ONES THAT CAME OUT OF THE LUNAR CURTAIN AND ALUS-SAN'S STAFF...
SUKU (STAND)

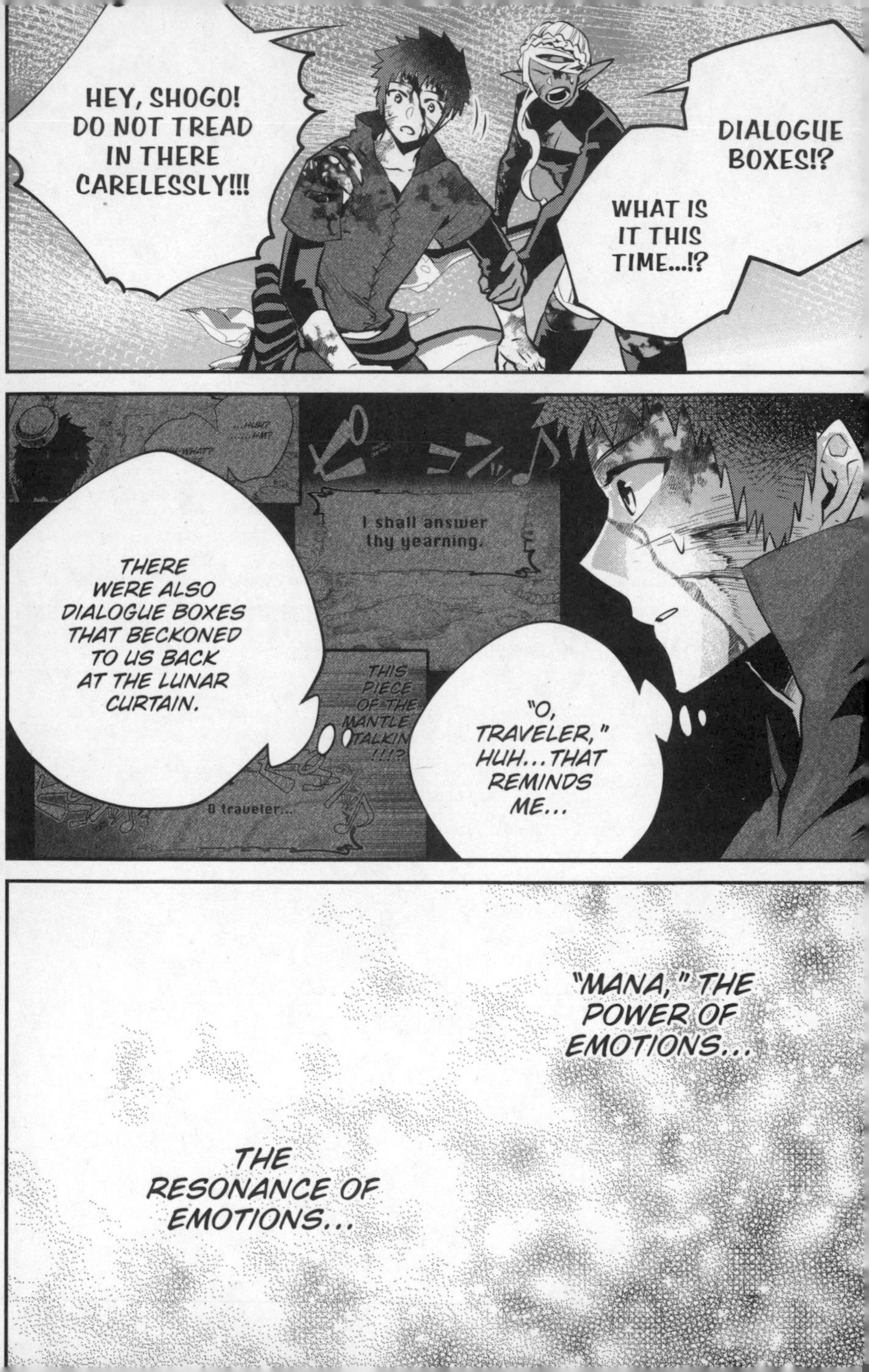
DIALOGUE BOXES!?
WHAT IS IT THIS TIME...!?
HEY, SHOGO! DO NOT TREAD IN THERE CARELESSLY!!!
"O, TRAVELER," HUH...THAT REMINDS ME...
I shall answer thy yearning.
THERE WERE ALSO DIALOGUE BOXES THAT BECKONED TO US BACK AT THE LUNAR CURTAIN.
THIS PIECE OF THE MANTLE TALKIN !!!?
O traveler...
"MANA," THE POWER OF EMOTIONS...
THE RESONANCE OF EMOTIONS...

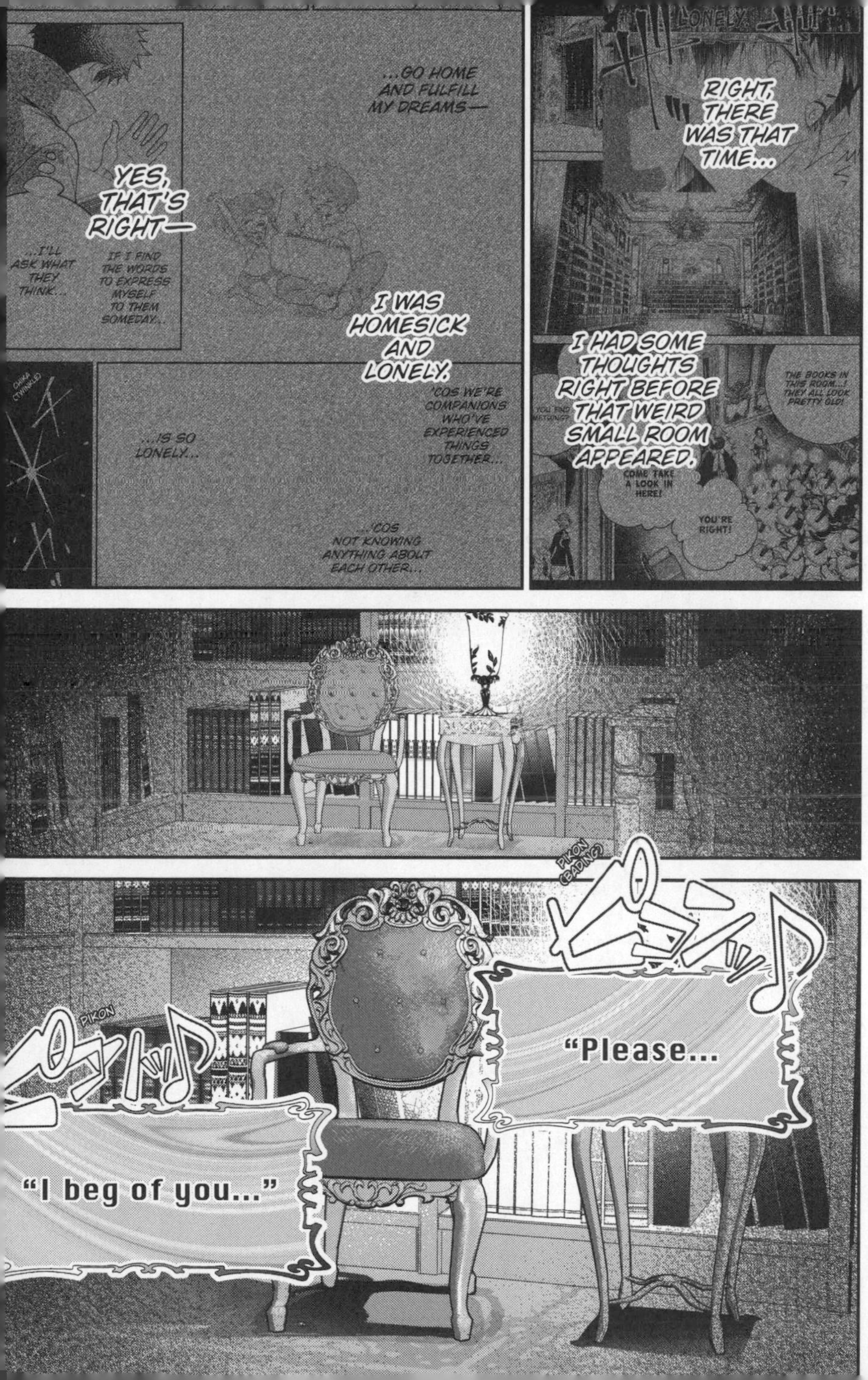
LONELY.
RIGHT, THERE WAS THAT TIME...
I HAD SOME THOUGHTS RIGHT BEFORE THAT WEIRD SMALL ROOM APPEARED.
THE BOOKS IN THIS ROOM...! THEY ALL LOOK PRETTY OLD!
COME TAKE A LOOK IN HERE!
YOU'RE RIGHT!
...GO HOME AND FULFILL MY DREAMS—
YES, THAT'S RIGHT—
IF I FIND THE WORDS TO EXPRESS MYSELF TO THEM SOMEDAY...
...I'LL ASK WHAT THEY THINK...
I WAS HOMESICK AND LONELY.
'COS WE'RE COMPANIONS WHO'VE EXPERIENCED THINGS TOGETHER...
...IS SO LONELY...
...'COS NOT KNOWING ANYTHING ABOUT EACH OTHER...
CHIKA (TWINKLE)
PIKON (BADING)
"Please...
PIKON
"I beg of you..."

...BE ABLE TO MAKE SOME SENSE OF THIS.

REI... I THINK I MIGHT JUST...

WHAT...!?

UNFROZEN TIME...

HIS DECEASED WIFE...

THE MAGE ELMO...

ELMO'S NOTES...

THE LANTERN WITH A WARM FLAME...

NOTES OF MAGE ELMO

"...IT'S B
THREE DAYS S

ree days since I stumbled
miliar library room.
es have appeared
ut they're weak
hey're no problem

THIS FLAME FEELS WARM...

"...MY
BELOVED,
DEAD
WIFE."

THE NOTES END HERE!

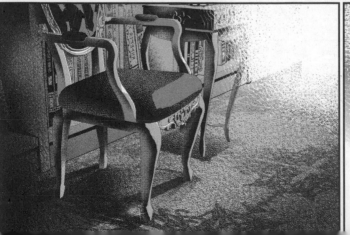

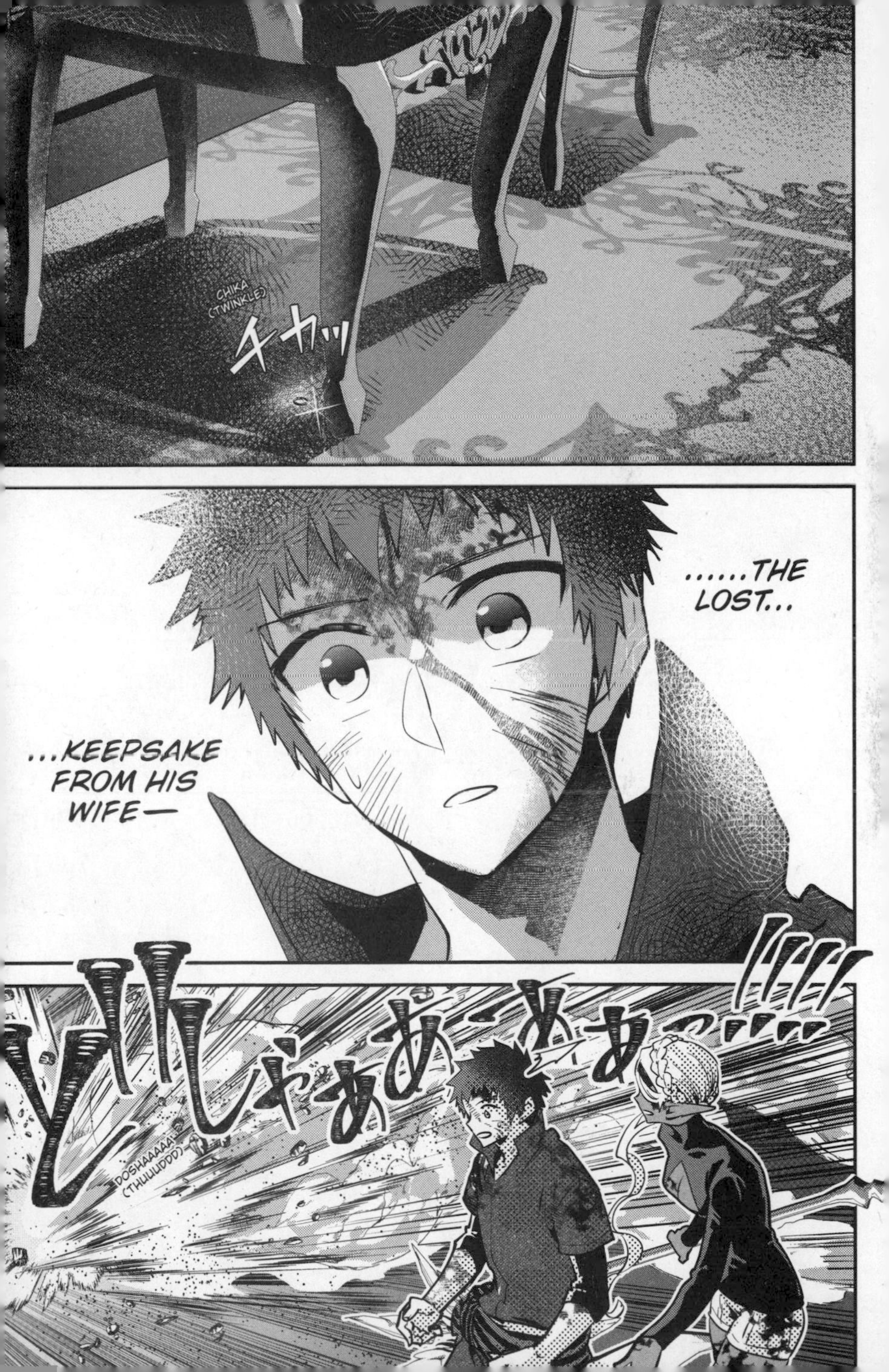
CHIKA (TWINKLE)
チカッ
......THE LOST...
...KEEPSAKE FROM HIS WIFE—
どしゃああーああっ!!!!
DOSHAAAAA (THUUUDDD)

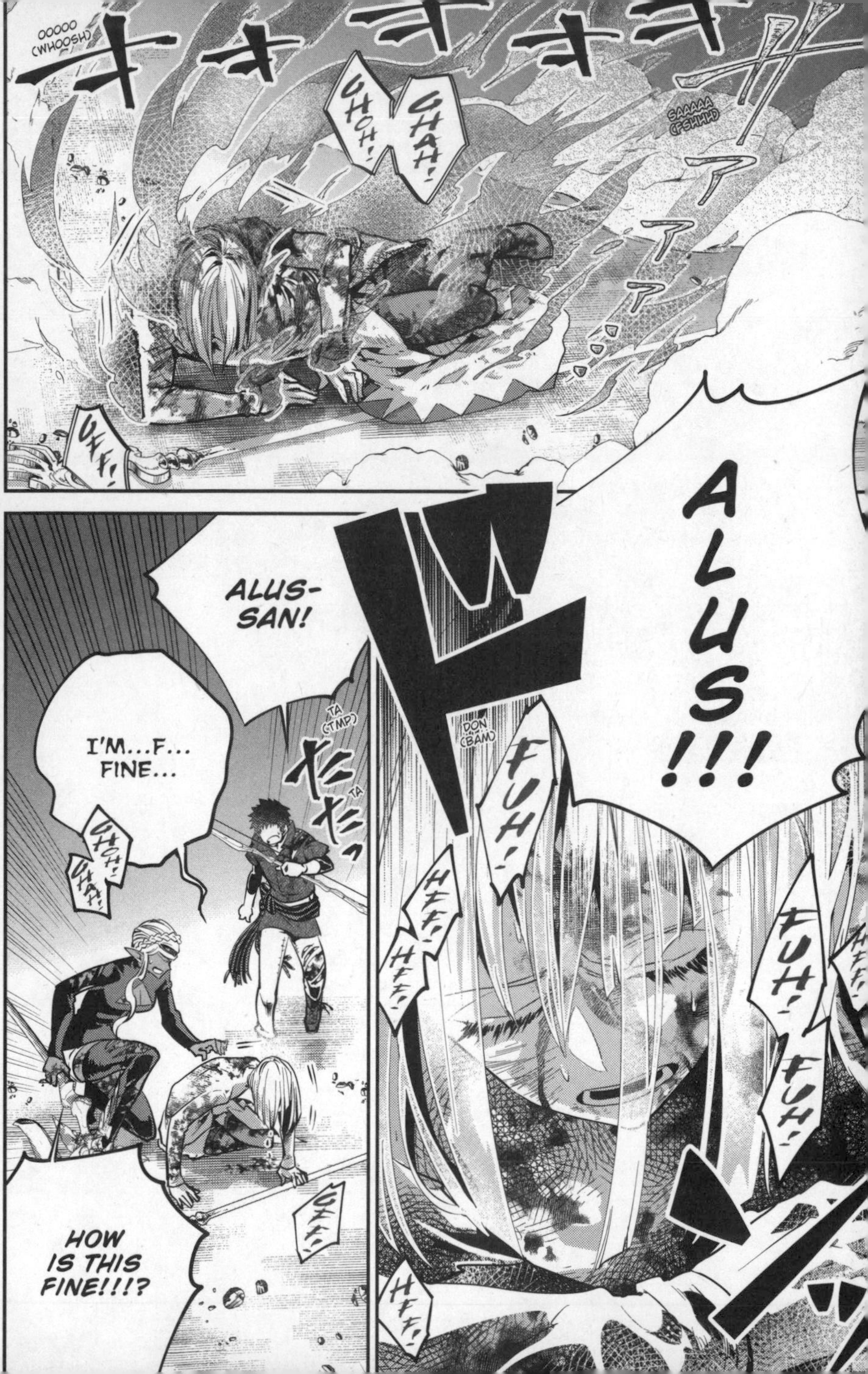
SAAAAA (FSHHH)
GHAH!
UHOH!
OOOOO (WHOOSH)
UFF!
ALUS!!!
DON (BAM)
FUH!
HFF!
HFF!
FUH!
HFF!
FUH!
HFF!
ALUS-SAN!
TA (TMP)
TA
I'M…F… FINE…
UHOH! UHAH!
GFF!
HOW IS THIS FINE!!!?

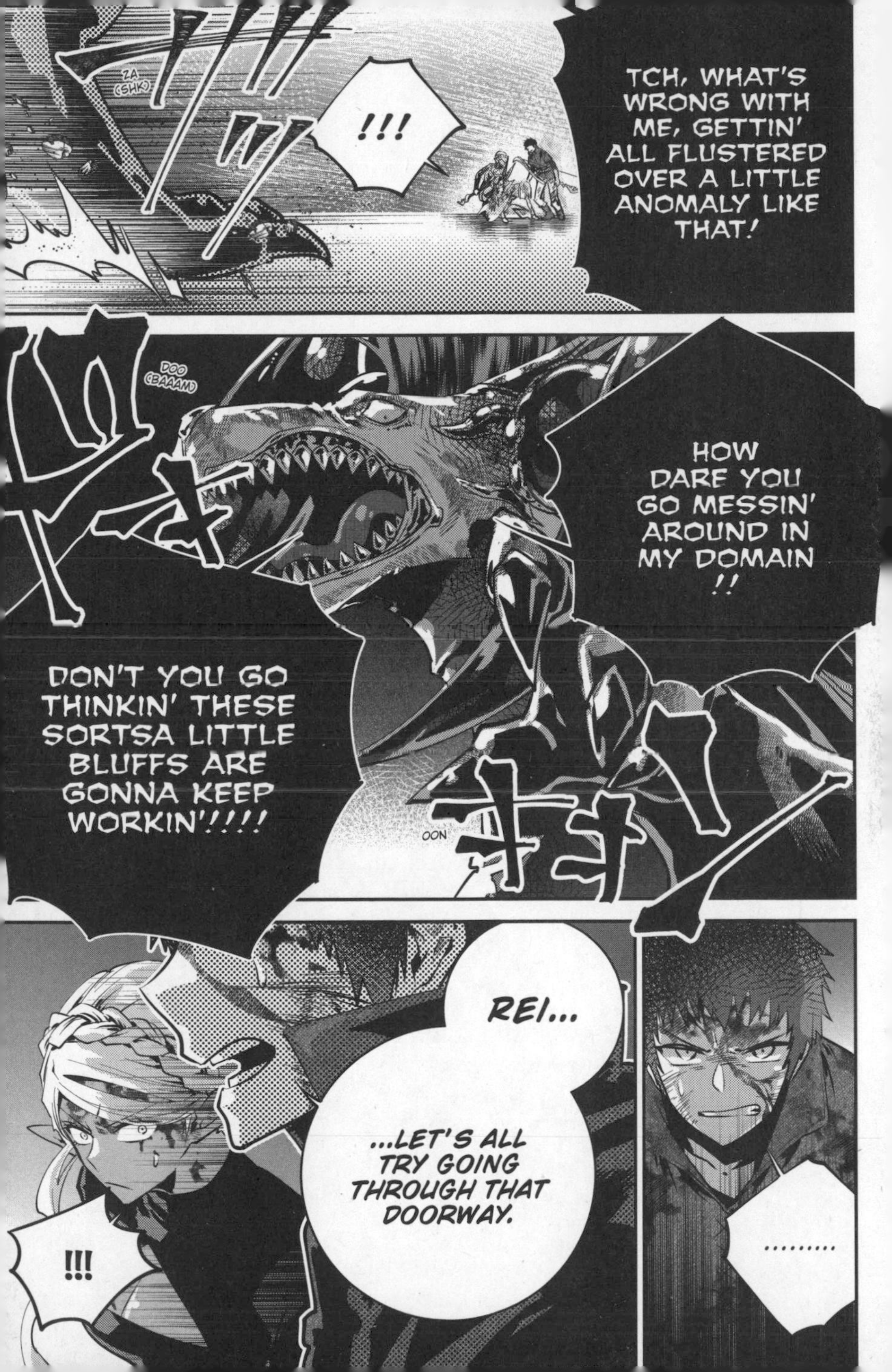
TCH, WHAT'S WRONG WITH ME, GETTIN' ALL FLUSTERED OVER A LITTLE ANOMALY LIKE THAT!
!!!
ZA (SHK)
HOW DARE YOU GO MESSIN' AROUND IN MY DOMAIN !!
DOO (BAAAM)
DON'T YOU GO THINKIN' THESE SORTSA LITTLE BLUFFS ARE GONNA KEEP WORKIN'!!!!!
OON
.........
REI...
...LET'S ALL TRY GOING THROUGH THAT DOORWAY.
!!!

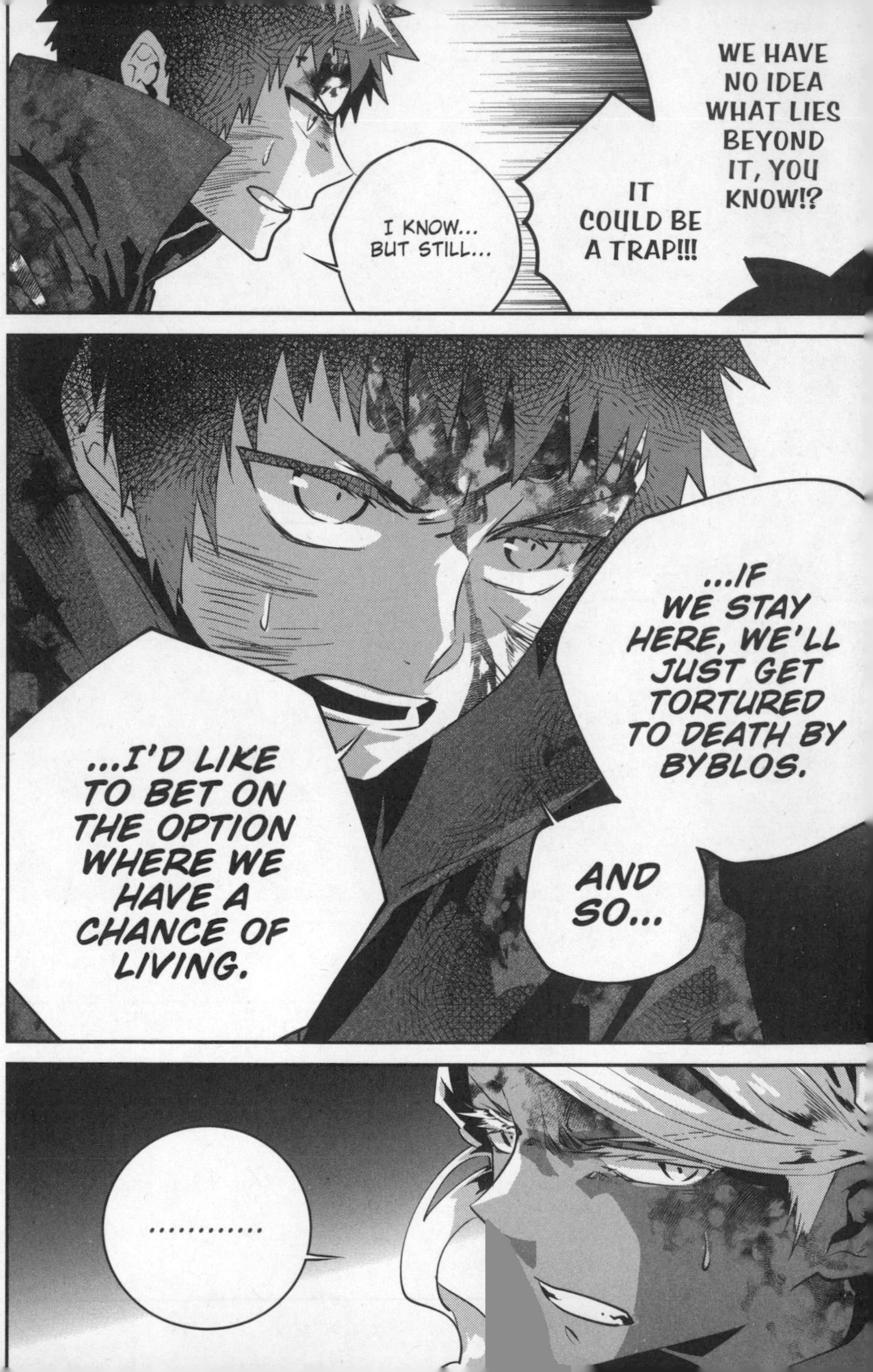
WE HAVE NO IDEA WHAT LIES BEYOND IT, YOU KNOW!?
IT COULD BE A TRAP!!!
I KNOW... BUT STILL...
...IF WE STAY HERE, WE'LL JUST GET TORTURED TO DEATH BY BYBLOS.
AND SO...
...I'D LIKE TO BET ON THE OPTION WHERE WE HAVE A CHANCE OF LIVING.
............

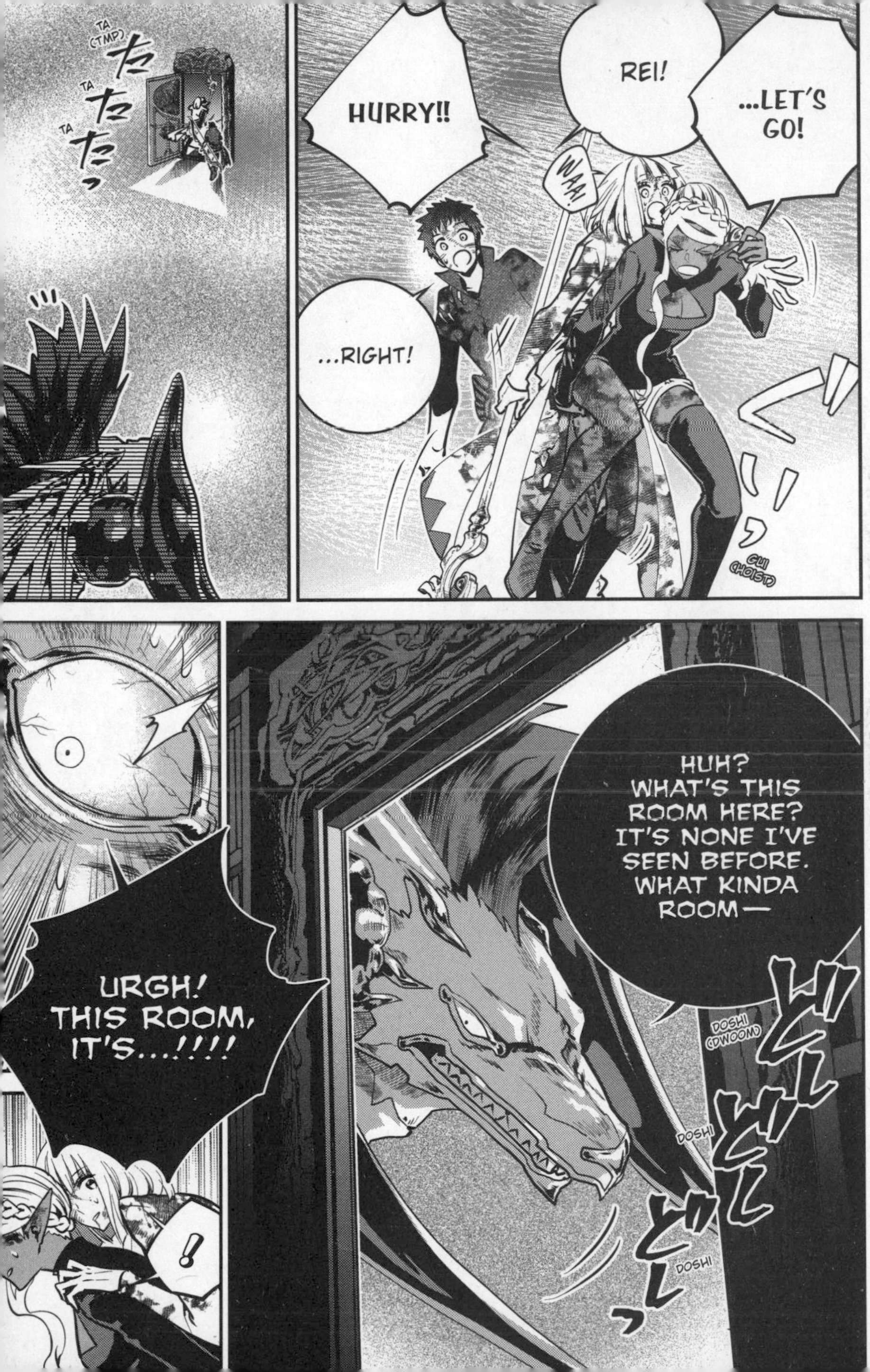

...LET'S GO!
REI!
HURRY!!
WAA!
...RIGHT!
GUI (HOIST)
TA (TMP)
TA
TA
HUH? WHAT'S THIS ROOM HERE? IT'S NONE I'VE SEEN BEFORE. WHAT KINDA ROOM—
DOSHI (DWOOM)
DOSHI
DOSHI
URGH! THIS ROOM, IT'S....!!!!
!

PIKON (BADING)
"Please...
PIKON
"I beg of you...
PIKON
"Unite us.
"Please unite us...
PIKON
PIKON
"I wish to be as one."

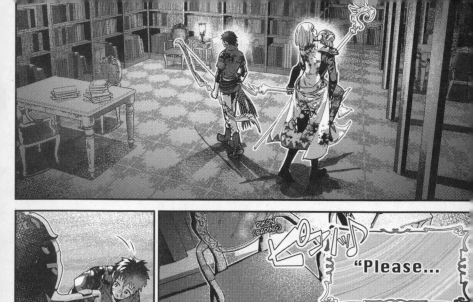

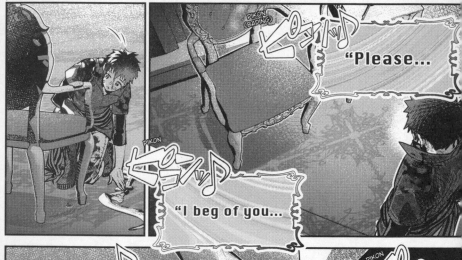

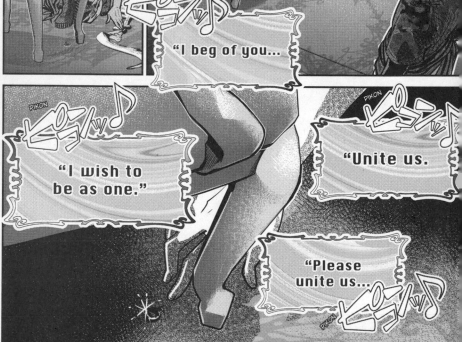

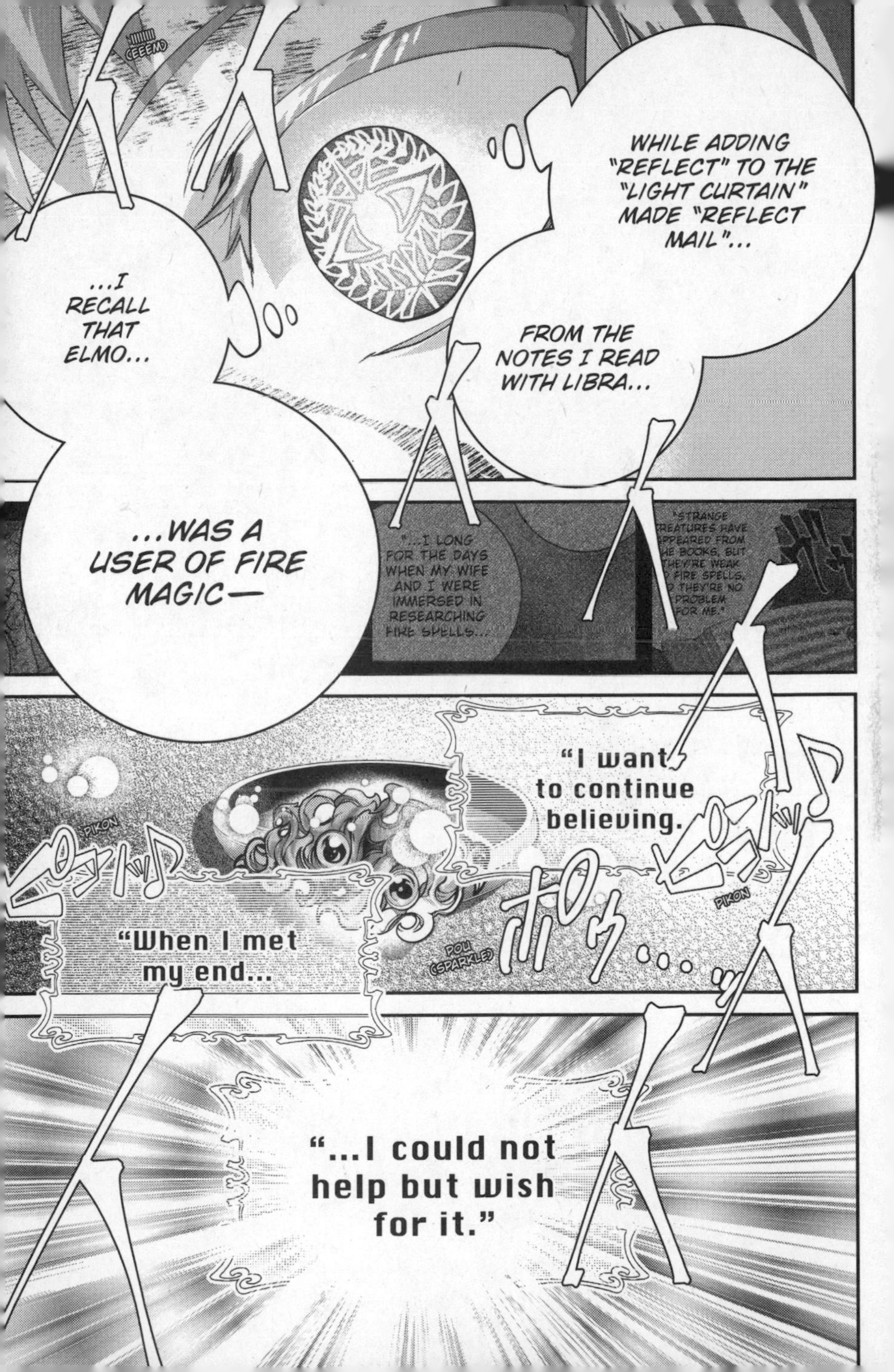

CEEEMD
WHILE ADDING "REFLECT" TO THE "LIGHT CURTAIN" MADE "REFLECT MAIL"...
FROM THE NOTES I READ WITH LIBRA...
...I RECALL THAT ELMO...
...WAS A USER OF FIRE MAGIC—
"STRANGE REATURES HAVE PPEARED FROM HE BOOKS, BUT THEY'RE WEAK O FIRE SPELLS, D THEY'RE NO PROBLEM FOR ME."
"...I LONG FOR THE DAYS WHEN MY WIFE AND I WERE IMMERSED IN RESEARCHING FIRE SPELLS...
"I want to continue believing.
PIKON
POU (SPARKLED)
PIKON
"When I met my end...
"...I could not help but wish for it."

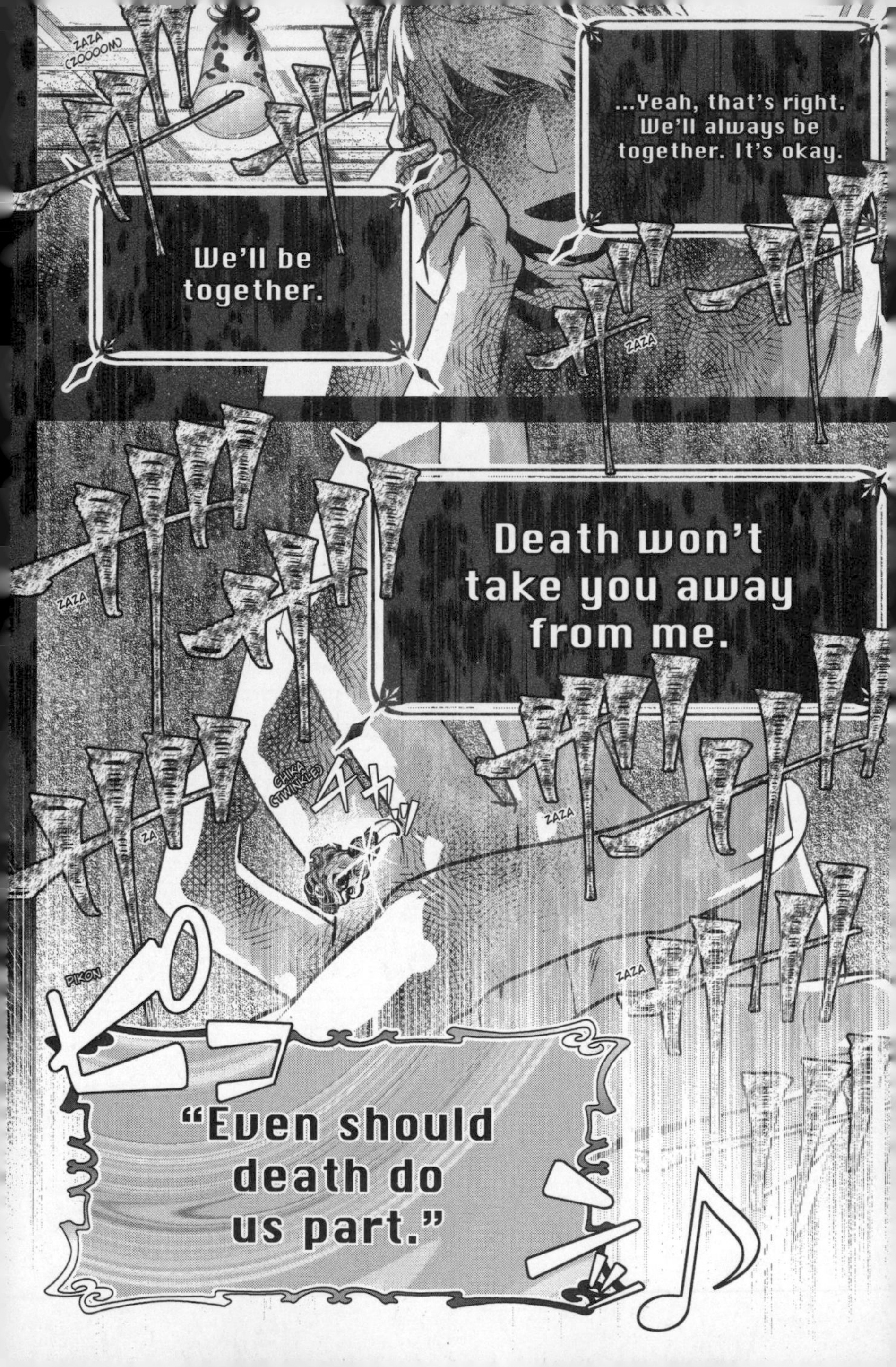
...Yeah, that's right. We'll always be together. It's okay.
ZAZA (ZOOOOM)
We'll be together.
ZAZA
Death won't take you away from me.
ZAZA
ZAZA
CHIKA (TWINKLE)
ZAZA
ZA
ZAZA
PIKON
"Even should death do us part."

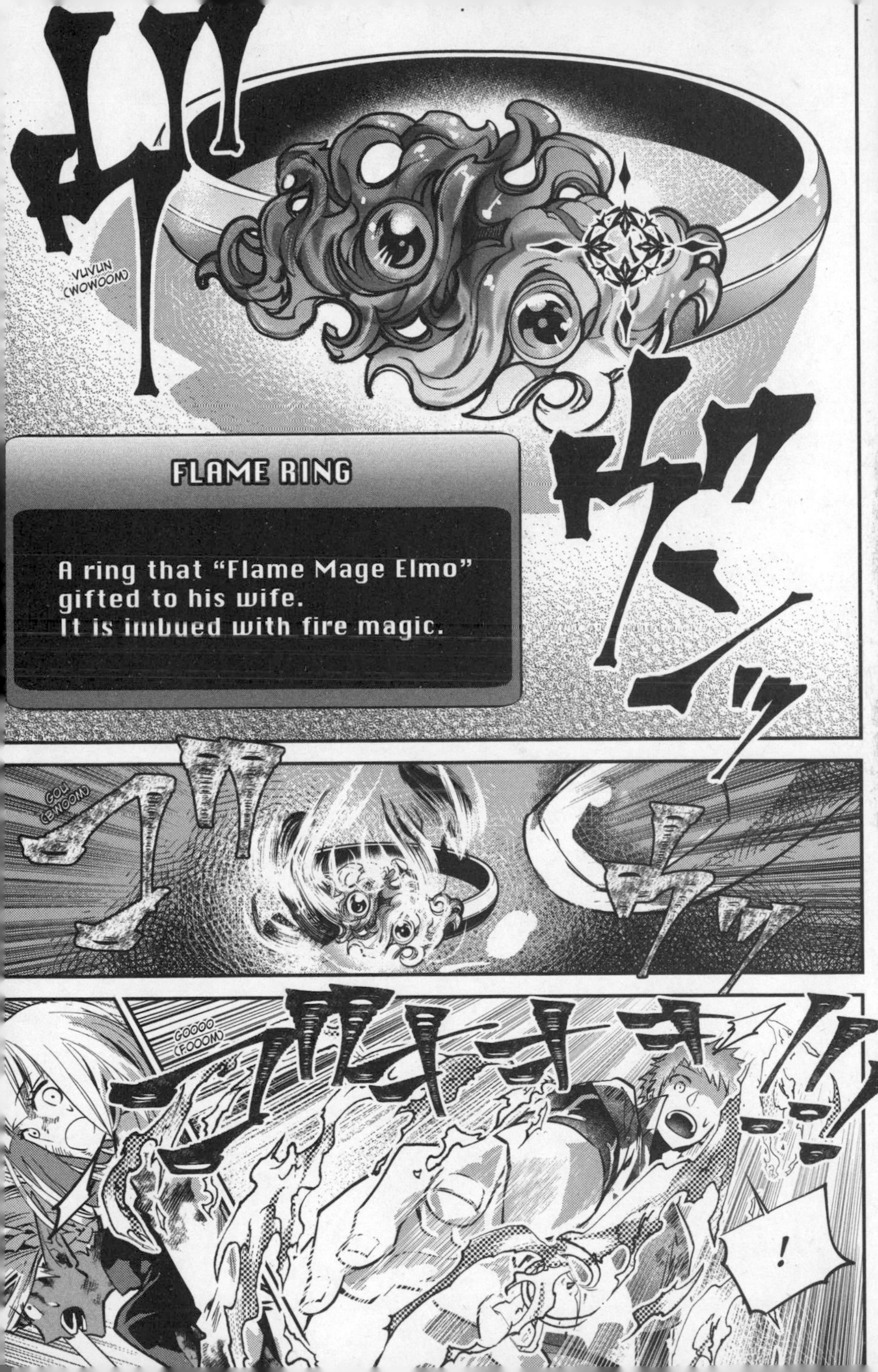
VUVUN (WOWOOM)
FLAME RING
A ring that "Flame Mage Elmo" gifted to his wife.
It is imbued with fire magic.
GOU (BWOOM)
GOOOO (FOOOM)
!

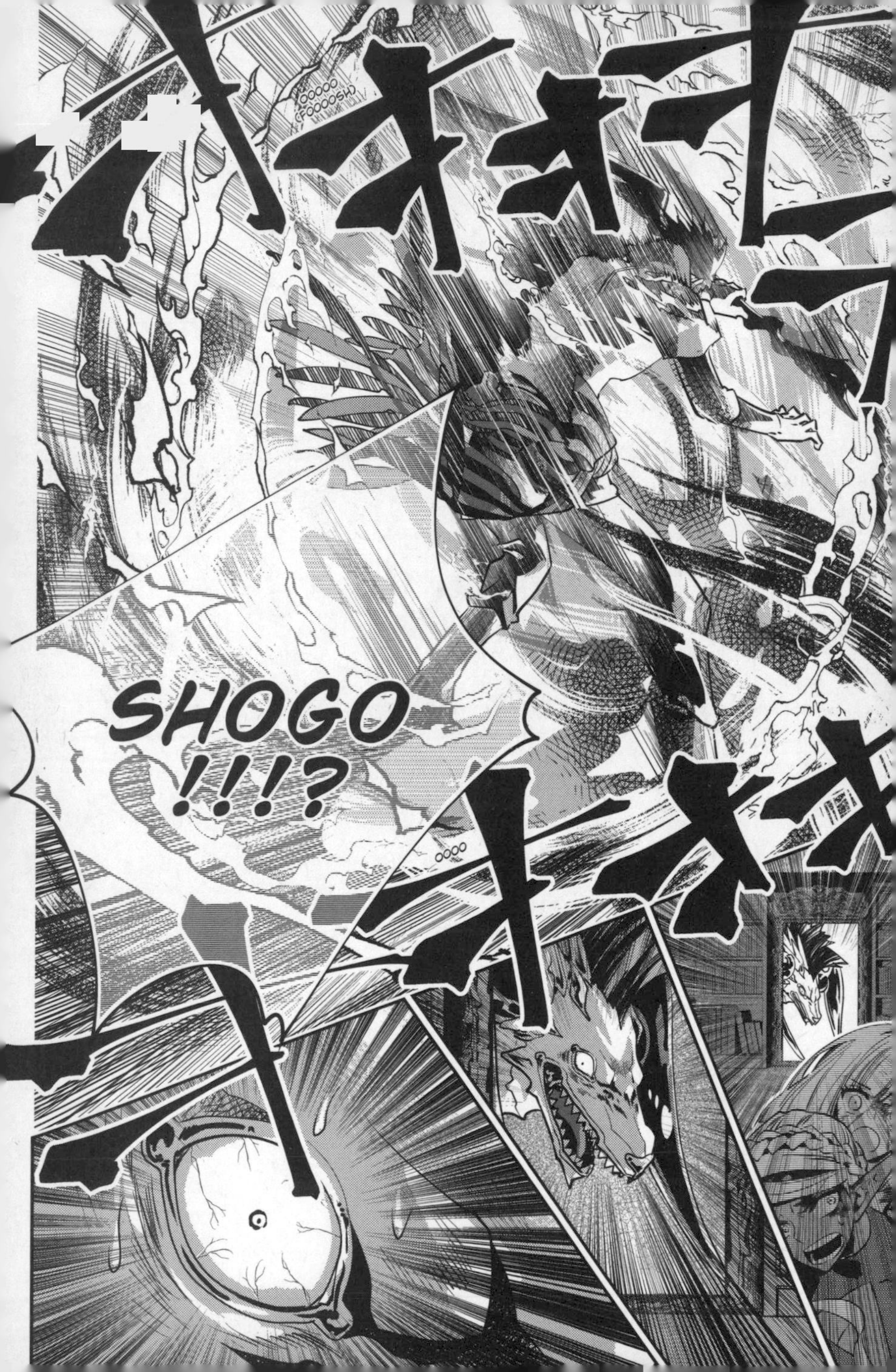

OOOOO
(FOOOOSH)
SHOGO !!!?
OOOO

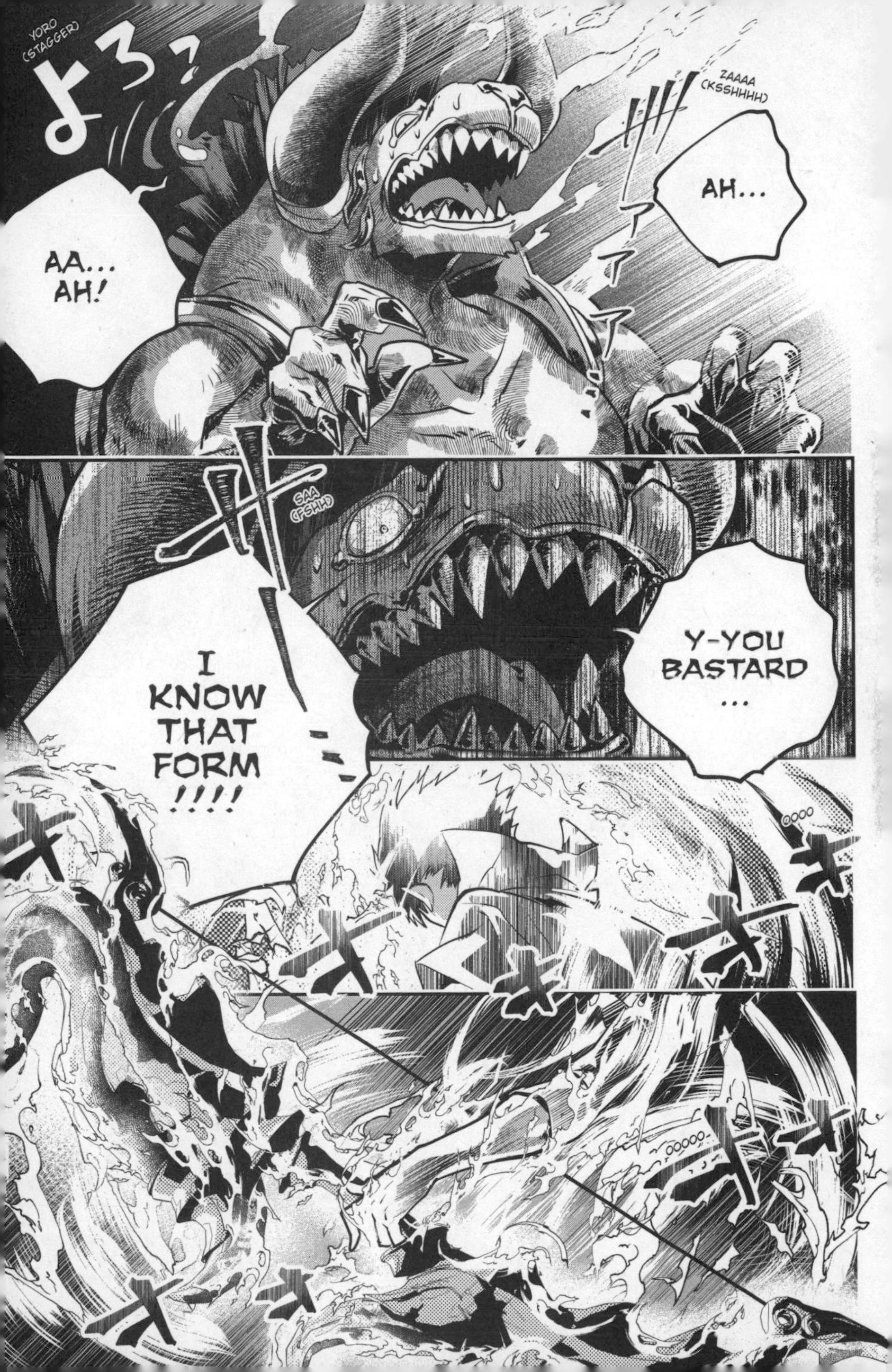
ZAAAA (KSSHHHH)
AH...
YORO (STAGGER)
AA... AH!
Y-YOU BASTARD...
SAA (FSHH)
I KNOW THAT FORM!!!!

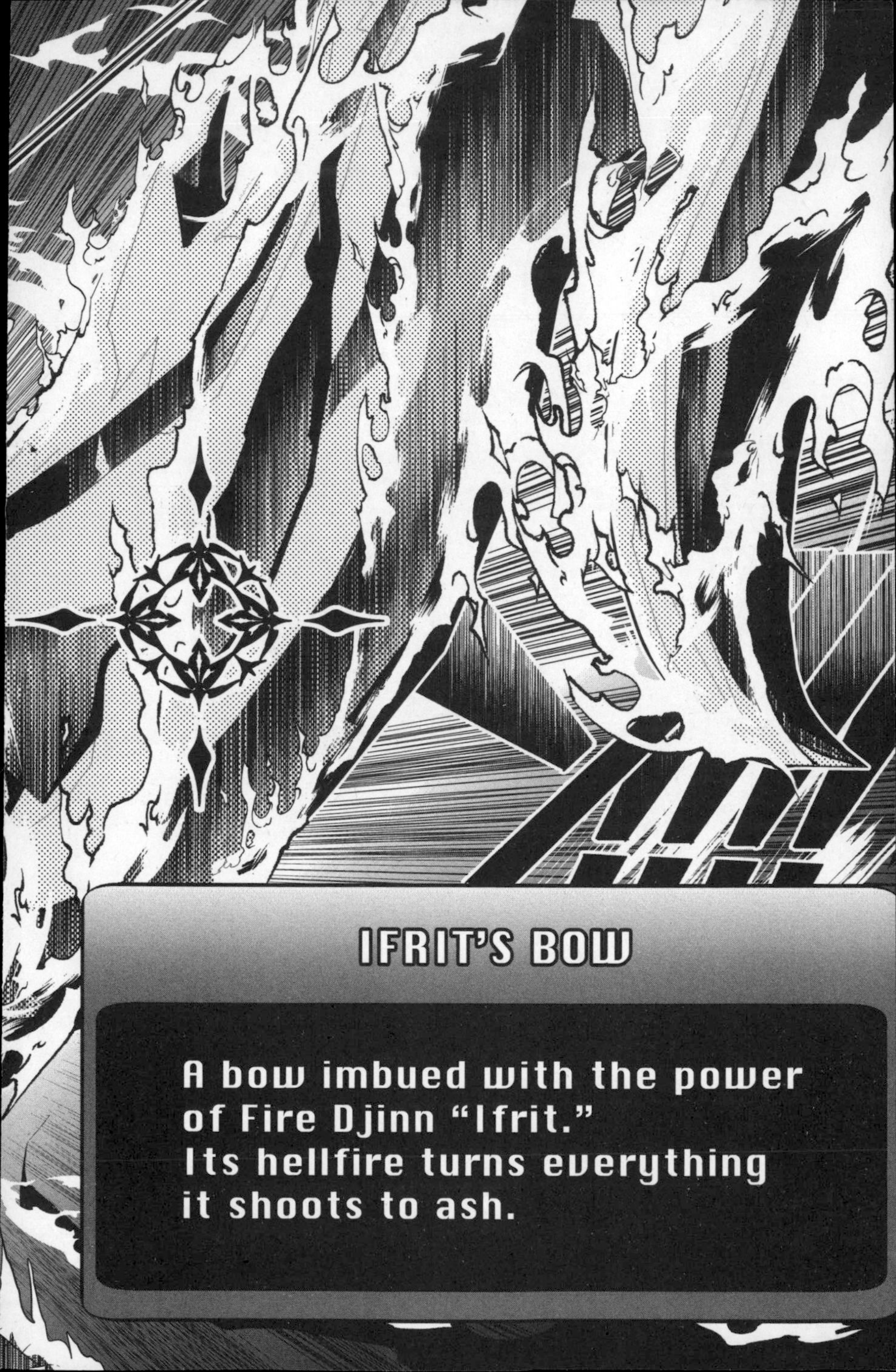
IFRIT'S BOW
A bow imbued with the power of Fire Djinn "Ifrit."
Its hellfire turns everything it shoots to ash.

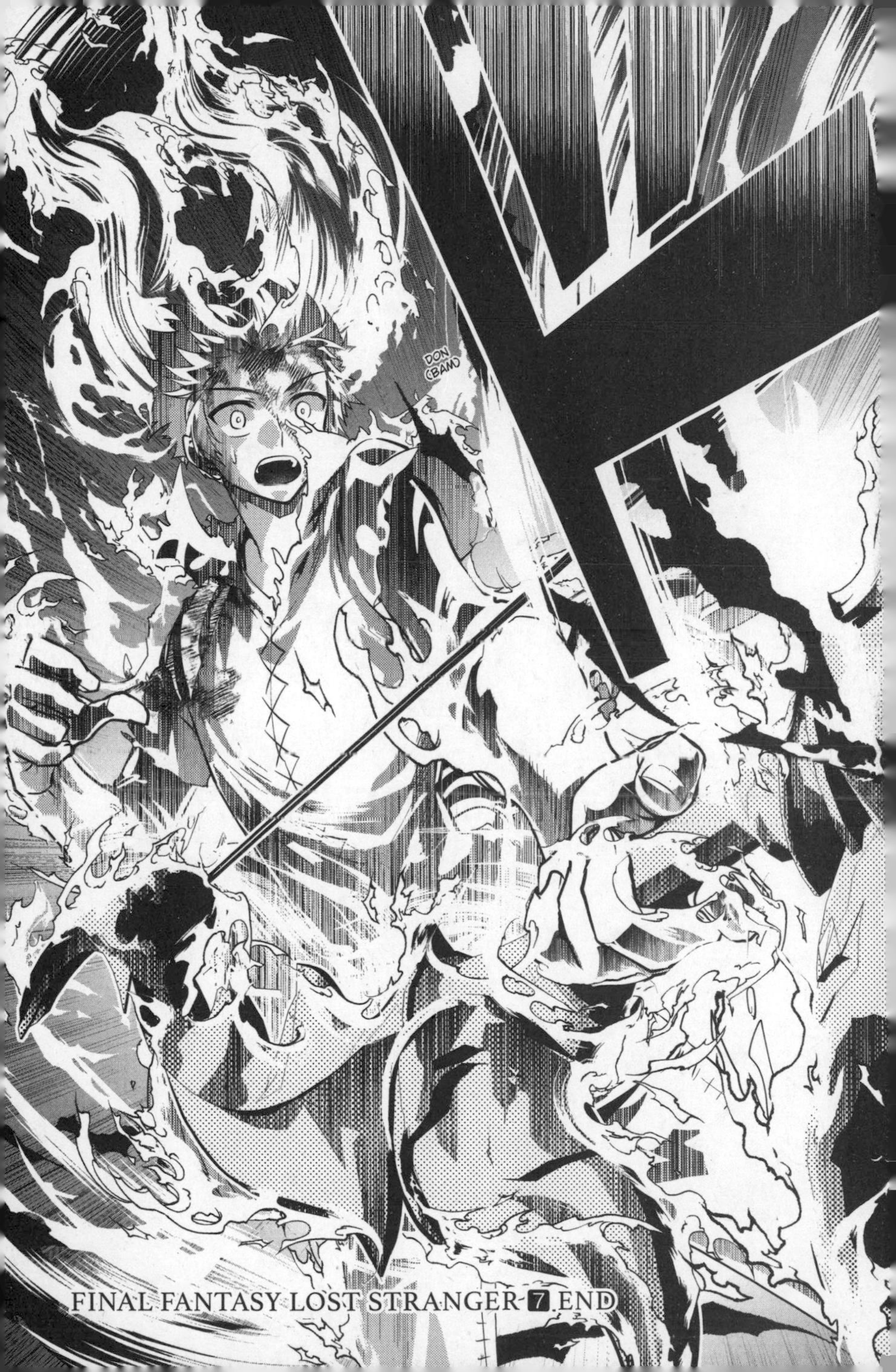
DON (BAM)
FINAL FANTASY LOST STRANGER 7 END

Preview

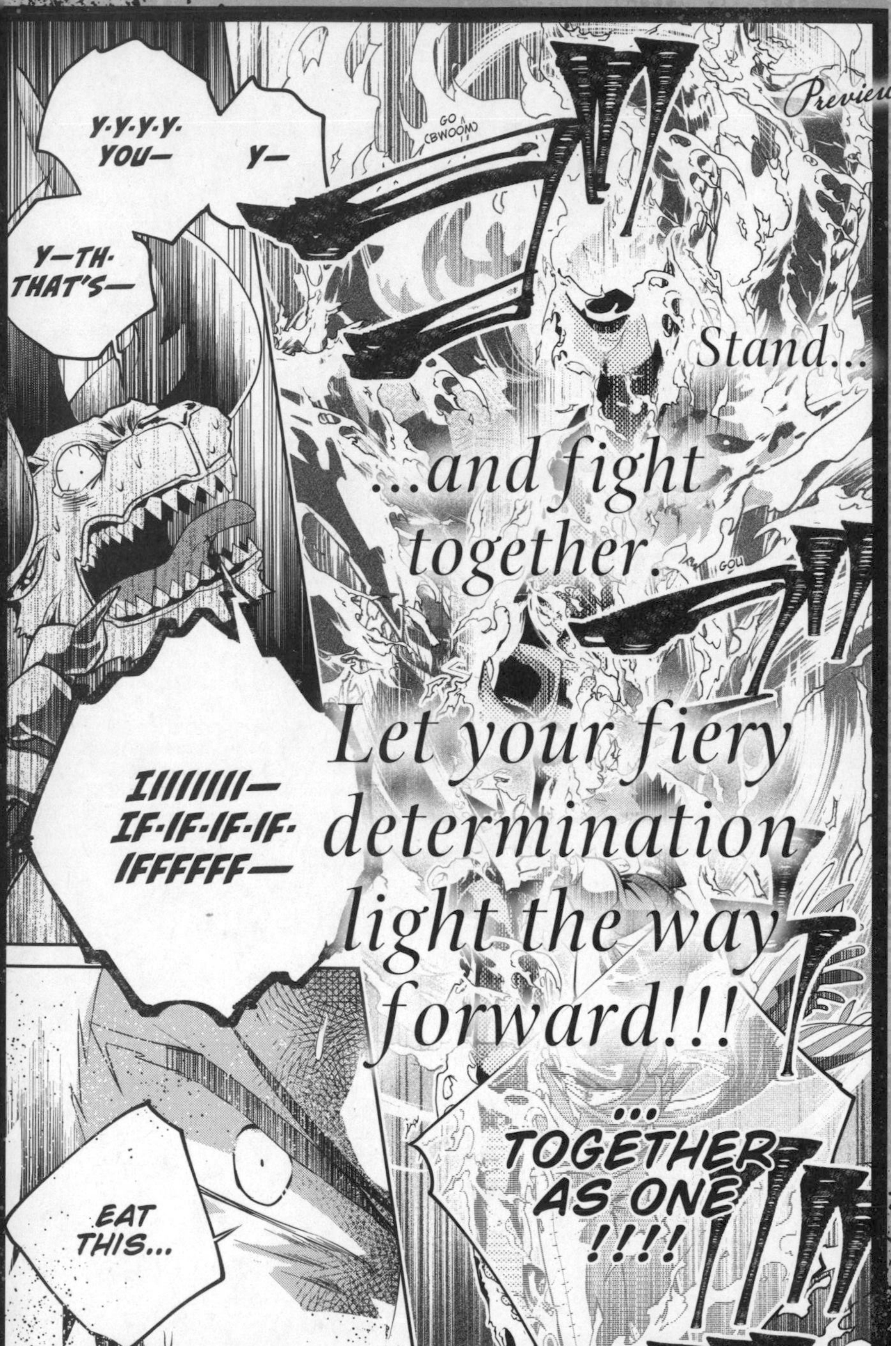
GO (BWOOM)
Stand...
...and fight together.
GOU
Let your fiery determination light the way forward!!!
...TOGETHER AS ONE !!!!
Y-Y-Y-Y. YOU— Y—
Y—TH. THAT'S—
IIIIIII— IF-IF-IF-IF- IFFFFFF—
EAT THIS...

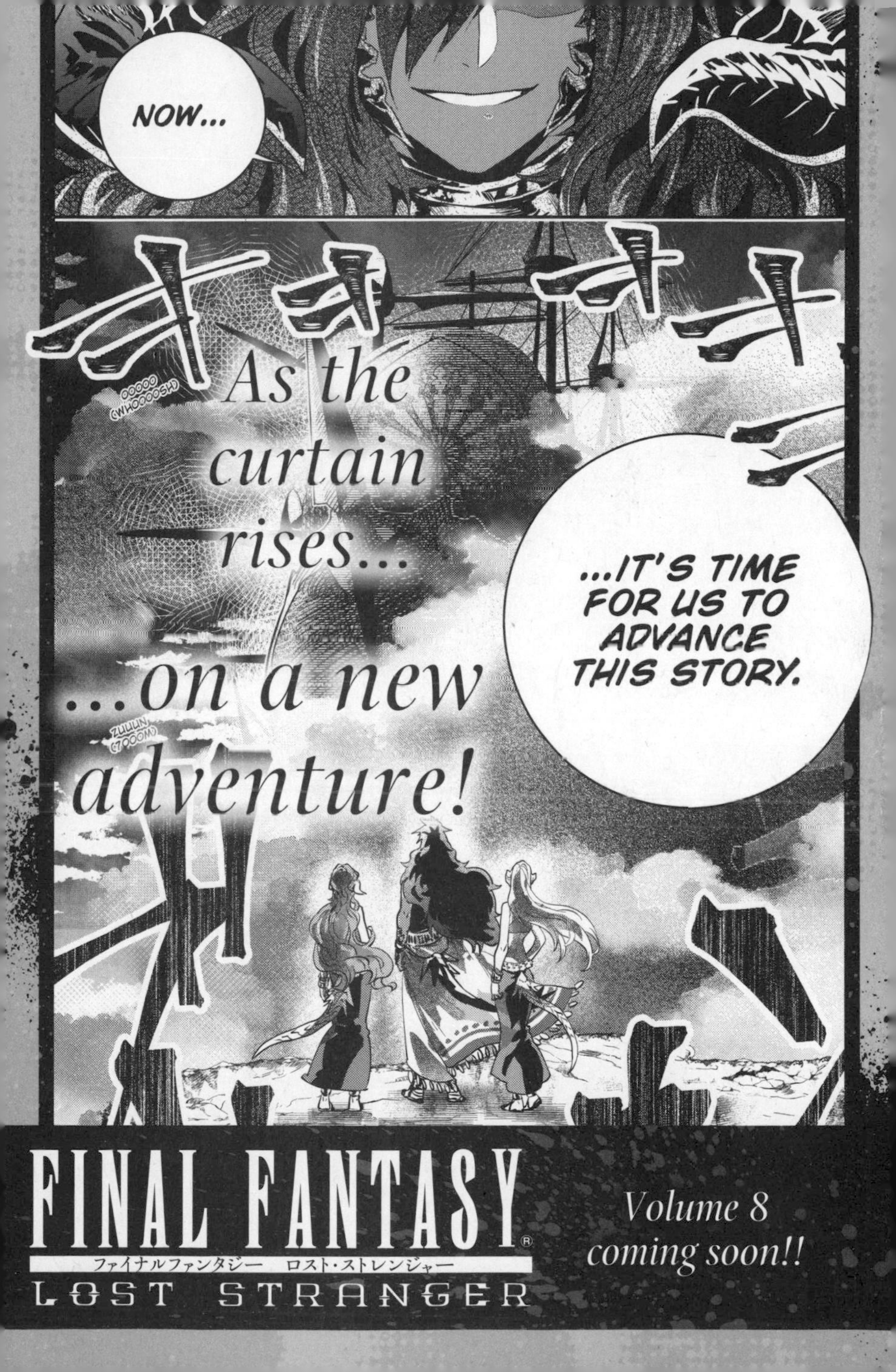
NOW...
OOOOO
(WHOOOOSH)
As the curtain rises...
...IT'S TIME FOR US TO ADVANCE THIS STORY.
...on a new adventure!
ZUUUN
(ZOOOM)

# FINAL FANTASY®

ファイナルファンタジー　ロスト・ストレンジャー

LOST STRANGER

Volume 8
coming soon!!

# TRANSLATION NOTES

## COMMON HONORIFICS

**no honorific:** Indicates familiarity or closeness; if used without permission or reason, addressing someone in this manner would constitute an insult.

**-san:** The Japanese equivalent of Mr./Mrs./Miss. If a situation calls for politeness, this is the fail-safe honorific.

**-kun:** Used most often when referring to boys, this indicates affection or familiarity. Occasionally used by older men among their peers, but it may also be used by anyone referring to a person of lower standing.

**-chan:** An affectionate honorific indicating familiarity used mostly in reference to girls; also used in reference to cute persons or animals regardless of gender.

**-sensei:** A respectful term for teachers, artists, or high-level professionals.

**Onii-chan:** An affectionate term used for older brothers or brother figures.

### ✦ PAGE 5

The Japanese title of this chapter translates to "indomitable sentiments," but it's also the name of the *FF14* track "Invisible," which plays during the second phase of the Hades boss battle.

### ✦ PAGE 43

The Japanese title of this chapter translates to "An Unraveled Spell and Melted Hearts," but it's also the name of the *FFIX* track "Broken Spell, Healed Hearts," which plays during important scenes involving Lady Hilda and Cid.

### ✦ PAGE 62

"Land of mercy, loosen tight fists!" is the *Final Fantasy Tactics* incantation for the Time Magic spell "Float." In Japanese, "Float" is known as "Levitate."

### ✦ PAGE 68

"Join the Froggers!" is the *Final Fantasy Tactics* incantation for the spell "Toadja."

### ✦ PAGE 69

"Impart light to fight our holy war" is the *Final Fantasy Tactics* incantation to summon the eidolon "Carbuncle." However, this is a truncated version of the original Japanese incantation, as the full translation would not have fit in the PlayStation game's speech bubble. This chapter features the translation of the full incantation.

### ✦ PAGE 77

The title of this chapter shares its name with the *FFVI* track "Awakening," which serves as the game's main theme.

# TRANSLATION NOTES

### PAGE 82
Carbuncle is a recurring summoned creature from the *Final Fantasy* series that typically possesses healing abilities.

### PAGE 84
The background of the first panel shows Terra from *Final Fantasy VI*, a character who is capable of using the "Trance" ability.

### PAGE 121
The title of this chapter shares its name with the *FFXIV* track "Bibliophobia," which plays during the Great Gubal Library (Hard) dungeon in the game's *Heavensward* expansion

### PAGE 155
The English name of the "FlareWave" ability changes between iterations of *Final Fantasy III*. Due to text length limitations, the original Nintendo release called it "FlareWave," but in newer editions of the game, it becomes "Particle Beam." In Japanese, it's always called *hadouhou*, which directly translates to "Wave Cannon."

The title of this chapter shares its name with the *FFXIV* track "A Thousand Screams," which plays during the Thousand Maws of Toto-Rak dungeon in the base game.

### PAGE 156
The boss Shogo is fighting onscreen is Cloud of Darkness. The NES version of *Final Fantasy III* uses the name DarkCloud due to text length constraints.

### PAGE 183
The title of this chapter shares its name with the *FFX* track "Wandering," which plays at the Zanarkand Dome and the Farplane. The literal translation of the chapter title is "Wandering Flame."

### PAGE 207
Shogo's quote differs from the quote that is said in *Final Fantasy V*. The exact quote Shogo is referring to is "All memories... dimensions...existence... All that is shall be returned to nothing." Also, in the Japanese version of the game, the order of the three items is memories, existence, dimensions.

# FINAL FANTASY

ファイナルファンタジー　ロスト・ストレンジャー

## LOST STRANGER